# ASIAN
# SECURITY
# REASSESSED

# ASIAN
# SECURITY
# REASSESSED

EDITED BY
**STEPHEN HOADLEY** AND **JÜRGEN RÜLAND**

**Institute of Southeast Asian Studies**

First published in Singapore in 2006 by ISEAS Publications
Institute of Southeast Asian Studies
30 Heng Mui Keng Terrace
Pasir Panjang
Singapore 119614

*E-mail:* publish@iseas.edu.sg
*Website:* <http://bookshop.iseas.edu.sg>

---

### ISEAS Library Cataloguing-in-Publication Data

---

Asian security reassessed / edited by Stephen Hoadley and Jürgen Rüland.
   (Issues in Southeast Asian security)
   1.   National security—Asia.
   2.   Asia—Strategic aspects.
   I.   Hoadley, Steve.
   II.   Rüland, Jürgen, 1953–
   III. Series
UA830 A843            2006

ISBN 981-230-357-X (soft cover)
ISBN 981-230-400-2 (hard cover)

---

Typeset by Superskill Graphics Pte Ltd
Printed in Singapore by Oxford Graphics Pte Ltd

# Contents

# Acknowledgements

Given the dispersed home bases of the editors, authors, and publisher, the publication of this book is a triumph of global communication over physical separation. Nor has the diversity of the authors' academic backgrounds and analytical approaches prevented a satisfying degree of conceptual convergence. In view of the many other commitments engaging editors, authors, and publisher alike, the book's completion may be seen as a triumph of professional commitment and persistence.

But authors hardly write in a vacuum, or should we say in pristine cyber-space. Robust on-the-ground institutions were needed to provide financial, administrative, and editorial support to make possible the composing, editing, and publishing of this book. The editors would like to thank the following institutions for their generosity: the University of Auckland Research Committee for an International Collaboration Grant; the University of Auckland's Political Studies Department and General Library for administrative support, bibliographic resources, and online access; the University of Freiburg's Faculty of Humanities and Department of Political Science, and the Arnold-Bergstraesser-Institute Freiburg for providing institutional support to five of the contributors; the Universitas 21 consortium for providing a network linking the contributors; the two anonymous reviewers nominated by the Institute of Southeast Asian Studies (ISEAS) for constructive comments, and the editorial and publications staff of ISEAS, Singapore for encouragement, valuable advice, and professional editing, formatting, and presentation.

Many individuals including sponsors, mentors, colleagues, spouses, family and friends provided the editors and authors with material assistance, advice or personal support, including enhancement of their human security. But they are too numerous, and their contributions too varied, to name separately, so the editors and authors would like to acknowledge their help with a blanket "thank you" and leave specific gratitude to those concerned. Nevertheless, the dedicated and careful proofreading of Julia Übelhör, Benjamin Köhler, Dennis Mutschler, Henning Vogelsang, and Daniel Walter deserves specific mentioning. The editors express their sincere gratitude to them. The editors would also like to thank each of the authors for taking time out of their teaching and research programmes to write on their areas of security expertise and then to endure the editors' sometimes substantial amendments with good grace.

And finally the editors would like to thank each other for sincere dedication to the joint project, to which each made an invaluable contribution over a three-year span, never doubting, even as themes were modified and deadlines set back, that the initial vision would yield a worthwhile volume in the end. They are pleased to be able to share the fruits of their labours with security-policymakers, scholars, students, and interested readers everywhere.

Stephen Hoadley                                      Jürgen Rüland
Auckland                                             Freiburg

# About the Contributors

**Jörn Dosch** is Senior Lecturer and Head of Asia-Pacific Studies at the Department of East Asian Studies, University of Leeds. He has been associated with the Asia/Pacific Research Center of Stanford University, the East-West Center, Hawaii, the International University of the Social Sciences (LUISS Guido Carli) in Rome, and the Institute of Political Science at the University of Mainz. His publications include *The New Global Politics of the Asia-Pacific* (RoutledgeCurzon, 2004) and forty books and articles on international relations in the Asia-Pacific, U.S.-Asia and EU-Asia relations, ASEAN, and democratization in Southeast Asia.

**Julie Gilson** is Senior Lecturer, Department of Political Science and International Studies, University of Birmingham (UK). Her publications include *Japan and the European Union* (Macmillan 2000) and *Asia Meets Europe* (Edward Elgar 2002). Her current research interests include Sino-Japanese relations and Japanese political and economic interests in Southeast Asia.

**Jürgen Haacke** is Lecturer in the Department of International Relations at the London School of Economics and Political Science. He is the author of *ASEAN's Diplomatic and Security Culture: Origins, Development, and Prospects* (RoutledgeCurzon, 2003). His research interests have focused on the international politics of Southeast Asia, China-ASEAN relations and Myanmar's politics and foreign policy. He is currently leading an ESRC-funded research project on how regional security cultures mediate the responses of regional organizations to transnational challenges.

**Stephen Hoadley** is Associate Professor of Political Studies at the University of Auckland. He is Senior Fellow of the Centre for Strategic Studies,

Victoria University, and has taught at the Chinese University of Hong Kong and Kobe Gakuin University, Japan. His recent publications include *New Zealand and Australian Security Management in the South Pacific* (CSS: NZ, 2005), *New Zealand and France: Politics, Diplomacy and Dispute Management* (NZIIA 2005), "Chinese and American Naval Strategies in the Western Pacific" (RNZN 2004), *Negotiating Free Trade: The New Zealand Singapore CEP Agreement* (NZIIA, 2002) and *New Zealand United States Relations: Friends No Longer Allies* (NZIIA, 2000).

**Anja Jetschke** is Assistant Professor of International Relations at the Faculty of Political Science at the University of Freiburg. She has been associated with the European University Institute, Florence, and a project on international human rights norms and domestic political change directed by Thomas Risse for the Deutsche Forschungsgemeinschaft. Her publications include: "Linking the Unlinkable: International norms and nationalism in Indonesia and the Philippines", in Risse, Sikkink, and Ropp, *The Power of Human Rights: International Norms and Domestic Change* (Cambridge, 1999) and "Culture on the Upswing: Meanings, Values and Action Repertoires in International Relations", in *Zeitschrift für Internationale Beziehungen*. Her current research interests are constructivism in International Relations and the international relations of Southeast Asia.

**Rod Lyon** is Senior Lecturer in the School of Political Science and International Studies at the University of Queensland in Brisbane. In 2004 as a Fulbright scholar he researched the future of alliances and coalitions in U.S. security policy at Georgetown University, Washington. His recent publications focus on alliance relations, nuclear strategy and Australian strategic policy, and include *Alliance Unleashed: Australia and the US in a New Strategic Age* (ASPI, 2005). His research and teaching responsibilities include international and regional security, the future of conflict, and civil-military relations.

**Bernd Martin** is Professor of History at Freiburg University. He stayed as a research-associate at the East-Asia Institute of Harvard University in 1976 and taught at Oxford University St. Antony's College, in 1982. He was the first German Visiting Professor of History in Beijing in 1988. He is author of *Japan and Germany in the modern world* (Berghahn Books,

1995). For several years he has been engaged in research and educational and cultural exchange in China, Japan, Korea and Thailand.

**Mia Mikic** was a Senior Lecturer in Economics at the University of Auckland and Professor of International Economics at the University of Zagreb before joining the United Nations ESCAP in February 2005. She was a visiting fellow at the Universite Lumiere, Lyon and Oxford University. She is the author of *International Trade* (Macmillan, 1998) and has published in the *Zagreb International Review of Economics and Business, Southern Economic Journal, New Zealand Economic Papers, Economic Journal of Development Issues, European Studies*, and *Financijska praksa*. Her work focuses on the impacts of preferential and multilateral trade liberalization on developing and least developed countries of Asia and the Pacific.

**Jürgen Rüland** is Professor of Political Science at the University of Freiburg, and Director of the Arnold-Bergstraesser-Institute for Social Research, Freiburg. He has spent more than six years as a researcher and visiting professor in Southeast Asian countries including the Philippines, Thailand, Indonesia, Malaysia, Singapore and Vietnam. He has published widely on the Asia-Pacific region and is an co-athour of *Parliaments and Political Change in Asia* (ISEAS, 2005 forthcoming). His is also an editor of and contributor to *Asia-Pacific Economic Cooperation (APEC): The First Decade* (RoutledgeCurzon, 2002) and of *Interregionalism in International Politics* (Routledge 2005 forthcoming).

**Dominique Schirmer** is Research Associate at the Institute of Sociology, University of Freiburg. Her recent publications include "Globale chinesische Kultur? Überlegungen zu Ort und Raum der chinesischen Identität" [Global Chinese culture? Reflections on place and space of Chinese identity] in Peter Haslinger, ed., *Regionale und nationale Identitäten. Wechselwirkungen und Spannungsfelder im Zeitalter moderner Staatlichkeit* (Würzburg, 2000). Her current research focus is on sociological methodology, Chinese sociology, gender and everyday life, and Pacific Asia community development.

**Hermann Schwengel** is Professor of Sociology and Dean of the Faculty of Humanities at the University of Freiburg. He has published on globalization.

Among his major publications is *Globalisierung mit Europäischem Gesicht. Der Kampf um die politische Form der Zukunft*, Berlin: Aufbau Verlag, 1999.

**Clem Tisdell** is Professor of Economics at The University of Queensland, Brisbane. He is associated also with the People's University of China and the Institute of Development Studies, Orissa. He has published widely on environmental, ecological, development and tourism economics and serves on editorial boards of numerous journals. His recent books include *Economics of Conserving Wildlife and Natural Areas* (Elgar, 2002) and *Ecological and Environmental Economics* (Elgar, 2003).

**Clevo Wilson** is a Lecturer in the School of Economics and Finance, Queensland University of Technology (QUT), Brisbane, Queensland, Australia. His main research interests are in environmental and resource economics. He obtained his Ph.D. from the University of St Andrews, Scotland, UK. He also has an MSc from the University of Glasgow, an MPhil from the University of Cambridge and a B.A. (Economics) from The University of Peradeniya, Sri Lanka.

**Jian Yang** is Senior Lecturer in Political Studies at the University of Auckland. His publications include *Congress and US China Policy* (2000) and numerous shorter pieces on China's foreign policy. His research and teaching interests are foreign policy-making, U.S.-China relations, security in Asia-Pacific, international relations theory, and Chinese politics.

# List of Abbreviations

| | |
|---|---|
| ABM | Anti Ballistic Missile |
| ABRI | Angkatan Bersenjata Republik Indonesia |
| ACAMM | ASEAN Chief of Army Multilateral Meeting |
| ADB | Asian Development Bank |
| AF | Agreed Framework |
| AFTA | ASEAN Free Trade Area |
| AGAM | Angkatan Gerakan Aceh Merdeka |
| AMMTC | ASEAN Ministerial Meeting on Transnational Crime |
| ANZUS | Australia, New Zealand, United States Security Treaty |
| APC | Asia-Pacific Consultations on Refugees, Displaced Persons, and Migrants |
| APEC | Asia-Pacific Economic Cooperation |
| APT | ASEAN Plus Three |
| ARF | ASEAN Regional Forum |
| ARMM | Autonomous Region of Muslim Mindanao |
| ASC | ASEAN Security Community |
| ASEAN | Association of Southeast Asian Nations |
| ASEAN+3 | ASEAN + China, Japan and South Korea |
| ASEANAPOL | ASEAN Chiefs of National Police |
| ASEM | Asia Europe Meeting |
| ASNLF | Aceh Sumatra National Liberation Front |
| ASPC | ARF Security Policy Conference |
| BMA | Bangsamoro Army |
| BMD | Ballistic Missile Defense |
| CBM | Confidence-Building Measure |
| CCP | Chinese Communist Party |
| CIA | Central Intelligence Agency |
| CSBM | Confidence and Security Building Measure |

| | |
|---|---|
| CSCAP | Council on Security Cooperation in the Asia-Pacific |
| CSCE | Conference on Security and Cooperation in Europe |
| CSIS | Center for Strategic and International Studies |
| DDII | Dewan Dakwah Islamiyah Indonesia |
| DMZ | Demilitarized Zone |
| DOM | Daerah Operasi Militer |
| DPD | Dewan Perwakilan Daerah |
| DPRK | Democratic People's Republic of Korea |
| EAGA | East ASEAN Growth Area |
| EEP | Experts and Eminent Persons |
| EMIS | Electromagnetic Isotope Separation |
| ESCAP | Economic and Social Commission for Asia-Pacific |
| ESRC | Economic and Social Research Council |
| EU | European Union |
| FDI | Foreign Direct Investment |
| FMIA | Front Mujahidin Islam Aceh |
| FPI | Front Pembela Islam |
| FTA | Free Trade Area |
| GAM | Gerakan Aceh Merdeka |
| GATT | General Agreement on Tariffs and Trade |
| GDP | Gross Domestic Product |
| GNP | Gross National Product |
| HFO | High Frequency Oscillator |
| HMI | Himpunan Mahasiswa Indonesia |
| IAEA | International Atomic Energy Agency |
| ICCPR | International Convention on Civil and Political Rights |
| ICESCR | International Convention on Economic, Social and Cultural Rights |
| ICJ | International Court of Justice |
| IDSS | Institute of Defence and Strategic Studies |
| ILEA | International Law Enforcement Cooperation |
| ILO | International Labour Organization |
| IMF | International Monetary Fund |
| IOM | International Organization on Migration |
| ISEAS | Institute of Southeast Asian Studies |
| ISG | Intersessional-Support Group |
| ISIS | Institute of Security and International Studies |
| ISM on CT-TC | Inter-sessional Meeting on Counter-Terrorism and Transnational Crime |

| | |
|---|---|
| ITB | Bandung Institute of Technology |
| JBIC | Japan Bank for International Cooperation |
| JCLEC | Jakarta Center for Law Enforcement Cooperation |
| JDA | Japan Defence Agency |
| JI | Jemaah Islamiyah |
| KEDO | Korean Peninsula Energy Organization |
| KISDI | Komite untuk Solidaritas dengan Dunia Islam |
| KMM | Kumpulan Mujaheidin Malaysia |
| KOPASSUS | Army Special Force Command |
| KOSTRAD | Army Strategic Reserve Command |
| LDP | Liberal Democratic Party |
| LWR | Light Water Reactor |
| MERCOSUR | Mercado Común del Sur |
| MILF | Moro Islamic Liberation Front |
| MIM | Mindanao Independence Movement |
| MMI | Majelis Mujaheidin Indonesia |
| MNLF | Mindanao National Liberation Front |
| MOFA | Ministry of Foreign Affairs |
| MUI | Majelis Ulama Indonesia |
| NATO | North Atlantic Treaty Organization |
| NGO | Non-Governmental Organization |
| NMD | National Missile Defense |
| NPT | Non-Proliferation of Nuclear Weapons Treaty |
| NUCD | National Union of Christian Democrats |
| OIC | Organization of Islamic States |
| OSCE | Organization for Security and Cooperation in Europe |
| OSS | Office of Strategic Services |
| PACOM | U.S. Pacific Command |
| PBB | Partai Bulan Bintang |
| PD | Presidential Decree |
| | Preventive Diplomacy |
| PDI | Partai Demokrasi Indonesia |
| PKO | Peace Keeping Operation |
| PLA | People's Liberation Army |
| PLO | Palestine Liberation Organization |
| PMO | Prime Minister's Office |
| PPP | Partai Persatuan Pembangunan |
| PRC | People's Republic of China |
| RA | Republic Act |

| RATS | Regional Anti-Terrorism Structure |
| RCC | Regional Consultative Commission |
| ROK | Republic of Korea |
| RTZ | Rio Tinto Zinc |
| SAR | Special Administrative Region |
| SARS | Severe Acute Respiratory Syndrome |
| SCAP | Supreme Command for the Allied Powers |
| SCC | Security Consultative Committee |
| SCO | Shanghai Cooperation Organization |
| SDF | Self-Defence Force |
| SEAC | South East Asia Command |
| SEARCCT | Southeast Asia Regional Center for Counter Terrorism |
| SEATO | South East Asia Treaty Organization |
| SME | Small and Medium-Sized Enterprises |
| SOM | Senior Official Meeting |
| SPCPD | Southern Philippines Council for Peace and Development |
| TAC | Treaty of Amity and Cooperation |
| TCOG | Trilateral Coordination and Oversight Group |
| TMD | Theater Missile Defence |
| TNC | Transnational Cooperation |
| TNI | Indonesian Armed Forces |
| UK | United Kingdom |
| UN | United Nations |
| UNDP | United Nations Development Programme |
| UNEP | United Nations Environment Programme |
| UNHCR | United Nations High Commission for Refugees |
| UNSC | United Nations Security Council |
| USARPAC | U.S. Army Pacific Command |
| USSR | Union of Soviet Socialist Republics |
| WFP | World Food Program |
| WHO | World Health Organization |
| WMD | Weapons of Mass Destruction |
| WTO | World Trade Organization |

# Preface

Thousands of books have been written on how to achieve security. But the victims of insecurity since World War II have numbered in the tens of millions, nearly half of them in Asia, caught in armed conflicts and attendant famine or disease, and the damage has cost trillions of dollars. Another book on security is hardly superfluous but instead an additional asset in the search for a less lethal and destructive way of conducting inter- and intra-state relations, not least in the Asian region. It is our belief that fresh thinking about security concepts can lead to more perceptive studies by security scholars and more discriminating policies by Asian leaders and those of governments dealing with Asia such as the United States. We have endeavoured to produce a book that spans not only a variety of security threats and policies in a number of Asian countries but also a generous interval of time, thus achieving a measure of historical perspective as well as geo-political scope. We have been less concerned to quantify concepts, test hypotheses, or survey Asian countries systematically than to inform the reader of pressing issues, illuminate important themes, and put forward promising conceptual innovations in the fields of security studies and security policies. Building on the works of our academic predecessors, we hope this volume will be of value to our contemporaries and successors in the ongoing intellectual project of sharpening analysis and motivating research. We hope also to reach out to the security-policy community to contribute to improving Asian security not only at the regional and state levels but also in the economic, ethno-cultural and community spheres, ultimately enhancing human security.

# Part One

## Approaches to Asian Security

Chapter One

# The Evolution of Security Thinking: An Overview

Stephen Hoadley

## INTRODUCTION

Few topics can be more important to more people than security, not least in Asia. Unfortunately for those who live there, Asia has been one of the world's most belligerent regions since the end of World War II. Of the approximately two hundred armed conflicts registered between 1945 and the present, nearly one-third took place in Asia. Two of the deadliest among them were fought in Asia. More than three million people died in the Korean War (1950–53) and over two million in the Vietnam War (1965–73). The Indochina death toll would reach three million if we add the victims of the first Indochina War (1946–54) and the Cambodian conflict (1979–91).[1] Great power rivalry, arms races, communist insurgencies, ethnic rebellions, genocide, massive refugee flows, widespread human rights violations, terrorism, banditry and piracy have added to the apprehensions over Asia's security.

The end of the Cold War has not defused many of these conflicts in Asia as it has those in other parts of the world such as Europe. Even worse, new threats have emerged to frustrate the efforts of Asian governments and international organizations to create a peaceful security environment in the region. The nature of these threats has been aptly summarized by the *2001 Quadrennial Defense Review* of the United States Department of Defense. The report describes Asia as a region containing:

> a volatile mix of rising and declining regional powers. The governments of some of these states are vulnerable to overthrow by radical or extremist internal political forces. Many of these states field large militaries and possess the potential to develop or acquire weapons of mass destruction.[2]

In a globalized world the consequences of these conflicts may easily spill over into other world regions. Asia's security problems have thus become a prime focus for study by policymakers, scholars of international relations and the media, both inside and outside the region. This volume contributes to this policy-relevant study. It seeks to assess the changes in the Asian security environment since the end of the Cold War and the shifts in the perceptions and strategies of managing the threats in the region.

## GROWING URGENCY OF SECURITY STUDIES

The subject of this book has gained additional urgency for at least three reasons. First, since the end of the Cold War in 1990 our understanding of the nature of security itself has been changing rapidly. Some scholars perceive a paradigm shift while others are more comfortable devising ways to encompass new perceptions within a familiar realist framework, and debate between the two camps is lively. What is evident is that the security policy community is rethinking security, not taking the traditional assumptions of the Westphalia system for granted. Second, the intensification of globalization and the appearance of its malignancies in the form of the Asian financial crisis of 1997/98 have reminded us of the importance of economic security. Manifestly, economic security has implications for political security and ultimately for international security, as the popular disturbances that led to Indonesian President Suharto's resignation and the surrender of East Timor to United Nations tutelage seem to show. Third, the terrorist attack against the United States on 11 September 2001, and subsequently against Asian targets, most notably in Bali and the Philippines, and the launching by Asian governments of counter-terrorism campaigns, have raised worries about terrorism to the top of the agenda. Not only are bombers of concern but also their confederates and supporting organizations, many of which are more properly termed criminal gangs or secessionist movements.

These are just three events of many that have signalled the changing nature of security and attracted efforts to meet threats to it. There are others, including the worsening of atmospheric pollution seen most dramatically in the annual "haze" blankets of insular Southeast Asia, the exhaustion of natural resources, most notably land, trees and potable water, the displacement of people from their homes on a growing scale by environmental despoliation, economic hardship, and armed conflict, and the surging of illegal migrants from one country to another. Then there are familiar security threats presented in new guise. These include inter-state military rivalries — those between North and South Korea, China and Taiwan, and India and Pakistan come immediately to mind — that consume economic and human resources that could better be used for economic and social programmes. Few Asian states are not upgrading their military establishments and the sophistication of the arms at their disposal. Add to the growing lethality of conventional arms the possibility of nuclear weapons delivered by intermediate or long-range missiles or more modest means such as a shipping container. Less ambitious regimes might be tempted by chemical and biological weapons because they are cheaper and more easily obtained.

But it is possible more people will be threatened by conflict closer to home, from the rival ethnic group in the neighbouring district, or the local gang. Asia is rich in ethnic, religious, and linguistic diversity, which if not managed can deteriorate into riot, pogrom, civil war and secession. The only weapon needed for local mayhem is a *kris*, machete, two-by-four, or lighted match, and there seems to be no shortage of small arms and explosives. Ethnic strife makes common cause with terrorism and both may be exploited by organized crime and entrepreneurial piracy. Together these undermine economic and physical security and generate refugees. These conditions not only threaten basic human rights in themselves but also trigger reactions by overzealous and heavy-handed governments that inadvertently may destroy livelihoods and civil liberties, rend the fabric of civil society, and replace communal coexistence with suspicion and conflict. Illegitimate and ineffective governance can breed economic and social insecurity and ultimately disorder, rebellion, and flight, which in turn can render previously stable governments unsteady.

## CLARIFICATION AND QUALIFICATIONS

At this point the obvious questions must be asked and the normal qualifications and clarifications must be made. What do we mean by security? How far does Asia extend? Which are the states, institutions, and peoples with which we are to be concerned? As the introductory discussion has hinted, the nature of security is protean. Note also that the above passages highlighted threats to security, not security as such. Unless one is a social philosopher, it is more difficult to describe its essence than to inventory threats to it. In fact most common definitions cast security as the absence of various sorts of threats, leaving the essential nature of security as a residual conceptual space. Perhaps an analogy with the concepts of freedom, happiness, or love is useful: One feels them intuitively, and knows when they are lacking and what detracts from them. But their nature is axiomatic, not derivative, so cannot be expressed in terms of other concepts, only in terms of their opposites. It is normal for a government to speak of national security as the absence of threat of attack by another government. In a similar vein, the recently established United Nations Commission on Human Security has drafted its work plan in terms of threats to security such as inequality, discrimination, persecution, displacement, and violence.[3] As the subtitle of this book suggests, most of the contributors will be considering not security itself but various threats to security and the policies that might alleviate these threats. Nevertheless an examination of the positive nature of security does appear in the interstices of some contributions, and constitutes a welcome intellectual link to deeper exegeses elsewhere.

Turning to the Asian locus of security challenges, the editors decided to direct the attention of contributors to Pacific Asia, that is, East Asia and Southeast Asia. The regions of South Asia and Southwest Asia, Australasia and Oceania are not the focus of this book, although mention may be made of states or events therein as appropriate. Our reasons are pragmatic rather than judgmental. We acknowledge the importance of security in all parts of Asia and its linkages to the security of neighbouring regions and indeed the whole world, but found that the interests and expertise of our contributors centred most comfortably on East and Southeast Asia. Therefore we chose to focus rather than disperse our resources and to leave other parts of Asia to the many able specialists in the field of security studies.

Within the Asian regional envelope posited above, which entities is this book to be concerned with? The spotlight falls naturally on states as the most visible and powerful players in the region. These states number fifteen and range from Japan, the two Korean states, and the three Chinese governments, then south to the ten member states of the Association of Southeast Asian Nations (ASEAN). Neighbouring Russia, Mongolia, East Timor, Papua New Guinea, and the states of South and Central Asia may merit mention in specific contexts but are not central to our survey. One other state is external to the region but nevertheless central to a study of the security of Asia, and that is the United States of America. The U.S. presence in Asia has roots that go back two centuries and branches that extend not only to military bases and forces afloat but also a vigorous economic presence — trade, direct foreign investment, tourism — and a strong cultural influence. Recent military initiatives in the Middle East suggest that U.S. influence will grow also in Pacific Asia, for better or for worse. Thus the U.S. contribution to Asian security deserves specific attention. This is done explicitly in the chapter by Jörn Dosch but also constitutes an important element in other chapters of Part II and Part III, and in the conclusion.

Regional and international organizations are also important entities in the security network. Certainly the activities of ASEAN, the Asia-Pacific Economic Cooperation (APEC), and the ASEAN Regional Forum (ARF) deserve attention and will receive it, and the same may be said of the International Monetary Fund (IMF), the World Bank and the Asian Development Bank (ADB), the World Trade Organization (WTO), and the United Nations (UN) and its many specialized affiliates. Besides states and inter-governmental organizations one finds other salient institutions, notably transnational corporations and their local affiliates on the one hand, and non-governmental organizations (NGOs) on the other, often at odds with each other and with the host governments as well.[4] On the "wrong side of the law" but nevertheless very significant in any analysis of security are criminal gangs, pirates, terrorists, black marketeers, poachers, money-launderers, and networks of drug-, gun-, and people-smugglers. Less institutionalized are ethnic, religious, and regional groups with potential for mobilization for political action, or for outbursts of inchoate violence. Each of these categories is of interest to the security analyst, particularly if it is guided, assisted, or inspired by outsiders.

This brings us to "the people". It is asserted by many, for example adherents to the "human security" approach, that the concept of security is morally anchored to the security of individual human beings rather than states or other collective entities or socio-cultural groups. At one level this is self-evident; human beings are the irreducible unit by which all social and political organizations are constituted. The logical prescription is to judge all institutions by their ability immediately to relieve individuals from threats to their security. This logic taken to an extreme by radical critics leads to branding corporations and states as structurally incompatible with human security, and then to a utopian anarchy based on direct democracy led by NGOs. But at another level social and political organizations culminating in the state are more than the individuals that comprise them, and one must acknowledge intangible qualities such as heritage, icons, inspiration, trust, and justice to account for these constructs, for without them one has nothing more than a sheet of sand, as Sun Yat Sen asserted. To put it another way, threats to security are constrained not only by armies, police and courts but also by social values, networks and regimes, and by the institutions of civil society which are interactive with states. Following from that, the security of individuals may be visualized as intertwined with the security of benign civil organizations and states, and that which threatens the security of a benign state also threatens the security of its citizens.

Here we have the core antinomy of the study of security, indeed of much of political philosophy. On the "right" of the political spectrum stand those who accept the state and its agencies, including corporations and other national economic institutions, as a framework within which all people must work if they are to have any hope of security in an anarchic and dangerous world. These pessimistic analysts are called realists. On the far "left" stand those who suspect the state and allied corporations of self-interest and oppression of the people, thus a threat to human security, and in need of fundamental reform if not outright disestablishment. They place their faith in direct democracy, NGOs and opposition movements. We might call these advocates radicals.[5] Between realists and radicals stand those who rely neither on the state nor on NGOs but rather on the "international community", usually manifested by the United Nations, as the best hope of achieving security on a global basis. We call these optimistic thinkers liberal-internationalists or simply liberals, although in some circles they might be called idealists.

More recently, a fourth school of thought called constructivism has emerged.[6] Although not developing their own paradigm of security, constructivists have added a cognitive dimension to the understanding of security issues. They explain security issues as the result of inter-subjective interactions which have embedded themselves in the collective memory of a nation and society and guide decision-makers in their actions. Historical legacies and cultural traditions, role perceptions of self and others derived from them, and ideas and norms circulated and propagated by international institutions are thus key components of a socially constructed concept of security. However, argues William Tow, constructivism is derived from Western experience and developed by European and American theorists, so its application to Asia is not yet mature.[7] Consequently it does not feature explicitly in the analyses of this book. Yet, constructivist approaches on the one hand, and the rationalist schools mentioned earlier on the other, despite resting on different epistemological and ontological foundations, are not mutually exclusive, but may fruitfully complement each other. For example, synoptic realism as conceived by Kindermann in 1986 and the concept of institutional learning inherent in neo-functionalist and neo-institutionalist approaches have provided convincing evidence of such combinations of theoretical approaches. Furthermore, approaches that stress the influence of ideas and norms on social and political leaders' decisions are consonant with constructivist insights, and implicitly appear in several of the chapters to follow, particularly those by sociologists Schwengel and Schirmer.

In the context of this brief theoretical clarification, the editors have opted to invoke mainly the first two paradigms, realism and liberalism, to orient the contributions to this book. Our purpose is to offer the reader a straightforward, familiar, and historically grounded conceptual map and a common vocabulary that can be useful for navigating the chapters that follow on specific aspects of security. The contributors have been invited to draw upon the concepts, approaches and terminology implicit in realism and liberalism when conducting their analyses, but pragmatically, to the extent that they enhance the clarity and coherence of the work without imposing rigidity or arbitrariness. Nor are elements of radicalism and constructivism excluded where useful to advance an argument or sharpen an analysis. Nevertheless the overall result is eclectic inasmuch as the substance and texture of each chapter reflect each author's unique academic experience, analytical judgment and intellectual creativity. We trust that the resulting variety, vitality, informativeness and policy relevance of the chapters will compensate for departures from paradigmatic uniformity.

## SECURITY PARADIGMS AND APPROACHES

Many analysts have observed that the concept of security is in the midst of a paradigm shift. The dominant paradigm since World War II has been the realist paradigm.[8] The realist paradigm is state-centric and political-military-power oriented. Realists believe that the international environment is anarchic, that states struggle with each other for survival and advantage, and that power defined by military prowess is the ultimate arbiter. The best mechanism to preserve peace is a balance of power. To this end or — in the words of Stephen Walt — to establish a balance of threat, cautious cooperation is undertaken in military alliances, which were replete during the Cold War period and survive today, notably the North Atlantic Treaty Organization (NATO) and in bilateral alliances linking Japan, South Korea, and the Philippines to the United States, and China to the Soviet Union, North Korea, and North Vietnam. These were crafted as instruments to increase partners' security primarily by formalizing and encouraging military consultation and cooperation with other powers. Treaties are thus manifestations of the realist paradigm of international relations studies.

At the other end of the conceptual spectrum is liberalism. The liberal paradigm rests on the assumption that states have common interests that can best be realized by cooperation and that those interests transcend physical security to encompass economic prosperity, human welfare, and sustainable environmental management. The liberals put less emphasis on states and military power and more emphasis on inter-governmental and supranational organizations, international norms and laws, and transnational consensus. Whereas realists tend to be competitive and exclusive, liberals tend to be cooperative and inclusive. As expressed in an aphorism popular among international relations progressives, realists focus on the balance of power, whereas liberals focus on the balance of interests.

The polarity of the realist and liberal paradigms and the spectrum between them provide a useful framework within which to fit the discourses about Asian security concepts as they have evolved in the past three decades. The following passages trace in chronological order the origins of a series of security concepts. These may overlap at some points, but are nevertheless moving the paradigmatic centre of gravity along the realist-liberal continuum in the direction of the latter. The concepts include:

National security
Collective security
Common security
Confidence and security building measures (CSBMs)
Cooperative security
Comprehensive security
Human security

## NATIONAL SECURITY

The concept coming closest to a purely realist view of security is national security. It was the dominant security concept in Pacific Asia during the early Cold War period until the end of the Vietnam War in the mid-1970s. National security emphasizes the physical aspects of security. It is primarily defined in terms of military power and geopolitical constellations. Thinking in these terms classically reproduces what John Herz has called the "security dilemma". The quest of the "security state" to attain military superiority over imagined or real rival powers for the sake of national security is perceived by the latter as a potential threat which can only be contained by even more military power. The mutual distrust translates into a spiralling arms race which heightens tensions and increases the threat level. Relations with other states are seen as a zero-sum game and exclusively assessed on the basis of relative gains.

The national security approach subordinates everything to military strength even if this means sacrifices in economic development and of welfare for large segments of the population. The results are excessively high defence expenditures as a percentage of Gross Domestic Product (GDP). Typical examples are the former Soviet Union, Vietnam until the end of the Cold War, and present day North Korea and Myanmar (Burma). The economic dimension of national security is autarky in strategic economic sectors, in particular, heavy industries, even if this is equivalent to a highly inefficient allocation of scarce resources. National security requires the primacy of foreign policy, which is viewed as an entirely executive prerogative and usually surrounded by an aura of secrecy. Political leaders often display a tendency to paranoid behaviour and to view the outside world through the lens of conspiracy theories. The domestic equivalent of the "security state" is an authoritarian order and the maintenance of an extensive intelligence apparatus which tends to denounce political dissent as subversion. Not surprisingly, national security regimes often correlate with dismal human rights records and low levels of human security.

## COLLECTIVE SECURITY

Pure realists are of course hard to find, because most states find cooperation mutually beneficial, mainly in trade, but also in inter-governmental organizations. The United Nations has survived because it has served mutual interests in achieving order. One of the conceptions guiding the United Nations is collective security. Its manifestation in the United Nations has given it an aura of permanence. Collective security is a conceptual extrapolation from defensive alliances, positing a universal alliance that included all actors, dedicated to keeping order among its parties rather than directed against an outsider. Collective security is a popular concept because not only "soft" realists but also liberals are comfortable with it. It is realist inasmuch as it assumes the primacy of the state and the central role of sovereign military power, but is liberal inasmuch as it assumes also that states have common interests in deterring or defeating an aggressor, and can actually cooperate long enough to achieve these goals. It is more liberal than collective defence, exemplified by treaties such as NATO, which appear to be directed overtly or tacitly against a particular non-member presumed to be hostile.

Collective security in contrast presumes universality; all relevant states will join and play their part; and there is no presumed enemy. Historically, collective security is associated with the League of Nations and the United Nations with particular reference to the UN Charter's Article 51. Also, Article 1 refers to "collective measures for the prevention and removal of threats to peace, and for the suppression of acts of aggression…." Collective security has not always worked as conceived, but two of its most successful applications were in Korea in 1950 and in the Iraq-Kuwait War in 1991. Nevertheless Asian leaders have not been enthusiastic about its application to themselves or their region.

## COMMON SECURITY: EUROPE

A later refinement of collective security was called "common security". This is a European concept. Its usage originated with the report by the Independent Commission on Disarmament, chaired by Sweden's Prime Minister Olof Palme. The Palme Report, *Common Security: A Blueprint for*

*Survival,*[9] stressed interdependence, "common responsibility", and "security with" instead of "security against" an adversary. It rejected unilateral deterrence and pluri-lateral alliances as modes of security and stressed instead non-provocative and non-offensive defence postures and collective security. Common security as a paradigm structured debate between realists and liberals for a decade. Its core principles were incorporated into the Conference on Security and Cooperation in Europe (CSCE) which was successful in bringing the Soviet Union into a dialogue with Western Europe, which now has been institutionalized in the Organization for Security and Cooperation in Europe (OSCE).

Common security tilts strongly towards the liberal pole; under the CSCE and OCSE it evolved into a full-fledged security regime with binding rules, verification procedures and sanctions in case of non-compliance. Although common security maintains a state-centric focus, the comparatively high level of precision, obligation and centralization characterizing it demand from members sacrifices in national sovereignty reaching beyond the collective security concept of the UN. Precisely because of the curtailment of national sovereignty and the high level of institutionalization of the CSCE process, common security has not caught on in Asia. Moreover, unlike in Europe in the mid-1970s, territorial disputes in Asia were shelved but not resolved. Finally, Asians also rejected the normative underpinnings of the CSCE and, later the OSCE. The CSCE's first basket, for instance, formulated human rights norms which were at variance with the then popular Asian values hypothesis which claimed that Asian societies rest more on collective economic and social rights than individual political rights as in the West. In short, Asia was not Europe, and an Australian initiative to import common security into the Asia-Pacific region failed.

## CONFIDENCE AND SECURITY BUILDING MEASURES (CSBMs)

The next step was to move Common Security and Cooperative Security from abstractions to practical outcomes by means of policy instruments. One of the most widely discussed and sometimes employed means by governments was a congeries of measures collectives called Confidence and Security Building Measures, or CSBMs for short. These practices were initiated in the context of the CSCE process in Europe, and some of them found favour in the Asia-Pacific, not least because the ASEAN states had already employed some close equivalents. The notion of CSBMs goes back at least to President Eisenhower's 1955 "open skies" proposal to the Soviet Union, and other agreed-upon provisions for military exercise notification and observation, then called confidence-building measures.[10] Other "transparency" measures were negotiated in the Mutual and Balanced Force Reduction talks in the period 1975–86. The specific term "CSBM" first came into use in 1982 at an inter-governmental conference held in Madrid.

The CSBM concept was taken up by the Asian security community in the early 1990s. It was mentioned formally in ASEAN Regional Forum (ARF) discussions in Bangkok in 1994, although the Japanese suggested the alternative term "Mutual Reassurance Measures" and the Australians suggested "Trust-Building Measures". The Track II network Council on Security and Cooperation in the Asia-Pacific (CSCAP) in 1995 established a working group on CSBMs. The CSCAP Working Group concluded in 1995 that "CSBMs, if properly devised and executed, can promote peace and stability in the Asia-Pacific" and recommended them for ASEAN Regional Forum (ARF) consideration.[11] Subsequently they have become a regular item on the agendas of the ARF and other Asia-Pacific inter-governmental security consultations.

CSBMs may be defined as "measures to make military intentions more explicit by increasing transparency and predictability, thus reducing the risk of war by accident or miscalculation".[12] They fall into three broad categories:

- Declaratory measures — statements of intent including commitments not to attack or use certain types of weapons first. An example might be the signing by nuclear weapon states of the protocols of the South Pacific Nuclear Free Zone Treaty (Treaty of Rarotonga).
- Transparency measures — including exchange of information, notification, and observation/inspection invitations, such as publication of facts on defence expenditures, order of battle, and arms sales.
- Constraint measures — including exclusion or separation zones and risk reduction regimes, for example, DMZs and nuclear weapons free zones.

Thus it is seen that CSBMs are soft realist in character, presupposing negotiations between sovereign governments, narrow focus on military matters, and voluntary unilateral compliance. CSBMs are useful means of pursuing collective, common, cooperative, or comprehensive security, but are not comparable in quality to these overarching concepts.

## COOPERATIVE SECURITY: CANADA AND AUSTRALIA

The concept of cooperative security is identified with an initiative by Canada's Foreign Minister Joe Clark in 1990.[13] It bears a close resemblance to common security, and indeed, inasmuch as Australia's Gareth Evans invoked it with approbation in 1993, cooperative security might be called an Anglo-Pacific variant of Europe's common security. It differs from collective and common security because it does not presuppose institutionalization; rather, it is an interim precursor to some yet unspecified multilateral security arrangement for the Asia-Pacific. Thus it leans towards multilateralism, but cautiously and incrementally, so as to avoid alienating individualistic (and realist) Asian governments. It is realist inasmuch as it rests on existing bilateral and balance-of-power arrangements and works through them in the interim while encouraging multilateralism and the transcendence of the military dominance of the security dialogue to evolve. Cooperative security shares with common security an appreciation of the need for inter-governmental cooperation, although it encompasses a wider set of concerns and modes of interaction. By nurturing the "habit of dialogue" it seeks to create a new security framework geared toward reassurance rather than deterrence and prevention rather than reaction.

Australia's Foreign Minister Gareth Evans in his speech to the UN General Assembly in September 1993 summed up his understanding of cooperative security, and the key passage is reproduced in expanded form (bullet points added) to portray the contrast between the realist and the liberal paradigms. Cooperative security emphasizes:

- Reassurance rather than deterrence;
- It is inclusive rather than exclusive;
- Favours multilateralism over unilateralism or bilateralism;
- Does not rank military solutions over non-military ones;
- Assumes that states are the principal actors in the security system but accepts that non-state actors have an important role to play;
- Does not particularly emphasize the creation of formal security institutions, but does not reject them either; and
- Stresses the value of creating habits of dialogue.

On the other hand, cooperative security shares with comprehensive security, to be discussed below, the broader vision of security and the notion of common interests between states, including issues such as large population movements, illicit flow of drugs, technology, or information, equitable access to scarce resources, markets, and strategic minerals, air, land and marine pollution and degradation, global ecological changes, and human rights abuses. Thus, along with comprehensive security, it is a useful bridging concept shifting attention from the security of states to the security of people.

## COMPREHENSIVE SECURITY

The term comprehensive security was first used by officials and think-tank analysts in Japan.[14] In 1978, motivated by the relative decline of American dominance in the Western Pacific as the Soviet Union and China built up their military forces, and by Japan's increasing dependence on resources and markets distant from the Northern Pacific region, Prime Minister Masayoshi Ohira proposed a policy of comprehensive security that incorporated not only military elements of national power but also factors such as economy, diplomacy, and politics. Ohira in April 1979 set up a task force to elaborate Japan's policy of "comprehensive national security". The task force's *Report on Comprehensive National Security* of July 1980 proposed that "Pax Americana" was over, replaced by a new era of "peace maintained by shared responsibilities", in which Japan could no longer pursue its own economic interests without cooperation with other states. Therefore security required initiatives at three levels: efforts to turn the overall international environment into a favourable one; self-reliant efforts to cope with threats, and intermediary efforts linking the national and international levels. Thus far his conception barely transcended the realist paradigm. Six objectives were set, including attainment of energy security, achievement of food security, and measure for coping with earthquakes as well as orthodox security goals such as territorial defence and cooperation with the United States. Also stressed were assumptions that economic interdependence was a precondition for security and that knowledge and intelligence were vital means to anticipating and dealing with security threats.

While the individual elements of the report were familiar to policymakers and analysts, and reflected two decades of rising awareness of non-traditional security concerns,[15] their consolidation in a single document was a departure from customary Japanese cautious, indirect, and reactive foreign policies. It fundamentally changed the Yoshida Doctrine of separation of economics from politics (*seikei bunri*), in which Japan pursued its economic interests but left foreign policy and defence initiatives to the United States, by rejoining the two policy sectors with an assertion of self-reliance. In a curious reversal of Western thinking that relegated economics to "low politics", the Japanese had placed economic diplomacy at the top of their foreign policy agenda. In the 1980s however, Japan began to accept international politics and defence as legitimate elements of their security paradigm, alongside economic diplomacy.

The 1980 Ohira Report was widely accepted, albeit not without controversy, by Japanese policymakers and security analysts, and provided a common vocabulary of discourse. More importantly, the concept engendered public legitimacy for more vigorous participation in international affairs in the 1980s including increased economic aid and support of the United Nations, and paved the way for the unprecedented peacekeeping deployments, then cautious military support to the United States, in the 1990s. It was also used by Japanese political leaders to justify raising defence expenditures to just over 1 per cent of GNP on the grounds that defence self-reliance and regional stability were complementary.

## Southeast Asian Views of Comprehensive Security

Southeast Asian governments embraced the concept about the same time, although they preferred to use the terms *national resilience* (*ketahanan nasional*) and *regional resilience* (*ketahanan regional*), with initial stress on domestic self-strengthening. As the government of Indonesia proclaimed it in 1973, "National resilience is an inward-looking concept, based on the proposition that national security lies not in military alliances but in self-reliance deriving from domestic factors such as economic and social development, political stability, and a sense of nationalism".[16] It is the "ability of a nation to cope with, endure and survive any kind of challenges she meets in the course of her struggle to achieve her goals."[17] Prime Minister Dato Hussein bin Onn noted that Malaysia's security threats included communism, insurgency, subversion, armed separatism, economic slowdown or recession, drug addiction, illegal immigration, and religious extremism and racial strife; they included "political, socio-cultural, psychological and economic dimensions — thus emphasizing the total or comprehensive nature of Malaysia's national security". His successor

Mahathir bin Mohamad subsequently declared, "National security is inseparable from political stability, economic success, and social harmony". Singapore in 1984 launched its new doctrine of total defence, whose five elements included economic and social defence as well as military, civil, and psychological defence.[18]

The decline of insurgency and secessionism in the 1960s, and the success of ASEAN in moderating disagreements between members in the 1970s and assisting in the peace process in Cambodia in the 1980s, encouraged a more externally-oriented security policy by the Southeast Asian governments, which began to resemble the characteristics of comprehensive security as conceived in Japan and elsewhere. This was called regional resilience. Notably, while ASEAN continued to subordinate security issues to economic and social matters, by 1990 the ASEAN Post Ministerial Conferences with non-ASEAN states began to include political-military matters on their agendas. This practice grew to the point where a separate body, the ASEAN Regional Forum (ARF), was established in 1993 to bring together officials from the ASEAN states and the dialogue partner states to confer regularly on security issues. At its August 1995 meeting the Chairman's Statement included the observation that "the ARF recognizes that the concept of comprehensive security includes not only military aspects but also political, economic, social and other issues".[19]

## The Track II Process

Asian non-governmental figures, notably university scholars, research institution staff, thoughtful journalists, and NGO leaders, were also active in thinking about security issues in their countries and region. By the mid-1980s, institutes of strategic studies had been established in almost every East and Southeast Asian country. In 1991 these institutes initiated a series of conferences on "Security Cooperation in the Asia-Pacific" which led in 1993 to the establishment of the Council for Security Cooperation in the Asia-Pacific (CSCAP). The CSCAP agenda focused on four issues, for each of which a working group was appointed:

- Maritime Cooperation,
- North Pacific Dialogue,
- Confidence and Security Building Measures, and
- Cooperative and Comprehensive Security.

## The CSCAP Memorandum No. 3

Further CSCAP initiatives cumulated in its 1996 Memorandum No. 3 on "The Concepts of Comprehensive and Cooperative Security". This document distilled the consensus of Asia-Pacific non-officials (and officials acting in an unofficial capacity) at mid-decade. As it represents a milestone in the thinking of leading academics and researchers in the region still valid today, it deserves close analysis. Its main points are summarized below.

The memorandum noted that the new strategic situation offered a "window of opportunity" to develop fresh concepts and policies of security, and set out to provide "an over-arching organizing concept for the management of security in the region which might be agreeable to states in the Asia-Pacific". That concept was comprehensive security.

The new concept was to go beyond the balance of power and collective security of states. It was to:

* Build consensus and encourage cooperation between states;
* Link regional security to global security; and
* Link external security to domestic security.

In a nutshell, "comprehensive security is the pursuit of sustainable security in all fields (personal, political, economic, social, cultural, military, and environmental) in both the domestic and external spheres, essentially through cooperative means".

The memorandum acknowledged two unanswered questions: (1) how to distinguish a security threat from an ordinary problem and (2) how to implement comprehensive security. Regarding the first, it suggested that a security threat has the "clear potential to threaten the vital interests or core values of the person, the community, or the state". But governments would ultimately have to make judgments, sometimes subjectively, where to draw the line. Regarding the second question, the answer was that all governments and inter-governmental organizations should work towards comprehensive security simultaneously. "Comprehensive security cannot be implemented by a single process either regionally or domestically". But the ASEAN Regional Forum is singled out as a key forum.[20]

All these manifestations of comprehensive security, while gradually moving to varying degrees towards international institution-building and liberal concepts of security, are still firmly anchored in realist categories. True, the more advanced notions of comprehensive security transcend the exclusively state-centric security concepts of realism by conceding a role to transnational actors and international institutions. Yet, the "soft" institutions established in the last decade are not allowed to deepen because Asian states are not prepared to transcend inter-governmental cooperation. Institution-building ends where it engenders a loss of national sovereignty and policy-making autonomy. In some cases, the incipient multilateralism created by the efforts to promote comprehensive security is little more than a tactical move and a diplomatic mechanism of institutional balancing. This must be assumed in the case of China and previously also Indonesia. For these countries, a peaceful security environment is not an end in itself, rather a means to buy time for modernization. Compared to the earlier concept of national security, the relationship between economy and military power has reversed. Economic prowess is now seen as a prerequisite for military power which is still a major component of security. Behind such reasoning stands a thinly veiled desire for national greatness which can only be satisfied by playing a regional or — even better — a global leadership role.

## HUMAN SECURITY

Human security emerged in the 1990s as an attractive new concept, seemingly in tune with the post-Cold War devaluation of power politics and the proliferation of international humanitarian and human rights initiatives. It is a manifestation of the individualization of international law, which increasingly accepts that not only states but also individuals can be subjects of international law. In its most progressive form human security has been incorporated into the concept of collective security. Based on this reasoning the international community is not only called upon to move against aggressors, but also to intervene in cases of severe crimes against humanity. The concept of human security thus provides legitimacy to the contentious instrument of humanitarian intervention. As humanitarian intervention marks a profound interference into the domestic affairs of states, human security is seen by many to undermine the presumption of absolute sovereignty on which more traditional security concepts are founded. It is the security concept most advanced towards the liberal pole on the realism-liberal continuum, and elements of radicalism may be found in it. Not surprisingly, it is championed by liberals and radicals and resisted by realists.

Human security also addressed sub-state security threats increasingly highlighted by international news media. Like other new security concepts, it turns out to have substantial historical roots. The human security notion arose in development studies in the 1960s out of the dissatisfaction with the orthodox growth model and the failure of benefits to "trickle down" to powerless groups and individuals. Alternative thinking led to theories of radical structuralism, empowerment, and community-focused development, and to a focus on poverty alleviation and provision of basic human needs in development and aid policies. In the 1970s, the humanist perspective was adopted by scholars of global development particularly in the World Order Model and the Club of Rome projects.[25] Further elaborations of the concept, albeit under different labels, were made by the Independent Commission on International Development Issues (the Brandt Commission) in 1980 and the Independent Commission on Disarmament and Security Issues (the Palme Commission) in 1982.[26] The concept of Comprehensive Security developed by Japan in the 1980s and CSCAP in the 1990s included elements of what we now call human security. In the 1990s the notion of human security was at the core of the Stockholm Initiative on Global Security and Governance in 1991, the UNDP's *Human Development Report* in 1994, and the report of the Commission on Global Governance in 1995.[27] The governments of Canada and Norway in the later 1990s formally adopted human security as an element of their foreign policies and sponsored a human security network.[28] And in 2001 the government of Japan jointly with the United Nations and the Rockefeller Foundation sponsored and funded establishment of a United Nations Commission on Human Security.[29]

Scholars have now taken up the concept and are attempting to refine, measure, and assess its policy relevance. Particularly prominent are groups of scholars at Harvard University's John F. Kennedy School of Government and the University of British Columbia's Centre for Human Security. They and others are also attempting to fit human security into the framework of traditional and transitional theories of international relations and security approaches including those sketched earlier in this chapter.[30] Canadian scholar George MacLean summarizes the principal issues of human security as follows in Figure 1.1.

Of particular interest to the editors and contributors to the present book are works applying the notion of human security to the Asian region and its states and societies.[31] Anthony Burke, for example, has suggested

**Figure 1.1**
**Principal Issues of Human Security**

---

Personal security of the individual from violence or harm
Access to the basic essentials of life
Protection of the individual from:
    Crime and terrorism
    Pandemic diseases
    Political corruption
    Mass migration
Provision of human rights
Freedom from violation based on gender
Rights of political and cultural communities
Political, economic, and democratic development
Preventing the misuse and overuse of natural resources
Environmental sustainability and efforts to curtail pollution

---

Source: George MacLean, "The Changing Perception of Human Security", in *Canada on the Security Council* 1999–2000, Table 3, found at <www.unac.org/en/link_learn/canada/security/perception.asp>

that the Asian human security agenda could most usefully focus on four priority areas:

- Intrastate and ethnic conflict,
- Economic instability, development, and inequality,
- Domestic transformation in democracy, governance, and human rights, and
- Environmental problems and sustainable development.[32]

From a slightly different perspective Snitwongse and Bunbongkarn note with approval that ASEAN has broadened its agenda from state, economic and societal security to include comprehensive and human security issues such as:

> Environmental degradation,
> Mass migration,
> Energy security,
> Drug trafficking, and
> Cyber crime.[33]

These issues are discussed in the chapters that follow.

## COMPARISONS

To clarify the differences between the different approaches to security, Canadian scholar George MacLean offers a dichotomous comparison of traditional and human security concerns along seven dimensions (see Figure 1.2).[34]

Roland Paris proposes to analyse human security in a four-cell matrix with types of threats (military versus non-military) as one dimension and actors that might be victims of threats (states versus societies, groups or individuals) as the other dimension. This allows him to group traditional security studies of inter-state conflict in the first cell,[35] studies of non-traditional threats to the state including economic and social turbulence in the second cell,[36] studies of sub-state armed conflict in the third cell, and non-violent threats to human groups and individuals in the fourth cell, as shown in Figure 1.3.[37]

Our own summary of the several concepts of security employs the familiar realist-liberal polarity and places security concepts along a one-

**Figure 1.2**
**Dimensions of Traditional and Human Security**

| Dimension | Traditional Security | Human Security |
| --- | --- | --- |
| Spatiality | Territorially sovereign | Not necessarily spatially oriented |
| Target | State | Community and individual |
| Subject-matter | Diplomatic and military | Socio-political, socio-economic, environmental |
| Patterns of control | Institutionalized | Non-institutionalized |
| Decision-Making | Formal (political) | Informal (intuitive) |
| Potential threat | Structured violence | Unstructured violence |
| Responses | Diplomatic and military; unilateral | Scientific, technological; multilateral governance |

**Figure 1.3**
**Grouping of Studies by Type and Victim of Threat**

| Traditional security threat studies | Non-traditional security threat studies |
| --- | --- |
| Studies of sub-state armed conflict | Studies of non-violent threats to human security |

dimensional axis between the two paradigms. Figure 1.4 displays this placement. Each concept is followed by its proponent in brackets.

This list is neither categorical nor unidirectional nor exhaustive. Its categories are porous and overlapping, that is, states may pursue realist and liberal policies simultaneously, in different sectors or circumstances. The policies of states, initially realist, may tentatively and rhetorically expand to encompass elements of liberalism, and then move back to a realist stance, as Jürgen Rüland shows in his discussion of neo-traditionalism in Chapter 15. While the policies of most states will be found in the above spectrum, thinking about security in the new millennium will progress beyond it. The discussions by Martin (Chapter 2), Schwengel (Chapter 13) and Schirmer (Chapter 14) move towards constructivism and beyond inasmuch as they propose culturalism, public goods, and communities, respectively, as post-liberal notions around which to orient security thinking and reform.

To conclude this section, we would stress three points, one analytical, the second normative, and the third axiomatic. First, the concepts, spectra and diagrams presented above are analytically complementary, not mutually exclusive. We offer them without discrimination to show the widening possibilities open to scholars and analysts that partake of the new security

**Figure 1.4**
**A Spectrum of Security Concepts**

REALISM
|
Unilateral deterrence and defence (ultimate posture of most states)
|
Balance of power, alliances, collective defence
(Western states during Cold War)
—
Collective security (UN Security Council system)
|
Common security and CSBMs (proposed by Europe in CSCE and OSCE)
|
Cooperative security (proposed by Canada, Australia)
|
Comprehensive security (proposed by Japan, CSCAP)
|
Human security (proposed by UNDP and Commission on Human Security)
|
LIBERALISM

thinking, but acknowledge that which taxonomy is chosen and how it is employed will be influenced by its appropriateness to the analytical task at hand, which we would not wish to prejudge. Second, implicit in our discussion is a presumption that human security should be privileged to a greater extent than it has been in the past, when realism prevailed. After all, each of us is an individual human being seeking survival, protection, sustenance, and rights. In a word, we seek security. Contrariwise, to privilege the state, corporate entities, or religions or ethno-cultural groups over the individuals that comprise and animate them would deny our humanistic belief in the ultimate value of the human person. It follows that the contributors to this book incline to the liberal paradigm, where cooperative and human security are emphasized.

But, third, we do not underestimate the continued importance of traditional security, that is, the stability and authority of states and institutions, for we are convinced, like Thomas Hobbes, that individuals cannot achieve security or justice in a state of nature. Several of the chapters that follow, principally in Part II and the book's final chapter, are grounded on a realist approach inasmuch as their focus is states and inter-governmental institutions. But the assumption implicit in each is that state and institutional security will enhance human security, or at least minimize threats to it better than any conceivable alternative arrangement. Indeed, we assume a mutually reinforcing dynamic between state, societal, and individual security. And we can confidently turn the argument around to assert that enhancing human security will make societies and states more secure in the long run. Thus, despite frequent clashes between leaders of states and leaders of human rights and aid NGOs, we see no ultimate contradiction between the maintenance of secure states and socio-economic institutions on the one hand, and the encouragement of initiatives to enhance human security on the other. Traditional and new concepts of security should remain distinct for analytical and policy purposes, but their potential for mutual reinforcement should be kept firmly in view.

## POLICY IMPLICATIONS

To ask national leaders to keep the entire spectrum of security concepts on their policy agendas is unrealistic. But it is not unreasonable to recommend a progressive broadening of their security agendas to take account of new security concerns as they arise. To be sure, decision-makers must prioritize attention and concentrate scarce resources. Trade-offs must be undertaken.

This is most clearly illustrated by the debate in modern states over allocation of military resources between conventional defense, peace support operations such as peacekeeping, and constabulary tasks associated with post-conflict nation-building. Then there are demands to address pollution, conservation, financial, migration and human rights issues. More recently the shift of focus by the United States and the United Nations Security Council to counter-terrorism and WMD counter-proliferation has seen yet another call for the reallocation of human and material resources. And more broadly the human security advocates would shift the emphasis from guarding state security to building up socio-economic protection, amelioration and equity programs as the preferred route to long-term security. No government can cover all threats to security simultaneously. But every government should at least be aware of all plausible threats, and consider all policy instruments that could enhance security in the short, intermediate, and long runs. Small but timely allocations to meet nascent problems can yield disproportional gains, or at least avoid disastrous losses, in the longer term.

It is in this regard that academics and analysts can assist, by mapping future or alternative scenarios of threats and suggesting appropriate security policies, as an ideational exercise preliminary to effective action. While each government must assess threats and take actions in its unique security environment, its officials and leaders can learn from their counterparts, and from analysts, about new vectors of concern, new concepts for assessment, and new techniques of leadership and management. The editors and authors of this book aim to contribute in some measure to this common endeavor, not by compiling policy recipes and check-lists for crisis response, but by developing historical and comparative insights that, in the longer term, can improve the perceptions that underpin good policies.

## OVERVIEW OF CONTRIBUTIONS

In this book we take an eclectic view, one that acknowledges the validity of each of the several approaches to security in Asia sketched above. Far from rejecting the traditional concept of state security, we reply to interrogations by our liberal and constructivist colleagues that the state continues to be the ultimate guarantor of security by providing protection and order, and that well-run states will remain crucial in distributing justice and the guaranteeing the material prerequisites for human survival, sufficiency and dignity. But far from accepting realism uncritically, we are painfully aware of the ineffectiveness, corruption, and oppressiveness of some states, and the virtual collapse of others, and thus the need to address the security of societies, groups and individuals directly, not as a derivative of state security. In these cases we need to acknowledge the essential contributions of transboundary institutions such as international NGOs, inter-governmental organizations, and international human rights covenants and courts to the security of those human beings whose states have failed them.

The contributions that follow tacitly derive conceptual inspiration from one or another of the paradigms presented in this introductory chapter. Their incidence and application are the consequence of each author's choices, guided only lightly by the editors. The privileging of one paradigm over another is rarely made explicit. Rather, each chapter implicitly if not explicitly deepens the understanding of the referent paradigms of security by providing fresh insights and timely information. Ours is not primarily a book of rigorous analysis of security theories, but rather a book about Asian security in which theories, analysis, narrative, and assessment are employed to help the reader better understand the variegated nature of security in Asia, and the possibilities for government policies and non-governmental initiatives to enhance security at various levels and in various sectors. Taken together, the chapters of this book constitute an inventory of security concepts, mid-level theories, and historical and contemporary examples that we hope will assist students, analysts and policymakers to organize the otherwise bewildering variety of facts and beliefs surrounding the subject of Asian security.

A brief note on the contributions that follow will place each into context and guide the reader where first to turn to explore issues of particular interest. The two parts that follow have been arranged to illuminate the realist and liberal approaches respectively, and to lead the reader from the former to the latter. The five chapters of Part II focus on traditional security management by leading states and inter-state institutions. Historian Bernd Martin introduces Asia's traditional concepts of security. Martin works within the realist paradigm to trace Asia's experiences of inter-state aggression and defence and the balance of power, deterrence, and alliance systems that have been fashioned to meet these traditional threats. The subsequent chapters by Julie Gilson, Jian Yang, and Jörn Dosch examine the contributions — negative as well as positive — that the governments of Japan, China, and the United States are making to order in Asia. Gilson notes Japan's recent deepening of defence ties with the United States to maintain a balance of power but acknowledges also Tokyo's commitment to economic diplomacy and its loans, aid, and sponsorship of cultural exchanges, elements of Japan's comprehensive (or liberal) security policies as described in Chapter 1. While not unaware of non-traditional aspects of human security, Yang and Dosch implicitly cast their analyses within a realist framework and explicate how statecraft and strategy bear on issues of regional security. They note the potential rivalry of the United States, a *status quo* power, with China, challenging its implicit subordination, as a looming threat to Asia's international order. Each usefully acknowledged the role that domestic politics plays. The chapter by Jürgen Haacke on regional institutions could be characterized as "soft" realism tending towards liberalism inasmuch as it implicitly advocates inter-governmental consultation and cooperation. While collective defence and collective security have not found as much favour in Asia as in Europe, the notions of common security, cooperative security, and especially comprehensive security have been taken up by some foreign policymakers, and it is in this vein that Haacke's chapter is cast.

Part III is an exploration of specific non-traditional threats to security. Its chapters are arranged so as to move in conceptual approach from realism towards liberalism. In the lead-off chapter of Part III, Rod Lyon identifies weapons proliferation, both conventional and mass destruction weapons, as a growing threat even in the era of relative peace since the Vietnam War, and illuminates the unique, persistent, and seemingly intractable challenge posed by North Korea. Consistent with his realist standpoint, Lyon prescribes firmness by responsible states in arms control negotiations and creation of verifiable regimes. Inasmuch as arms control is both a traditional and non-traditional issue, Lyon's chapter may be seen as a bridge between Parts II and III.

Adopting a more liberal perspective, Clevo Wilson and Clem Tisdell note that struggle for resources, and the related problem of despoliation of the environment, are rising in the security agenda, and may cause, or be caused by, conventional armed conflict, illustrating the interaction of traditional and new security threats. Wilson and Tisdell stress the need for international and regional attention to inter-state resource conflicts, since they are embedded in history, complex socio-ethnic tensions, and political commitments beyond the capacity of any one government to resolve. Jürgen Rüland notes similarly that resource conflicts (among several other causes) may precipitate ethnic rivalries and separatism, which can shade off into criminality, and are sometimes characterized not only by armed clashes but also terrorism. Rüland elaborates the cases of Indonesia and the Philippines as the most severely plagued by these sub-state armed threats and as examples of the vulnerability faced by many Southeast Asian states given four unfavorable circumstances, which he outlines.

Stephen Hoadley notes that the above threats generate refugees and "economic migrants" who often turn to illegal channels of migration to escape their insecurity. Hoadley points out that those illegal migrants not only become vulnerable to deprivation and exploitation, but also exacerbate economic, social and political tensions in the destination countries, and thus exemplify security threats at multiple levels. Inter-governmental agreements and UNHCR initiatives to protect refugee rights while maintaining border security are proliferating, but a coherent migration regime, very much needed, is yet to emerge in Pacific Asia.

That security has an economic dimension is illuminated by Mia Mikic in her review of the Asian financial crisis. This crisis, and other economic dislocations consequent upon globalization, are sources of human hardship. Furthermore, they can precipitate violence and unexpected political change, as in Indonesia in 1999. Anja Jetschke surveys human rights standards and international agreements but notes that adherence to these by Asian states is patchy, particularly in Indonesia whose example she illuminates. Jetschke, reflecting a liberal view, advocates initiatives by a combination of international, regional, and sub-state actors, ranging from the United Nations to NGOs, and including other concerned governments, to ameliorate the plight of victims of human rights abuses by their own governments.

Part IV of the book opens with two inter-disciplinary perspectives and concludes with a discussion of main themes broached in the book and their policy implications. In an implicit critique of realist notions, theorist Hermann Schwengel points out that security dilemmas are deeply embedded in the history of the rival states of Asia, and exacerbated by current changes, mainly globalization. Schwengel then explores conceptually how to escape from them, adopts a post-liberal notion of security as a global public good, and finds in a thickening web of Asian regional, national, and local networks a promising route from conflict to cooperation. In emphasizing non-institutional modes of regional interaction he thus complements a prior chapter by Haacke on formal inter-governmental associations. In the next chapter Dominique Schirmer adopts liberal and some constructivist ideas to spotlight the importance of sub-state and supra-state communities in moderating geo-political interactions. In describing how communities form and strengthen, she illuminates some of Schwengel's insights. Then steering the discussion into the human security realm, she shows how social networks, NGOs, media, other elements of civil society can encourage convergence of values, or at least tolerance of divergence, thus making possible political dialogue as well as human dignity. Schwengel's and Schirmer's chapters may be read as alternate but convergent visions of pathways to security, grounded on regimes rather than governments.

In the book's final chapter Jürgen Rüland discusses the persistence of realism that results from not only current international uncertainty borne of globalization and terrorism but also, amplifying Schwengel, pre-colonial values casting their shadows on contemporary political and foreign policies. Rüland attributes the hesitancy of regional inter-governmental cooperation to a tactic of rational risk-aversion on the part of Asian decision-makers. The rise of American unilateralism in world affairs under the Bush administration is an influential model reinforcing self-interested behaviour by Asian leaders. While acknowledging that progress has been made in academic and NGO circles towards a broader concept of security, Rüland finds that Asian governments' practices lag far behind the new security thinking. The reforming of traditional practices and their reconciliation with new concepts regarding security in Asia may await a change of policy in Washington and reciprocal innovations by enlightened new leaders in Pacific Asia.

## CONCLUSION

In the meantime, this book represents a call for inclusiveness and clarity in security thinking. While not anticipating an embrace by Asian governments of comprehensive and human security policies in the short term, the contributors nevertheless encourage policymakers to keep in touch with the fresh approaches being developed in academia, research institutes, NGOs, and thoughtful media. They are convinced that security can be achieved only if power is guided by vision to the enhancement of human values. While differing in their approaches, they converge in advocating a judicious blend of power, vision, and values in the pursuit of Asian security with an increasing comprehensive and human emphasis. And they invite their colleagues in Asia and elsewhere to join the dialogue on how to accomplish this worthwhile goal.

## NOTES

1. Ruth Leger Sivard, *World Military and Social Expenditures 1993* (15th edition, Washington: World Priorities, 1993); Nils Petter Gleditsch and Håvard Strand "Armed Conflict 1946–99: A New Dataset". Paper prepared for session WB08 "New Data on Armed Conflict" 42nd Annual Convention of the International Studies Association, Chicago, IL, 20–24 February 2001, found at <http://www.isanet.org/archive/npg.html#_ftn1>. Accessed 24 January 2004.

2. *Asia Yearbook 2002* (Hong Kong: Far Eastern Economic Review, 2002), p. 16.

3. Commission on Human Security homepage <www.humansecurity-chs.org> (accessed March 11 2003).

4. Along with NGOs one should acknowledge the adversarial roles *vis-à-vis* the establishment played by political parties not in government, occupational and family guilds, ethnic and neighbourhood associations, sporting clubs, and occasionally city and provincial governments.

5. Alternative labels are structuralists, dependency theorists, or neo-Marxists.

6. Emanuel Adler, "Seizing the Middle Ground: Constructivism in World Politics", *European Journal of International Relations* 3, no. 3 (1997): 319–63, Ted Hopf, "The Promise of Constructivism in International Relations Theory", *International Security* 23, no. 1 (Summer 1998), Alexander Wendt, *Social Theory of International Politics* (Cambridge: Cambridge University Press, 1999).

7. William T. Tow, "Alternative Security Models: Implications for ASEAN", in *Broadening Asia's Security Discourse and Agenda*, edited by Ramesh Thakur and Edward Newman (Tokyo: United Nations Press, 2004).

8. On realism and its counterpart idealism as paradigms in the study of international relations see James E. Dougherty and Robert L. Pfaltzgraff, *Contending Theories of International Relations* (Philadelphia: J. B. Lippincott, 1971), Paul R. Viotti and Mark V. Kauppi, *International Relations Theory: Realism, Pluralism, Globalism* (New York: Macmillan, 1987), Robert Jackson and Georg Sorensen, *Introduction to International Relations* (Oxford: Oxford University Press, 1999), John Baylis and Steve Smith, *The Globalization of World Politics: An Introduction to International Relations* (2nd edition, Oxford: Oxford University Press, 2001).

9. (New York: Simon and Schuster, 1982).

10. Susan Pederson and Stanley Weeks, "A Survey of Confidence Building Measures", draft background paper for CSCAP dated 15 September 1994.

11. CSCAP Memorandum No. 2, *Asia Pacific Confidence and Security Building Measures* (1995).

12. Pederson and Weeks, cited above, p. 5.

13. See David Dewitt and Alan Dupont, "Concepts of Security" in *Unresolved Futures: Comprehensive Security in the Asia-Pacific*, edited by Jim Rolfe (Wellington: Centre for Strategic Studies, 1995), p. 9.

14. The following passage draws from Robert W. Barnett, *Beyond War: Japan's Concept of Comprehensive National Security* (Oxford: Pergamon, 1984) and Alan Rix, "Japan's Comprehensive Security and Australia", *Australian Outlook* (August 1987), pp. 79–86. My Figure 1 is based on Rix's diagram on his p. 79, with modifications.

15. The "Basic Policy for National Defence" proclaimed in 1957 included principles of support of the United Nations, international cooperation, and promotion of public welfare. See *Defence of Japan 1993* (Tokyo: Japan Defence Agency, 1993, p. 65).

16. This passage draws from David Dewitt, "Common, Comprehensive, and Cooperative Security", *The Pacific Review* 7, no. 1 (1994): 1–16.

17. Dewi Fortuna Anwar, *Indonesia and the Security of Southeast Asia* (Jakarta: Center for Strategic and International Studies, 1992), p. 13.

18. Steve Hoadley, "Singapore's Security Policies", *New Zealand International Review* (September/October 1988), pp. 19–22.

19. CSCAP Memorandum No. 3 (Kuala Lumpur: CSCAP, August 1995) p. 1.

20. The definitive work on CSCAP and the Track Two process is Desmond Ball, *The Council for Security Cooperation in the Asian Pacific: Its Record and Its Prospects* (Canberra: Strategic and Defence Studies Centre, Australian National University, October 2002).

21. See David Dewitt and Alan Dupont, "Concepts of Security" in *Unresolved Futures: Comprehensive Security in the Asia-Pacific*, edited by Jim Rolfe (Wellington: Centre for Strategic Studies, 1995), p. 9.

22. Pederson and Weeks, op. cit.

23. CSCAP Memorandum No. 2, op. cit.

24. Pederson and Weeks, op. cit., p. 5.

25. Saul B. Medowitz, ed., *On the Creation of a Just World Order* (New York: The Free Press, 1975) and Rajni Kothari, *Footsteps into the Future* (New York: The Free Press, 1974); Donella H. Meadows et al., *The Limits to Growth* (New York: Universe Books, 1979).

26. The Independent Commission on International Development Issues, *North-South: A Programme for Survival* (Cambridge: The MIT Press, 1980), Independent Commission on Disarmament and Security Issues, *Common Security: A Blueprint for Survival* (New York: Simon and Schuster, 1982).

27. Stockholm Initiative on Global Security and Governance, *Common Responsibility in the 1900*, published by the Prime Minister's Office, Government of Sweden, Stockholm, 1991; United Nations Development Programme, *Human Development Report 1994 New Dimensions of Human*

*Security* (New York: Oxford University Press, 1994); Commission on Global Governance, *Our Global Neighbourhood* (Oxford: Oxford University Press, 1995).

28. <www.humansecuritynetwork.org>.
29. <www.humansecurity-chs.org>.
30. Nicholas Thomas and William T. Tow, "The Utility of Human Security: Sovereignty and Humanitarian Intervention", in *Security Dialogue* 32, no. 2 (2002): 177–93; Alex Bellamy and Matt McDonald, " 'The Utility of Human Security': Which Humans? What Security? A Reply to Thomas and Tow", in *Security Dialogue* 33, no. 3 (2002): 373–77. See also articles in *Security Dialogue* such as Astri Suhrke, "Human Security and the Interest of States", 30, no. 3 (September 1999) and *International Security* touching on the human security debate.
31. William T. Tow, Ramesh Thakur, and In-Taek Hyun, eds., *Asian Emerging Regional Order: Reconciling Traditional and Human Security* (Tokyo: United Nations University, 2000); William T. Tow, "Alternative Security Models: Implications for ASEAN", in *Non-Traditional Security Studies in Southeast Asia*, edited by Andrew T. H. Tan and J. D. Kenneth Boutlin (Singapore: Institute of Defence and Strategic Studies, 2001), Alan Dupont, *East Asia Imperiled: Transnational Challenges to Security* (Cambridge: Cambridge University Press, 2001), and Thakur and Newman, eds., *Broadening Asia's Security Discourse and Agenda* (2004) cited above.
32. Anthony Burke, "Caught Between National and Human Security: Knowledge and Power in Post-crisis Asia" in *Pacifica Review* 13, no. 3 (October 2001): 215–39.
33. Kusuma Snitwongse and Suchit Bunbongkam, "New Security Issues and Their Impact on ASEAN", in *Reinventing ASEAN*, edited by Simon S. C. Tay, Jesus P. Estanislau, and Hadi Soesastro (Singapore: ISEAS, 2001).
34. George MacLean, "The Changing Perception of Human Security" in *Canada on the Security Council* 1999–2000, Table 3, found at <www.unac.org/en/link_learn/canada/security/perception.asp>.
35. We would place the concepts of collective security, common security, cooperative security, and CSBMs in this cell as well.
36. We would place the concept of comprehensive security in this second cell as well.
37. Roland Paris, "Human Security: Paradigm Shift or Hot Air?" *International Security* 26, no. 2 (2001): 98–99. In contrast to the enthusiasm of his security-study colleagues, Paris is sceptical that human security constitutes a discrete paradigm for theoretical study. But he acknowledges that it is a potent normative notion that motivates useful research, and therefore should be incorporated, even if it cannot be integrated, in the field of international relations research.

# Part Two

## Security Management by Asian States and Regional Institutions

Chapter Two

# Asia from Colonialism to Culturalism

Bernd Martin

## INTRODUCTION

This chapter builds on the observation that the past leaves a legacy, and that that legacy will influence contemporary security perceptions and security policies. This theme is always implicit, and often explicit, in the chapters that follow, for which this chapter serves as a historical introduction. However, the course of history is neither a progressive one as Westerners tend to believe, nor a cyclic one, as Asians under the influence of Buddhism tend to believe. It is rather a winding road, and those travelling it have difficulty detecting the turning points or most important milestones. Sometimes the past seems totally forgotten, no longer affecting politics. But with sudden changes in international affairs the national past can re-emerge into view, be freshly interpreted, and even be deliberately molded to support a particular response to a security crisis. History, as constructivists warn us, is not a monolith but rather a quarry where the stones are chosen and shaped by policymakers for a political purpose.[1]

An example will illustrate the point and also lead the discussion to the body of this chapter. In the eyes of United States policymakers, the Pacific countries have been an American sphere of influence, a U.S. security and economic "*mare nostrum*", for almost 150 years. This outlook was challenged by the great European powers in the age of imperialism and was contested again by Asian leaders in the post-colonial era. Because of their Asian colonial heritage, British, French and Dutch historians often tend to glorify the colonial past, which in turn legitimated their governments' later searches for privileges in the region.[2] Contrariwise, Asian leaders find little virtue in the colonial past but reached back to pre-colonial kingdoms and cultures to underpin their authoritarian and nationalistic policies.

## THREE SCHOOLS OF SECURITY THINKING

Considering these varying national perceptions, contemporary historians and political scientists have developed three schools of thinking about security that are applicable to East Asia.[3] These have been foreshadowed also by the discussion in Chapter 1 of this book. The school of realism focuses on power-politics, a derivative of Bismarck's "realpolitik", to achieve security. European statesmen and historians, quite familiar with the continental record of permanent wars, have developed the idea of challenge and response or, in military terms, of attack and counter-attack, and also of threat and deterrence. In these concepts cultural differences or economic diversities count for little. The school of liberalism, however, sees security achieved by interdependencies created by economic exchange and diplomatic institution-building at regional and international levels. This is a very modern conception. In contrast, a third school is of older provenance. It may be termed culturalism, and it emphasizes the deep differences between cultures, religions and historical experiences, and therefore the need for bridges of mutual understanding as prerequisites to international security. Inasmuch as culturalism presupposes that different security perceptions and values spring from different cultures, it is analogous to the modern international relations school of constructivism. The doctrine of culturalism has been set forth by scholars and politicians from Asian countries with thousands of years of indigenous culture like China and Japan, sometimes in the guise of the "Asian values" assertion. At best culturalism can stabilize governments and give them self-confidence in their external dealings, thus enhancing security. But if exaggerated it can produce a clash of cultures and non-material disputes between governments not susceptible to rational mediation, thus reducing security.

## ASIA: CONCEPTIONS AND LABELS

The dimensions of Asia, like security perceptions, depend on viewpoint. A geographer might take Asia as stretching from Russia and Pakistan east through the Japanese and Indonesian archipelagos, encompassing India and Sri Lanka. The classical heartland theories, developed by the German geo-political theorist Karl Haushofer and taken up by Japanese scholars as reinforcing their notions of a Greater East Asia led by Japan, identified Asia with the Eurasian continental block from Gibraltar to Yokohama.[4] Europe was associated but South- and Southeast Asian territories were neglected, and, in the inter-war period, were relegated to unimportance as colonial annexes of the great powers. In the colonial period the Japanese idea of a continental block resisting the challenge of the Anglo-Saxon sea powers was compelling but in the post-World War II period this view seemed archaic. But it may have re-emerged in response to the U.S. attack of Iraq and other assertive policies, fostered by the Chinese advocacy of anti-hegemony and multi-polarity and the advent of the Shanghai Cooperation Organization and the China-ASEAN economic cooperation talks, as sketched by Haacke below. This time Japan, intimidated by and dependent on the United States, tends to stand aloof and isolated.

The term Far East, still used occasionally today, stems from classical colonial times when the British capital London was regarded as the centre of the world. Within the British Empire the possessions in the Far East like Hong Kong, Malaysia and Singapore were farthest away from London. The Middle East, mostly referring to Persia and the Persian Gulf, was half-way while the Near East with the British mandates Palestine and Iraq lay closest to Britain. The proclamation of the Greater East Asia Co-Prosperity Sphere by the Japanese in August 1940 erased the term "Far East". Imperial Japan was now to become the new centre of the world with Tokyo as the new capital. The eight corners of the world (*hakko ichiu*) should be united under one roof — Japan — and eternal peace established. Maps of the world printed in Japan even today depict Tokyo as the centre of our globe, not the Greenwich zero meridian internationally accepted in 1884.

Nevertheless the term East Asia for the region to be dealt with in this chapter is the most neutral and widely accepted. This region includes the Eastern parts of Russia, China and Myanmar as the cornerstone in the South-West, while the islands of New Guinea and East Timor comprise the borderline in Southeast Asia.[5] By this definition India, continental

Russia, Australia and New Zealand and the Pacific islands do not belong to East Asia. From a historical perspective it is significant that this area is almost identical (save for the islands) with the frontiers (Russia excluded) of Japan's wartime empire.

The term Asia-Pacific, in contrast, originates from the United States and reflects the outcome of the Pacific War. Although World War II in Asia was both a naval war and a land war, the latter with fiercest battles in China, the Americans tend to look only at their own maritime battlefields and their former allies in the war against Japan. The term Asia-Pacific was picked up by Australia and its economic partners when they established the Asia-Pacific Economic Cooperation (APEC) forum in 1989. It now denotes all member states that border on the Pacific, including Canada, Australia, New Zealand, and the Pacific coast states of Latin America but not the Pacific island states. The term Asia-Pacific is thus a conscious politico-economic construction, devised to serve the interests of the APEC members, and insofar as it reflects neither political nor economic realities, only aspirations, it is an illustration of the constructivist paradigm at work.

## THE SETTING: FORCED OPENING, UNEQUAL TREATIES AND EARLY COLONIALISM

The legacy of colonial rule in Asia, especially in the tropical regions, still has a strong influence on the security policies of the new Asian nations. Even in countries not colonized like China and Japan, the former encroachments by the West have left deep traces in the political culture of the two nations. Notable is an undercurrent of rebellion against all things Western, which for example in Imperial Japan led to the Pacific War and in China led to Mao's Cultural Revolution. Attempts to westernize the two traditional monarchies of East Asia by force resulted in destabilizing the whole region and eventually in war. Colonizing the peoples of Southeast Asia living in smaller feudalist political regions resulted in upheavals and the triggering of national movements, often supported by Japan until 1945 and afterwards by Communist China.

It all started with the forced opening of China for Western trade by the Treaty of Nanjing in 1842 and Japan by the Treaty of Kanagawa in 1858. Formerly private colonial rule was replaced by state-controlled colonialism by Britain in the Opium War with China (1842). The contracts imposed on China and Japan provided for a new form of indirect commercial dominance by the Western powers. The provisions of these "unequal treaties" also included extra-territorial rights, like consular jurisdiction for foreigners and, more important, in the long run the loss of tariff autonomy. The Chinese markets, and fifteen years later those of Japan, lay open to cheap Western industrial products; the typical five per cent duty *ad valorem* on Western imports was no obstacle. The unequal treaties and the foreign settlements demonstrated to the local population that their countries had partly lost their sovereignty.[6] Great Britain as the leading political power, the richest trading nation, and last but not least ruler of the seas by virtue of its navy, was most prominent in the Western penetration of East Asia. The bad image of Britain as the propagator of and profiteer from inequality lasted for about a hundred years until 1943 when the unequal treaties with China were finally abolished. But the negative impression has prevailed. The former leading colonial power, starting with the acquisition of Singapore in 1823 and the seizing of Malaysia, Brunei and Burma in Southeast Asia, still symbolizes the superiority asserted by the white man; Britain's colonial past in China and its former colonies casts long shadows right up to the present.

Japan, on the other hand, was forced by an American naval squadron in 1853 to accept the United States as liberator from the feudal past and protector against the colonial ambitions of the European powers. America's opening of Japan and its "manifest destiny" bringing Western civilization to a backward country have to be seen in the context of the frontier movement of American civilization first across the continent and then from California across the Pacific Ocean to Hawaii and the coasts of Japan. The special relationship between the United States and Japan is not so much the result of the Pacific War but rather, stems from the days of the opening the country.[7] For more than 150 years, the United States has claimed a kind of patronage over Japan. This self-assumed role evoked strong opposition in Japan and eventually led to the clash of the two countries in World War II. Educating the "misguided Japanese" in the benefits of civilization again became a key element of American occupation policy, to which the Japanese reaction has remained ambivalent to this day.

America's colonial concept in the Philippines did not differ much from the one carried out in Japan. In 1898 the Philippine islands were to be liberated from European colonial rule.[8] Spanish colonialism, backward as it was with the feudal *hacienda*-system in the countryside, was to be replaced by a more liberal agrarian order where the local elite collaborating with the Americans gained unrestricted control over their holdings and better profits out of them. The Philippine people were to be educated for democracy and guided to independence under American protection. America in the eyes of its leaders was not a colonial power at all but the herald of liberty.

French colonial rule entered Southeast Asia in the guise of protecting the Catholic missions in Annam in 1858 and soon spread to the local monarchies. Cambodia, Vietnam and Laos officially became French protectorates where the Catholic religion and French-European culture would be spread unhampered. The Dutch had exploited their East India possessions by monopolizing the export trade of spices and other raw materials like rubber since about 1600. Tolerating the religious beliefs of the native Muslim population, aligning themselves with local rulers, and crushing local rebellions ruthlessly, they ruled the islands pragmatically for two centuries before they conquered the last autonomous states and took possession of the entire archipelago in the second half of the nineteenth century.

Despite different colonial concepts and different attitudes towards the semi-colonial domination of China, and, in the beginning, Japan as well, the legacy of Western intrusion or Western rule may be summed up in the following points:

- Traditional trade was disrupted. Indigenous political leaders and merchants were co-opted, or were eliminated or forced to adapt to Western hegemony.
- The economy changed from subsistence production to a market economy based on exports and imports, which had been non-existent or unimportant previously.
- The local elite, bereft of their economic basis, lost political power and acted as puppets of Western interests. Only Japan managed to avoid this further restraint of national sovereignty by a radical anti-Western reform programme, the Meiji Restoration. The kings of Siam did likewise, but less radically.
- Alien ethnic groups, mainly Chinese and Indians, were imported by the colonial administration, for example in Singapore, to control the local populations or perform economic roles. Christian missionaries, as in China, played pacifying and educating roles. Ethnic diversity and religious variety in many East Asian countries, therefore, result from colonial policies.
- The educational system, especially higher learning, was opened to Western concepts. British traces can still be found in its former colonies

while the French system prevailed in former Indochina despite communist rule. American and German influence in China can be seen during the inter-war period and again during the period of communist reforms. Japan was strongly influenced by the Prussian educational system but was forced after 1945 to turn to American models.

- The political values of the West forced upon the Asian countries reflected their European or American origins and were resisted by the traditional elite, most strongly in Japan, thus fostering anti-Western nationalist movements.

- The colonial powers maintained peace only as long as they did not fight each other, but their colonial practices destabilized the local economic and political units and led ultimately to disorder.

Thus the colonialists' concept of Western (often American) civilization led to the first clash of different cultures as early as during the second half of the nineteenth century. This first attempt at including East Asia in the "civilized world" was bound to fail. But it was soon followed by fresh attempts. These five phases may be entitled (1) The Framework, (2) The Vision, (3) The Alternative, (4) The Vision Renewed, and (5) Upheaval and Balance.

## THE FRAMEWORK: GREAT POWERS DURING THE AGE OF IMPERIALISM

In the era of imperialism the traditional European colonial powers and the new missionary nation, the United States, were joined by Tsarist Russia, itself for the largest part of its territory an Asian nation, and by the two imperialist late comers, Japan and Germany. The common object of all the powers involved in East Asia was to exploit China, now unprotected by its crumbling monarchy.

Japan took its first steps as an expansionist power[9] first in Taiwan (1895) then in Korea (1910), where it opened markets, settled Japanese, and tried to impose liberation and modernization. Since the kingdom of Korea lay within the Chinese tributary system, the Japanese moves antagonized the Manchu government in Beijing. The traditional rivalry between China (the big brother) and Japan (the little brother) reached a new dimension with the struggle over Korea which ended in the first modern war between the two neighbouring nations in 1894/95. The great Japanese victories, in naval campaigns as well as in land warfare, seemed to corroborate the country's modernization programme. Korea became the first Asian country to be officially liberated from the Chinese feudal chains. But now Russia claimed interests in Northern Korea.

Before a new conflict could emerge, the Boxer movement in China threatened all imperialist powers and finally united them in their first joint military intervention against the Chinese rebels and the government of the Emperor that supported them. From 1897 with the acquisition of Qingdao (Tsingtao), Wilhelmine Germany had joined the imperialist powers in the scramble for China. Western imperialism, imitated and joined by Japan, reached its climax in 1900 when all the nations involved in China sent troops under a joint command headed by a German field marshal.[10] The crushing defeat of ill-equipped and poorly trained Boxer soldiers and regular units was a humiliating blow to the old monarchy. Modern nationalist thought spread among Western-trained Chinese scholars who like Dr. Sun Yat-sen soon turned to become revolutionaries.[11] The Boxers as the first effective anti-foreign movement were admired in retrospect as patriotic soldiers by their fellow-countrymen. Modern Chinese nationalism saw, and in Communist China still sees, its military origins in the Boxers fighting the foreign devils. In the monument of the People's Liberation Army, situated on Tiananmen Square in Beijing, the Boxers are remembered as the forerunners of today's armed forces.

However, only four years later Western imperialism in China was halted. The Russo-Japanese war, fought over who would influence Manchuria and Korea, was actually a struggle for regional leadership and, the Japanese believed, for the liberation and self determination of the East Asian countries. The total defeat of Russia, one of the leading military powers of the world, by a non-white race and a country which had been modernizing for only one generation, dealt a decisive blow to Western superiority. Imperial Japan claimed to be the "light of Asia" bringing a bright future to all Asians under direct or indirect Western rule. Henceforth national leaders from India to Shanghai put their faith in Japan as the only anti-colonial power. Now the centre of the East Asian orbit, traditionally the capital of the Central Kingdom of China, shifted from Beijing to Tokyo. Before the First World War the Japanese Empire was commonly regarded, even by the Western powers, as the leading nation of East Asia, and the guarantor of peace and stability.[12]

Thus the legacy of the age of imperialism up to the outbreak of World War I consists of the following main points:

- A permanent conflict arose between Japan and Russia over their border and spheres of interest. For almost a hundred years the struggle over a mutually recognized frontier-line could not be resolved. The issue of the Kurile Islands lingers on and still destabilizes the region of the North Pacific.
- The cultural and ideological rivalry between China and Japan became a political issue with the question of leadership unresolved up to our time, even as the centre of East Asia seems to be gradually shifting back to Beijing.
- China's decline and revolution in 1911 produced a period of turmoil after the First World War. By actively fomenting Chinese disorder Japan gradually replaced Great Britain as China's arch enemy.
- The traditional European colonial powers started to retreat, joined by Germany and Russia. But Japan stepped in, closely observed and soon followed by the United States, each with its own liberation mission in the new slogan of "open door" in China.

## THE VISION: THE FAILURE OF THE WILSONIAN ORDER IN EAST ASIA

World War I deeply affected East Asia, not so much on the military field but rather in the political arena. Allied to Britain, Japan immediately joined the Entente powers. The siege of the German leasehold of Tsingtao was to win Japan permanent access to Central China. The German model colony was compelled to surrender to an overwhelming Japanese siege force. Japan took over the German possessions which, like Tsingtao, were valuable for extending trade with China or, like the Pacific islands, could be used as naval bases. After military victory Japan strove for political hegemony over China and in January 1915 confronted the weak Chinese central government with the notorious "Twenty-one Demands". In the shadow of the bloody trench war in Europe Japan tried to subjugate China as a semi-colony. Only when America's support stiffened Chinese resistance did the Tokyo government eventually drop its demands for political surveillance and police control in China.

The expansion of Japanese hegemony in East Asia was watched with suspicion by the United States, which was pursuing similar goals. In order to back China against further Japanese demands, the U.S. government led by President Woodrow Wilson pressed China to sever diplomatic relations with the German Reich and finally enter the war as an ally of the Entente powers, as America had done in April 1917. The weak Chinese Government in Beijing finally gave in, hoping for equal treatment as an ally at the peace conference. The return of Tsingtao to China and the abrogation of the unequal treaties were the two most important Chinese war aims. But both issues failed at the Paris peace conference as Wilson could not fulfil his former promises. Doggedly pursuing his vision of eternal peace, Wilson betrayed China. Japan was needed for the founding of the new collective security system, the Covenant of the League of Nations, so the demands of China, backwards and weak, were sidestepped.[13]

When the provisions of the Versailles Treaty became known in China, the first nationwide protest campaign erupted. The May Fourth movement shook and changed the whole country. In what is regarded as the first Cultural Revolution, Chinese intellectuals with students of Beijing University in the vanguard turned away from the Western powers as their counterparts in Japan had done before. China was thrown back on its own feet and forced to find its own way, which proved to be a revolutionary one. The rise of the Kuomintang, the national revolutionary movement under the guidance of Sun Yat-sen and the founding of the Communist Party soon to be led by Mao Tse-tung, were the results of the betrayal of the Versailles peace treaty.

China refused to sign the Western document and strove for a separate treaty with Germany which might serve as a substitute and a model for ending all foreigners' special rights. The German *Reich* was the first Western power to give up all its former privileges. For the first time modern China signed a treaty on equal terms with a former colonial power. No longer an imperialist power, the Reich gained tremendous influence in nationalist China.[14] Germany's special role did not end with the Pacific War but rather, was revived by the communist regime when defending China against American or Japanese economic threats. To this day there still is some stabilizing effect of Germany acting as the mediator concerning Western influence in China, as can be seen by the communiqué issued after Chancellor Schroeder's visit in China in 2002.[15] On the occasion of the opening of the German-built Transrapid railway line in Shanghai, both sides stressed the point of having no political differences at all.

While China was accepted at least by the German Reich as an equal, Japan was pushed back to the rank of a regional power at the Washington Conference in 1921–22. America's second attempt to check Japan's extension on the Asian mainland finally succeeded. Handing over Tsingtao to China and retreating from Siberia, where the joint American-Japanese intervention against Bolshevism starting in 1917 had long failed, ended Japan's continental ambitions at least temporarily. The *status quo* was re-established again and the principle of the open door was reconfirmed. Japan had to submit to American preponderance in China and even gave in to an agreement limiting naval arms. Because of an unfavourable ratio imposed on Japan, the combined American and British navies had three times the strength of the Imperial Navy. The agreement worked until 1934 when Japan cancelled its obligations as a result of rising international tensions. The only disarmament agreement in the inter-war period had not been worked out multilaterally by the League of Nations but rather was imposed by the United States, using the traditional European methods of unilateral pressure, persuasion and promises in diplomatic talks lasting for months. This U.S. *realpolitik* method departed starkly from Wilsonian ideals.

Nevertheless it worked for the time being. In 1922 Japan was back under American tutelage. The United States again ruled the Pacific and exercised strong influence on the countries bordering the ocean. In accordance with the armaments agreements, Britain had to give up all military strongholds east of Singapore. The over-extended British Empire could no longer be controlled from London by military means, and the first self-imposed imperial retreat started in East Asia.[16] However, America step-by-step took over the British political and economic positions.[17] America had begun to succeed Great Britain, and its imperial power first took shape in the Pacific region, to be completed by the end of World War II.

American leadership and the Americanization of Japan manifested themselves in a Western lifestyle and democracy in the Taisho period (1912–25), but they stirred strong opposition in traditional ruling circles like the military and the court. The national ideology of the Japanese (*kokutai*), the *Tenno* (Emperor) system and the traditional agrarian-based social order seemed to be endangered by America.[18] The Japanese felt threatened and further humiliated by American immigration laws excluding all Asian people.[19] This racial discrimination by the West fostered the increase of national myths in Japan. As heirs of the sun-goddess, the Japanese felt called upon to fulfil their divine mission in liberating the Asian countries from Western and increasingly American influences and thereby leading the world to eternal peace.

The first step on this way was the incident staged by the Imperial Army at Mukden on 18 September 1931 and the subsequent occupation of Manchuria. This action became a turning point both in Japanese domestic and international politics. With the military in power, all attempts to transform Japan into a democratic Western state came to an end. On the international level, moreover, the whole system set up at Versailles collapsed. The vision of collective security, promulgated by the League of Nations, had been destroyed by a founding member and victorious power of World War I — imperial Japan. The Wilsonian idea failed, as did America's unilateral power politics in East Asia. The Chinese-Japanese antagonism widened with the Mukden incident bringing both countries to the brink of war.[20] The traditional Western powers, France and Great Britain, turned out to be too weak to confront the Japanese challenge, and the United States, who could have done so, did not want to be entangled in foreign affairs at a time when millions were out of work. So the road from Mukden led to Munich. Western appeasement of the totalitarian states, first with Japan and later on with Hitler's Germany, further helped to destabilize the Pacific region as well as Europe in the 1930s.

## THE ALTERNATIVE: JAPAN'S GREATER EAST ASIA CO-PROSPERITY SPHERE

The West, represented in Asia by the United States and still partly by Britain, and the East led by imperial Japan, were turning away from each other. Different concepts of political order and security, at home as well as abroad, led the two sides to a final clash. But the differences were more than those over power politics and international organizations. The origins of the Pacific War cannot be understood without taking into account cultural or ideological aspects, as taught by the third school of security and order thinking cited above. The American-propagated order based on individualism, political liberalism and capitalism was rejected, not only by Japan but also by all emerging nationalist movements in China as well as in the colonies of the region. Instead of Western concepts, Asian people strove for a New Order based on the traditional values of collective harmony, spirituality and economic partnership. Japan's proclamation of a New Order on 22 December 1938, after the Munich conference, certainly aimed at regaining the leadership in Northeast Asia which Tokyo was forced to give up in 1922.[21] The New Order slogan was also a propaganda tool to win over the Chinese who then were bitterly fighting the Japanese. Open war had broken out in

July 1937, and severe fighting and bloody atrocities committed by the Japanese troops — like the rape of Nanjing, had cost hundreds of thousands of lives. Brutal warfare, therefore, was covered up by a visionary phrase about a bright future for Asia under Japan.

But the slogan contained the nucleus of a different political programme the West totally failed to grasp. The think tank of Prime Minister Konoye, Japan's leading politician in the 1930s, had worked hard on combining traditional national values and the new social necessities brought about by industrialization in an indigenous political programme. Former Marxists still supported the idea of a socialist revolution, but now within the nationalist context of regional hegemony. Social reforms, the longed-for second Showa Restoration, and the expansion on the Asian mainland should be combined, and Japan should lead the way by liberating itself and the Asian countries from Western influence. Having advocated a programme of re-Japanization for a long time, the traditional elite shared these thoughts and, as long as their social position was not endangered, supported the programme of expansion.[22]

This lofty aim did not attract the Chinese people suffering under brutal Japanese rule but it did attract the liberation movements all over Southeast Asia and also the Indian Congress movement. The enlarged version of the New Order, the "Greater East Asia Co-prosperity Sphere" proclaimed by the Konoye government at the end of July 1940, underlined Japan's aim of controlling all East and Southeast Asia.[23] The programmatic contents of the slogan further increased the hopes of the colonial peoples to shake off the white man's yoke. On the other hand the proclamation of a sphere of influence was to be an equivalent to the concept of Hitler's New Europe, propagated after the fall of France in summer 1940. Setting the borders of their respective spheres of influence served as a basis for a mutual understanding among the "young fascist countries" jointly fighting the Western dominated world order. The Tripartite Pact formalized this alliance in September 1940.[24] The world was then divided into two camps, the liberal democratic one and the fascist-totalitarian one, with the communist Soviet Union standing to one side.

Historians and politicians have continued to debate whether the "Greater East Asia Co-prosperity Sphere" was a cleverly designed propaganda slogan to exploit the natural resources of Southeast Asia,[25] a lofty idealist aim, or a kind of military strategy to disguise Japan's military and economic weakness. But Western scholars tend to neglect the alternative order that thoughtful Japanese leaders were striving for, while Japanese and Asian authors tend to defend this political vision but overlook the excesses of this political strategy and its victims.

The declaration of the Greater East Asia Conference in Tokyo in November 1943 about the liberation of Asia was intended as a counter-proclamation to the Western allies' Atlantic Charter.[26] It provided not a parliamentarian system but a paternalistic order in East Asia with benevolent rulers, and was modelled on the Japanese Empire. The semi-divine Japanese emperor was bound to rule the family of nations. All exploitation and racial discrimination should cease, and Western norms replaced by indigenous ones. Above all, the rule of the white man should once and for all come to an end. Despite its shortcomings this liberation concept did not fail completely. Japan granted independence to Burma, the Philippines and to the Free Indian Government led by Subhas Chandra Bose and encouraged national liberation movements in the formerly Dutch and British possessions, notably Indonesia. With the surrender of Singapore on 15 February 1942, which Churchill called the greatest military defeat in British history, British colonial rule was shattered.[27] The slow process of de-colonization of prior decades was speeded up by the Japanese military victories and the accompanying concept of Co-Prosperity.

The foundations of the neo-traditionalist political systems of present day Southeast Asia were laid by the Japanese. The new national leaders, Aung San in Burma, Sukarno in Indonesia, Bose in India, Phibul Songkhram in Thailand and Laurel in the Philippines, all rejected the political order of their former colonial masters, thus refuting Western democratic ideas. Asian nationalists like their counterparts in the Arabian world favoured "fascist" ideas about national unity and, like their models had done, tried to combine nationalism with socialism. Fascist Italy under Mussolini served as a European model and, racial discrimination conveniently ignored, so did Hitler's national-socialist Germany.[28] In the view of civilian nationalists, developmental dictatorships were to be established in order to lead the colonies to independence and to cope with the colonial legacy and the turmoil brought about not only by colonial forces but also by brutal Japanese occupation forces.

The destruction of the plantation economy in the Dutch East Indies and in the Philippines had a devastating effect on the whole economy of these colonies. International trade was totally disrupted because the Japanese were unable to ship stockpiled raw materials to Japan or other destinations within the new sphere because of non-military shipping shortages and

U.S. submarine warfare. Subsistence economy could neither feed the local population nor the greedy Japanese occupation force. Unemployment, mass migration to the urban districts and finally starvation marked Japanese occupation policy[29] and thus encouraged, as in badly devastated China, communist movements striving for a radically different third way to shaping the political-economic order.

Because of the unfavourable military situation, Japan's Greater East Asia Co-Prosperity Sphere had no chance. But it left its mark. The rise of nationalist liberation movements and of communist ideas was Japan's war heritage to Asia. The return of the West and the pacifying of the region in accordance with Western democratic and liberal norms seemed almost impossible despite Japan's unconditional surrender on 2 September 1945.

## THE VISION RENEWED: ALLIED WAR-TIME PLANNING AND ITS RESULTS

The "Germany First Strategy" decided upon by Roosevelt and Churchill even before the United States entered the war relegated the war in China and the mounting crisis in the Pacific region to second place. In American eyes, Hitler and national-socialism (Nazism) were considered the real enemies while the Japanese just misbehaved and under economic pressure would give in. If Japanese aggression could not be halted then, at least, it could be used as a back door to war. Having outlined their war aims in the Atlantic Charter, the Roosevelt administration and the now-weakened Churchill government strove for one world of liberalism and capitalism like the Wilson government had done in World War I. The United States could lead the other nations in a new crusade for democracy. The Fascist powers had to be completely defeated and their economies integrated into a system of worldwide free trade, the terms of which were to be set by the United States.[30] The alternative economic orders of the combined have-not nations, such as their state controlled capitalist structure and the system of barter trade, were to be eradicated. Economic competition by the Axis powers in Central and South America had cut into American trade. The trading terms of the Axis powers, payment of industrial goods and weapons in return for deliveries of raw materials, were much more attractive to underdeveloped countries than the American terms insisting on payment in foreign currency, which those countries were usually lacking. America again, as in World War I, supported the idea of decolonization and this time, with Britain dependent on American war material and support and unable to resist, succeeded. Nevertheless, the renewed vision of a united world under American guidance had two weak points: The economic and geo-strategic challenge by communist Russia to a liberal-capitalist world, and the political challenge by Asian nationalists set up by the Japanese military.

A new collective security system embodied by the United Nations (UN) was set up to replace the former League of Nations that had failed to guarantee a stable world order, not least because the United States had stood aside. This time, the regional stabilizing role assigned Japan in 1919, was transferred to nationalist China. Despite its weakness and the communist threat China was to become one of the four policemen, with decision (and veto) power in the UN Security Council to act against aggressors. For the first time in its history the American Government would join and support a new global security institution. The United States, now the leading military and political power, would move from isolationism to internationalism and take up the task of world security.

At the Cairo conference in November 1943, the future order of East Asia was decided upon by Roosevelt and Churchill[31] without consulting Stalin. All unequal treaties or Western privileges in China would be abrogated by the Western powers. After a hundred years of humiliation China got back its full sovereignty. But in a concession to the British, Hong Kong would remain a Crown Colony. Japan would be limited to its original borders, returning to China all conquered territories such as Manchuria and Formosa (Taiwan). The Korean Peninsula would be liberated from Japanese rule and put under temporary trusteeship of the United Nations pending elections and self-government. Furthermore, Japan would remove its troops from the conquered colonies of the Western powers and hand these possessions back. The liberation of India and the independence of Southeast Asian nations that Japan had advocated were to be revoked in response to British wishes. The American Secretary of State, Cordell Hull, summed up the war aims of the United States in the Pacific when proclaiming: "After the people who have come under domination on Japan's armed forces are liberated our task will be that of making the Pacific and Eastern Asia safe — safe for the United States, safe for our Allies, safe for all peace-loving nations."[32] Again, the Pacific would become an American-controlled sea, foreshadowing its later characterization by Ravenhill as an "American lake".[33]

In February 1945, at the conference at Yalta,[34] Soviet demands could no longer be ignored. The Roosevelt administration, which since the Pearl

Harbour attack had been asking for a Soviet intervention against Japan, had to accept special Soviet rights in China in exchange for Moscow finally declaring war on Japan three months after the end of hostilities in Europe. Soviet Russia wished for a restitution of the former Tsarist Empire's borders in East Asia. The North Manchurian railway, the shortcut of the Trans-Siberian railway from Vladivostok to Irkutsk, should be returned to Russia as well as its former leasehold, the naval base of Port Arthur. Furthermore, Southern Sakhalin and the Kurile Islands should be ceded by Japan. Soviet Russia[35] pursued imperialist aims at exactly the moment when the West had given up all its privileges from the golden days of colonialism. Once again, like at the end of World War I, China felt like a loser and humiliated.

"The beginnings of a permanent structure of peace" as Roosevelt characterized the results of the Yalta conference, did not comply with the real situation in China.[36] By giving in to all Soviet demands in a treaty signed in Moscow on 15 August 1945, the nationalist government of Chiang Kai-shek was further weakened. The disintegration of China and the re-emergence of the communists led to civil war. America's mediation efforts failed, corruption within the armed forces of the national government reached new heights and the People's Liberation Army, supported by the impoverished peasants, was on the road to victory. Even with the Japanese surrender, China could no longer be relied upon as one of the future four policemen of the world. The whole region, therefore, from the Kuriles down through China to Indochina and insular Southeast Asia had been destabilized by the outcome of the Pacific War.

The final event of the war, the surrender of Imperial Japan on the battleship *USS Missouri* on 2 September 1945, obscured the disastrous political situation in Asia, at least temporarily. With Commodore Perry's ensign displayed, the ceremony evoked memories of the first opening of Japan by force in 1853, which had obviously failed. The second attempt, after a great American victory, now would finally lead the country to democracy and Western reforms. The American protectors were back to guide their Japanese wards to the Western way of life and virtue. Occasionally seeming to stage the occupation as a show, the American "shogun" General MacArthur with decisiveness and flamboyance initiated basic reforms and personally rewrote the constitution. The idealism of the American reform bureaucrats stemmed from the heady days of the New Deal movement since many reformers, no longer needed in the United States, were transferred to the Occupation (SCAP) authorities in Japan.[37]

The British in their traditional, colonial way commented on the restless American activities that they were not sure that the Americans "realise what they are doing in their enthusiasm for freedom"[38] while the newly elected Prime Minister Yoshida, a former career diplomat, kept complaining about unnecessary and un-Japanese reforms at the headquarters. The formerly occupied countries, too, criticized the rule of the American authorities in Japan, for its alleged kindness and benevolence. The re-education process was finally stopped with the outbreak of the war in Korea. Political reforms and political purges came to an abrupt end. The second attempt of totally Westernizing Japan according to the American model succeeded only partly. With the Peace Treaty of San Francisco in 1951 sovereignty was restored to the former aggressor, but with limits. Japan was bound by a security treaty to the United States and henceforth served as a rear base for the American military and indirectly became entangled again in affairs on the Asian mainland. Since then, for more than fifty years the United States has been guaranteeing Japan's security, with all the implications for political controversy of such an unequal alliance.[39]

## UPHEAVAL AND BALANCE:
## EAST ASIA AFTER WORLD WAR II

The United States could block Soviet aspirations for a separate occupation zone in Japan's northern island of Hokkaido, but Washington could not stop the former colonial powers, the British, French and Dutch, from returning to their war-worn former possessions. The West European states had experienced military defeat and even humiliating occupation at the hands of the Germans and the Japanese. They had been devastated by the war and needed their colonies back to support their re-emergence as major powers.

The Dutch colonial forces had been interned after their surrender to the Japanese in March 1942. In Indochina,[40] the French colonial administration had been deposed and the few remaining French soldiers still loyal to the Pétain government taken captive by the Japanese as late as March 1945. The power vacuum emerging in North Vietnam was immediately taken advantage of by the communist liberation movement, the Vietminh, for a brief time supported by the American Office of Strategic Services (OSS) and supplied with American war materials in their resistance to Japanese forces. Only the British had fought their way back through Burma. The capital Rangoon had been liberated with the assistance of the Japanese trained Burma National Army changing sides. The Southeast Asia Command, led by the British Admiral Mountbatten, could not spare any troops to recapture the naval base at Singapore. Therefore, the formal surrender of the Japanese in Southeast Asia was delayed until 12 September 1945, when at least a symbolic British force had arrived in Singapore nearly a month after the armistice was signed.[41]

The British Southeast Asia Command (SEAC) soon was nicknamed "Save England's Asian Colonies".[42] As the British lacked power and soldiers and the new Labour Government no longer had any colonial visions, the British had to rely on the Japanese forces to keeping public order in the Dutch East Indies and in French Indochina (which they garrisoned until token British forces arrived). Having granted independence to Indonesia on the very last day of the Pacific War, the remaining Japanese troops after fighting for the liberation of Asia were by no means keen to pave the way for the impending return of the white man. Therefore, Sukarno's national movement in Indonesia as well as the Vietminh led by Ho Chi Minh and communist partisans gained momentum. The scene was set for a colonial war.

Indochina on the other hand had been divided along the 16th Parallel by the Potsdam Conference. The Northern part would be supervised by national China while the Southern part would be controlled by Britain until the French could take over the whole colony again. Both occupation forces left in January 1946 when the French finally returned and immediately denied the independence of all the three countries (Laos, Cambodia and Vietnam). Colonial war was inevitable. Even the Americans, having reconquered the Philippines in the beginning of 1945, had to actively fight the pro-communist Hukbalahap partisans before granting again independence to the country on (American) Independence Day in 1946.[43] With a kind of modern unequal treaty the United States secured special economic rights and leased twenty-three military bases for ninety-nine years in the Philippines, reminding historians of the practices of the former colonial powers in China. Having been forced under colonial rule again, Southeast Asia soon became a region of radical movements, armed uprisings, and prolonged fighting.

In China, post-war fighting set in as well. With the Soviet occupation of Manchuria in August 1945, a rear base was provided to communists to enable their armed struggle to resume. Captured Japanese arms and equipment were freely distributed to the People's Liberation Army by the

Soviet authorities. American mediation — the Hurley and Marshall missions — came to no effect. The demoralized and pauperized soldiers of the Kuomintang fled or went over to the communists. After four years of civil war Chiang Kai-shek's government and troops together with about a million refugees retreated to the island of Taiwan, and Mao Tse-tung proclaimed the People's Republic of China on 1 October 1949.[44] Despite the Truman Doctrine of containment, first enunciated on 12 March 1947, East and Southeast Asia seemed to be on the verge of turning communist.

With the invasion by North Korean troops of South Korea the danger of communism spreading through Asia seemed imminent. After the country had been hastily divided at the 38th Latitude for the purposes of occupation in 1945, two separate governments had developed. A communist takeover in the North accompanied by radical purges and the socialization of basic industries had been sponsored by the Soviets. The Americans in the South, after briefly discouraging independence, gave their support to the autocratic long-exiled national leader Syngman Rhee and had left the country in 1948. But they hastily returned under the command of General MacArthur to fight back the North Korean army backed by Chinese "volunteers" until the cease fire restored the former demarcation line in 1953.[45]

To this day no formal peace treaty or any other form of political settlement between the two Korean governments has been achieved. The unsolved Korean question has been endangering peace in East Asia for more than fifty years. Japan too, as America's "deputy", has been heavily involved in the crisis. As the former colonial oppressor who transferred two million Koreans to do forced labour in Japan during the war, the Japanese now suffer an extremely hostile image in Korea. In South Korea too, the legacy of the Japanese colonial policy has only recently given way to steps towards reconciliation. Japan's *"Nordpolitik"* has not proved as convincing as West Germany's *"Ostpolitik"*. The remaining Koreans in Japan, about 640,000, are still discriminated against socially and in many cases legally regarding their immigration status. The textbook issue, in which Japanese educational writers gloss over colonial and wartime atrocities, also aggravates the Koreans, as it does the Chinese as well.

The colonial wars were eventually ended in Indonesia (1949) and in Malaysia (1952), but not in Indochina. The Geneva settlement of the French-Vietnamese war in 1954 — the partition of the country along the 17th Latitude — was not signed by the American Government and its new ally, the corrupt South Vietnamese regime. The United States extended its policy of containment to Southeast Asia. Security treaties with Japan and the Philippines (1951) and Australia and New Zealand (ANZUS) implicitly signalled American hegemony in the Pacific, decisively displacing Great Britain as the centre of a global empire. Bilateral defence agreements followed with Taiwan and South Korea in 1954. When the French had been beaten and in American eyes had surrendered to communist pressure at Geneva, the United States sponsored a military alliance, the Southeast Asia treaty of collective security, known as the Southeast Asia Treaty Organization (SEATO), after the organization that it set up in Bangkok, in September 1954. United in the common struggle against communist aggression were the former colonial powers Britain and France, Australia and New Zealand (members of the British Commonwealth), and Pakistan together with Thailand and the Philippines. They formed a very heterogeneous alliance. Even though a global balance against further communist expansion in Asia was eventually achieved, the American-led treaty system did not deter Ho Chi Minh's government from intervening in South Vietnam, the ensuing Vietnam War, victory by the North in 1975, and the unification of the country under a communist government. And the treaty system was irrelevant to those newly independent countries of Southeast Asia that did not join but strove for their own zone of freedom, liberty and neutrality as proclaimed at the Bandung Conference in 1955. This conference of twenty-three Asian and African "non-aligned" nations had refuted any kind of hegemony, American as well as Soviet, and opted for neutrality.

## AMERICA AND ANTI-AMERICANISM

Finally, because of the unfavourable outcome of the war in Vietnam, the Americans started to retreat. President Nixon in his famous Guam Doctrine statement in July 1969 proclaimed the Vietnamization of the war. Secretary of State Henry Kissinger summed up the military realities — "A conventional army loses if it does not win, a guerrilla force wins if it does not lose" and negotiated a ceasefire with North Vietnam in 1973. The United States subsequently withdrew its forces and left the South Vietnamese to their fate.[46] Vietnam was united under communist rule in 1976, and the United States, having attempted to impose its own version of order in Asia, was widely perceived to have failed.

The same might happen in Iraq where guerrilla warfare has been endangering the American liberator ever since their brilliant military victory in 2003. Western policy has always failed in the Arab world and certainly will fail again as has been the case in East and Southeast Asia. Security, whether domestic or on the inter-state level, could not be provided under American protection. The dominance of the United States in the Pacific region ever since 1945 has provoked stern opposition, even hatred finally leading to fundamentalist terrorism against all Westerners.

The "axis of evil" including Iran, Syria and North Korea and formerly Iraq, Libya and Afghanistan, has a historical dimension. It was proclaimed by President George W. Bush but actually forged by previous American leaders. Although political terrorism has a long record in European history with the anarchical and nihilist movements in Tsarist Russia and Spain, the modern form of suicide attacks goes back to the Pacific War. This new global terrorism of today based on crude Islamic beliefs of a holy war and personal resurrection, has one of its roots in the Japanese Kamikaze squadrons. Overwhelming American materialistic superiority on the battlefields in the Pacific led the Japanese to strengthen their spiritual virtues. The nationalist ideology of a god-like nation and the stern belief of the military, the vanguard of the Imperial Throne, as being divine and worshipped at the Yasukuni Shrine after death in action, led to a strategy of self-sacrifice. The ideological and real enemy then with the Japanese military and nowadays with the Arab terrorists, has been America.

During the last year of the Pacific War, the Japanese army trained and socialized many Koreans to sacrifice their life for the Emperor on suicide missions. According to the well researched study of the Israeli historian Croitoru,[47] the strategy of Kamikaze attacks survived in North Korea for similar reasons after the war. The arch enemy, the United States, prevailed and the communist state was hopelessly inferior to the mighty American super-power. Suicide missions were accomplished by squads from the North in the Korean War and against politicians from South Korea, like blowing up half of the government on a visit to Rangoon in 1983. At the same time within the frame of anti-imperialist (=anti-American) campaigns Palestine fighters were trained in camps in North Korea. They started to fulfil their "missions" in suicide attacks against the Israeli when the holy war ("*Jihad*") had been formally declared. Most Arab people, in Iraq as well as in Iran, have been looking on the Jewish state as an outpost of America and its hated civilization.

The two Gulf Wars have given rise to anti-American feelings within the whole Islamic world, extending from Turkey to Indonesia. Deluded Arab terrorists have been further encouraged to fight against "Western evils" on a global scale. Since September 11, therefore, East and Southeast

Asian states had to take stern anti-terrorist measures. Japan even joined the United States in sending special units to Iraq thereby giving up, step by step, the status of a peaceful and non-belligerent nation as confirmed in the Constitution of 1947. Especially in Indonesia, the country with the largest Islamic population,[48] suicide attacks as the one in Bali against Western tourists on 12 October 2003 have endangered the whole region. Ethnical conflicts, so far submerged in Southern Thailand, Malaysia or even Singapore, may erupt any time and, in the end, could disturb the whole of Southeast Asia and depress its growth trajectory.

## THE UNEASY ASIAN BALANCE OF POWER

The dire scenario of neighbouring countries falling to communism like a row of dominoes did not transpire even after American withdrawal from Vietnam. One reason lies in the growth of indigenous Asian initiatives in conflict management. The Association of Southeast Asia Nations (ASEAN) was founded in 1967 without Western participation and soon evolved as a significant regional stabilizing factor. ASEAN leaders are fond of the word resilience to describe their style of dealing with domestic conflict without depending on intervention by neighbouring or Western governments. Although severe ideological schisms and deadly ethnic conflicts persist in many Asian countries, their governments have fallen back on their own political resources to begin managing their own security affairs in their own way. This is true regardless of whether they embrace or reject the continuing American military hegemony in the Pacific region, which remains an international fact of life.

Nevertheless the Asian order remains a brittle one. The verdict of Samuel Huntington in 1999 that "Asia has replaced Europe as the principal area of instability and political conflict" sounds very harsh but might prove right in the long run.[49] As legacies of a long history, the political tensions surrounding the northern frontiers (the Kurile islands and the Amur and Ussuri rivers ), and of Korea divided between South and North and China between Taiwan and the mainland, have not been dissolved yet, and no end is in sight. With China's economy booming and Japan's receding, the traditional rivalry between the two Asian great powers has been revitalized, and a new East Asian struggle for hegemony could flare up, into which the United States would be drawn inevitably. The treaty of peace and friendship between China and Japan, finally signed in 1978, resembled an earlier treaty between the two nations of 1885 when both sides refrained from hegemony. Both agreements have become obsolete in the course of history. This suggests that formal treaty-making along Western lines is plainly not the key to security, but rather deeper, more autochthonous and historically-rooted modalities are needed.

## CONCLUSION: HEGEMONY OR CULTURALISM?

To sum up, Western intervention in Asia, and thus the Asian resistance to Western tutelage, started with the first colonial intrusions and accelerated with the forced opening of Japan by America in 1853 and subsequent American expansion into the region. Asian resistance has adopted different forms ranging from avoidance and adaptation to revolution and war, and was taken up by various Asian leaders at different phases of their countries' development. And it has not ended yet. But reflections on history and on historical self-consciousness familiar to Western philosophers have been few in Asia. From the point of view of Western historical researchers, the horrors of the past are brushed aside, not only in Japan's dealing with a criminal past of aggression and atrocities but in the selective official memories of China,[50] Cambodia and Indonesia as well.[51] It is as if the eternal Buddhist cycle of life prevails, and tolerance and tranquility are elevated above justice to supreme virtues. Unlike in the West, there seem to be no guilty nations or individuals, and no moral self-doubts. Therefore, without reflection and repentance, as in Germany, the cycle of violence might repeat itself in East Asia.

Does the solution to latent violence lie in benign American tutelage, as in the occupation of Japan, and U.S. political-military hegemony, as in the current balance of power in the Western Pacific?[52] The United States, the strongest military power in the region, maintains a presence in East Asia for economic and security reasons. But the American way of life, the secular consumer society, has been rejected by many Asian leaders and their compatriots. Globalization, seen as Americanization in disguise, has not dissolved the sovereign states with their centralized governments in Asia yet. Neo-traditionalism, most explicitly the Singapore model, but also reflecting Indonesian, Vietnamese and Burmese views, resists an American-controlled global economy. The consumer society of the West has been accepted in some circles, but only superficially, as was Christianity a century ago. Despite all the outward Americanization of capital city malls, American lifestyle and American political leadership will not be accepted in the long run by Asian leaders who represent their diverse communities and are true to their unique histories. And many Asian security problems such as ethnic strife and fundamentalist terrorism are simply not susceptible to the American way of warfare or American material-rationalist political reasoning.

But there is another view emerging. It is based on the fact that Asian communications are steadily deepening, communities are gradually evolving, and Asian governments are increasingly working together, as is shown in the following chapters of this book. A new security order is being formed by Asian leaders themselves. With reference to the three schools introduced above, the new Asian security order has its basis partly in realism, that is sovereign state-to-state relations, but increasingly also in liberalism, that is regional and international inter-state cooperation and institution-building. And a neo-traditional basis we have called culturalism is emerging. This connotes the convergent values and arrangements that are arising out of cultural interactions and mutual understanding and respect. As McCloud has observed, "neo-traditionalism represents the restatement of basic values drawn by indigenous history and captured in its cultural milieu, in a contemporary context, which is the only way South East Asian society can modernize".[53] This can be as true for East Asia as it is for Southeast Asia.

Consequently Asian history can be read not only as an endless cycle of inter-state wars and intra-state violence but also as a salutary point of reference, teaching valuable lessons for the future security of the region. The centuries of destabilizing Western interference can be transcended by creative interpretations of the pre-colonial past. Quarrying and molding the past can provide the building blocks for a more promising future, one that does not reject history and traditional mores but sublimates them in a new security amalgam that blends the paradigms of realism, liberalism, and culturalism. Examples of how these paradigms manifest themselves in the security policies of Asian states may be found in the chapters that follow. The emerging amalgam will be unique to Asia, and it will stand firmly on the premise that Asia's security can only be established by Asians themselves.

## NOTES

1. Commemorating the fiftieth anniversary of the outbreak of war in the Pacific, the eminent American scholar, James Moreley, observed of his fellow historians that: "They either lie or create myths". Quotation from Chihiro Hosaya, ed., *Fifty Years After: The Pacific War Reexamined: Conference papers, Lake Yamanaka/ Mount Fuji, Japan, 14 November 1991* (Tokyo: University of

Tokyo Press, 1993). I concur that historians often falsify history and — as Morley might have added — thereby help to legitimize national initiatives such as Japan's attack on Pearl Harbour or the United States' retaliatory war on Japan. History "story-tellers" have almost always reflected the nationalist mainstreams of their countries' political and foreign policies and have even submitted to censorship in times of war.

2. The German approach might be regarded as a more neutral one, since German colonial possessions and entanglements in East Asia came to an end with World War I. Regarding the German "model-colony" of Tsingtao, see Mechthild Leutner and Klaus Mühlhahn, eds., *"Musterkolonie Kiautschou":* *Die Expansion des Deutschen Reiches in China. Deutsch-chinesische Beziehungen* *1897–1914. Eine Quellensammlung* (Berlin: Akademie-Verlag, 1997). On Germany's loss of colonies in the South Seas, see Hermann Joseph Hiery, *The* *Neglected War: The German South Pacific and the Influence of World War I* (Honolulu: University of Hawaii Press, 1995).

3. Derek McDougall, *The International Politics of the New Asia Pacific* (Boulder, Colorado: Lynne Reinner Publishers, 1997).

4. Christian Spang, "Karl Haushofer und die Geopolitik in Japan. Zur Bedeutung Haushofers innerhalb der deutsch-japanischen Beziehungen nach dem Ersten Weltkrieg" in *Geopolitik. Grenzgänge im Zeitgeist, vol. 1, 1890–1945,* edited by Irene Diekmann et al. (Potsdam: Verlag für Berlin-Brandenburg, 2000).

5. East Asia is often sub-divided into Northeast Asia and Southeast Asia by area specialists and policymakers.

6. For Prussia's part in the forced opening of China, Japan, and Siam see Bernd Martin, "The Prussian Expedition to the Far East (1860–1862)", *Journal of* *the Siam Society* 78 (1990): 35–43.

7. Edwin Palmer Hoyt, *Japan's War: The Great Pacific Conflict, 1853–1952* (London: Arrow Books, 1989).

8. For an account of colonial rule and decolonization, see Rudolf von Albertini, *Decolonization, The Administration and Future of the Colonies, 1919–1960* (New York: Africana Publishing Company, 1982). The Philippines is covered on pp. 473–87.

9. Bernd Martin, "The Politics of Expansion of the Japanese Empire — Neo Imperialism or Pan-Asiatic Mission" in *Japan and Germany in the Modern* *World,* edited by Bernd Martin (Oxford and Providence RI: Berghahn Books, 1995), pp. 79–106.

10. Bernd Martin and Susanne Kuss, eds., *Das Deutsche Reich und der Boxeraufstand* (München: Judicium, 2002).

11. June Grasso et al., *Modernization and Revolution in China. From Opium War* *to World Power* (New York: Sharpe, 2004). Jürgen Osterhammel, *China und* *die Weltgesellschaft. Vom 18. Jahrhundert bis in unsere Zeit* (München: Beck, 1989).

12. David Wells and Sandra Wilson, eds., *The Russo-Japanese War in Cultural Perspective, 1904–05* (New York: St. Martin's Press, 1999). Bernd Martin, "Der Untergang des zaristischen Russlands. Tsushima, 27. und 28. Mai 1905", in *Schlachten der Weltgeschichte. Von Salamis bis Sinai*, edited by Stig Foerster et al. (München: Beck, 2002), pp. 264–78.

13. Bruce Elleman, *Wilson and China. A Revised History of the Shandong Question* (London: Sharpe, 2002). More critical is Russell Fifield, *Woodrow Wilson and the Far East: The Diplomacy of the Shantung Question* (Reprint. Hamden, Conn.: Archon Books, 1965.).

14. Bernd Martin, "Germany as a Model? The Abrogation of the Unequal Treaties Between the German Reich and China" in *Guomin zhengfu feichu bupingdeng tiaoyue liushi zhounian jinian Guoji xueshu taolunhui lunwen [Commemorating the sixtieth anniversary of the National Government and the Abrogation of the Unequal Treaties. International Academic Colloquium of the Archive of the Guomindang Party]* (Taipei: 2002), pp. 75–92. Also see Bernd Martin, *Die deutsche Beraterschaft in China 1927–1938. Militär — Wirtschaft — Außenpolitik [ The German Advisory Group in China 1927–1938]* (Düsseldorf: Droste, 1981).

15. Presse und Informationsamt der Bundesregierung, *Bulletin* (2002).

16. T. G. Fraser and Peter Lowe, eds., *Conflict and Amity in East Asia. Essays in Honour of Ian Nish.* (London: Macmillan, 1992).

17. David Reynolds, *The Creation of the Anglo-American Alliance 1937–1941. A Study in Competitive Co-operation* (London: 1981). Donald Cameron Watt, *Succeeding John Bull. America in Britain's Place 1900–1975* (Cambridge: Cambridge University Press, 1984).

18. Klaus Antoni, *Der Himmlische Herrscher und sein Staat. Essays zur Stellung des Tenno im modernen Japan* (München: Judicium, 1991). Stephen Vlastos, *Mirror of Modernity: Invented Traditions of Modern Japan* (Berkeley: University of California Press, 1998).

19. Roger Daniels, *The Politics of Prejudice: the Anti-Japanese Movement in California and the Struggle for Japanese Exclusion* (Berkeley: University of California Press, 1962).

20. Akira Iriye et al., eds., *American, Chinese, and Japanese Perspectives on Wartime Asia, 1931–1949* (Wilmington, Del.: Scholarly Resources Inc., 1990).

21. The "New Order of East Asia" was restricted to North East Asia, encompassing Japan proper, Manchuria, northern parts of China and the Japanese colonies Korea and Formosa. This concept generally is seen as a forerunner of the "Greater East Asia Co-Prosperity Sphere". Text of the proclamation in *Japan's Greater East Asia Co-Prosperity Sphere in World War Two*, edited by Joyce C. Lebra. *Selected Readings and Documents* (London: Oxford University Press, 1975), pp. 68–70.

22. Miles Fletcher, *The Search for a New Order. Intellectuals and Fascism in Prewar Japan* (Chapel Hill: The University of North Carolina Press, 1982).
23. Peter Duus et al., eds., *The Japanese Wartime Empire, 1931–1945* (Princeton: University Press, 1996).
24. Bernd Martin, "The German-Japanese Alliance in the Second World War" in *From Pearl Harbour to Hiroshima. The Second World War in Asia and the Pacific, 1941–1945*, edited by Saki Dockrill (London: Macmillan, 1994) pp. 153–74.
25. Scornfully called The Greater East Asia Robbery Sphere by its victims and opponents.
26. Akira Iriye, *Power and Culture. The Japanese-American War, 1941–1945* (Cambridge: Harvard University Press, 1981).
27. Bernd Martin, "Die Verselbständigung der Dritten Welt. Der Prozess der Entkolonialisierung am Beispiel Indiens", in *Saeculum* 4 (1983): 165–86.
28. Paul W. Frey, *Faschistische Fernostpolitik. Italien, China und die Entstehung des weltpolitischen Dreiecks Rom-Berlin-Tokio* (Frankfurt: Peter Lang, 1997).
29. Bernd Martin and Alan S. Milward, eds., *Agriculture and Food Supply in the Second World War* (Ostfildern: Scripta Mercaturia, 1985).
30. Detlef Junker, *Kampf um die Weltmacht. Die USA und das Dritte Reich 1933–1945* (Düsseldorf: Droste, 1988). Bernd Martin, "Amerikas Durchbruch zur politischen Weltmacht. Die interventionistische Globalstrategie der Regierung Roosevelt" in *Militärgeschichtliche Mitteilungen* 29 (1981): 57–98.
31. Warren Kimball, *The Juggler. Franklin Delano Roosevelt as Wartime Statesman* (Princeton: University Press, 1991). R. A. C. Parker, ed., *Winston Churchill. Studies in Statesmanship* (London: Brassey's, 1995).
32. Roger Buckley, *The United States and the Asia-Pacific since 1945* (Cambridge: Cambridge University Press, 2002), pp. 7 and 232.
33. John Ravenhill, ed., *No Longer an American Lake?* (Sydney: Allen & Unwin, 1989).
34. Jost Dülffer, *Jalta, 4. Februar 1945. Der Zweite Weltkrieg und die Entstehung der bipolaren Welt* (München: dtv, 1998).
35. Alexander Lukin, *The Bear Watches the Dragon. Russia's Perception of China and the Evolution of Russian-Chinese Relations Since the Eighteenth Century* (New York: Sharpe, 2003).
36. Buckley, op. cit., p. 12.
37. Michael Schaller, *The American Occupation of Japan: The Origins of the Cold War in Asia* (Oxford: Oxford University Press, 1985).
38. Buckley, op. cit., p. 19.
39. See Julie Gilson's article in this volume. Also see Timothy P. Maga, *Hands Across the Sea. US-Japanese Relations, 1961–1981* (Columbus, Ohio: Ohio Universtity Press, 1997) and Gerald C. Curtis, ed., *The United States, Japan, and Asia* (New York: Columbia University Press, 1994).

40. James P. Harrison, *The Endless War. Vietnam's Struggle for Independence* (New York: Columbia University Press, 1989) and Marc Frey, *Geschichte des Vietnamkrieges* (München: Beck, 1998).

41. Rolf Tanner, *A Strong Showing. Britain's Struggle for Power and Influence in South-East Asia 1942–1950* (Stuttgart: Franz Steiner, 1994).

42. Buckley, op. cit., p. 22.

43. Henry W. Brands, *Bound to Empire. The United States and the Philippines* (New York: Oxford University Press, 1992).

44. Odd Arne Westad, *Decisive Encounters. The Chinese Civil War 1946–1950* (Stanford: Stamford University Press, 2003).

45. Bruce Cumings, *The Origins of the Korean War* (Second edition, Princeton: Princeton University Press, 1991) and Janshieh Joseph Wu, ed., *Divided Nations. The Experience of Germany, Korea, and China* (Taipei: National Chengchi University, 1995).

46. Buckley, op. cit., p. 142.

47. Joseph Croitoru, *Der Märtyrer als Waffe. Die historischen Wurzeln des Selbstmordattentats* (München: Hanser, 2002).

48. Mike Miiard, *Jihad in Paradise. Islam and Politics in Southeast Asia* (New York: Sharpe, 2002). Paul J. Smith, *Terrorism and Violence in Southeast Asia. Transnational Challenges to States and Regional Stability* (New York: Sharpe, 2004).

49. Samuel Huntington in *Daily Yomiuri* (Tokyo) 6 January 1999; quoted by Buckley op. cit., p. 230.

50. Bernd Martin, "From the Pacific War to a Policy of Good Neighbourliness? Japan's Way of Dealing with the Past", in *Dialogue and Cooperation*, vol. 2 (Singapore: Friedrich-Ebert-Stiftung, 2003), pp. 71–77.

51. Partial exceptions may be found in Taiwan, Singapore, Philippines and South Korea, which not coincidently are the most Westernized of the Asian countries.

52. Chalmers Johnson, *Blowback. The Costs and Consequences of American Empire* (New York: Metropolitan, 2000) and also by Johnson, *The Sorrows of Empire. Militarism, Secrecy, and the End of Republics* (New York: Metropolitan, 2003).

53. Donald G. McCloud, *Southeast Asia — Tradition and Modernity in the Contemporary World* (Boulder: Westview, 1995), p. 146.

# Chapter Three

# Japan and East Asian Regional Security

Julie Gilson

## INTRODUCTION

This chapter examines Japan's changing regional security context at the start of the twenty-first century. Japan's own approach to security issues throughout the post-war period has been simultaneously constrained by particular domestic forces and buffeted by international pressures. Forced to renounce the use of conventional and nuclear forces in the region in the wake of defeat and occupation after 1945, the Japanese Government adopted what became known as a "pacifist" constitution and the Japanese people supported the later introduction of Japan's so-called three non-nuclear principles.[1] At the same time, since regaining its independence in 1952 Japan has been pushed to assume greater international military burdens.[2] These contradictory forces, as will be shown below, have facilitated an often pragmatic and changing security posture by the Japanese government, within its region and beyond.

This chapter will examine the principal issues related to Japanese security concerns with the region, particularly since the ending of the Cold War. The first section provides a brief historical overview of how Japan's security relations in its region have developed over time. The second section looks at the main issues concerning Japan's security at the start of the new century and examines the more frequent adoption of security alternatives. Section 3 looks at three major security concerns: anti-terrorism in the wake of 11 September 2001, North Korea and the war in Iraq. The conclusion assesses the extent to which Japan's pragmatism is capable of dealing with this changing security environment, and examines how far the Japanese Government may be seen to be developing a "comprehensive security" strategy.

## HISTORICAL OVERVIEW

In the wake of defeat in 1945 Japan was occupied for almost seven years by the Supreme Command for the Allied Powers (SCAP). This predominantly American presence on Japanese soil ensured that the processes of demilitarization and democratization were set in train.[3] Despite later U.S. calls for the rearmament of Japan, the revised Constitution of 1946 set in place what became the mantra of the Japanese security élite: Article Nine. This reads as follows:

> Aspiring sincerely to an international peace based on justice and order, the Japanese people forever renounce war as a sovereign right of the nation and the threat or use of force as means of settling international disputes.

> In order to accomplish the aim of the preceding paragraph, land, sea and air forces, as well as other war potential, will never be maintained. The right of belligerency of the state will not be recognized.[4]

This document has underpinned public opinion and political choices since that time. However, with the onset of the Cold War and Japan's close ties with the United States, cemented by the 1952 U.S.-Japan Security Treaty, Japan's renunciation of war would nevertheless be accommodated under the military umbrella of U.S. protection.[5] Prime Minister Yoshida's economics-first doctrine and the much vaunted "UN-centred diplomacy" of the 1950s could not supplant this overarching relationship.[6] The security treaty remains in place today, but changing bilateral relations and global conditions have given Japan opportunities to explore alternative vehicles for regional security. The Conclusion will assess the extent to which events since 2001 have influenced these changes.

The 1980 Study Group on Comprehensive National Security was designed to enhance military cooperation with the United States, but also to persuade the USSR that Japan was not a threat. This study placed new issues on the "security" agenda for the first time. Its notion of comprehensive security included energy security, food security and crisis management and thereby located diplomacy and economic stability at the heart of security itself. Within Japan, it has developed as a supplement to more traditional forms of security and was validated in the 1990s by new United Nations (UN) proposals on human security, as well as by the rise of local conflicts and new approaches to their resolution that resulted from the collapse of Cold War structures (see Chapter 1). The government of Japan thus "began reviewing its security posture",[7] and commenced operationalizing its comprehensive security processes in the 1990s. However, a concurrent need to address Japan's inability to function as a "normal" state militarily and assume its share of what was perceived to be an international security burden was highlighted by its refusal to participate fully in the Gulf War of 1990–91. This burden, particularly over the issue of sending troops to participate in peace-keeping operations, will be examined further below.

## FORMULATING SECURITY POLICY

According to the 2003 *Diplomatic Bluebook*, the principal goal of Japan's foreign policy is to "secure the safety and prosperity of Japan and the Japanese people".[8] Despite such broad aspirations, however, the actual mechanisms for formulating foreign security policy remain limited, while the number of significant actors is similarly small. Constitutional constraints and the dominant relationship with the United States remain at the core of Japan's security concerns. Moreover, in spite of the fact that an increasing number of non-state actors (such as the media and non-governmental organizations) have begun to play a minor role in influencing security debates, Japan's security policy continues to be dominated by the Ministry of Foreign Affairs (MOFA), the Prime Minister's Office (PMO) and the Japan Defence Agency (JDA).

Overall responsibility for security policy resides with MOFA, which "functions in many ways as the coordinator of Japan's international relations and as the state's window upon the world".[9] The ministry is itself divided into functional bureaus (including Foreign Policy and Intelligence and Analysis) and regional bureaus, which include Asia and North America. The latter is the most powerful bureau and ensures a continued pro-U.S.

stance in Japan's foreign policy orientation. Interestingly, as Hook *et al.* note, the Asia bureau increasingly challenges the North America bureau and is itself gaining substantial powers as the region becomes more important in Japan's overall foreign security policy-making.[10] MOFA devises and implements overall foreign security policy, by gathering information, assessing security threats overseas and consulting other ministries and bureaus abroad. Its representatives also liaise directly with the U.S. Department of Defence and Department of State and they participate in regional security fora such as the ARF.[11] However, MOFA remains under-staffed and under-budgeted, with roughly one third of the personnel of the U.S. Department of State and this makes it weak in gathering security information effectively. Linked to this, with poor representation in the Diet, MOFA has little political power or incentive to challenge the centrality of U.S.-driven foreign policy. With the pro-U.S. Liberal Democratic Party (LDP) retaining central political influence, this is unlikely to change in the near future. At the same time, however, Diet members may also participate in security affairs through, for example, the Dietmen's Leagues for the Promotion of Japan-North Korea Friendship, Japan-China Friendship and Comprehensive Security. Such groupings are important for gathering information and strengthening international linkages.

The PMO provides executive leadership but has a limited staff and tends to be run by people drawn from the main ministries. Through study groups, with a greater voice at international summit meetings and with what Hook *et al.* label "moral authority", the prime minister can, nevertheless, exercise some authority on particular issues.[12] Prime Minister Koizumi led with executive authority on the difficult decision to support the United States in Iraq and to send SDF there, as will be illustrated below.

The JDA implements Japan's defence policy and manages the defence budget, but lacks substantial decision-making power when compared with MOFA. In particular, as a result of Japan's particular history and constitutional arrangements, the SDF come under direct control of the prime minister and the JDA itself does not have full ministerial status but resides within the administrative framework of the PMO. Its role, especially with regard to peace-keeping operations, is gaining a higher profile as it works more closely with MOFA and it remains to be seen whether it will begin to accrue greater decision-making powers. Recently, many of these various actors have begun to coalesce around the policy formula put forward by Foreign Minister Yoriko Kawaguchi, for Japan to turn its attention to "comprehensive conflict prevention" as part of the promotion of the "consolidation of peace".[13] This proposal is a reassertion of Japan's comprehensive security, with an emphasis on post-conflict reconstruction and humanitarian assistance as part of the security agenda.

## CURRENT SECURITY ISSUES

In terms of security participation in the region of East Asia, Japan's bilateral alliance with the United States continues to determine many of the parameters of Japanese action.[14] This relationship may indeed have been reinforced as a result of the 2001 attacks in the United States. At the same time, however, greater regional dialogue and agreement on a range of economic and political concerns have precipitated closer multilateral cooperation on non-traditional security issues.[15] As Segal noted in 1995, "East Asia is at a crucial moment in shaping its international affairs".[16] On the one hand, the "dangerously vague" strategy of the United States in the region and ever-growing military acquisitions by regional states provided the context for greater insecurity.[17] On the other, the growth in regional trade and the need to address collectively trans-border security concerns meant that new mechanisms for dialogue were already becoming increasingly significant. But, as Ball notes: "It could well take more than a decade for the developing dialogue processes within the region to produce sufficient mutual understanding, confidence and trust for resolving or managing substantive regional security issues".[18] Both sides of this security approach will be examined below, but it is worth indicating first what is meant by the alternative agenda that sits at the core of many interpretations of comprehensive security and the consolidation of peace.

## COMPREHENSIVE SECURITY?

Japan's economic penetration of the rest of East and Southeast Asia since the 1970s in particular is well documented.[19] Increasingly, Japanese business involvement (particularly since the many wholesale business relocations as a result of the Plaza Accord of 1985), tourism and cultural exports have reinforced Japan's presence across the continent. Notwithstanding these developments, the difficult legacy of history and the political posturing of leaders and their use of symbols (from honouring the war dead at the Yasukuni Shrine to authorizing school textbooks denying Japanese war atrocities throughout the region) have perpetuated the sense of regional suspicion of the possibility of a remilitarized, and indeed nuclear, Japan. In part to assuage some of these concerns, and in part to be seen to be playing a burden-sharing role, the Japanese Government since the 1990s began actively to seek new ways of cooperating to promote regional security.

The most visible evidence of this posture has been Japan's proposal for, and involvement in, the ASEAN Regional Forum (ARF). The ARF is designed to act as a *de facto* confidence-building measure (CBM) and to provide the location for a dialogue on issues as diverse as anti-terrorist cooperation, the fight against drugs trafficking and the sale and transfer of conventional weapons.[20] Similar issues have also been raised in the Asia-Europe Meeting (ASEM), while the recently instituted ASEAN+3 (APT) grouping could eventually become an important focus for intra-regional discussions on these kinds of issues.[21] In addition to these institutional arrangements, the Japanese Government has been active in the development of a debate over "human security". Based on the UN Development Programme (UNDP) reports of the mid-1990s, this attempt to widen the scope of activities embraced within the "security" debate has once again been influential at a number of levels. Indeed, with the rise in salience in the post-Cold War era of so-called "soft" security issues and the UNDP reports examining them, scholars began to integrate into traditional explanations of security a close scrutiny of the concept of the individual and the community.[22]

Thomas provides a definition that encapsulates the Japanese Government's understanding of these changing circumstances, when she notes that human security "describes a condition of existence in which basic material needs are met, and in which human dignity, including meaningful participation in the life of the community can be realised".[23] These forms of human security place a premium, as noted in the 1994 UNDP report, on addressing issues related to, for example, job and income security, health, environment and a crime-free society.[24] A Commission on Human Security was established, co-chaired by Sadako Ogata, former United Nations High Commissioner for Refugees and Amartya Sen of Cambridge University. Its final report was adopted at its last meeting in February 2003 in Tokyo and submitted to the Secretary-General of the UN. While the Japanese Government has failed to offer a central role to non-governmental organizations (NGOs) as part of the development of a human security agenda, it has, nevertheless, used these themes to promote a more active, if limited, foreign policy role.[25] Foreign Minister Kawaguchi proposed consolidation of peace can be viewed as a reiteration of these principles. The principal channels of Japan's contribution to this form of security have been Japan's bilateral aid-giving and contributions through multilateral mechanisms, such as the United Nations Environment Programme (UNEP), the United Nations Economic and Social Commission for Asia-Pacific (ESCAP), the Asia Pacific Economic Cooperation (APEC) forum, the UN Commission on Human Security, and the UNDP. The rationale for this type of commitment is founded upon the basis that, under the safe umbrella of "human security", Japan has been able to make a more constructive contribution in the international arena, from the Balkans, to the Middle East and Afghanistan.[26] No longer, according to this view, is Japan simply paying the bills, an action for which it was so roundly criticized at the time of the Gulf War of 1990/91. Actions in Iraq have further asserted this position.

One of the most significant steps made by Japan in this regard, and an area that straddles conventional and "new" security agenda, is in peace-keeping. The 1991 Gulf War forced the Japanese Government to review its provisions for sending SDF on UN peace-keeping operations. In the aftermath of this conflict, Prime Minister Kaifu put forward a bill to extend the participation of Japanese SDF personnel. His aims in part were to counter criticisms of Japan's "checkbook diplomacy" and to demonstrate that Japan was becoming a "normal" power in the international security arena.[27] The first proposed UN Peace Cooperation Bill of October 1990 was defeated, but in June 1992 a third attempt by the ruling Liberal Democratic Party (LDP) succeeded in getting the UN Peace-Keeping Operations (PKO) Cooperation Bill through the Diet. In the event, the first troops sent as part of PKO activities went to Cambodia in 1992. However, the strict conditions of PKO participation included the following:

- A ceasefire must be in place;
- Disputing parties must agree to a Japanese presence as part of the PKO;
- The operation must be neutral;
- Japanese forces must withdraw if these change; and
- The use of weapons must be restricted to a minimum self defence.[28]

Successive prime ministers have sought to advance this issue and former Prime Minister Obuchi (1998–2000) was particularly active in his attempts to have legal restrictions lifted, in order for Japanese personnel to participate more fully. It was, however, under Prime Minister Junichiro Koizumi that changes were put into place. While these items gained currency within regional and international fora during the 1990s, more recent crises, including the September 2001 terrorist attacks in the United States, have focused attention on the need for military responses. In these ways, the imperatives of a military response to new security challenges were accommodated uneasily within a more nuanced Japanese approach to broadening concepts of security. However, over ten years after the introduction of the 1992 PKO law, Koizumi managed to enact revisions in 2001 that served to "de-freeze" certain activities, such as the monitoring of disarmament, stationing and patrolling in buffer zones, the collection and disposal of abandoned weapons and also expanded the scope of the use of weapons. The ensuing dispatch of SDF to Timor-Leste (formerly East Timor) represented a new phase in Japanese peace-keeping. In fact, according to Gorjão, the dispatch of 690 members of the Engineer Group of the SDF troops and other personnel there as part of UN peace-keeping operations "became a significant test case, not only of Tokyo's commitment to Asia's regional security, but also of Japan's desire to be a more important player on the international political stage".[29]

If changed conditions since the ending of the Cold War have seen the Japanese Government attempt to recreate its comprehensive security architecture, there has been, however, little agreement as to exactly what shape cooperative security arrangements could take. Segal notes that it "seemed to be no more than that the term should cover economic well-being and social stability, as well as military power".[30] Japan's own attempt to redefine its security parameters echoes the general, "largely abstract" debate over contemporary security.[31] However, U.S. calls for greater military involvement in the region continue to top Japan's foreign policy agenda.

## REGIONAL SECURITY AND STABILITY

In terms of military security and regional stability, Alagappa summarizes some of the key preoccupations in East Asia:

> New apprehensions, rivalries, and tensions are also surfacing, due in large part to uncertainty about the future positions and behavior of China, Japan, the US, Russia, and India and about the state of relations among these countries.[32]

These very real security tensions have been exacerbated by what some scholars perceive to be an arms race and by new issues of major concern relating to terrorism and North Korea. These will be addressed separately below. To begin with, according to Ball the regional growth in the acquisition of arms during the 1980s resulted from rapid economic growth combined with a need for greater self reliance, especially in light of a perceived reduction of the U.S. military presence in the region and from middle power concerns over the rise of the larger powers in the region. The subsequent threat and development of regional conflicts heightened the issue still further.[33] Although regional institutions such as the ARF are important in alleviating some of these tensions, Ball is correct to assert that informal dialogue alone will be insufficient to establish the basis for talks on multilateral arms control.[34] In Northeast Asia, in particular, the proliferation of weapons of mass destruction (WMD) and ballistic missiles continued throughout the 1990s, when North Korea's threat (later to become a reality) of developing WMD and its missile activities came to be viewed as a destabilizing factor for Japan's own security as well as that of the region.

Of equal importance has been the role of the United States in the region. Even before the events of 11 September 2001, representatives of the U.S. government promised to continue a policy of "robust engagement" in the region, and reasserted the fact that the U.S.-Japan alliance "remains the linchpin of our security strategy in Asia".[35] The 1995 review entitled *United States Security Strategy for the East Asia-Pacific Region* (otherwise known as the "Nye Report", named after Joseph S. Nye, Assistant Secretary of Defence for International Security Affairs, under whose supervision it was written) confirmed the continued presence of U.S. troops in Asia and on Japanese soil in particular. The 1997 revision of the 1978 defence guidelines between the United States and Japan that resulted in part from this report were intentionally vague, in the hope that "they might act as a deterrent to something like a Chinese attack on Taiwan", while the U.S. East Asian Strategy Reports of both 1995 and 1998 made it clear that security "is like oxygen: You do not tend to notice it until you begin to lose it".[36] Despite domestic discussions over the continued validity for Japan of the security treaty and in spite of public hostility in Okinawa over decisions to renew leases for the use of the U.S. military, the United States is generally viewed by the Japanese and their neighbours, as playing a "stabilizing role" in the region.[37] Some observers, such as Solomon and Drennan, are in no doubt that the removal of this restraining element would lead Japan to remilitarize and would engender Sino-Japanese confrontation.[38] Others note that a trend is already visible, in that the decision to revise the U.S.-Japan defence guidelines in 1997 actually led

Japan's neighbours to conjecture that "Japan was to take a bigger military role in the region".[39]

This concern, held in particular by the Chinese Government, is illustrative of the mutual wariness between Tokyo and Beijing about real and potential increases in military capabilities and changed intentions. China's nuclear tests in 1995, military exercises to intimidate Taiwan in 1996, China's inclusion of the Senkaku Islands in its 1992 Territorial Waters Law and its crossing of the meridian line in the South China Sea, all added to growing Japanese concerns over the potential security implications of China's rapid economic growth.[40] Furthermore, Japan's constrained military forces relegate it to the status of an "incomplete major power" when compared with the capabilities of its giant neighbour, which has the potential to become "East Asia's pre-eminent strategic power".[41] China, for its part, is chary about the revised defence guidelines, about further Taiwanese moves towards claiming greater international recognition and about Japan's agreement to participate in U.S. President Bush's missile defence programme. Roy assumes that these conditions set Japan and China as "natural rivals" and that Chinese actions could in fact precipitate a military build up in Japan.[42] These bilateral tensions, however, are only part of an increasingly complex picture of potential instability in the region, as the following section illustrates.

## CURRENT TENSIONS

Three important issues that exercise the Japanese Government in terms of security today are the after-effects of the 11 September 2001 terrorist attacks, the behaviour of North Korea, and the war in Iraq.

### Terrorist Attacks

The 11 September 2001 terrorist attacks on the United States "became an opportunity to further review Japan's role in the world and its contribution to international security".[43] Most interesting for the purpose of this current discussion, these events allowed Japan to pass new legislation, even in the face of domestic constraints. Immediately following the attacks, Prime Minister Koizumi went to Washington D.C. to show his solidarity with U.S. President George W. Bush. On his return, the so-called Anti-Terrorism Special Measures Law was enacted on 29 October 2001 and came into force on 2 November. According to the *Diplomatic Bluebook* of 2002, this law was "designed to enable Japan to contribute actively and on its own initiatives to the efforts of the international community for the prevention and eradication of international terrorism". Specifically, Japan would cooperate through:

- SDF cooperation and support for U.S. and other armed forces;
- Search and rescue for combatants; and
- Relief activities to assist affected people.

Subsequent measures taken in the name of this law have included the dispatch of Maritime SDF destroyers on information-gathering exercises in November 2001 and assistance in the refuelling of U.S. and British naval ships.

On 20 November 2001, Koizumi backed a bill to expand the scope of SDF participation in UN peace-keeping operations and to ease the restrictions on the use of weapons during such missions.[44] According to this bill, SDF personnel would be permitted to:

- Monitor ceasefires;
- Disarm local forces;
- Patrol demilitarized zones; and
- Dispose of abandoned weapons.

The Lower House passed the bill on 30 November 2001 and the Upper House passed it on 7 December and it has had important repercussions in the case of Iraq, as will be seen below. Gorjão regards this as a "major shift" in Japan's security contributions.[45] Indeed, it was important for two reasons. First, it gained the support of other states, notably Australia and Indonesia. In this way, international pressure and the need for cooperation served, as did the financial crisis, to remove previous taboos on greater Japanese commitment to the region. As announced in October 2002, these new forms of involvement by SDF personnel include:

- Immigration control
- Aviation security
- Customs cooperation
- Export control
- Police and law enforcement
- Measures against terrorist financing.[46]

These types of cooperation are entirely consistent with Japan's alternative security agenda, despite the fact that they are being applied as means of stopping the proliferation of conventional and nuclear weapons by terrorist groups. The subsequent impact of the war in Iraq on peace-keeping will be examined below.

Second, the Japanese supported the U.S. position in the wake of the terrorist attacks and agreed at the U.S.-Japan Security Consultative Committee (SCC) meeting in December 2002 that continued cooperation in the fight against terrorism should be accorded the "highest importance". This cooperation is tempered by growing Japanese cooperation with its East Asian neighbours with regard to North Korea.[47] Indeed, even in the pursuit of anti-terrorist activities, the Japanese government has been keen to emphasize that "Japan attaches particular importance to the Asian region and is collaborating with the Asian countries. For example, Japan has held a working-level ASEAN Regional Forum workshop and seminars for officials of law enforcement agency in Asian countries".[48] Thus, the Japanese Government continues to ally itself with the United States, while also paying greater heed to the East Asian regional dimension of its own foreign policy decisions.

## North Korea

From 1995 until 2002 the United States participated alongside Japan and others as part of the Executive Board of the Korean Peninsula Energy Development Organization (KEDO).[49] Within that role, the Japanese Government committed over 116 billion yen in loans to KEDO and disbursed over US$300 million through the Japan Bank for International Cooperation (JBIC), as well as almost US$10 million for KEDO's payment of interest to the JBIC. In addition, Japan has contributed US$29 million to help cover the administrative expenses of the KEDO office. In these ways, Japanese economic diplomacy served as an important foundation for military ends. North Korea's declaration of its enriched plutonium programme, the unilateral lifting of its freeze on nuclear-related facilities (set by the terms of the U.S.-North Korea Agreed Framework of 1994) and its 10 January 2003 decision to withdraw from the Treaty of Non-Proliferation of Nuclear Weapons (NPT) and the Safeguards Agreement with the International Atomic Energy Agency (IAEA) have tested this stance, but representatives of the Japanese Government have continued to stress that "the problem of North Korea is not a problem between the United States and North Korea but a problem of the international community as a whole".[50] In response, U.S. Deputy Secretary of State, Richard Armitage, told reporters in Tokyo in December 2002 that the

United States was committed to diplomacy to manage the North Korea threat.[51] The Japanese Government has continued to support the strengthening of international institutions such as the NPT, the Biological Weapons Convention, the Chemical Weapons Convention and the Comprehensive Test Ban Treaty.[52] Throughout negotiations to date, the Japanese Government has reinforced the role of multilateral cooperation in this process:

> Japan will strongly urge North Korea to immediately retract its decision and take prompt action to dismantle its nuclear development programs. To this end, Japan will closely coordinate with the US and the Republic of Korea and cooperate with other concerned countries and the IAEA.[53]

The Japanese Government also attaches great importance to the Trilateral Coordination and Oversight Group (TCOG) process among Japan, the United States and South Korea, which was designed to coordinate policies towards North Korea, including security issues such as ballistic missile issues.

Interestingly, given particular historical issues linking Japan and North Korea, and the topic of the so-called "abductees" from Japan, Prime Minister Koizumi has simultaneously pursued bilateral channels with Pyongyang. On 17 September 2002, during an unprecedented visit by a Japanese prime minister to North Korea, the Japan-Democratic People's Republic of Korea (DPRK) Pyongyang Declaration was signed, as a framework for Japan to resolve a number of concerns between Japan and North Korea, including the abduction issue and security issues. In this context, the Japanese Government has continued to emphasize the importance of normalizing relations with North Korea alongside its multilateral goals. Prime Minister Koizumi was also forthright in suggesting that he had made it clear to President Bush that Japan preferred North Korea not to become a second Iraq:

> I believe that the U.S., at an early date, should resume talks with North Korea and I shall continue to maintain close contacts with President Kim of the Republic of Korea and President Bush of the United States on these matters. I shall also continue to address this question of normalization of relations with North Korea, with the understanding that we have a trilateral common stance amongst Japan, the Republic of Korea and the United States.[54]

Notably in this speech, Koizumi used the term "comprehensive approach", which, he said "makes efforts bearing in mind policies and measures in

such fields as politics, security, the economy, society, and development".
The reiteration of this type of approach demonstrates how the Japanese
Government continues to interweave its own pragmatic security policy
with contemporary demands for its SDF to play a greater military role in
response to new challenges.[55]

## Iraq

The crisis over and in Iraq has forced Japanese policymakers to challenge
many foreign policy assumptions. On the one hand, the overriding strength
of the bilateral relationship with the United States has been underlined by
Prime Minister Koizumi and his cabinet's agreement to support American
actions. On the other, the whole issue of the war and the post-war
reconstruction of Iraq raises questions — in the public as well as in the
official domain — surrounding Japan's position with regard to the UN
and to the sending of SDF to the region in an expanded capacity.

From the start of the growing crisis, the Japanese Government was
keen to pursue diplomatic ends through the UN, in order to secure the
unconditional entry of weapons' inspectors into Iraq, consistent with UN
Security Council (UNSC) resolution 1441.[56] As part of an active period of
shuttle diplomacy, the government also sent former MOFA ministers and
the senior vice minister for foreign affairs to meet with key counterparts in
the Middle East and Europe as special envoys of the Japanese prime
minister, with the aim of strengthening the "solidarity of the international
community".[57] Foreign Minister Kawaguchi also pressed upon her Iraqi
counterpart the need to accept the unconditional resumption of UN
weapons' inspections, although this met with a cool response. When this
approach failed and the U.S. decided to assemble a "coalition of the
willing" and enter Iraq without UNSC approval, Japan continued to
support its leading ally. By way of explanation in March 2003, Prime
Minister Koizumi outlined the bases for his support:

> This is not other people's affairs, I felt. It is extremely dangerous now
> that we came to the conclusion that there is no willingness to disarm on
> the part of the Hussein regime. I deem it appropriate to support the use
> of force by the United States.[58]

At the same time, however, he stressed the role that Japan would play in
that coalition and re-emphasized that Japan's contribution would come
in the form of humanitarian assistance, as part of the policy of

consolidating peace, on behalf of the "peace and stability of the international community".[59]

In spite of Koizumi's categorical promises, one of the most significant consequences of the war in Iraq for Japan has been the decision to send about one thousand SDF troops, including 600 main ground units and 400 air force and naval logistical support units to the relatively peaceful town of Samawah in southern Iraq.[60] Their duties involve general reconstruction tasks, providing clean water and creating infrastructure. From the time in December 2003 when Prime Minister Koizumi expressed his intention to send the troops, the government has been trying to justify its actions to its many sources of opposition, For example, the deputy permanent representatives of Japan to the UNSC in May 2004 observed that "Japan fully understands the fundamental importance of peacekeeping as a tool for conflict resolution and continues its active support. We are prepared to accept a new operation if a Peace Keeping Operation (PKO) is justified and its mandate appropriate."[61] Despite the glowing rhetoric, however, there was significant initial public hostility to the idea of sending SDF to Iraq and the government ensured that the troops were dispatched without a huge media following. In fact, it was observed that the "initial low-key coverage partly reflects the Japanese public's ambivalence over the deployment, which the government has linked to larger goals of moving the nation from pacifism toward an embrace of military commitments".[62] The JDA went as far as to ask all media to leave Iraq and to threaten a local blackout of information if there are any "problems".[63]

To those detractors, including fellow LDP members, who attacked the prime minister for participating in any activity without a UN mandate, Prime Minister Koizumi responded that there "might be a phase that doesn't require a resolution" and he noted that "We can always discuss the issue [of] whether the resolution is required, once we agree to work with the UN". He further insisted that "No new Japanese law is needed to help reconstruct Iraq as long as Japan's contribution is non-military in nature".[64] Interestingly, despite a growing public acceptance of the need to participate in the reconstruction of Iraq, Prime Minister Koizumi continues to argue the case for peace-keeping operations on the grounds of the legitimacy of the war itself.[65]

The whole issue of peace-keeping has gained salience in public and private debates in Japan as a result of these activities. For example, the necessary rise by 60 per cent of the UN's PKO budget has been of major concern to the Japanese Government.[66] Among the public in Japan, not only has the issue of sending troops been widely debated, but the implications for the very constitution of Japan have come under scrutiny, according to observers like Gerald Curtis.[67] Around the rest of Asia, although countries such as South Korea and Singapore have expressed approval at Japan's actions, there has been some disquiet expressed in the media in China and North Korea that such actions hold the potential seeds of renewed Japanese militarism.[68] This case, although based on the fundamental goals of comprehensive security and with the aim of consolidating a peace process, raises additional concerns about Japan's military, domestically, within the region and beyond.

## CONCLUSION

This chapter has illustrated how Japan continues to confront a range of apparently contradictory pressures in its regional security environment. First, the Japanese Government continues to face a public that cherishes Article Nine (the no-war clause), with the result that the strengthening of peace-keeping activities has been, and is likely to continue to be, incrementally and carefully charted. Second, those who worry about a reduced U.S. role in the East Asian security architecture may be premature in their assessments. The effects of 11 September 2001 appear to have further reinforced U.S. involvement in the region and secured the close treaty linkages with Japan, while Prime Minister Koizumi's unwavering support for President Bush with regard to Iraq confirms their alliance. Third, and in possible contradiction to the second factor, Japan has been careful to underline its East Asian regional credentials in addressing the issue of North Korea and in continually advocating a dialogue-based solution. Fourth, and at the same time, East Asian responses to Japan's military and security initiatives have relaxed, if only to a limited extent, to provide in some circumstances a more accommodating stance for greater Japanese military involvement and other forms of cooperation within the region, as well as its increased military presence in international peace-keeping operations. Finally, the Japanese Government has begun to shape an alternative security orientation by initiating and enhancing policies related to non-traditional forms of security, as a supplement for more traditional security approaches.

This developing comprehensive security framework is likely to lead Japan in a number of directions. First, the pursuit of multilateral engagements — whether in the all-embracing forum of the UN, the regional arrangement of the ARF, the more limited remit of the G8 or the narrowly conceived TCOG dealing with North Korea — continues to be supported strongly by Tokyo. Only in this way will the greater participation of the SDF be more palatable to domestic constituents and accepted by the rest of East Asia. Second, the U.S.-Japan Security Treaty is likely to remain the centre-piece of Japan's regional security participation for the medium term. However, as Koizumi's assertions regarding North Korea and Iraq attest, it is increasingly becoming a vehicle for the joint leadership of regional issues. Japan's greater activities within the APT, ARF, ASEM and other regionally-oriented dialogues are likely to enhance this role. Third, the international nature of terrorism with the possibility of attacks on their own soil, and Tokyo's anti-terrorist responses, make the Japanese public more accepting of a greater role for their SDF abroad, to deal with problems that cannot be managed within national territorial borders. Similarly, the very idea of Japanese participation in peace-keeping operations is viewed more and more in the public domain as part of a necessary humanitarian contribution to international stability. In summary, as Berger noted in 1998, while a "culture of anti-militarism" may persist at home, the reality of a growing regional security role for Japan, which may involve greater regional military re-engagement, is now taking centre stage in government policy.[69]

## NOTES

1. Glenn Hook, Julie Gilson, Christopher W. Hughes and Hugo Dobson, *Japan's International Relations*, second edition (London: Routledge, 2005).
2. See Sueo Sudo, "Japan and the Security of Southeast Asia", *The Pacific Review* 4, no. 3 (1991): 333–44.
3. W.G. Beasley, *The Rise of Modern Japan* (Tokyo: Charles E. Tuttle, 1990).
4. Glenn Hook and Gavan McCormack, *Japan's Contested Constitution* (London: Routledge, 2001).
5. Reinhard Drifte, *Japan's Foreign Policy in the 1990s* (London: Macmillan, 1996).
6. Ronald Dore, *Japan, Internationalism and the UN* (London: Routledge, 1997).
7. Drifte, op. cit., p. 54.
8. *Diplomatic Bluebook 2003*, Tokyo: Ministry of Foreign Affairs, chapter 3. Available at <http://www.mofa.go.jp/policy/other/bluebook/2003/chap3-a.pdf>, visited on 10 August 2004.
9. Hook, et al., op. cit. p. 45.
10. Ibid.

11. Christopher W. Hughes "Japan's Subregional Security and Defence Linkages with ASEAN, South Korea and China in the 1990s", *The Pacific Review* 9, no. 2 (1996): 229–50.
12. Hook et al., op. cit., p. 49.
13. *Diplomatic Bluebook 2003*, op. cit.
14. See Peter Gourevitch, Inoguchi Takashi and Courtney Purrington, eds., *United States-Japan Relations and International Institutions: After the Cold War* (San Diego: University of California, 1995).
15. Sueo Sudo, *The International Relations of Japan and South East Asia: Forging a New Regionalism* (London: Routledge, 2002), pp. 81–93.
16. Gerald Segal, "'Asianism' and Asian Security", *The National Interest* 42 (1995/1996): p. 61.
17. See Richard K. Betts, "Wealth, Power and Instability", in Michael E. Brown, Sean M. Lynn-Jones and Steven E. Miller, eds., *East Asian Security* (Cambridge MA: MIT Press, 1998), p. 35. See also Desmond Ball, "Military Acquisitions in the Asia-Pacific Region", in Brown et al., op. cit., pp. 76–110.
18. See Ball, op. cit., p. 107.
19. Richard Doner, "Japan in East Asia: Institutions and Regional Leadership", in *Network Power: Japan and Asia*, edited by Peter J. Katzenstein and Takashi Shiraishi (Ithaca: Cornell University Press, 1997), pp. 197–233; James Reilly, "Japan: A New Security Posture Raising Concerns", <www.fpif.org/commentary/2002/0202japan_body>, 14 February (2002).
20. Pauline Kerr, "The Security Dialogue in the Asia-Pacific", *The Pacific Review* 7, no. 4 (1994): 397–409.
21. Richard Stubbs, "ASEAN Plus Three: Emerging East Asian Regionalism?", *Asian Survey* 42, no. 3 (2002): 440–55.
22. Mark Webber and Michael Smith, eds., *Foreign Policy in a Transformed World* (Harlow: Prentice Hall, 2002), p. 42; Keith Krause and Michael C. Willliams, eds., *Critical Security Studies: Concepts and Cases* (Minneapolis: University of Minnesota Press, 1997); Julie Gilson and Phillida Purvis, "Japan's Pursuit of Human Security: Humanitarian Agenda or Political Pragmatism?", *Japan Forum* 15, no. 2 (2003): 193–207.
23. Caroline Thomas, *Global Governance, Development and Human Security* (London: Pluto Press, 2000), p. 6.
24. UNDP (United Nations Development Programme), *Human Development Report* (New York and Oxford: Oxford University Press for the United Nations Development Programme, 1994), p. 3.
25. Gilson and Purvis, op. cit.
26. Julie Gilson, "Japan in Kosovo: Lessons in the Politics of Complex Engagement", *Japan Forum* 12, no. 1 (2000): 65–75.
27. See Hook et al., op. cit., passim.
28. Sudo, op. cit. (2002), p. 85.

29. Paulo Gorjão, "Japan's Foreign Policy and East Timor, 1975–2002", *Asian Survey* 42, no. 5 (2002): 754.

30. Segal, op. cit., p. 61.

31. Muthiah Alagappa, ed., *Asian Security Practices: Material and Ideational Influences* (Stanford: Stanford University Press, 1998), p. 11.

32. Alagappa, op. cit., p. 1.

33. Ball, op. cit., passim.

34. Ball, op. cit., p. 107.

35. <www.defenselink.mil/pubs/easr98>, visited on 31 January 2003.

36. Cited in Frank Langdon, "American Northeast Asian Strategy", *Pacific Affairs* 74, no. 2 (2001): 173.

37. Richard H. Solomon and William M. Drennan, "The United States and Asia in 2001: Forward to the Past?", *Asian Survey* 41, no. 1 (2001): 2.

38. Solomon and Drennan, op. cit., p. 11.

39. Langdon, op. cit., p. 173.

40. Greg Austin and Stuart Harris, *Japan and Greater China: Political Economy and Military Power in the Asian Century* (London: Hurst and Company, 2001), p. 93.

41. Austin and Harris, op. cit., p. 89. See also Denny Roy, "Hegemon on the Horizon?", in Brown et al., op. cit., p. 115.

42. Roy, op. cit., p. 127.

43. Gorjão, op. cit., p. 766.

44. Ibid., p. 767.

45. Ibid., pp. 767–69.

46. <www.mofa.go.jp/policy/un/disarmament/approach0209.html>, visited on 13 January 2003.

47. <www.usinfo.state.gov/regional/ea/easec/usjapanscc>, visited on 31 January 2003.

48. Toshimitsu Motegi (Senior Vice-Minister for Foreign Affairs), "The Munich Conference on Security Policy", 8 February 2003, <http://www.mofa.gov.jp /policy/terrorism/speech0302.html>.

49. Langdon, op. cit.

50. Motegi, op. cit.

51. <www.usinfo.state.gov/regional/ea/easec/armiitage2120902>, visited on 23 February 2003.

52. <www.mofa.go.jp/policy/economy/apec/2002/announce-2>, visited on 13 January 2003.

53. <www.infojapan.org/announce/press/2003/1/0110>, visited on 13 January 2003.

54. <www.mofa.go.jp/ policy/economy/apec/2002/announce-a.html>, visited on 13 January 2003.

55. See S. Javed Maswood, *Japan and East Asian Regionalism* (London: Routledge, 2001), passim.
56. See <www.mofa.gov.jp>, 26 November 2002, visited on 8 August 2004.
57. <www.mofa.gov.jp>, visited on 9 August 2004.
58. Ibid.
59. Ibid.
60. <www.yomiuri.co.jp/newse/20040810wo01.htm>, visited on 10 August 2004.
61. <www.mofa.go.jp/announce/speech/un2004/un0405-6.html>, visited on 10 August 2004.
62. <www.csmonitor.com/2004/0120/p08s01-woap.html>.
63. Ibid.
64. <www.atimes.com/atimes/Japan/EC28Dh01.html>, 28 March 2003, visited on 10 August 2004.
65. The troops themselves have contributed to greater public support by growing moustaches to fit in with Iraqi locals and by being seen to integrate well with their new local surroundings. One local Iraqi resident was reported to have observed: "What a magnificent moustache. He looks just like an Iraqi!" <www.news.bbc.co.uk/go/pr/fr/-/2/hi/asia-pacific/3461643.stm>.
66. H.E. Mr. Toshiro Ozawa, Ambassador of Japan to the United Nations, to the Fifth Committee Fifty-eighth session of the United Nations General Assembly, 3 June 2004, New York.
67. *Tokyo Shimbun*, 8 February 2004.
68. <http://news.bbc.co.uk/go/pr/fr/-/2/hi/asia-pacific/3413769.stm>, visited on 10 August 2004.
69. Thomas Berger, *Cultures of Antimilitarism: National Security in Germany and Japan* (Baltimore: Johns Hopkins University Press, 1998).

# Chapter Four
# China's Security Strategy and Policies

Jian Yang

## INTRODUCTION

The past decade or so has witnessed a dramatic change of China's security perceptions, which is rooted in the sea change of the international system and China's opening up. While the disintegration of the Soviet Union and the end of the Cold War provided a peaceful international environment for its economic development, China found that its strategic importance to the United States decreased dramatically. China's opening up and economic reforms since 1978 have resulted in its economic take-off and integration with the world economy. Meanwhile, the Chinese have been exposed to Western values which inevitably have had a strong impact on their perceptions of the world and China's political future.

This chapter will first discuss the evolution of China's understanding of its security requirements, followed by a reassessment of China's security environment. The chapter will then look at China's grand strategy and policies concerning its national security, and conclude with three dilemmas that China must manage.

## DEFINITION AND SCOPE

Not surprisingly, China defined its national security in excessively narrow military terms in the Cold War years. After all, China was under constant threat from the United States and then the Soviet Union. Beijing's ideology-oriented worldview determined that it would always have a strong sense of military insecurity.

In the post-Cold War world, as noted by Chris Brown, "As concern over military security becomes less pressing, so a wider conception of security has come to the fore."[1] In the West, more attention is given to non-military security threat, such as depletion of the ozone layer, mass unemployment, large-scale drug trafficking and the arrival of large numbers of refugees. The focus of "security" is contested. Should it be traditional national and international security or individual security such as denial of human rights and poverty, societal security like regional integration and ethnic conflicts, or global security like a breakdown of the global monetary system and global warming?

The security debate in the West has influenced the Chinese understanding of national security. Chinese analysts accept that security now means "comprehensive security" (*zonghe anquan*). It no longer equals to national defence and diplomacy and is no longer limited to the defence of national sovereignty and territorial integrity. In addition to traditional military security, national security now includes, among other things, economic security, political security, societal security, environmental security, human security, and technological security. One Chinese analyst says that "Basically, every aspect of human life can be regarded as a part of national security, such as energy, resources, food, environment, population, ecology, space, drug trafficking, epidemic disease, cultural rubbish, cross-boundary crimes, international terrorism, etc."[2]

The fundamental change in China's understanding of national security is the realization that without a strong economy, the military dimension of national security is not sustainable. This understanding contributed to China's concept of "comprehensive national power" which has constituted the foundation of China's foreign and domestic policies. The emphasis on economic security, however, should not overshadow military security. "Military security is no less important [than economic security]. It still is an effective guarantee of comprehensive security and the last resort," says a Chinese analyst.[3]

## SECURITY REASSESSED

The Chinese Government's security map is different from those of many other governments in that Beijing has to take care of not only China's external and internal security, but also the mind-boggling Taiwan issue.

### External Security Environment

In the 1980s, an increasingly pragmatic Beijing re-examined world politics and believed that peace and development were the twin dominant themes of the time. Political crisis in 1989 and the end of the Cold War ushered in some uncertainties. The events highlighted the West's political threat to the rule of the Chinese Communist Party (CCP). The end of the Washington-Beijing-Moscow grand triangle also reduced China's strategic importance to the United States. Although Beijing later decided that it did not face any imminent military threat and economic development was still the top priority, its perception of its external security environment has experienced a rather dramatic evolution.

China tried to re-define its main potential threats in the years immediately after the end of the Cold War. According to some analysts, Japan was likely to replace the Soviet Union/Russia to become the Chinese leadership's major concern.[4] China's perceptions of security threats became more complicated after 1996 when the Taiwan Strait crisis made clear the possibility of a military clash between China and the United States over Taiwan.[5] Just one month after the dangerous escalation of the Taiwan Strait crisis, U.S. President Bill Clinton and Japanese Prime Minister Ryutaro Hashimoto held a summit meeting in Tokyo and signed the U.S.-Japan Joint Declaration on Security — Alliance for the 21st Century. The crisis and the joint declaration as well as subsequent revision of the 1978 Guidelines for U.S.-Japan Security Cooperation deepened China's suspicion of U.S. motives regarding Taiwan and, in the longer term, U.S. strategy toward a rising China.

Many Chinese analysts tend to perceive the United States as a competitor rather than a threat. A basic assessment is that "in short and medium terms the United States will not publicly challenge the overall integrity of our territory and sovereignty by using force."[6] But the relatively benign view has been challenged from time to time. Shortly after George W. Bush came to office, China-U.S. relations experienced a dramatic downturn. A series of events seriously strained the bilateral relationship. From the very beginning, the Bush administration made it clear that it would push forward the national missile defence (NMD) system. Beijing deems it an attempt that will neutralize its limited nuclear deterrent. Washington also did not hesitate to re-cast Beijing as a "strategic competitor" rather than a "strategic partner". While these were by and large what had been anticipated, the mid-air collision between a U.S. EP-3 surveillance plane and a Chinese interceptor surely caught the world by surprise. During the eleven-day tense standoff over the 24 American crew members, Beijing demanded a U.S. apology which Washington, claiming its right to fly in international space, refused to offer. Shortly after the stand-off, Bush promised the biggest arms sales to Taiwan in a decade and pledged to do "whatever it took" to help Taiwan defend itself against a mainland military attack.

Some Chinese analysts started to question the assessment that peace and development are the dominant themes of the time. They argue that it underestimates the "severe" (*yanjun*) security environment China now faces. The assessment was against the background that the United States did not regard China as its main rival and the two countries even had strategic cooperation. To continue to emphasize peace and development may result in miscalculation in security strategy.

To the relief of the Chinese, the 11 September terrorist attacks on America and the subsequent U.S. "war on terror" helped improve China-U.S. relations. In the short and medium term, it is believed, U.S. efforts against terrorism will help ensure the stability of the bilateral relationship. Chinese leaders see no major military clashes between China and other great powers before 2020. They have deemed the next twenty years "a period of important strategic opportunities" (*zhanlue jiyuqi*) for China's economic development. The understanding, however, should be put in perspective. Firstly, it can be challenged by the Taiwan issue and possible U.S. involvement. Secondly, it does not mean that China has become very much relaxed with its strategic environment. In fact, a number of Chinese analysts have alerted policymakers that China's strategic environment has become more complicated. One analyst notes that the United States is still regarding China as a potential main rival. With troops in Central Asia, it is now in a position to "squeeze China from both East and West". Japan has become more active militarily while India is determined to seek a world power status. Both are making changes to their military strategy to guard against the rise of China.[7]

## Internal Stability

For Chinese leaders, more imminent security concerns are not from without but from within. As an undemocratically elected government in a globalized world, Beijing is acutely aware of its vulnerability. Marxism or communist utopia is no longer appealing to the Chinese and the Chinese economy is now more capitalist than socialist. Beijing has a persistent sense of internal crisis. It faces a number of explosive issues, especially the widening gap between the rich and the poor, mass unemployment, and rampant corruption.

The biggest threat to China is that internal and external threats combine forces. China's late paramount leader Deng Xiaoping used to remind his comrades that the 1989 Chinese students' anti-government demonstrations were the result of the combination of external environment and internal problems. Externally, the West had been trying to "peacefully change China" by exporting Western values to China. Internally, anti-government forces had played upon China's social problems, such as corruption and inflation. Similarly, Falungong and separatists in Tibet and Xinjiang have all been accused of plotting with foreign hostile forces for anti-China activities.

What should also be mentioned is that the deadly severe acute respiratory syndrome (SARS) epidemic has alerted the Chinese that they need a more sophisticated non-traditional security system. As mentioned earlier, China had been talking about non-traditional security issues, including epidemic diseases. The SARS crisis is the most dramatic event that has driven home China's vulnerability to non-traditional security threats.

## The Taiwan Issue

The Taiwan issue is closely related to China's external security and internal stability. Externally, a military clash across the Taiwan Strait could end up with a China-U.S. military conflict. Internally, a soft stance on the Taiwan issue could trigger off social instability and power struggle in China.

With the end of the Cold War and the subsequent decrease of China's strategic importance to the United States, some major diplomatic conflicts over Taiwan have erupted between Beijing and Washington. Taipei scored a few major breakthroughs in its relations with Washington. The first was President George Bush's 1992 decision to lift a decade-old ban and sell 150 F-16s to Taiwan. The sale smoothed the way for other U.S. arms sales to

Taiwan. A much more important breakthrough was that, under congressional pressure, the Clinton administration changed the sixteen-year-old U.S. policy of barring Taiwanese leaders from the United States and granted the then Taiwan President Lee Teng-hui a visa to visit America.

Lee's U.S. visit resulted in deep crises in Sino-American relations and across the Taiwan Strait. Beijing "indefinitely" recalled its ambassador to Washington. It conducted ballistic missile tests in waters close to Taiwan and staged large-scale military exercises in the coastal areas facing Taiwan. In March 1996, in an attempt to influence Taiwan's presidential election, Beijing staged guided-missile tests and conducted live-fire military exercises at the southern end of the Taiwan Straits. To send a warning signal to Beijing, Clinton ordered two aircraft carriers and their battle groups to waters off Taiwan.

In his second term, Clinton was more accommodating to Beijing and was willing to resist congressional pressure on the Taiwan issue. In his visit to China in late June 1998, Clinton became the first U.S. president to articulate the "three no's" policy — no support for Taiwan's independence, no support for "two Chinas", or "one Taiwan, one China", and no support for Taiwan's entry into international organizations for which statehood is a requirement. The Clinton administration also distanced itself from Lee Teng-hui's "state-to-state" theory that described Taiwan and China as two virtually equal states.[8] Clinton told Chinese President Jiang Zemin that Lee "had made things more difficult for both China and the United States".[9]

The Taiwan issue came back as a focus of dispute between Beijing and Washington shortly after George W. Bush entered the White House. In late April 2001, Bush promised new submarines, destroyers, and aircraft to Taiwan, then pledged to help Taiwan defend itself against a mainland military attack. One month later, much to Beijing's anger, Taiwan President Chen Shui-bian from the pro-independence Democratic Progressive Party had a three-day stopover in New York. The Bush administration's support for Taiwan remains firm despite China's support for U.S. war on terrorism. In March 2002, Washington allowed a working visit to the United States by Taiwan's defence minister for the first time since 1979 when Washington switched its diplomatic relations from Taipei to Beijing.

The controversial victory of Chen Shui-bian in the 2004 presidential elections further deepened Beijing's concerns. It warned that Taiwan's independence timetable is Beijing's reunification timetable. Beijing has made it clear that it will not tolerate Taiwan independence just for the sake of the mainland's economic development and the 2008 Olympic Games in Beijing.[10]

Beijing's warnings should not be dismissed. The Taiwan issue is China's core national security concern. What happened in the past decade has increased China's sense of urgency and has been a key factor for Chinese military's strong political influence and a key driving force for China's military modernization.

## THE GRAND STRATEGY

According to Michael Swaine and Ashley J. Tellis, a grand strategy is a country's "basic approach to political-military security".[11] Swaine and Tellis also argue that China's grand strategy seeks to preserve domestic order, defend against external threats, and eventually attain geo-political influence as a major, and perhaps, primary state. This is largely in line with the above discussion which demonstrates that China's security concerns include external security, internal stability and the Taiwan issue, and that China's overall goal is to enhance its "comprehensive national power".

China's grand strategy thus consists of at least two main components — national security strategy and national development strategy. National reunification strategy is also an important component but is largely embodied in two other main strategies (See Figure 4.1).[12] National security strategy is based on diplomatic strategy and national defence strategy. National development strategy is more complicated. It encompasses economic, political, technological, social and cultural development strategies.

National security strategy and national development strategy are inter-related. As mentioned earlier, the Chinese are aware that a strong economy is the foundation of the military dimension of national security. Economic development is also the key to internal stability. Indeed, it has been widely accepted in China that to develop the economy remains China's "ultimate solution (*genben chulu*) to all internal and external problems".[13] Internally, to claim its legitimacy, the Chinese Government has to substantially raise the living standard. Externally, economic development is a key to comprehensive national power. The Chinese often remind themselves that the Soviet Union lost the Cold War to the West mainly because the Soviet economy was not able to sustain the conflict. Military modernization therefore must be based on economic modernization. With regard to the Taiwan issue, military coercion is necessary but may not be effective. In fact, it has further strengthened the "China threat" theory. Economic competition and integration with Taiwan is emerging as a more acceptable and effective strategy.

Without dismissing the importance of economic development, an increasing number of Chinese analysts now argue that it is time to pay more attention to national security strategy. After all, development needs a peaceful environment. More importantly, economic development will not automatically result in security. On the contrary, in line with the notion of "security dilemma", economic development may result in insecurity as China's development can be taken by other states as a source of threat.

One Chinese analyst notes that the goal of China's security strategy is threefold. Firstly, to help realize China's interest in development. Secondly, to realize China's interest in sovereignty and reunification. Thirdly, to realize China's interest in international participation, that is, China should actively participate in regional and world affairs and become an influential regional and world power.[14]

On the reunification issue, Beijing has made efforts to accommodate Taipei's requests.[15] However, the fundamental principle of China's reunification strategy has remained unchanged. That is, Beijing will make every effort to seek peaceful reunification but will retain the right to using force.

## POLICIES

China embarked on its military modernization when it started its reforms and opening up in the late 1970s. However, it soon realized that it was impossible for China to catch up with the United States as a military power by focusing on re-equipping and retraining the existing forces due to Chinese military industry's severe institutional deficiencies. It is noted that "China's leaders accepted the need to reduce the size of the forces substantially, and to rely on a steady growth in the national economic and technological base, coupled with a non-confrontational diplomacy, to secure the country's strategic interests."[16]

What has been influential is Deng Xiaoping's sixteen-character principle set after the 1989 Tiananmen Square crackdown, namely *tao guang yang hui* (be skillful in hiding one's capacities and biding one's time), *shan yu shou zhuo* (be good at the tactics of low profile diplomacy), *jue bu dang tou* (never take the lead) and *you suo zuo wei* (take proper initiatives). The

**Figure 4.1**

China's Grand Strategy

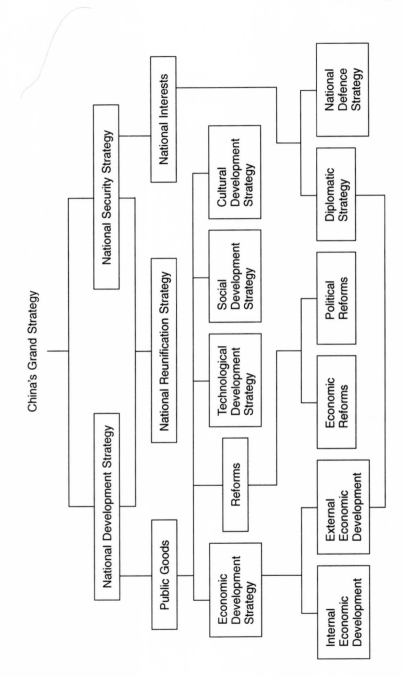

principle has been carried out rather faithfully. This is reflected in China's relations with some major players in the region.

## Relations with Major Players

While China has been making efforts to improve relations with all peripheral states, it has paid special attention to major players in the region, including the United States, Japan, Russia and the Association of Southeast Asian Nations (ASEAN). For China, relationship with the United States is undoubtedly the most important bilateral relationship. Japan as a neighbour and economic superpower also occupies an important place in China's diplomacy. Russia as a possible counterweight against U.S. dominance is useful in forming a "united front". As for ASEAN, it plays a crucial role in China's pursuit of a peaceful external environment, regional influence and a multipolar world.

### The United States

The Chinese have long maintained a "love-hate" sentiment toward the United States. Historically, America piggy-backed on concessions won by Great Britain after the Opium War of the early 1840s that started China's "century of humiliation". Yet at the same time, America made efforts to protect China's territorial integrity against powers like Japan, although arguably the efforts were mainly for America's own interests. The Korean War of the early 1950s resulted in strong hatred among the Chinese for "American imperialists" in the following two decades. The hatred was then quickly replaced by their affection for America after President Richard Nixon's 1972 visit to Beijing. Notwithstanding some problems, the love affair between China and America continued until the Tiananmen Square crackdown in June 1989. Then the Cold War ended in the early 1990s, which resulted in a dramatic decrease of China's strategic importance to America. Since then, as Washington pressured Beijing on a range of issues, the Chinese started to view America with suspicion. That suspicion turned into hatred in May 1999 when U.S. planes bombed the Chinese embassy in the Yugoslav capital, Belgrade. The bombing stirred up fervent nationalism in China.

Unlike U.S. policy toward China which is often criticized for lacking consistency, China has consistently shown restraint and caution to avoid unduly antagonizing the United States. In spite of Chinese suspicions toward U.S. strategic intentions, the top leadership has refrained from publicly endorsing any of the alarmist views.[17] The Chinese leadership knows well that China can ill afford a rupture in its relations with the United States. Thus, in the case of the mid-air collision incident of April 2001, despite its strong rhetoric, Beijing ultimately yielded without the apology that it had demanded.

The biggest challenge to the Chinese leadership with regard to U.S. policy is the Taiwan issue. As a nation that historically suffered abuse at the hands of foreign powers, China is acutely sensitive to infringements of its sovereignty. As a government that can no longer ignore public opinion, Beijing could also find its hands tied in dealing with Washington. After all, no Chinese leader is ready to be regarded in Chinese history as the "criminal of all time" by losing Taiwan. All this determines that Beijing has to be firm in dealing with Washington over Taiwan. At the same time, however, Beijing is constrained by its desire to have a good relationship with Washington.

While making efforts to strengthen relations with the United States, China has made it clear that it abhors U.S. hegemonism. The Chinese are no strangers to concepts like the balance of power. In fact, Chinese strategic thinkers "think more like traditional balance-of-power theorists than do most contemporary Western leaders and policy analysts".[18] Therefore, to promote multipolarity to balance off U.S. power has also been China's consistent policy. However, it is observed that Beijing's countermeasures against U.S. hegemony "do not amount to a robust balancing strategy explicitly designed to dislodge the U.S. hegemonic position" and "Beijing's balancing has been overall hesitant, low-key, and inconsistent".[19] After all, many other powers tend to jump on the U.S. bandwagon and China cannot afford open confrontation with the United States.

## Russia

For Beijing one way to power balance the United States is to have alliances with other reliable and strong allies. Russia is an obvious potential ally. Sino-Russian relationship improved dramatically since 1994. In January that year, the then Russian President Boris Yeltsin sent a letter to Jiang Zemin, proposing a "constructive partnership aimed at the twenty-first century". The two countries have since institutionalized the relationship and maintained frequent high-level contacts, including a number of summits. Of these summits, Yeltsin's visit to China in April 1996 deserves special attention. The Chinese highly value this visit largely because, among other things, Yeltsin suggested an enhancement of the already prepared Sino-Russian Joint Declaration, changing the "constructive partnership" into "strategic partnership". Vladimir Putin, Yeltsin's successor, has continued the momentum and extended Yeltsin's China policy.

Anti-hegemonism which targets the United States has been one of the key factors driving China and Russia closer. In November 1997, the two countries' heads signed the Joint Statement of China and Russia Concerning World Multi-Polarization and Building a New International Order. The joint statement of November 1998, Sino-Russian Relations at the Turn of the Century, also expressed the common views and standpoints of both sides on multi-polarization, the diversification of world civilization, the globalization of the world economy, the United Nations, and post-Cold War great-power relations. Anti-hegemonism is the first area of cooperation in the Treaty for Good Neighbourliness, Friendship and Cooperation of 2001.

China, however, is well aware of the limits of its ties with Russia. While it believes that it is in its interest to rally with Russia in its anti-hegemonic strategy, it has no intention to enter a formal military alliance with Russia. In fact, Chinese analysts have all along been careful in defining "Sino-Russian Cooperative Strategic Partnership". They play down its role as a counter-balance against the United States and the West. " 'Partnership' is a popular word in recent international relations", a Chinese analyst noted. "So long as there is no enemy-us relationship (*diwo guanxi*) between two countries or groups, then the relationship could be called partnership.... It is another name for friendly relationship."[20]

The Chinese do not have the illusion that in the foreseeable future Russia-U.S. relations will deteriorate dramatically and thus benefit China. They believe that although Russia is disappointed with the United States, its reforms have determined that it has to rely on the support and aid of the U.S.-led West. Russia's economy has been transformed from an isolated and centralized economy into an open market economy closely linked to the international economic system. Its national strategy has evolved from seeking unlimited national security boundaries to focusing on foreign policies conducive to its economic interests. This will inevitably make Russia heavily dependent on the United States and other Western countries. In fact, the Chinese do not believe that Russia's policy of emphasizing the importance of both the West and East is practical. The generally accepted view is that Russia will not stop tilting toward the West. They will not be surprised if Russia someday decides to sacrifice Russia-China relations for its relations with the West.

## Japan

China's perceptions of Japan are more complicated. While many Chinese analysts believe that the upgraded U.S.-Japan security alliance is a major step for the United States to strategically contain China, they are more concerned about Japan's greater role in the alliance. As noted by Thomas J. Christensen, "Although they [Chinese analysts] harbour suspicion toward the United States, they view Japan with even less trust and, in many cases, with a loathing rarely found in attitudes toward America."[21]

Japan's aggression and atrocities committed in China in the first half of the twentieth century continue to bedevil Sino-Japanese relations. The Chinese tend to note that Japan has not adequately acknowledged and apologized for its aggression and atrocities. Although Prime Minister Tomiichi Murayama in 1995 for the first time used the word "apology" in his statement about Japanese aggression, the Chinese tend to emphasize the facts like the Japanese Diet's failure to pass a resolution apologizing for Japan's wartime crimes and the refusal of Japan to offer a full, written apology. They find that their dissatisfaction is further justified by the sharp contrast between Japan's attitude toward the past and that of Germany. The Chinese today remain acutely sensitive to any efforts which they believe attempt to deny, cover or embellish historical facts, such as Japanese school history textbooks that appear to play down Japanese war crimes, and Japanese officials' visits to the Yasukuni Shrine which enshrines Japan's 2.5 million war dead, including class-A war criminal Hideki Tojo, Japan's wartime prime minister.

The past might not be that important if Japan were not so powerful. Japan is an economic superpower and its military, Chinese observers believe, is much stronger than it appears. They stress that Japan's Self-Defence Force (SDF) is the best-equipped military force in Asia and that Japan's defence spending is the second biggest in the world. The high proportion of officers in Japan's otherwise small force is seen as giving Japan the ability to expand rapidly in war time.

Notwithstanding a security concern, Japan plays an important role in China's political and economic strategies. Although Chinese leaders' worldview since the end of the Cold War has been less ideology-oriented,

"Westernization" is still regarded a major threat to the Chinese Government. The fact that Japan lifted sanctions not long after the Tiananmen Square crackdown shows that Japan poses little political threat to Beijing and may well be used to foil the West's pressure. Economically, Japan plays a vital role in China's economic reform and development. In 1993, Japan became China's largest trading partner while China emerged as Japan's second largest after the United States. The trade volume between the two countries rose over 160 times in thirty-two years, soaring from US$1.04 billion in 1972 to US$167.89 billion in 2004. Japan remains one of the largest investors in China.

Basically, China's policies toward Japan reflect its mainstream perceptions. Beijing maintains vigilance against Japan's militarism and is concerned about Japan sending its military overseas in peace-keeping operations. It emphasizes that due to historical reasons, Japan's sending troops abroad is a very sensitive issue. While warning against "revitalization of Japanese militarism", the Chinese Government has been careful not to let the history issue derail the bilateral relationship. However, with an increasingly assertive Japan and a strong anti-Japanese sentiment in China, the history issue will remain a major challenge to Beijing.

## ASEAN

Southeast Asia is important to China in that firstly, it is a key to China's regional influence, especially *vis-à-vis* that of Japan. One Chinese strategic thinker notes that so long as China is able to pre-empt Japan in Southeast Asia and the Korean Peninsula, Japan will be in no position to compete with China in Asia.[22] Secondly, Southeast Asia has its own geo-political significance. After all, much of China's trade and oil from the Middle East pass through the region. Thirdly, with a population of 450 million and growing economies, Southeast Asia has obvious economic importance.

Southeast Asia's importance to China also lies in other considerations. Firstly, ASEAN is crucial to Chinese strategy of promoting multipolarity. Secondly, Southeast Asia is important in China's effort to counter the perceived U.S. containment strategy. China has used the ASEAN Regional Forum (ARF) as a means to question U.S. bilateral alliances in the region. Thirdly, Southeast Asia offers one of the best opportunities for China to discredit the persistent "China threat" theory. Former Malaysian Prime Minister Mahatir Mohamad's statement that "China should be viewed as a country with enormous opportunities rather than perceived as a threat" is the message China endeavours to send.[23] Fourthly, Southeast Asia could be China's ally in resisting Western pressure on issues like political liberalization and human rights. Finally, closer relations with Southeast Asian nations would make it harder for Taiwan to build up its political ties with these nations.

China's relations with ASEAN experienced a dramatic improvement in the past decade. In August 1990, China restored its diplomatic ties with Indonesia, followed by the establishment of diplomatic relations with Singapore two months later. It then established diplomatic relations with Brunei in September 1991, and normalized party-to-party relations as well as state-to-state relations with Vietnam in November 1991. In July 1996, China became a full dialogue partner of ASEAN. Despite the Chinese leadership's initial hesitation, China joined the ARF in 1994, and in the following year started regular senior officials meetings with the ASEAN states at the deputy foreign minister level.

The major security issue between China and ASEAN is the South China Sea disputes. Although negotiation will not be easy and conflicts may intensify from time to time, it is unlikely that those conflicts will run out of control in the near future. In December 1997, a summit meeting was held between the ASEAN states and China. In the joint statement released after the summit, it was announced that the two sides had established a partnership of good-neighbourliness and mutual trust. Both parties pledged to resolve their differences and disputes through peaceful means, and not to allow existing differences to obstruct the development of friendly and cooperative relations between them. China's signing of the Declaration on the Conduct of Parties on the South China Sea in 2002 and its earlier-than-expected accession to ASEAN's Treaty of Amity and Cooperation in October 2003 are further indications that China is making efforts to defuse the tension over South China Sea and to strengthen its relations with ASEAN.

China's increasing economic power is perhaps the most important factor for its closer relations with ASEAN. Given that some ASEAN members have been concerned about China's economic threat, China has been trying to convince these countries that its economic development is an opportunity rather than a threat. China's decision not to devalue its currency during the 1997–98 Asian financial crisis won it praise in Southeast Asia. The relationship made yet another giant step forward with the signing of the historic agreement between China and ASEAN in November

2002 to create the world's largest free trade area, embracing 1.7 billion people and trade worth US$1.2 trillion.

## Internal Stability

Foreign policy is often an extension of domestic policy. Much of China's effort to seek a peaceful international environment is based on its domestic demand for economic growth. Economic development is an effective way to alleviate people's dissatisfaction with other pressing issues, including the widening gap between the rich and the poor, mass unemployment, corruption and most importantly, the CCP's legitimacy.

China's economic development has dramatically enhanced China's national strength and has substantially improved Chinese people's living standard. The achievement did not come without a price. The Chinese Government has claimed that a pre-condition for economic development is stability. "Stability prevails over everything" is what the government has been saying. The CCP learned a lesson from the experience of the former Soviet Union. Soviet Leader Mikhail Gorbachev's dramatic political reforms led to the collapse of his communist regime and the disintegration of the Soviet Union. On the other hand, the economic plight that the Russians experienced after the disintegration of the Soviet Union discouraged the Chinese from pushing for political reforms. China's gradualist approach to economic and political reforms has worked well. After rapid economic growth for over two decades, the Chinese are confident that China is able to maintain a growth rate of 7 to 8 per cent for another two decades.

The Chinese Government today faces daunting challenges though. On the one hand, domestic socio-political problems demand a high economic growth rate. On the other hand, with a more open society, pressure for political reforms has increased. As demonstrated by the SARS crisis, it is now much harder for the Chinese Government to conceal information from the people. The rationale of "stability prevails over everything" is in question. The Chinese state still maintains a good control over the Chinese society. But a fundamental shift in the balance of power between the two is underway.

Despite the challenges, it is unlikely that China will collapse. It was rather popular in the 1990s to predict "China's coming collapse". One observer even made a specific prediction in 1995 that China would have a "terminal crisis" within ten to fifteen years.[24] The Chinese Government under the CCP did experience extraordinary political, economic and social difficulties. Thanks to its pragmatism and adaptability, the government has survived. It will make efforts to maintain continued economic growth and to continue to reinvigorate legitimacy and popular support. Instead of a sudden collapse, we may say with confidence that "China stands a reasonable chance of completing the inevitable economic and political transitions to modernity in peace and stability."[25]

## The Taiwan Issue

Beijing has demonstrated its impatience over the Taiwan issue after Lee Teng-hui's 1995 U.S. visit and, more importantly, Lee's "state-to-state" theory in 1999. Beijing's 11,000-word White Paper on Taiwan, "The One-China Principle and the Taiwan Issue" published in late February 2000 stated that Beijing would take over Taiwan by force under three conditions: Taiwan declares its independence; Taiwan is invaded and occupied by foreign countries; and Taiwan refuses indefinitely to negotiate a peaceful settlement with Beijing. The last condition had long been Beijing's implicit policy but had never been so clearly stated. The White Paper was intended to warn Taiwan's voters not to elect a candidate who might declare Taiwan's independence. Beijing was targeting Chen Shui-bian, the candidate of pro-independence Democratic Progressive Party. However, the White Paper failed to deter the Taiwanese from electing Chen to Taiwan's presidency in March 2000. Beijing was very much restrained during Taiwan's 2004 presidential elections. To the disappointment of the mainland Chinese, Chen retained his power despite the controversy over the legitimacy of the elections. The pressure on Beijing became ever greater.

Beijing may well decide to resort to force if Taiwan declares its independence. In the eyes of most mainland Chinese, the CCP could hardly justify itself if it failed to protect national sovereignty. Surveys consistently show that over 90 per cent of mainland Chinese would support the use of force if Taiwan declared its independence.

To be sure, for Beijing to resort to force over the Taiwan issue is the worst case scenario. "China is operating very much at the psychological or political, rather than military, level of conflict," it is observed.[26] And Beijing is not simply targeting Taipei. It has been China's "international political strategy" to ensure that "there is no retreat, especially by the major powers, from the position of refusing to recognize Taiwan as a sovereign state."[27]

Beijing has made adjustments to its reunification strategy and has been strengthening its economic leverage over Taiwan. The strategy has succeeded in making Taiwan's economy increasingly dependent on the mainland. However, closer economic relations have so far failed to stop Taiwan from drifting away from the mainland politically. Beijing is therefore preparing for the worst.

## CONCLUSION

Few observers see China as an immediate military threat to its neighbours. China does not see any immediate external threat to its national security either. There is a good chance that China's external environment will remain largely peaceful in the years to come. China is likely to continue to focus on economic development and to enhance its comprehensive national power. Meanwhile, it will keep a watchful eye on other big powers, especially the United States and Japan.

China's foreign policy has been deeply influenced by domestic political necessity. That China has endeavoured to improve its relations with great powers, especially the United States, and its neighbours is largely due to the necessity of maintaining high levels of economic growth, on which the Chinese Government has been basing much of its appeal. Continued high levels of economic growth have so far helped reinforce the legitimacy of the CCP's rule. China's efforts to integrate into international society are driven also by the pursuit of economic development.

China's biggest security concern is the Taiwan issue. The Chinese are worried about a growing sentiment for the independence of Taiwan and the seemingly deepening U.S. involvement in the issue. Beijing may well be determined to prevent at any cost, Taiwan from becoming independent. A direct military clash with the United States, however, is the last thing it wants.

China's security perceptions are therefore of multiple dimensions, reflecting the changes in world politics. While the military dimension remains a key element, especially because of the Taiwan issue, the political and economic dimensions have become more prominent. China is now in a process which it can barely control. Its decision more than two decades ago to open up and to make economic reforms has substantially enhanced its national power. During the process, however, its economy has become more and more integrated with the world economy and its people are increasingly exposed to Western values. China now has no choice but to further integrate into the international community. It feels the pressure of accepting the rules of the game and acting as a responsible power. Chinese analysts thus note that China has lost some of the strategic freedom that it enjoyed in the Cold War years.

China also faces a number of dilemmas regarding its national security. Firstly, it wants to become an important member of the international society and play a more active role in international affairs, which may consolidate its national security. Yet at the same time, to be deeply involved in international conflicts may derail China's economic development. Secondly, China wants to actively participate in building the international system, which may well benefit its national security. On the other hand, it does not want to be tied up by the system and lose its own autonomy. Thirdly, to counter the "China threat" theory, China has an interest in international security cooperation. However, given its territorial disputes with a number of countries and the Taiwan issue, China is wary of paying "excessive prices" that might jeopardize its sovereignty.[28] These dilemmas are likely to persist for some time.

## NOTES

1. Chris Brown, *Understanding International Relations* (Second edition, Basingstoke, England and New York, N.Y.: Palgrave, 2001), p. 238.

2. Lin Limin, "A Few Points on China's National Security Strategy in the 21st Century", *Jiangnan Shehui Xueyuan Xuebao* [*Journal of Jiangnan Social College*], no. 2 (2002): 23.

3. Geng Mingjun, "China's National Security under Globalisation", *Dangdai Shijie yu Shehui Zhuyi* [*Contemporary World and Socialism*], no. 2 (2003): 57.

4. Chu Shulong, "The PRC Girds for Limited, High-Tech War", *Orbis* 38, no. 2 (Spring 1994): 180–83; David Shambaugh, "The Insecurity of Security: The PLA's Evolving Doctrine and Threat Perceptions towards 2000", *Journal of Northeast Asian Studies* 13, no. 1 (Spring 1994): 6.

5. For more information, see Jian Yang, *Congress and U.S. China Policy, 1989–1999* (New York: Nova Science, 2000).

6. Chu Shulong and Wang Zaibang, "Some Thoughts on Several Major Issues about International Situation and Our External Strategy", *Xiandai Guoji Guangxi* [*Contemporary International Relations*], no. 8 (1999): 5.

7. Wei Ling, "An Analysis of the Current Security Soundings of China", *Renmin Daxue Xuebao* [*Journal of People's University*], no. 3 (2003): 133–35.

8. *Los Angeles Times*, 14 July 1999, p. A14.

9. *Washington Post*, 12 September 1999, p. A27.

10. Xing Zhigang, "Taiwan: Don't Test Beijing's Resolve", *China Daily*, 29 July 2004, p. 1.

11. Michael D. Swaine and Ashley J. Tellis, *Interpreting China's Grand Strategy: Past, Present, and Future* (Santa Monica, CA: RAND, 2000), p. ix.

12. Based on Zhou Jianming and Wang Hailiang, "National Grand Strategy, National Security and National Interest", *Shijie Jingji yu Zhengzhi* [*World Economy and Politics*], no. 4 (2002): 22.

13. Chu and Wang, p. 6; Yan Xuetong, "International Environment and Thoughts on Diplomacy", *Xiandai Guoji Guangxi* [*Contemporary International Relations*], no. 8 (1999): 10.

14. Lin, p. 24.

15. For more information, see Sheng Lijun, *China and Taiwan: Cross-Strait Relations under Chen Shui-bian* (London and New York: Zed Books; Singapore: Institute of Southeast Asian Studies, 2002).

16. International Crisis Group Asia Report No. 54, *Taiwan Strait II: The Risk of War*, 6 June 2003, p. 4.

17. Yong Deng, "Chinese Perceptions of U.S. Power and Strategy", *Asian Affairs, An American Review* 28, no. 3 (Fall 2001): 150–55.

18. Thomas J. Christensen, "Chinese Realpolitik", *Foreign Affairs* 75, no. 5 (September–October 1996): 37.

19. Yong Deng, "Hegemon on the Offensive: Chinese Perspectives on U.S. Global Strategy", *Political Science Quarterly* 116, no. 3 (Fall 2001): 343–465.

20. Qin Yongchun, "A Few Questions about Sino-Russian Strategic Cooperative Partnership", *Heping yu Fazhan* [*Peace and Development*], no. 4 (1997): 23.

21. Christensen, p. 41.

22. Jin Xide's comments on Japan in Yan Xuetong, "Our Situation after 9/11: Changes and Continuity", *Shijie Zhishi* [*World Knowledge*], no. 1 (2002): 39–40.

23. As quoted in Dana R. Dillon, "Contemporary Security Challenges in Southeast Asia", *Parameters* 27, no. 1 (Spring 1997): 129.

24. Jack A. Goldstone, "The Coming Chinese Collapse", *Foreign Policy*, no. 99 (Summer 1995): 35–52.

25. Yasheng Huang, "Why China Will Not Collapse", *Foreign Policy*, no. 99 (Summer 1995): 55.

26. International Crisis Group, p. i.

27. Ibid.

28. Meng Xiangqin, "On the Changes of China's International Role and the Fundamentals of China's Security Strategy", *Shijie Jingji yu Zhengzhi* [*World Economy and Politics*], no. 7 (2002): 12–13.

## Chapter Five
# United States Security Policies in Asia

Jörn Dosch

## INTRODUCTION

The United States was a Pacific power long before it became an Atlantic one. In the early 1840s the United States intensified its commercial engagement in East Asia. Under the terms of the Treaty of Wanghia (1844), America gained the right to trade in Chinese ports. More decisively, in 1853 Commodore Matthew Perry terminated Japan's self-imposed isolation and forced the country to enter into trade with the United States. Both events paved the way for America's later colonial involvement in the region, which took shape with the takeover of the former Spanish colonies in the Philippines and Guam in 1898. In only a dozen decades the United States had experienced a metamorphosis from a colony to a colonial power. Since the late nineteenth century the United States has maintained a pre-eminent position in the Asia-Pacific, only briefly interrupted by imperial Japan's attempts to establish a "Greater East Asian Co-Prosperity Sphere", which precipitated the Pacific War.

The defeat of Japan in August 1945 was followed by the emergence of an Asia-Pacific Pax Americana in the post-World War II era. Although the Cold War in the Asia-Pacific was characterized by a tripolar structure with the United States, China and Russia as its poles and shifting power relativities within this triangular order, its dominant element was nevertheless American primacy or, as some argue, hegemony. Unlike Western Europe where the United States' leading security role was embedded in a multilateral structure centred on the North Atlantic Treaty Organization (NATO), a collection of bilateral alliances with Japan, South Korea, Republic of China on Taiwan and the Philippines served as the *ad hoc* structure of security relations in the Asia-Pacific.[1] Among those, the U.S.-Japan axis emerged as the most important. In 1951 the United States and Japan signed the San Francisco Peace Treaty and the Mutual Security Treaty. While the first formally ended the American occupation of Japan, the second enshrined Japan's position as Washington's principal Asian ally or, according to some, military satellite. In 1960 a bilateral defence pact between the two nations raised Japan's status because it eliminated earlier provisions allowing the United States to intervene in Japanese politics, provided a nuclear umbrella and obliged the United States to defend Japan if attacked. The pact also required Washington to consult Tokyo regarding use of U.S. military bases in Japan. At the same time the defence pact further integrated Japan as a key element of America's global Cold War security and defence strategy.[2]

Has anything really changed since then from an American point of view? Does the management of East Asian security in the post Cold War era differ markedly from previous decades? Are there any new challenges at all that would require new policy responses? At first glance, the answer to all three questions is yes. The clear Cold War structure of tripolarity, comprising the United States, Russia and China as the main regional and also competitive powers, is gone and has been replaced by what seems to be an asymmetric multipolar system. The Association of Southeast Asian Nations (ASEAN) as the only collective actor in East Asia with a track record, a more active and assertive Japan and emerging nuclear powers such as China and North Korea, have all influenced international security relations in the 1990s and the beginning of the twenty-first century. A new mix of hard and soft security issues, with religious fundamentalism and terrorism as its main ingredients, seems to require revised foreign policy strategies. The first Clinton administration gave impetus to structural change by applying a strategy of "engagement and enlargement" towards East Asia and the region's actors.

In retrospect, however, Clinton's neo-Wilsonian enthusiasm for multilateral forums such as the ASEAN Regional Forum (ARF) and the

Asia-Pacific Economic Cooperation (APEC) already looks like nothing more than a footnote in the history of American foreign relations. The widespread perception among foreign policymakers of China as a strategic competitor, the joint American-Japanese development of a sea-based missile defence system within the Theater Missile Defence (TMD)-framework, and the debate on eliminating current and future threats to the American national interest in a unilateral manner modelled on Operation Iraqi Freedom points to a general pattern of Washington's approach in security relations with East Asia. As Marvin Ott has concluded:

> at the most basic level, United States objectives in East Asia have remained consistent over the last five decades: Prevent the emergence of a regional hegemon; keep open the sea and air routes that transit the area; maintain commercial access to the economics of the region and the peace and stability that commerce requires; and preserve and strengthen security ties with allies and friends in the region.[3]

In a similar vein, this chapter will argue that despite emerging new security challenges in the post-Cold War regional security order, the general pattern of U.S. interests and policy strategies towards East Asia has been remarkably consistent over time because it is been embedded in a persistent, multi-dimensional structure that has defined Washington's relations with the regions since the early days of American involvement in East Asia. In the passages to follow I will outline the major events in U.S.-East Asia security relations and Washington's policy priorities towards the region since the end of the Cold War. I will then highlight, firstly, a trio of variables that have formed a consisted pattern of America's involvement in the Asia-Pacific, and, secondly, explain why the United States has been able to sustain its pre-eminent power position in the Asia-Pacific for more than a century.

## THE UNITED STATES AND THE POST-COLD WAR SECURITY ORDER IN THE ASIA-PACIFIC

The Cold War security architecture of the Asia-Pacific was strikingly different from the one in Europe not only in terms of its structure but even more with regards to its implications. While the American-Soviet balance of power kept Europe relatively secure and stable, the ideological-political antagonism between the two super powers resulted in armed conflict by proxy in the Asia-Pacific. In fact, the two "hot wars" of the Cold War were fought in East Asia, in Korea (1950–53) and Vietnam (1963–75). When the Cold War finally came to an end it was clear from an American perspective that any new world order would have to be built along the lines of U.S. supremacy and be consistent with American values and beliefs. However, the United States entered the post Cold War era as a weaker power than previously, especially in economic terms. The decline in U.S. economic power had two reasons, the trade deficit and the budget deficit. The U.S. trade deficit with Japan was in the region of US$50 billion, and with other Asian countries around US$25 billion in the early 1990s. At the same time, the U.S. Government was running a massive fiscal deficit, which necessitated a further reduction in spending on welfare programmes and the military. Both facts pointed to a continued decline in U.S. influence in the region. Strong signals began to emerge in some sections of the U.S. political elite which favoured either a military drawdown from Asia, or increased host country contributions to defray the cost of U.S. bases in countries like Japan and South Korea. According to the standard argument, the extremely successful economies of East Asia were now in a position to defend themselves without U.S. assistance. As a result, the future of the bilateral alliances became uncertain.

## NEW STRATEGIES IN THE LIGHT OF CHANGED STRUCTURES: THE EMERGENCE (AND DECLINE) OF MULTILATERALISM

In the wake of structural changes and uncertainties, many key foreign policy actors in Washington perceived the need for new mechanisms to cope with the emerging challenges. In the early days of the first Clinton administration, the Assistant Secretary of State for East Asian and the Pacific Affairs, Winston Lord, wrote an influential memo to Secretary of State Warren Christopher, warning that the United States was in deep trouble in Asia. Some Asian states had started to oppose American engagement in the region and perceived Washington an "an international nanny if not bully", as one senior official within the administration put it.[4] U.S. officials favoured the promotion of multilateralism as a strategy to keep the United States involved in the region and to strengthen both credibility and legitimacy of Washington's position *vis-à-vis* other major regional actors. Unlike the administration of George Bush, a majority of relevant actors of the first Clinton administration welcomed multilateralism as a supplement (but never as an alternative) to existing bilateral arrangements. Hence, the United States supported the approaches of strengthening existing multilateral dialogues (APEC) and creating new ventures, such as the ASEAN Regional Forum (ARF).

In contrast to transatlantic experiences and maybe for the first time in modern history, in the Asia-Pacific a multilateral system of interstate relations was initiated by weak actors and not by the dominant regional powers. At the same time, it is important to note that the role of the United States was crucial to the emergence of multilateralism in the region, even though Washington did not initiate the process. Instead, the ASEAN states take credit as the architects of the regional security dialogue. ASEAN saw the ARF concept as a way of keeping the United States engaged in the region and as a restraint to the rising powers such as China and Japan. In the first half of 1993 the United States and Japan signalled their support for a multilateral security forum. Washington was interested in creating a vehicle to encourage dialogue between South Korea and Japan in the absence of any suitable bilateral forum. Japan was driven by the political will to search for supplementary ways to ensure its security without seeming to be too active, thus avoiding any reminders of the bitter days of Japanese imperialism. Hence, both Japan and the United States welcomed ASEAN's initiative to take the diplomatic lead in setting up a multilateral venture.[5] When the *Washington Post* on 26 July 1994 reported after the first ARF meeting that the new institution had been built "along lines advocated by President Clinton", it ignored the fact that the new forum was obviously more Asian-driven. Moreover, in a speech to the South Korean National Assembly in July 1993 Clinton endorsed security dialogues among Pacific countries. He proposed a number of overlapping security activities, from multilateral discussion on specific issues such as the Spratly Islands dispute to confidence-building measures such as discussion of defence doctrines, transparency in weapons acquisitions, and conflict management. This proposal, which was part of Clinton's neo-Wilsonian "engagement and enlargement strategy", marked a fresh phase in U.S. foreign policy towards the Asia-Pacific.

The first half of the 1990s were the blossoming of the "Pacific dream" when the terms future, prosperity and Asia-Pacific became almost synonymous. No actor, certainly not the United States, wanted to lose out on the "coming Pacific century". In his critical assessment of the Asia Pacific vision, Rob Wilson wrote:

> Asia-Pacific is a utopic discourse of the liberal market, an emerging signifier of transnational aspirations for some higher, supra-national unity in which global/local will meet in some kind of "win-win" situation and the open market will absorb culture and politics into its borderless affirmative flow.[6]

Since the mid-1990s, however, regional multilateralism has gradually lost momentum primarily as a result of the Asian financial crisis which clouded the perception of the Asia Pacific as the economic powerhouse of the twenty-first century. At the same time, however, APEC, ARF and other multilateral forums remain relevant. In the absence of other suitable mechanisms they continue to provide a valuable framework for regular high level meetings between states and non-state actors that otherwise would find it difficult to communicate. The dyads China and Taiwan, Japan and South Korea, and the United States and North Korea are cases of dialogue in point. Furthermore, the current crisis on the Korean Peninsula demonstrates the U.S. administration's interest in pursuing multilateral strategies as long as direct and immediate threats to core elements of the American national interest are not at stake. When the North Korean regime admitted to having a nuclear program in October 2002, Pyongyang stated on various occasions that it would only hold bilateral talks with the U.S. Government. The Bush administration, however, has made it clear that it will only engage in multilateral talks and has sought to engage the United Nations Security Council on the matter. North Korea eventually agreed on discussing the implications of its nuclear ambitions within a multilateral setting.

Why has the Bush administration favoured a multilateral approach towards North Korea whereas it followed a unilateral strategy in the case of Iraq? Both states were indicted as members of the so-called axis of evil. Unlike Iraq under Saddam Hussein, North Korea has been isolated since the end of the Cold War when its traditional allies the Soviet Union/Russia and China withdrew support. Furthermore, in April 2003:

> Moscow for the first time said it would consider imposing economic sanctions against North Korea if it didn't back down from developing atomic weapons. Beijing has also been reported by diplomats in China as having made subtle threats toward North Korea over its nuclear program, including temporarily shutting off an oil pipeline into the isolated communist country.[7]

In the absence of any international support for its position, and contained by South Korean and American military might, the risk that North Korea would make use of its weapons of mass destruction and pose a direct threat to the United States remains extremely small. Overall, however, multilateral approaches to regional security are the exception rather than the rule in the early twenty-first century.

In general terms and as far as the United States is concerned, the outbreak of the Asian financial crisis in 1997 dispelled worry about the possible decline of U.S. primacy. From the perspective of a strong America, multilateral cooperation lost its initial attraction and necessity as a means of promoting U.S. interests. Traditional unilateral, bilateral, and minilateral strategies regained importance. The successful redefinition of the U.S.-Japan alliance also influenced this change of perception. The renewed agreement significantly reduced the U.S. uncertainties of the early 1990s about Asia-Pacific's post Cold War security architecture. The alliance was again seen as the backbone of security relations in the area, thus reducing the need for supplementary strategies.

## THE REVIVAL OF TRADITIONAL U.S.-EAST ASIA RELATIONS: BILATERALISM PREVAILS

The predominance of bilateral approaches to security in the Asia-Pacific is clearly reflected by the U.S.-Japan Joint Declaration on Security: Alliance for the 21st Century of 16 April 1996. It describes in general terms the need for the two countries to "work jointly and individually... to achieve a more peaceful and stable security environment in the Asia-Pacific region".[8] The document stresses four major points:

- Cooperation with the People's Republic of China with the aim of encouraging China to "play a positive and constructive role in the region".
- Encouragement of cooperation with Russia's ongoing process of reform, and reaffirmation of full normalization of Japan-Russia relations as important to regional peace and stability.
- Continuation of efforts regarding stability on the Korean Peninsula in cooperation with South Korea.
- Development of multilateral regional security dialogues and cooperation mechanisms such as the ASEAN Regional Forum and eventually security dialogues regarding Northeast Asia.

A comparison of these points with the five "foundation stones" of U.S. Asia policy named by then Defence Secretary Caspar Weinberger in 1985 shows that Washington's priorities have not changed significantly:

- The key importance of the U.S.-Japanese security relationship;
- The U.S. commitment to stability on the Korean Peninsula;

- U.S. efforts to build an enduring relationship with China;
- U.S. support for ASEAN;
- The long-standing U.S. partnership with Australia and New Zealand.[9]

The Joint Declaration of 1996 and the new Guidelines for U.S.-Japan Defence Cooperation released in New York on 23 September 1997, stimulated a lively academic debate on the meaning of the alliance for security relations in the Asia-Pacific. Generally it is acknowledged that the renewed American-Japanese alliance represents more than ever the cornerstone of the region's security architecture. It guarantees peace and security not only for Japan but for the entire Asia-Pacific area. Most regard the alliance as the second-best option in the absence of a multilateral security and defence structure as can be found in Europe. At the same time many in Asia (and perhaps conservatives in the United States as well) perceive the alliance as a necessary counterweight against a potentially expansionist and aggressive China causes. But among liberals there is still concern that the alliance is provocative.

After the short interlude of multilateralism, neither the Clinton administration nor the succeeding administration of George W. Bush have questioned bilateralism on U.S. terms as the principal foreign policy approach towards the Asia-Pacific. If this policy were to change, then a concert of power could emerge as a working alternative. One popular scenario, which has been discussed both by political actors and academics, envisions the enlargement of the U.S.-Japan alliance.[10] South Korea (and maybe a future reunited Korea) and Australia are likely players in such a concert system that would give the U.S. allies significantly more duties and responsibilities than today. However, the key question is whether China will qualify as a partner in the concert — or as a rival. If the answer is a partner, then the Asia-Pacific could well resemble the increasingly inclusive trans-Atlantic security structure centred on an enlarged NATO.

## THE IMPACT OF SEPTEMBER 11 AND THE WAR ON TERROR

The post-11 September 2001 alternations to international relations point further in the direction of concerted efforts to establish a secure regional order in the Asia-Pacific. Despite unilateral tendencies in U.S. foreign policy in the wake of the terrorist attacks on New York and Washington, the ongoing war on terrorism needs partners in order to achieve anything.

How far do multilateral approaches go? According to a widely held view, the attacks of September 11 have reversed Washington's perception of ASEAN and greatly enhanced the organization's status as a major regional player. In fact, the U.S.-ASEAN Joint Declaration for Cooperation to Combat International Terrorism, signed in August 2002, has encouraged the perception of the U.S.-ASEAN axis as a major element in the global fight against terrorism.

However, although one cannot deny the growing U.S. attention ASEAN has enjoyed recently, Washington does not seem to perceive ASEAN as a central actor in its own right in the fight on terror but rather as a vehicle to support and strengthen crucial bilateral relations with key states in Southeast Asia. In other words, while Southeast Asia has undoubtedly re-gained its previously lost geo-strategic importance and priority on the U.S. foreign policy and defence agenda, the nature of Washington's approach to the region remains bilateral in mode. The National Security Strategy of the United States supports this view:

> The attacks of September 11 energized America's Asian alliances. … We have deepened cooperation on counter-terrorism with our alliance partners in Thailand and the Philippines and received invaluable assistance from close friends like Singapore and New Zealand.[11]

Reference to ASEAN is made only in the very last paragraph of a long list of U.S. policies to be adopted "to enhance our Asian alliances and friendships". This passage states:

> We will… build on stability provided by these alliances, as well as with institutions such as ASEAN and the Asia-Pacific Economic Cooperation forum, to develop a mix of regional and bilateral strategies to manage change in this dynamic region.[12]

Overall, the United States has followed a key-country approach in its post-September 11 relations with Southeast Asia, most notably with the Philippines. The Bush administration pledged US$100 million in military assistance and sent 650 American soldiers to Mindanao (Southern Philippines) in order to fight the Abu Sayyaf group, bandits with alleged but never proven links to the Al-Qaeda terrorist network and a radical Islamist-separatist agenda.

To be sure, the U.S.-ASEAN Declaration does provide a suitable basis for a prominent involvement of ASEAN as collective international actor. In terms of *realpolitik*, however, given the different degree of the member states' exposure to terrorism and diverging views on and policies towards the complex issue of terrorism in general and Islamic militancy in particular, it seems unlikely that the ten ASEAN states will be in the position to agree, either among themselves or collectively with the United States, on any specific action that goes beyond a general support for the war on terrorism, however morally it might be welcomed. In 2001, the APEC summit in Shanghai demonstrated that achieving any consensus on anti-terrorism strategies that exceeds the lowest common dominator is next to impossible. Despite Indonesia's and Malaysia's initial intention to support a proposed APEC declaration condemning international terrorism, the declaration did not materialize particularly because domestic constraints hindered both governments from officially sponsoring and signing such as document. Instead, the APEC summit produced only a very general statement on terrorism. As Jürgen Haacke further explains:

> from the perspective of some ASEAN states the military focus of the US war against terrorism is not necessarily welcome. Indeed, Singaporean analysts consistently remind the US policy community that the war against terrorism, as far as Southeast Asia is concerned, should not involve the alienation of moderate Muslims. An anti-terrorism strategy primarily emphasizing military force is widely deemed ineffective and possibly counter-productive.[13]

The cautious approach of some ASEAN states to anti-terror cooperation is illustrated by the U.S.-ASEAN Joint Declaration. The document includes a paragraph the U.S. side was initially unwilling to accept: "Recognizing the principles of sovereign equality, territorial integrity and non-intervention in the domestic affairs of other states". The paragraph was added in the declaration at the request of Indonesia and Vietnam, who feared that a robust anti-terrorism accord with the United States could legitimize the incursion of U.S. troops in Southeast Asia. In sum, the anti-terrorist agreement:

> glosses over intra-ASEAN policy disagreements as how to fight terrorist movements, and ... touches upon very sensitive national security issues which most ASEAN members are not prepared to discuss in depth with their neighbors. While it may be true that Washington has reassessed the strategic priority of Southeast Asia, which it considers a second front in the war against terrorism, and is now dealing with ASEAN as an entity, the agreement is couched in the language of "soft law" and does not create binding obligations for ASEAN members to co-operate closer among themselves.[14]

Recent developments further suggest that the United States will not drastically change its strategic approaches towards ASEAN as an actor and Southeast Asia as a region. Contrary to initial expectations, Southeast Asia was not rocked by widespread and violent protest against the war on Iraq and from a U.S. point of view does not need significantly intensified attention. Even in Indonesia, the world's most populous Muslim nation, the Islamic backlash was rather moderate which is in stark contrast to the large anti-American demonstrations in the aftermath of September 11 and the war against Afghanistan's Taliban regime.

This historical overview has shown that despite major structural evolutions, the United States has dominated the East Asian region since the dawn of the nineteenth century. The next part of this chapter focuses on the factors that have significantly influenced the American approach towards the region.

## THE DOMINANT U.S. ROLE IN THE ASIA-PACIFIC: THREE DETERMINANTS

Any enquiry into why the United States has been dominant in the Asia-Pacific has to take into account three structural factors. The first is the American claim to global leadership; the second is the U.S. perception of the Pacific Ocean as a natural zone of American influence, as "our lake"; and the third is the outcome of the dynamics of the U.S. political system, that is, the competition among a wide range of actors over the conduct of foreign policy.

## THE U.S. CLAIM TO GLOBAL LEADERSHIP

The claim to leadership which is manifested in worldwide, sometimes aggressive, promotion of democracy, human rights and market economy is typically justified on moral and special status grounds. These perceived rights are embedded in the strong belief in exceptionalism and moralism or, according to Stanley Hoffmann's classical definition, "the deep and lasting faith in the singular, unique, 'unprecedented' and 'unrepeatable' character of the United States…"[15] The idea of American exceptionalism dates back to the mystical concept of "manifest destiny", when in 1845 John L. O'Sullivan, a Democratic Party leader and influential editor, gave the Westward movement its name. In an attempt to explain America's thirst for expansion, and to present a defence for America's claim to new territories, he wrote of the right of our manifest destiny to over spread and to possess the whole of the continent which Providence has given us for the development of the great experiment of liberty and federative development of self government entrusted to us. It is right such as that of the tree to the space of air and the earth suitable for the full expansion of its principle and destiny of growth.[16]

The concept of manifest destiny, reflecting the missionary character of U.S. foreign policy, is still very much alive, and many observers have interpreted the war with Iraq as a continuation of manifest destiny.[17] Not surprisingly this role concept clashes with Asian interests *vis-à-vis* the United States. Political elites in many East Asian states do not necessarily take for granted the missionary character of U.S. foreign policy nor do they subscribe to the idea of U.S. hegemony. Singapore's former ambassador to the United States, Tommy Koh, attempted in 1995 to explain American perceptions to his fellow Asians as follows:

> Many Asians do not understand America. America is not a normal country. From the time of its birth, Americans have believed that their country was founded with a divine mission... Since this belief is an article of faith it is like America's secular religion. A believer on faith would not normally subject his beliefs to intellectual analysis or to the empirical test. Thus, Americans have never hesitated in their proselytizing mission abroad in spite of the vast discrepancies between American ideals and American realities at home.[18]

In some cases the notion of American exceptionalism is at odds with other nations' aspirations to equality, even superiority. China is a case in point. The following statement betrays this common Chinese misconception regarding U.S.-China relations: "China and the U.S. will always confront each other. One country claims to be capitalist, while the other claims to be socialist, they should collide."[19] A situation of competing economic systems may not provide an ideal framework for stable and peaceful bilateral relations but the impact and consequences of the capitalist-socialist/communuist cleavage has been widely over-estimated. At best, it is only part of a far more complex structure. The decisive element of this structure is rather the clash of self-perceptions and role-concepts in international relations. In short, due to historical, geo-political and ideological factors, both nations, the United States and China, cling to their respective belief of being legitimately superior to any other actor in the Asia-Pacific, superior in terms of value systems and cultural features and as the result of a long-term hegemonic role in the area. After all, the

Chinese tribute system lasted for many centuries in contrast to American pre-eminence that emerged only in the late nineteenth century.

## THE PACIFIC AS THE "AMERICAN LAKE"

The second and closely related variable of any American role in the Asia-Pacific is the perception of the Pacific Ocean as a natural zone of American influence, as "our lake". This concept dates back to the late nineteenth century when most strategic points of the North Pacific rim were in U.S. hands. The annexation of Hawaii and the colonization of the Philippines on the eve of the twentieth century marked the key stages of American expansion into the Pacific. Historians have coined the terms "empire by invitation"[20] or "reluctant imperialists"[21] to describe this politically controversial process, initially more unplanned than strategically envisioned. The result of the American imperial involvement in the Asia-Pacific region is undisputed, however. For more than a century the Pacific Ocean has been perceived as a prime area for U.S. opportunity. As an oft-repeated aphorism put it, "The Mediterranean is the ocean of the past, the Atlantic is the ocean of the present and the Pacific is the ocean of the future".[22] Secretary of State John Hay's early twentieth century account sounds strikingly similar to the prophecy of James Hodgson, then the U.S. ambassador to Japan, about eighty years later: "The now flourishing Pacific Region ... constitutes nothing less than one of the great developments in human history — from now on the words 'Pacific' and 'future' will be synonymous."[23]

## THE OBSTACLES IMPOSED BY THE AMERICAN POLITICAL SYSTEM

As Marvin Ott's quote in the introduction above suggests, the consistency of the United States approach to the Asia-Pacific seems remarkable. However, many observers and analysts both within and outside the United States have complained about the lack of direction in Washington's Asia-Pacific policy, and called for a comprehensive and coherent long-term security blueprint or strategy, for example an Asia-Pacific Marshall Plan. What is the reason for the alleged lack of direction in Washington's East Asia policy?

The foreign policy-making process in general and strategies towards the Asia-Pacific in particular involve a wide range of actors representing different interests and pushing diverse agendas. The best example is Washington's China policy. The fact that U.S.-China relations often appear to lack consistency and long-term vision is at least partly due to the large number of actors involved in Washington decision-making. Whereas the making of foreign policy in most European democracies is monopolized by ministries of foreign affairs elites, the U.S. Constitution — to use the famous phrase of Edward Corwin — creates "an invitation to struggle for the privilege of directing American foreign policy".[24] As a result, in the United States we can normally observe a contradiction between a more pro-China policy of the administration and more anti-China interests in Congress. During the Clinton presidency, for example, the administration favoured a strategy of engaging Beijing and actively supporting the integration of the People's Republic of China into the international community of states, whereby it hoped to make China's foreign policy behaviour more predictable and reliable. However, from 1994 onwards the Republican-dominated Congress had increasingly challenged and undermined Clinton's cooperative approach. In 1999, the "Cox Report", a congressional study alleging that China had acquired sensitive technology through commercial satellite contracts, contributed to the perception of China becoming the United States' principal post-Cold War adversary. Congress' tough stand on Beijing has been influenced by an anti-China coalition of (a) pro-human rights NGOs, condemning the People's Republic of China (PRC) for its poor human rights record, (b) unions eager to curb imports from China that allegedly threaten American manufacturing jobs, and (c) religious and environmental NGOs.

In addition to the administration-Congress controversy and disputes between pro- and anti-China lobbies, a third cleavage refers to conflicting views on U.S.-Taiwan relations. In 1995 influential pro-Taiwan activists among the political élite in Washington successfully pushed the administration to grant Lee Teng-hui, then president of the Republic of China on Taiwan, a visa for a visit to his alma mater, Cornell University. The visit was loudly criticized by the government in Beijing because it was interpreted as a step toward a diplomatic recognition of Taiwan. The matter eventually provoked serious tension in the Taiwan Straits in July of the same year.

Although George W. Bush's visit to Beijing in February 2002 and Hu's trip to the United States in April of the same year built on the spirit of post-September 11, two new congressional commissions stirred up anxieties and annoyances for the future. According to David Shambaugh the commissions — the U.S. China Commission and the congressional-executive commission on China which focus on trade relations and human rights respectively — are "going to be a permanent thorn in China's side".[25] Diverging views on China and competing strategic approaches do not only exist in executive-legislative relations but also within the administration. The Pentagon, for example, is known for its anti-China and pro-Taiwan position and related reluctance to support any far-reaching engagement strategies towards China. On the eve of Hu Jintao's visit to Washington Defence Department officials allegedly leaked intelligence details of Chinese missile deployments near Taiwan in an effort to embarrass Hu. On the other hand, the Chinese vice-president became the most senior official of his country ever to visit the Pentagon.

The whole picture of U.S.-China relations is no doubt more complex. Nonetheless, this brief outline demonstrates that the variety of interests makes consistency, comprehensiveness and long-term planning in the foreign and security policy field hard to achieve for any U.S. administration.

## HARD POWER AND SOFT POWER: ASPECTS OF U.S. PRIMACY

Having discussed the factors that determine the U.S. foreign policy approach towards the Asia-Pacific, we now need to ask why the United States has been able to maintain primacy in the region. The answer relates to a combination of hard power based on military might and soft power based on the attractiveness and model character.

First, hard power. Not only has the notion of the Asia-Pacific as a focal point of Washington's foreign policy strategy virtually remained unchanged, but also the key actors contributing to the lasting and profound Asia-Pacific engagement have been remarkably persistent. Among them, the U.S. Navy is one of the most important. Although the exercise of hegemony seems to be outdated in the globalized world of the post-colonial and post-bipolar era, most states in the Asia-Pacific, with the prominent exception of China and North Korea, still consider and favour the United States as the prime stabilizer, broker and balancer within the area. Since the end of World War II, U.S. hard power in the region has been based on maritime superiority. Today this structural advantage could be even more important than during the days of the Cold War. Australian strategist Paul Dibb is worth quoting a length on this key theme:

From a defense planning perspective, it is important to understand that in the Asia-Pacific region potential military operations *will be essentially maritime* in nature. Apart from the Korean Peninsula, U.S. military forces are not likely to be involved in large-scale ground-force operations. The dominant geopolitical change in the new security environment has been the virtual elimination for military planning purposes of allied continental commitments; the emerging struggle for power in Asia will focus on political fault lines that are maritime rather than continental in aspect. The development of China's military power and the response to it of India and Japan are likely to put pressure on the chain of America's friends and allies in the long littoral extending between South Korea and Taiwan in the north to the ASEAN countries and Australia in the south.[26]

Potential adversaries of the United States such as China might be able to build naval forces capable of partially denying American naval forces complete freedom of movement. But they lack the platforms and support systems to establish command of the sea on a comparable scale. The actual debate concerns the degree of American naval superiority rather than its fact.

The responsibility of the U.S. Pacific Command (PACOM) covers more than fifty per cent of earth's surface, reaching from the west coast of the United States mainland to the east coast of Africa[27] and from the Arctic to the Antarctic. Approximately 90,000 to 100,000 troops are currently forward-deployed in the Asia-Pacific, principally in Japan (especially on Okinawa where sixty per cent of the 47,000 U.S. troops in Japan are stationed), South Korea, Guam and Diego Garcia. U.S. naval power in the in this region is based on the presence and mission of the Seventh Fleet, which is part of the Pacific Fleet and the core force within PACOM. Established in 1943, the Seventh Fleet is the largest of the Navy's forward-deployed fleets, including 40–50 ships, 200 aircraft and about 20,000 Navy and Marine Corps personnel. Eighteen ships operate from the U.S. facilities in Japan and Guam, representing the spearhead of the deployed fleet. Other ships are deployed on a rotating basis from bases in Hawaii and the U.S. west coast.[28]

Unlike the Clinton administration, which produced two security strategies for the Asia-Pacific (1995 and 1998), the succeeding Bush administration has not formulated a defence outlook for the region in spite of the area's growing strategic importance as a theatre for the war on terrorism. The 1998 report survived the change of governments and remains the authoritative blueprint — a further indication of rather persistent American interests and policies towards the Asia-Pacific. The tenor of the current U.S. National Security Strategy (2002) confirms the principal policy approach based on a system of bilateral alliances which is partly supplemented by multilateral initiatives.

## CULTURE, VALUES AND IDEOLOGY

The acceptance by Asian leaders of a pre-eminent position of the United States in the Asia-Pacific has never been based on the sheer seize of its military presence alone. The export of American culture and technology has played an equally important part. This is what Joseph Nye has called "soft power", described as follows:

> If [a state's] culture and ideology are attractive, others will more willingly follow. If it can establish international norms that are consistent with its society, it will less likely have to change. If it can help support institutions that make states wish to channel or limit their activities in ways the dominant state prefers, it may not need costly exercises of coercive or hard power in bargaining situations. Or more to the point: "Soft Power is your ability to attract others to get the outcomes you want. Hard power is when I coerce you".[29]

While hard power manifests itself in military force or economic sanctions, soft power is based on the attractiveness of values, ideology and cultural features. The sources of American soft power are liberalism and democracy and — maybe to an even greater extent — specific consumer goods and services, films, and pop youth culture generally. According to a popular cliché, McDonalds, Starbucks, MTV and Hollywood are the U.S. faces of globalization. This is, of course, a simplifying metaphor but a very powerful one and not very far from reality. Until very recently in Bangkok a cup of coffee would cost the equivalent of about a quarter of a U.S. dollar in mid-2003. Today it is fashionable to have the same black brew for ten times its former price. Today it is called *latte* and it is from one of the uncounted Starbucks outlets that spread over the city. Last but not least, American universities are an important source of soft power as they attract more than 500,000 foreign students each year who get in touch with — and often absorb — American values and ideas before they return home. Joseph Nye argues that while the United States as a leading world actor needs to exert both hard and soft power, the information revolution and the phenomenon of globalization call for the exercise of more soft power than hard power. He consequently criticizes the unilateral military element in George Bush's foreign policy.[30]

There is, of course, a flip-side to American soft power. While I have argued that American soft power has actually strengthened the U.S. position in the region, soft power could also easily be interpreted as "cultural imperialism" that might make American predominance less acceptable. Could this be the reason why Japanese pop culture is more and more becoming a cultural alternative to "Americanization" in Northeast and Southeast Asia?

## CONCLUSION AND OUTLOOK

This chapter has tried to show that despite (a) changing actors in U.S. foreign policy-making and (b) significant alterations to the structures of global order, in sum both American interests and strategies towards East Asia have been remarkably persistent over the past decades. The driver of the U.S. approach to Asian-Pacific affairs has been the claim to American primacy which is based on military might, particularly naval power, and justified on moral grounds, that is, the perceived superiority of American political and societal values. A foreign policy strategy based on unilateralism and flexible bilateralism can be described as the default pattern of Washington's relations with East Asia. However, multilateralism has played an important role at times, and the future of relations between the United States and the Asia-Pacific will partly depend on the effectiveness and efficiency of existing and emerging multilateral arrangements.

Multilateral cooperation forums are not useless "talk shops" despite having been scorned by academic literature and news coverage. It is true on the one hand that the United States is no longer as euphoric about APEC or the ARF as Washington used to be during the Clinton presidency. At the same time, these forums do still play an important role because:

- In the absence of any other suitable institutionalized mechanisms they provide a framework for the harmonization of interests between the United States and its many partners worldwide;
- They have encouraged regular dialogues between governments that had difficult talking officially to each other prior to the early 1990s, mainly China and Taiwan, Japan and South Korea, and North Korea and South Korea;

- Most importantly from Washington's perspective, they can legitimize U.S. foreign policy interests and actions, making them appear less unilateral and more palatable: the recent "U.S.-ASEAN Joint Declaration for Cooperation to combat international terrorism" is a case in point.

Having said that, regional dialogue forums have been significantly weakened by the deterioration of the so-called ASEAN Way of cooperation (soft institutions, consensus-building, and non-binding decision-making) in the wake of the Asian financial crisis and, more recently, the war against Iraq. Both events demonstrated both the institutional inability of the regional forums and also the unwillingness of the actors involved to take concerted action. One of the most remarkable successes of ASEAN has been the ability of its member states to harmonize their foreign policies and often speak with one voice in international affairs. However, for the first time since the Cambodia conflict of the 1980s, ASEAN governments found it difficult to coordinate their respective interests and strategies. At a meeting in the Malaysian state of Sabah which took place immediately before the outbreak of the war against Iraq in March 2003, ASEAN foreign ministers could not reconcile their different views. While the Philippines and Singapore backed the United States and Thailand adopted a neutral position, the remaining seven members of ASEAN opposed the war.

The bottom line is that a disunited ASEAN is neither likely to challenge the United States in the Asia-Pacific nor be able to provide the necessary leadership to keep the multilateral forums alive and useful as a means of limiting U.S. unilateralism. While on the one hand any significant institutional strengthening of trans-Pacific co-operation seems unlikely, on the other hand the growing "Asianization" of East Asia's international relations could well supplement if not challenge to U.S. primacy. What does this mean? An important feature of APEC, ARF and other institutionalized meetings has been the prominent involvement of the United States. This, however, changed in 1997 when the heads of government of the ASEAN states, Japan, China and South Korea met for an informal summit, marking the beginning of an exclusive East Asian regional dialogue. Since then, the ASEAN + 3 Meetings (APT), as the new forum was named, has begun to institutionalize and establish itself as a potential major actor on the international stage. Some even see the APT as a step closer towards an East Asian alliance. The forum's most notable potential achievements are various currency swap arrangements among its members, plans to develop an Asian bond market and a proposed ASEAN-China Free Trade Area which might be followed by an ASEAN-Japan FTA. Although APT does not have any serious security related ambitions as yet, security cooperation might emerge on the multilateral agenda in the not too distant future. Would it have any impact on continuous U.S. primacy? Probably not.

If any single actor was to challenge the American position in the Asia-Pacific in the medium term of the next ten years or so, China is the most likely candidate. Predicting China's future position in the Asia-Pacific and its relations with the United States has exercised an uncounted number of pundits. While some believe that China's military potential is significantly overestimated, others see China as a military superpower in ten to twenty years time. We should be very careful with all sorts of speculation and predictions even if they seem to be based on hard empirical evidence at first glance. Few political scientists were able to predict the end of the Cold War even in mid-1989. Another striking example was the inability of the vast majority of renowned economists and international organizations such as the World Bank and the Asian Development Bank to critically assess the East Asian Economic miracle of the 1970s–1980s or the Asian financial crisis of the late 1990s. In many if not most cases forecasts are made for political purposes. Whether we regard China as an emerging threat or a peace-loving *status quo* power is a reflection of our own interests, or more specifically, the interests of governments, think tanks and their sponsors, NGOs, and international organizations. The same goes for the Chinese economy. Reliable economic facts and data are practically non-existent in the case of China and those figures put forward often reflect political agendas rather than objective and balanced assessments.

Where does all this leave us? Absent irrational leadership or a catastrophic attack, the most likely mid-term scenario for the U.S. security role in the Asia-Pacific is a continuation of the default pattern: Unilateralism and bilateralism based firmly on the alliance with Japan bolstered by the subordinate alliances with South Korea, Philippines, and Australia and supported by *ad hoc* arrangements with Singapore, Thailand, Taiwan, and other friendly governments as circumstances dictate.

## NOTES
1. The only attempt to multilateral alliance building during the Cold War failed: The Southeast Asia Treaty Organization (SEATO) was founded in 1954 and grouped Australia, Great Britain, France, New Zealand, Pakistan

(until 1973), the Philippines, Thailand, and the United States. Cooperation never really worked due to the high degree of diversity among the members. SEATO was finally dissolved in 1977.

2. For a comprehensive overview and analysis see Frank Umbach, "The Future of the U.S.-Japanese Security Alliance" in *International Relations in the Asia-Pacific. New Patterns of Power, Interest, and Cooperation*, edited by Jörn Dosch and Manfred Mols (New York: St. Martin's Press, 2001), pp. 111–54.

3. Marvin Ott, "East Asia: Security and Complexity", *Current History*, no. 645 (April 2001): 147–53, quoted from p. 152.

4. Robert A. Manning and Paula Stern, "The Myth of the Pacific Century", *Foreign Affairs*, 73, no. 6 (November/December 1994): 79–93, from p. 86.

5. Jörn Dosch, Die Herausforderung des Multilateralismus. Amerikanische Asien-Pazifik Politik nach dem Kalten Krieg. (Baden-Baden: Nomos, 2002), p. 96.

6. Rob Wilson, "Imagining 'Asia-Pacific': Forgetting Politics and Colonialism in the Magical Waters of the Pacific. An Americanist Critique", *Cultural Studies*, 14 (3 April 2000): 562–92, on p. 566.

7. Jay Solomon and Carla Anne Robbinds, "A Global Journal Report: Bush Notes North Korea's Shift on Negotiations — Both Sides Signal Talks May Be Possible on Ending North's Nuclear Program' ", *Wall Street Journal (Eastern Edition)*, 14 April 2003: A 14 (17?).

8. <http://www.mofa.go.jp/region/n-america/us/security/security.html>.

9. Lawrence E. Grinter, *Security, Strategy, and Policy Responses in the Pacific Rim*. (Boulder: Westview Press, 1989), p. 22.

10. See Ralph Cossa, ed., *U.S.-Korea-Japan Relations. Building toward a "Virtual Alliance"*. (Washington: Center for Strategic and International Studies (CSIS), 1999).

11. The National Security Srategy of the United States of America, Washington: The White House 2002, p. 29.

12. Ibid.

13. Jürgen Haacke. Implications of September 11 for Economic and Security Cooperation in the ASEAN Region. Paper presented at the workshop on Asia-Pacific Economic and Security Cooperation: New Regional Agendas?, University of Hull, UK, 5–6 September 2002.

14. Jürgen Rüland, "Asian Regionalism Five Years after the 1997/98 Financial Crisis: A Case of 'Co-operative' Regionalism?" In *Asia-Pacific Economic and Security Cooperation: New Regional Agendas*, edited by Christopher M. Dent (New York: Palgrave, 2003), 61–82, from p. 70.

15. Stanley Hoffmann, *Primacy or World Order: American Foreign Policy since the Cold War* (New York: McGraw-Hill, 1978), p. 6.

16. Alan Brinkley, *American History, A Survey*. Volume I (9th edition, New York: McGraw-Hill, 1995), p. 352.

17. For example Snyder 2003; Larres 2003; Morone 2003.

18. Tommy T.B. Koh, *The United States and East Asia: Conflict or Co-operation* (Singapore: Times Academic Press, 1995), p. 91.
19. Shen Dingli quoted in *Agence France Presse*, 31 March 2002, "Year after Spy Plane Crisis, China-US Ties Face New Uncertainty".
20. Geir Lundestad, "'Empire by Invitation' in the American Century". In *The Ambiguous Legacy. U.S. Foreign Relations in the "American Century"*, edited by Hogan, Michael J. (Cambridge: Cambridge University Press, 1999), pp. 52–91.
21. Marvin Kalb and Elie Abel, Roots of Involvement: The US in Asia 1784–1971 ( New York: W. W. Norton, 1971), Chapter 1.
22. Quoted from Ali Wardhana, 'The Pacific Rim Challenge'. In *Indonesian Perspectives on APEC and Regional Cooperation in Asia Pacific*, edited by Hadi Soesastro (Jakarta: CSIS, 1994), pp. 173–81, from p. 175.
23. Quoted from Ibid.
24. Edward S. Corwin, *The President. Office and Powers, 1787–1984* (5th edition, New York: New York University Press, 1984), p. 201.
25. Quoted from *Far Eastern Economic Review* (14 February 2002), p. 30.
26. Paul Dibb, "Strategic Trends. Asia at the Crossroads". *Naval War College Review* 56, no. 1 (Winter 2001), online edition: <http://www.nwc.navy.mil/press/Review/2001/Winter/art2-w01.htm>.
27. Excluding the waters north of 5° S and west of 68° E.
28. Jörn Dosch, "The Maritime Strategy for the Asia-Pacific Region of the United States of America". In *Maritime Strategies in Asia*, edited by Jürgen Schwarz et al. (Bangkok: White Lotus 2002), pp. 145–70, from pp. 151–52.
29. Transcript of an interview with Joseph Nye given to Harvard University radio station, 4 April 2002; <http://www.ksg.harvard.edu/news/nye_softpower_wbur_040402.htm>.
30. Joseph S. Nye, *The Paradox of American Power: Why the World's Only Superpower Can't Go It Alone.* (Cambridge: Cambridge University Press, 2001).

## Chapter Six

# Regional Security Institutions: ASEAN, ARF, SCO and KEDO

Jürgen Haacke

## INTRODUCTION

This chapter discusses East Asia's cooperative security arrangements and regional organizations insofar as they seek to make a contribution to regional security.[1] The chapter will focus on the Association of Southeast Asian Nations (ASEAN), the ASEAN Regional Forum (ARF), the Shanghai Cooperation Organization (SCO) and the Korean Energy Development Organization (KEDO). In doing so, it will outline the respective security agendas of these four institutions and provide an overview of their responses in the face of the security challenges of the post-Cold War period. Particular attention will be given to developments since the Asian financial crisis of 1997–98 and the terrorist attacks of 11 September 2001. Although the above regional security institutions will be discussed individually for the most part, it is also one of the aims of this chapter to provide a brief comparison between them in the concluding section.

Two points must be stressed from the outset. First, East Asia's security institutions neither have the same membership, nor do they all aspire to enhance regional and international security in the same way. Given the inter-governmental nature of cooperation, they moreover tend to be hostage to the national foreign policies of their respective members. This implies that their purpose and the decisions and actions taken by them reflect the consensus of their members. This consensus takes concrete form in the normative framework underpinning security cooperation, the agenda, and the resources and capabilities with which their members have invested them.

Second, when analysing cooperative security arrangements and regional organizations it is also necessary to bear in mind that relations between members and the major powers shape their development and achievements. For example, although states seeking security may be party to a security regime, they may also want to rely in some way on a major power for their defence, irrespective of whether the major power concerned is itself party to the security arrangement in question. This sort of reliance is particularly likely when the major power in question is in effect a hegemonic power that is capable of offering extensive security cooperation to another state or is otherwise enhancing its defence capacity and the security of the incumbent regime. In such a case, the significance of cooperative security arrangements may be severely reduced.

At the same time, a hegemonic or major power may itself choose to either join, promote, ignore or stymie the institutional development of organizations and institutionalized processes of regional security co-operation, be they nascent or long established, and hence behave as an "instrumental multilateralist".[2] It is for these reasons that — where relevant — this chapter highlights the role of major powers in the overview and discussion of recent institutional developments and responses of East Asia's major inter-governmental forums of security cooperation to the challenges of the post-Cold War era.

The chapter is divided into five sections. Attention in the first two sections will focus on the Association of Southeast Asian Nations (ASEAN) and the ASEAN Regional Forum (ARF). The chapter will then examine developments relating to the recently established Shanghai Cooperation Organization (SCO) and the Korean Energy Development Organization (KEDO). The fifth and final section will briefly highlight some of the similarities and differences in the management of regional security as undertaken by these four institutions before reaching provisional conclusions on their likely further trajectory.

## ASEAN

One immediate goal of the establishment of the Association of Southeast Asian Nations (ASEAN) was to bring about regional reconciliation between Indonesia and its neighbours.[3] ASEAN was also designed to help member states achieve domestic political stability and regime security through a combined emphasis on multilateral dialogue and economic cooperation. It is to ASEAN's credit that the association managed to advance as a security regime and diplomatic community, if not partial or nascent security community, by the end of the Cold War.[4] A key step in this regard was the signing in 1976 of the Treaty of Amity and Cooperation, which formalized the association's code of conduct for intra-regional relations. Key norms shaping intramural behaviour include non-interference, sovereign equality, the norm of not resorting to the use or threat to use force and the norm of not putting bilateral disputes between members on the ASEAN agenda. Although violated at times, particularly in the early year's of ASEAN's institutional experience, the norms in question over time matured into a diplomatic and security culture that has not seen major change even by the early twenty-first century.[5]

ASEAN's role in helping to bring to an end the Cambodian conflict has been considered particularly significant in support of its conceptualization as a diplomatic community. Notably, while acting as a diplomatic community, the association cannot be viewed as ever having truly functioned as a manager of regional security in the wider Southeast Asia, not even during the course of its involvement in the Cambodia conflict.[6] This assessment is primarily based on the argument that notwithstanding its diplomatic contributions to reverse Vietnam's intervention in Cambodia, ASEAN effectively outsourced responsibility for regional peace and stability to the great powers, particularly China.

Reacting to the uncertainties of the post-Cold War period, ASEAN states vowed to intensify their security cooperation. However, this commitment did not alter the association's status as a cooperative security arrangement,[7] not least because operational efforts to enhance regional security were largely undertaken either at the bilateral level between ASEAN members or in the context of other frameworks of security and defence cooperation. Meanwhile, the admission of Vietnam and the Bangkok Summit of 1995, which for the first time brought together all ten Southeast Asian heads of government, signaled a successful process of regional reconciliation between the Indochinese countries and the early ASEAN members in the context of a major regional economic boom.

With the onset of the Asian economic and financial crisis in 1997, the association suddenly found its security severely challenged on at least two major fronts. The first was the reality of financial globalization, which, as became most starkly visible in Thailand, Malaysia and Indonesia, could play a major part in undermining members' economic security and eroding political stability. The second key challenge involved intra-state developments in individual ASEAN countries with perceived negative cross-border security implications for other members, such as the "haze" emanating from Indonesian forest fires or the counter-insurgency operations in Burma/Myanmar that affected Thailand. Notably, ASEAN members disagreed over whether they should collectively embrace new understandings in relation to the norms that have historically mediated their interactions so as to meet the transnational security challenges. These differences were thrust into the spotlight when they overwhelmingly rejected the proposal of Thai Foreign Minister Surin Pitsuwan, put forward in the summer of 1998, whereby ASEAN collectively embrace "flexible engagement".[8] This was not the end of the matter, however. Indeed, in the second half of 1998, even ASEAN's status as an ascendant security community was called into question as — due to perceived infractions of ASEAN's code of intramural conduct — significant tension developed in (a) Singapore's respective relations with Malaysia and Indonesia, (b) Malaysia-Philippines ties, and (c) Thailand-Myanmar relations. These developments also raised questions about ASEAN's ability to maintain regional stability.

## ASEAN's Efforts to Re-establish its Credentials

ASEAN leaders generally had little interest to see the association stamped by outsiders as irrelevant or incapable of maintaining regional stability. Faced with severe extra-regional criticisms, they thus committed themselves to a number of steps that were designed to demonstrate that the association would in future take greater heed of their security interdependence of members and to meet cross-border and transnational security challenges. To promote economic security and to avoid a relapse into another regional financial crisis, for instance, ASEAN initiated a surveillance process (and developed its financial cooperation with the states of Northeast Asia). It also set up new processes of interaction at ministerial level, called "retreats", the purpose of which was to serve to re-evaluate ASEAN's processes, norms, and goals in the light of changing regional circumstances and external criticisms. The association also elaborated on an institutionalized response to future air pollution emanating from fires raging in Indonesia.[9]

While important to improve ASEAN's international image, these steps did not demonstrate ASEAN's willingness to manage regional security on an exclusive basis. ASEAN's reluctance to collectively intervene in the 1999 East Timor crisis is a pertinent illustration, in so far as only some ASEAN countries decided to participate in the international force authorized to restore peace and stability in the former Portuguese colony. That said, the violent events in East Timor following that territory's referendum on its future political status, and the role that the association played in the run-up to the plebiscite, as well as afterwards, were factors that led ASEAN in July 2000 to establish the ASEAN Troika. The troika was "to enable ASEAN to address in a timely manner urgent and important regional political and security issues and situations of common concern likely to disturb regional peace and harmony".[10] The year after, the association also introduced rules of procedure pertaining to the invocation of the ASEAN High Council. This step seemed designed to meet longstanding criticisms, particularly from outside the region, that members were shelving conflicts rather than actively facilitating the settlement of disputes and situations.[11]

However, ASEAN has been unable to draw in practice on the agreed mechanisms and procedures. A good example is ASEAN's disinclination to activate the troika. This unwillingness was apparent in September 2000 when, pointing to its principles of non-interference and consensus, the then Chair of the ASEAN Standing Committee, Vietnam, dismissed UN Secretary General Kofi Annan's suggestion that the grouping should look into the apparent mistreatment of Nobel prize laureate Aung San Suu Kyi. The troika was also not involved when long-standing border strife between Thailand and Myanmar briefly erupted into a direct military exchange between the two countries' armed forces in February 2001.[12] ASEAN's off-hand stance toward Indonesia's security challenges, not least armed conflict in Aceh, is similarly instructive in so far as ASEAN has been happy to confine itself to ministerial expressions of support for the continued territorial integrity of the Republic.[13] More recently, Myanmar foiled Jakarta's efforts to activate the Troika in the aftermath of the Depayin incident of 30 May 2003.[14]

There are at least two key reasons why ASEAN remains above all a cooperative security arrangement rather than a veritable manager of regional security. First, members have generally remained loath to involve themselves in the domestic affairs of their neighbours although they have reluctantly done so when these have impacted on the standing of the association. The communiqué agreed by the association's leaders at their summit meeting in October 2003 makes clear that no unequivocal consensus on generally adopting new practices in dealing with cases of intra-state conflict has been achieved. Indeed, the Bali Concord II provisions on the ASEAN Security Community can at best be interpreted as paving the way for the possible adoption of a weak form of "flexible engagement".[15]

Secondly, ASEAN countries are generally unwilling to see the association assume a vastly more ambitious new role in the management of regional security. This is underscored in part by their collective role in the war against terrorism.[16] Initially, the grouping produced a declaration denouncing global terrorism, which concealed serious differences in intramural opinion. Several months later, in May 2002, ASEAN governments outlined a related work plan, which has set the scene, for instance, for a series of seminars that are designed to enhance capacity-building through learning from best practice.[17] The association has addressed counter-terrorism in the context of the Ministerial Meeting on Transnational Crime (AMMTC), which is headed by ministers of home affairs. It has also done so in the context of meetings of ASEAN Chiefs of National Police (ASEANAPOL), the informal ASEAN intelligence chiefs, and the annual ASEAN Chief of Army Multilateral Meeting (ACAMM).

Sub-regional attempts to address transnational threats have equally attracted some support from within the ASEAN region, underlined again recently when Cambodia and Thailand joined the Agreement on Information Exchange and Establishment of Communication Procedures that was entered into by the Philippines, Malaysia and Indonesia in May 2002. This accord covers co-operation with respect to transnational security threats including terrorism, drug trafficking, money-laundering, illicit trafficking of arms, theft of marine resources, smuggling, piracy, hijacking, intrusion, and illegal entry.

In July 2002, ASEAN moreover issued an important declaration on anti-terrorism cooperation with the United States, signed at the time of the thirty-fifth ASEAN Ministerial Meetings in Brunei Darussalam.[18] One of the objectives of the cooperation was to prevent, disrupt and combat international terrorism through the exchange and flow of information, intelligence and capacity-building assistance. However, the declaration arguably did as much to highlight existing deficiencies that characterize

ASEAN's anti-terrorism capacity at a regional level as to emphasize members' shared commitment to enhance regional anti-terrorism cooperation. The political significance of the declaration for ASEAN has in any case been limited in that it is non-binding and in practice has allowed individual member states to pursue the war on terror in different ways.

Notwithstanding their considerable collective endeavours, ASEAN leaders have not necessarily regarded the association as the principal institutional vehicle to tackle terrorism or other security challenges. In most ASEAN countries, counter-terrorism has involved a range of national measures.[19] Also, cooperation with extra-regional countries has been regarded at least as — if not more — important than intramural counter-terrorism efforts, as exemplified by the approach taken by the Philippines which resulted among other things in Manila's counter-terrorism fighting capacity being strengthened by joint training with U.S. Special Forces.[20] Other initiatives, some of which rely on external funding, include the Jakarta Centre for Law Enforcement Cooperation (JCLEC) in Semarang, which opened on 3 July 2004, the International Law Enforcement Academy (ILEA) in Bangkok and the Southeast Asia Regional Centre for Counter Terrorism (SEARCCT) in Kuala Lumpur.

The limit of interest by individual ASEAN states in a larger managerial role for ASEAN is also illustrated by the compromise reached among ASEAN countries on the ASEAN Security Community (ASC). In its original — Indonesian — conception, the purpose of the ASC was to allow ASEAN over time to meet security challenges at the intra-regional, bilateral or even intra-state levels.[21] However, as the Bali Concord II makes absolutely clear, there is as yet no agreement within the association for a security approach that would make ASEAN an important or even the most important port of call for addressing security challenges. Indeed, it would appear that some of the smaller member states continue to harbour fears of sub-regional hegemony, while others are uneasy about the potential role that particular countries might wish to play in intramural disputes.

In sum, within only a few years ASEAN has had to respond to two sets of new security challenges. The first demanded enhancing the organization's capacity to engage one another without abandoning the grouping's diplomatic and security culture. The second has focused on enhancing homeland security and eliminating a regional terrorist presence. With respect to the former, ASEAN has under certain circumstances been prepared to embrace subtle changes to long-standing understandings in relation to non-interference at the conceptual level, but found such changes difficult to translate into practice. With regard to formulating and practically responding to the latter set of transnational challenges, ASEAN members have not sought to rely on the association as the most pertinent institutional vehicle. Overall, therefore, notwithstanding its sincere efforts in the aftermath of the Asian crisis to restore its reputation and respond to the threat of transnational terrorism, ASEAN has not assumed more than a limited role in the management of regional security. Indeed, one could argue that ASEAN countries have in many ways been divided over assuming such a role in the first place, with some preferring to rely first and foremost on the United States for their security against both traditional and more recent transnational challenges.

## ASEAN REGIONAL FORUM

The ASEAN Regional Forum (ARF) is the only regional security arrangement that boasts the membership of all the major regional powers, some of which are of course also members of the United Nations Security Council (UNSC). It is also the only regional institution in which a group of small and middle powers (the ten ASEAN states) explicitly plays the role of the "primary driving force" within a membership that involves the major powers. At present, the Forum has a total of 24 members, Pakistan being the latest to join in 2004.

The establishment of the ASEAN Regional Forum in 1993 marked a tremendous diplomatic achievement for the association. It signified a break with ASEAN's stated aspiration of a zone of peace, freedom and neutrality as formulated by the association in the 1971 Kuala Lumpur Declaration, which had given expression to members' determination to "exert initially necessary efforts to secure the recognition of, and respect for, South East Asia as a Zone of Peace, Freedom and Neutrality, free from any form or manner of interference by outside Powers".[22] In contrast, the establishment of the ASEAN Regional Forum was premised on the engagement rather than exclusion of the major regional states by Southeast Asian states. It was against the backdrop of the loss of U.S. bases in the Philippines, fears about the strategic and security implications of a rising China and the creeping "normalization" of Japanese foreign and defence policy that ASEAN policymakers reached agreement on such a joint strategy of multiple engagement with the major powers.

The purpose of the ARF was to improve the climate of regional relations both between ASEAN and the major powers and among the latter.[23] As a vehicle of cooperative security the chief method to achieve this aim was an inclusive multilateral security dialogue from which, it was hoped, would spring confidence-building effects. As outlined in the 1995 ASEAN concept for the ARF, however, security cooperation among ARF participants was agreed to proceed in stages from confidence building to preventive diplomacy before ultimately culminating in the elaboration of approaches to conflict.[24] Like ASEAN, then, the ARF was not designed as either a defence community or a collective security organization in the conventional sense. However, compared to ASEAN, the ARF's experience of cooperative security has been one of deeper institutionalization almost from the outset, as illustrated by the establishment of inter-sessional groups and meetings and their respective activities.[25] At the same time, the ARF has subscribed to the principles of non-interference and consensus in more or less the same way as ASEAN. Consequently, the ARF has in many ways also lacked both the means and mandate to function as a regional security organization that could be relied upon to manage regional security.

Significantly, the nature and pace of security cooperation in the ASEAN Regional Forum have been the source of much controversy since its inception. While most ASEAN countries and China have expressed support only for a focus on broadly conceived confidence building measures, Western participants have favoured quickly shifting the emphasis from confidence-building to a preoccupation with preventive diplomacy. This demand has seemed justified partly because numerous CBM proposals (albeit not of the constraining kind) have been successfully implemented in an ARF context and partly because Western governments see the region's security challenges as making this necessary. The first compromise on this issue emerged at the fourth ARF in 1997, when under the chairmanship of Malaysia's then Foreign Minister Abdullah Badawi, the forum produced a statement endorsing recommendations made at the preceding ARF Senior Officials' Meeting to identify areas in the overlap between confidence-building measures and preventive diplomacy. These areas focused on:

- An enhanced role for the ARF chairman, particularly the idea of a "good offices" role;
- The development of a register of experts or eminent persons among ARF participants;
- An annual security assessment; and
- Voluntary background briefings on regional security issues.

As was to be expected, exploring the overlap between confidence-building measures (CBMs) and preventive diplomacy (PD) soon again proved both controversial and time-consuming. However, by the beginning of this century some progress was recorded in relation to a number of issues. The eighth ARF meeting in 2001, for instance, adopted three papers that outlined members' consensus in relation to the possible trajectory of the forum's embrace of preventive diplomacy. The first paper focused on the concept and principles of preventive diplomacy. The second delineated details of an enhanced role of the ARF chair. And the third identified the opportunities for ARF experts and eminent persons to make a contribution to regional security.

Significantly, however, all three agreements remained consistent with principles linked to the extension of ASEAN's diplomatic and security culture to the forum. ARF members, for instance, defined PD as "consensual diplomatic and political action taken by sovereign states with the consent of all directly involved parties" to help: (1) prevent disputes and conflicts from arising between states that could potentially pose a threat to regional peace and stability; (2) prevent such disputes and conflicts from escalating into armed confrontation; and (3) minimize the impact of such disputes and conflicts on the region.[26] The proposed terms of reference for experts and eminent persons stressed the non-binding nature of their advice on matters of preventive diplomacy. And the enhanced role of the ARF chair, it was agreed, would evolve only on the basis of consultation, consent and consensus of ARF members. Underlying this compromise is ASEAN's realization that it needed both to respond to the criticisms of some countries that the ARF has not moved fast enough and to recognize the importance of giving other members, not least Beijing, a stake in the process of evolving regional security cooperation. This has implied the need to accommodate above all Chinese objections to proposed ways of developing preventive diplomacy within the ARF (as well as those mooted from within the association).

ASEAN's continued leadership role in the ARF, the lasting emphasis on non-interference and consensus, which largely accounts for the slow embrace of preventive diplomacy as the next stage of regional security cooperation and the limited extent of the ARF's institutionalization, have all remained controversial among members. Other critics of the ARF have also stressed the importance of strengthening ties between and among defense officials, including those in the uniformed services. Still others have bemoaned the relative lack of input that Track II processes have had on Track I diplomacy. Fearing a drift into insignificance of the ARF if these points were left unaddressed, scholars and officials of some ASEAN countries have proposed a range of efforts to make the forum more meaningful for all members interested in addressing regional security challenges.

The director of the Institute for Defence and Strategic Studies in Singapore,[27] for example, suggested the following series of reforms. These involved, first, moving from simply exchanging views to encouraging a culture of problem solving within the forum and, second, developing further the existing institutional framework for the implementation of preventive diplomacy, including a stronger "good offices" role for the troika of past, present and future ARF chairs. A further proposal was, third, to "de-synchronize" the ARF chair from the ASEAN chair and the possible co-chairing of the ARF by a non-ASEAN member. The purpose of this proposal was to give external powers a greater stake in the ARF process. A fourth suggestion concerned the creation of an ARF Secretariat in Singapore that could be chaired alternately by an ASEAN and a non-ASEAN member. This could initially build, it was argued, on an ARF unit within the ASEAN Secretariat. Other proposals sought to give defence officials greater input into the ARF process, either by dint of senior defence officials meeting concurrently with the foreign ministers, or by way of a concurrent separate convening of defence ministers during the ARF. Finally, it was suggested that the role of the Council for Security and Cooperation in the Asia Pacific (CSCAP) in conducting so-called Track II (non-official) diplomacy should also be expanded. Proposals in this regard focus on establishing a formal link between the ARF and CSCAP and on giving CSCAP a role in developing approaches to prevention of conflict and engaging civil society or so-called Track III actors.[28]

The events of September 11 have presented the ASEAN Regional Forum with additional challenges, broadly similar to those of the association itself, and reinforced existing pressures on ASEAN to keep or make the ARF relevant in addressing the changing security agenda. After all, having been supportive but less than enthusiastic about the ASEAN Regional Forum since its inception, the United States was believed to be keen to see the ARF do its bit in the global war on terror. To appreciate this point, it is also important to remember that Washington has never seen the ASEAN Regional Forum as more than a supplement to its "hub and spokes" system of bilateral alliances on which U.S. hegemony is in part based. And in the last few years preceding 9/11, Washington was far more interested in winning improved access to infrastructure and facilities in Southeast Asia than in promoting security cooperation in the ARF. The calculation of those within ASEAN supportive of the further development of the ARF appeared to be that if the forum did not offer "added value" in the post-2001 environment, the ARF would simply be bypassed on even more occasions than before, which would not necessarily be in ASEAN's interests. In the event, ARF foreign ministers in 2002 responded to this challenge by consensually identifying nine areas for development:

- As an immediate step, consolidating and strengthening measures to combat international terrorism.
- Enhancing intelligence-sharing, police cooperation and financial measures against international terrorism.
- Establishing Inter-sessional Group on International Terrorism and Transnational Crimes.
- Enhancing the role of the ARF chair and assign the ASEAN Secretariat to assist the ARF chairman in co-coordinating the work of the ARF.
- Developing and utilizing the Register of Experts/Eminent Persons.
- Strengthening CBMs.
- Widening engagement and involvement of security and defence officials, building upon the Singapore Concept Paper on Defence Dialogue within the ARF.
- Enhancing linkages between ARF and ASEAN-ISIS, CSCAP and other organizations.
- Providing substantive follow-up to the Paper on Concept and Principles of Preventive Diplomacy adopted in 2001.[29]

## The ARF Record Since 2002

As the following overview will show, ARF members have since 2002 achieved significantly more progress in some of the above nine areas than in others. For instance, following the initial statement by the ARF chair, then Brunei Darussalam, in relation to the attacks of September 11, ARF activities in the context of the war on terror have noticeably expanded from January 2002 onwards. The first important step in this regard was the 2002 ARF Statement on Measures against Terrorist Financing, which demands a range of practical responses from its members. Having been worked out in a workshop on Financial Measures against Terrorism hosted by the United States and Malaysia in Honolulu in March 2002,[30] the ARF statement obliges members to deny terrorists access to funds. For ASEAN agreement on the statement has proved congenial in two ways: First, it has allowed member countries to argue that, under its guidance, the ARF has actually embraced a practical form of preventive diplomacy long called for by its critics. Second, the statement has served as an appeal to non-ASEAN members to grant practical and financial support to ASEAN countries in implementing UN Security Council Resolution 1373. ARF participants also established an Inter-sessional Meeting on Counter-Terrorism and Transnational Crime (ISM on CT-TC) in March 2003.

Counter-terrorism cooperation in the ARF has focused on enhancing the capacity of participants in areas such as information exchange, legal assistance, financial measures, and practical law enforcement cooperation. One illustration is the ARF Statement on Cooperative Counter-Terrorist Actions on Border Security in relation to the movement of people, goods and document security.[31] In general terms, the ARF has also sought to establish de facto benchmarks for national counter-terrorism responses by looking for and drawing on best practice. Australia and Singapore, for instance, organized a workshop on managing the consequences of a major terrorist attack, held in Darwin in June 2003, which had the key objectives of reaching a common understanding among ARF members of the complex issues involved in managing the consequences of a major terrorist attack including one involving chemical, biological, radiological or nuclear weapons, and considering the scope for further practical cooperation for those agencies most directly involved in preparing for any future major terrorist attack in the region.[32] ARF members have also expressed their commitment to strengthening transport security, including, *inter alia*, the organization of simulation and joint exercises, with a view to enhancing institutional capacity building of coastal states (with regard to piracy and maritime and aerial terrorism) and building an intermodal transport security framework (so as to provide a new approach to cargo transport security).[33] This was the outcome of the second ARF ISM on CT-TC held in Manila in late March 2004,[34] where coordination on transport security and terrorism — be it among modes, private and public sector entities, or countries — was regarded as necessitating some degree of policy transparency.[35] Notably, the meeting also legitimized sub-regional approaches in relation to the conduct of border patrols.

In testament to further institutionalization of existing security cooperation, ARF members have now agreed to invite the ASEAN Secretariat to attend all ARF ISG and related meetings.[36] ARF members have also passed the Terms of Reference for an ARF Unit in the ASEAN

Secretariat to support the enhanced role of the ARF Chair. Although the ARF Unit within the ASEAN Secretariat is mainly to regularly update the ARF Register of CBMs and serve as the repository of ARF documents, it seems that the last word on its institutionalization has not yet been spoken.[37] On the other hand, while ARF ministers agreed in 2003 to support the idea of "friends of the chair" in assisting the chair in dealing with international situations affecting the peace and security of the region, this broad consensus did not make headway at the most recent ARF Ministerial Meeting in 2004. Still, following further consultations, the ARF also adopted new guidelines on the operation of the EEP.

Meanwhile, CBMs have continued without however progressing much. Most proposals for CBMs parallel long-standing or evolving policy positions of member states. The annual meeting of heads of defence colleges is to be given terms of reference. The Annual Security Outlook attracts a fair number of submissions, but not from all member states. The same is true for the voluntary background briefings. In short, while CBM initiatives still proliferate, these steps must not be confused with a deepening of CBMs in the ARF. No obvious embrace of constraining CBMs has occurred as yet.

Still, the involvement of defense officials in the ARF process, for long regarded as essential to the confidence-building process, has been boosted. This has involved going beyond the ARF defence officials' luncheon to embrace a formal Defence Officials' Dialogue, organized twice yearly. Notably, among the ASEAN countries it has been Singapore that has in particular been interested in augmenting the visibility and role of defence officials in the ARF process, who will now meet four times yearly (in addition to meetings outside the ARF framework).[38] Indeed, it was agreed that the ARF Defence Dialogue, as an integral component of the ARF process, should now consider the way forward to ensure that its contribution continues to complement and add value to that process. Some new ground has also been broken by virtue of China's 2003 push for an ARF Security Policy Conference in which both high military officials and government officers are to be invited to participate. In the event, ARF members endorsed China's proposal on the ARF Security Policy Conference (ASPC), but ensured that at least for now it would remain a less conspicuous element of ARF proceedings, not least by deciding that the ASPC should be convened back-to-back with the annual ARF SOM. Importantly, the ASPC will normally be hosted and chaired by the ARF chair country.

Since this is an ASEAN member state, the agenda setting formally remains in the hands of the association. China will host the first ASPC by the end of 2004, but it has agreed that Indonesia will chair this conference. The increasing participation of defence officials is particularly noteworthy given the institutional challenge of sorts to the ARF as posed by the annual IISS Security Conference.[39]

Efforts to enhance the relationship between Track I and Track II have been incremental at best although Canada has played a key role in advancing this agenda, particularly through leading discussions on the basis of concept paper "Strengthening Linkages between Track I and Track II in the ARF Context". Essentially, there has not been a major development of note since 2002. At the ISG on CBMs in Beijing in November 2003, stronger inter-linkages between Track I and II seemed less important to some members than better informal liaison with other regional and international organizations such as the UN, APEC, SCO and OSCE. A similar point was made at the subsequent ISG on CBMs in Yangon in April 2004.

Having recognized the importance of making further progress on PD, ARF ministers have repeatedly underlined that the ARF's work in tackling terrorism represents a milestone in the ARF's development of a preventive role. ARF members have also argued that their work on preventive diplomacy was being advanced through, among other measures, the actions that it had taken to address the situation on the Korean Peninsula and to enhance confidence and cooperation in addressing common security threats, including international terrorism, transnational crime, piracy and other maritime crimes, and the support given to the ARF chairman in carrying out the enhanced role of the chair.[40] Conceptual work on PD has meanwhile continued, and Japan has played an important role in this regard. Within the membership discussions on the principles and scope of PD are thus carried forward to ensure the continued relevance of the ARF to the changing global situation. However, there is as yet no agreement to deal with PD in separate ISG meetings.

In sum, then, it seems possible to argue that the ARF has been fairly successful in attempting to add value to the international war on terror and the joint struggle against transnational security challenges. In contrast, much of the forum's long-standing agenda in relation to enhancing the role of the ARF chair, the relationship between Track I and Track II or the further general conceptual exploration of PD has not as yet been significantly advanced. If the self-imposed agenda for the development of the ARF has been tackled with only partial success, it is little surprise that a substantial number of the recommendations issued by regional research institutions have also not been pursued to date.

Significantly, then, the basic character of the ARF has not changed since 2001. It remains in the first instance an institutional arrangement for the multilateral exploration of ideas as well as the development of norms and security practices rather than a security organization invested with the necessary resources enabling it to directly confront the gamut of existing traditional or non-traditional security threats. As such, the management of regional security for the time being remains largely outside its purview.

## THE SHANGHAI COOPERATION ORGANIZATION

Growing out of the "Shanghai Five" and the Sino-Soviet border negotiations of the early 1990s, the Shanghai Cooperation Organization (SCO) was established at the Summit of Heads of States of China, Russia, Kazakhstan, Kyrgyzstan, Tajikistan and Uzbekistan in Shanghai on 14–15 June 2001.[41] While the "Shanghai Five" was primarily associated with confidence-building, disarmament, and border security, the SCO set out by tasking itself to combat what in China are labelled the "three evil forces": Terrorism, (ethnic) separatism and (religious) extremism.[42] However, as the Declaration on the Establishment of the SCO stresses,[43] the SCO, apart from maintaining regional stability and security, is also designed to strengthen mutual trust, friendship and good neighbourly ties among its membership, and to encourage effective intramural cooperation across a range of issue areas including political affairs, trade, economic, transportation, and science and technology. Ultimately, the proclaimed task is even to promote the creation of a new, democratic, just and rational international political and economic order. For the moment, the SCO's focus is firmly on enhancing regime and economic security as opposed to human security.

The SCO has quickly developed a relatively elaborate institutional structure. This includes the Council of Heads of State, which meets annually, the Council of Heads of Government, the Council of Ministers of Foreign Affairs, a Conference of Heads of Agencies, and the Council of National Coordinators.[44] Since January 2004 the SCO also has a secretariat based in Beijing, and a Regional Anti-Terrorism Structure (RATS) that was fully launched in Tashkent later in the year. The Centre, which was originally to be established in the Kyrgyz capital of Bishkek, is composed of a Council and an executive committee. The general operating principles of the SCO are similar to those invoked by ASEAN or the ASEAN

Regional Forum. The norms of the United Nations Charter are meant to govern the interaction of SOC members, particularly respect for sovereignty, independence, territorial integrity and inviolability of borders, non-interference, the non-use of force or threat of force, and the equality of member states. All issues are to be resolved by joint consultations. Members also renounce unilateral military advantage in contiguous areas.

## China and the SCO

While the middle and small ranking powers making up ASEAN have had a key role in developing the agenda of the ASEAN Regional Forum, China and, albeit to a lesser extent, Russia have in many ways been the major players of the Shanghai Cooperation Organization. That said, this chapter is not arguing that the SCO is simply a vehicle serving the interests and objectives of these two major powers. Indeed, promoting regional security and stability in Central Asia, as well as combating and defeating international terrorism and other forms of transnational crime is a shared concern among SCO members.

Yet at the same time Beijing has arguably the keenest interest in its development, standing and success in so far as the organization provides the PRC with a vehicle to promote and legitimize the pursuit of China's goals in Central Asia. Having succeeded not least through bilateral border agreements in promoting a measure of mutual confidence in its relations with the former Soviet Republics, the SCO has been promoted by Beijing to serve as a vehicle to enhance cross-border cooperation to counter the longstanding separatist and terrorist challenge in the Xinjiang Uighur Autonomous Region. Xinjiang is of great geo-strategic significance to Beijing, but the latter has found dealing with the former to be a challenge.[45] With even heavy-handed tactics having failed to quell Uighur separatism, whose exponents have in the past been able to seek refuge and win material assistance in neighbouring states, the SCO has in part been designed to allow new impetus to be directed to this task, which was already on the agenda of the "Shanghai Five". The background to this is in part that China's attempts to ingratiate itself to the now defunct Taliban regime with a view to stemming arms smuggling and terrorist activities also proved fruitless, accentuating the need to confront the challenge in new ways. Limited bilateral military assistance provided to some of the Central Asian republics has helped to improve bilateral relations with some of China's neighbours, but has proved inadequate to root out the terrorist challenge, associated above all with the East Turkestan Islamic Movement.

From China's perspective, the establishment of the SCO was also to serve the promotion of a multipolar order and the prevention of the country's strategic encirclement.[46] Beijing has to some extent been successful in making the case that the SCO should declare its pursuit of the preservation of the global strategic balance and stability. However, in their joint declaration of 15 June 2001 SCO members have also made clear that the SCO does not constitute an alliance and that its members adhere to the principle of openness as regards possible accession to the organization. Indeed, as the St. Petersburg Summit declaration of June 2002 put it,

> The SCO member states have an inalienable right to independent choice of forms and methods of ensuring their own security, including the establishment of co-operation with other states. They will pursue this policy [so] as not to cause any adverse consequences for regional stability and security.[47]

Notably, from China's declared perspective there is no contradiction between this unambiguous formula and Beijing's long-term aim of building a multipolar order. Indeed, the SCO is regarded in China as an institutionalized expression of its "new security concept", which promotes inclusiveness and common security, but is also considered to strengthen China's political and economic hand over its periphery through a combination of closer political contacts, economic integration, and security cooperation in relation to non-traditional challenges in the first instance.

## The SCO after September 11

Not least due to China's insistence, and irrespective of the difficulties in immediately following up its initial diplomatic intervention, the SCO was one of the first regional international organizations to respond with a heads of government declaration to the events of September 11. However, it took an extraordinary meeting of foreign ministers the following January to develop the SCO's international profile. While generally supportive of the United States in the war against terrorism, SCO members warned that Afghanistan should not fall into "sphere of somebody's influence" and appealed to the respect for the sovereignty, territorial integrity and state unity of the country and to avoid interference into Afghan internal affairs.[48] Having proposed the neutralization of Afghanistan, SCO states also emphasized the need for global, regional and national anti-terrorism efforts to be pursued in parallel. They moreover argued that the leading role in the international struggle against terrorism should be with the United Nations Security Council. Raising these and other points allowed the Shanghai Cooperation Organization to develop a diplomatic position distinct from the larger international anti-terrorism coalition.

The January 2002 meeting of foreign ministers also proved an important step toward the early completion of the SCO Charter and the establishment of practical cooperative mechanisms, primarily the regional anti-terrorism structure (RATS). In June, the SCO heads of states signed documents on the organization's charter, the establishment of an anti-terrorism centre in Bishkek (originally provided for in the Shanghai Convention on Action to Combat Terrorism, Separatism and Extremism) and a joint declaration. As part of these agreements, members decided to locate the SCO Secretariat in Beijing. They also agreed that the purpose of the regional anti-terrorism centre would be to promote information exchange, joint commando operations and anti-terrorism training.[49] In October 2002 China and Kyrgyzstan were the first to conduct within the SCO framework a bilateral military exercise focused on counter-terrorism.

While the SCO thus struggled to develop for itself a part in the management of regional security in Central Asia, bilateral military cooperation between several Central Asian republics and the United States gained significantly in scope and depth. September 11 led to a considerable deployment of American forces in what until only a decade ago was the Soviet Union. This stemmed in large measure from the military requirements of the war against the Taliban regime in Afghanistan. However, Washington also seemed keen to end years of neglect of the region, not only to defeat terrorism and contribute to regional stability, but also to exploit economic opportunities, particularly in relation to regional energy reserves. The Central Asian republics were generally happy to respond to Washington's advances in the fields of military and anti-terrorism cooperation in return for financial, economic and technical assistance. Some offered basing facilities for U.S. and allied forces for military and humanitarian purposes — apparently without consulting other SCO states. The closest military cooperation evolved between Tashkent and Washington. Their bilateral cooperation built on Pentagon Special Forces training programmes since the mid-1990s and its intensified nature was defined in the U.S.-Uzbekistan Joint Security Consultations. Kyrgyzstan also allowed for the establishment of a temporary base at Manas involving approximately 2000 U.S. personnel. Significantly, the U.S. deployment happened with Russian consent. In view of American carrots extended in the process and those anticipated in the future, it is perhaps not surprising that the Central Asian members of SCO felt inclined to at least temporarily value the military arrangements with the United States over a more rapid implementation of the Shanghai Convention against Terrorism, Separatism and Extremism.

## Further Preparing the SCO for a Managerial Role

Following the Moscow Summit of 2003, which essentially reconfirmed previous decisions,[50] the SCO has taken further strides in both institutional development and practical security cooperation. In early August 2003, the SCO conducted its first multilateral anti-terrorism exercises in Kazakhstan and around Yili in Xinjiang, China.[51] These reportedly focused on hostage-release techniques and the destruction of a terrorist base. Meeting in Beijing in September, the prime ministers of all six SCO states approved the form and finance of the secretariat, which was launched in January 2004 and is headed by a Chinese diplomat. In October 2003, the RATS governing body started work, with the regional anti-terrorism structure executive committee in Tashkent formally launched at the Tashkent Summit in June 2004.

Tasks of RATS include maintaining working contacts within the SCO and strengthening coordination with international organizations on the "three evil forces" of terrorism, separatism and extremism; participating in preparing drafts of international legal documents on these threats; gathering and analyzing information provided by members, creating an anti-terrorism database and submitting proposals in the struggle against the "three evil forces", preparing and organizing relevant research conferences.[52] The Heads of State noted the expediency of carrying out joint antiterrorist maneuvers with participation of the law enforcement agencies and the special services. Notably, anti-terrorism cooperation aside, which continues to be at the top of the immediate agenda, not least given the situation in Afghanistan and the bombings in Tashkent and elsewhere in the first half of 2004, SCO heads of governments, with a view to strengthening regional security, have also increasingly turned their attention to Chinese proposals for deeper economic cooperation and integration in the medium and longer term.[53] Recognizing the problem of transnational drug trafficking, SCO members moreover signed the Agreement on Cooperation in Combating Illicit Trafficking in Narcotic Drugs, Psychotropic Substances and Precursors. The Tashkent Summit consensus was that members should also organize the drafting of a programme on developing cooperation within the SCO in addressing new challenges and threats.

At the same time, the member states expressed unambiguously the view that regional stability and security in many ways will depend on the economic development of Central Asia and beyond. Consequently, the SCO is also committed to develop a larger and effective role in this area. Notably, environmental protection issues with a security dimension, such as a rational and effective utilization of the water resources, have also been identified as possible additions to the agenda for cooperation development within the organization. These developments notwithstanding, the success of the SCO is by no means assured when it comes to advancing as a cohesive diplomatic community and security organization.

## Challenges Facing SCO Cooperation

There are several reasons why successful substantive SCO cooperation is not yet assured. One is that the institutional structures put in place cannot per se be regarded as a guarantee for members delivering on the SCO agenda. Much will depend on whether intramural consensus is achieved on developing security cooperation. In this context, it is still unclear to what extent the Central Asian republics will feel able to respond to the focus and pace of regional cooperation proposed by China. In addition, intra-SCO relations are not free from disagreement, suspicions and conflicting strategic interests.

There are four points here. First, strife continues to characterize relations among the Central Asian members.[54] Uzbekistan, for example, has in past years had water and territorial disputes with all of its neighbours and has used its geographic location and significance for regional communications and trade as leverage in dealings with them. Its membership from 2001 onwards was the matter of some controversy. Even after 2001 problems linked to the unilateral management of border security have persisted. For example, Tajikistan against its will has become a staging ground for the oppositionist Islamic Movement of Uzbekistan. In response, Tashkent has apparently set up unmarked minefields along its borders. The potential for misunderstanding, recrimination, and escalation thus exists.

Second, SCO cooperation has also been subject to strains and stresses in relations between individual republics and the two major powers, China and Russia. These are in part structural given both Beijing's and Moscow's economic and military power position that predestines them for leadership of the SCO. Not too long ago, for example, Tashkent indirectly warned China against seeking to promote multipolarity through the SCO if this would call into question the U.S. regional presence. This was a message relayed by President Karimov without much ambiguity during the St. Petersburg summit in June 2002. Uzbekistan has also called for a nuclear-free Central Asia. This is in part noteworthy given the importance of the Xinjiang Uighur Autonomous Region for the development of China's nuclear forces. Having insisted on pursuing security in the ways it chooses, Tashkent has merely pledged not to do so in a potentially destabilizing manner. What is or is not destabilizing is of course likely to be a matter of perspective. China has thus been interested in strengthening Uzbekistan's stake in the SCO. More recently, there are indications of Taschkent's relations with China warming up as Washington has cast a more critical eye on Uzbekistan's human rights issues and bomb blasts in the country have made the regime appreciate the merit in strengthening anti-insurgent cooperation. Significantly, as with the other Central Asian republics, Uzbekistan is also becoming increasingly receptive to China's economic agenda. At the time of the 2004 Tashkent Summit, President Hu Jintao revealed that China would be making available US$900 million in credit loans to Central Asian members of the SCO. In the event, Beijing and Tashkent firmed up their relationship in the form of a joint statement detailing their cooperation.[55]

Third, the SCO is not necessarily immune to great power discord. True, Moscow and Beijing have for years now worked toward achieving a strategic partnership of substance. This has not been attained, however, the rhetoric and even cooperation in important areas notwithstanding. Indeed, mutual suspicions remain as Moscow wearily watches China's ascendancy and Beijing is nervous about Russia's growing strategic ties with the West, as expressed for instance in the establishment of the NATO-Russia Council and bilateral consultations on Central Asia between Moscow and Washington. A complete congruence of interest in this region is in any case unlikely, now and in future. At the very least,

Russia and China have competing energy interests in Central Asia.[56] Russia also has its own agenda in this part of its "near-abroad" and is clearly interested in reaffirming its presence in Central Asia, illustrated in part by the permanent military base established in Kant, Kyrgyzstan, in the autumn of 2003. Meanwhile, while China does not wish to openly challenge Russia in Central Asia, Beijing is clearly keen to pursue its own strategic interests in this region.

Fourth, success of the SCO is not assured given the existing institutional platforms of which Russia and Central Asian states also are already a part. All have a stake in the NATO Partnership for Peace framework, whereas China and NATO only recently established contact. Moreover, Kazakhstan, Kyrgyzstan and Tajikistan have membership in the Russian-led Collective Security Treaty Organization, established in 2002, which already boasts a rapid deployment force of about 1500 soldiers.[57] The Commonwealth of Independent States also has an anti-terrorist centre in Moscow, with a branch office in Bishkek. Although institutional co-existence is of course possible between these organizations and the SCO, only the future can tell what priorities are accorded to individual organizations.

In short, during its short existence the SCO has for the most part devoted its energies to institutional development, the articulation of a consensual regional diplomatic discourse, and steps toward the development of practical forms of security cooperation. The SCO has not as yet assumed a crucial role in the management of regional security, however. Whether it will do so in the future, remains to be seen. Contrary to the ASEAN Regional Forum, the SCO has been promoted first and foremost by great powers, primarily China. To further push forward regional co-operation in security matters China's President Jiang Zemin propagated the "Shanghai spirit". This stands for mutual trust, mutual benefit, equality, consultation, respect for diverse civilizations, seeking common development, and actively promoting a fair and rational new international political and economic order that will advance regional security and stability.[58] The successor of President Jiang, Hu Jintao, has continued to appeal to the "Shanghai spirit". Given the complexities of the international politics of Central Asia, the jury is still out whether he is appealing to anything more than a chimera when it comes to operational substance of inclusive multilateral cooperation within the SCO. That said, with the SCO only just having entered the stage of pragmatic substantive cooperation, judgment is perhaps rightly suspended for a little while longer. In the meantime, Beijing may already celebrate the growing bilateral ties with individual Central Asian countries, irrespective of whether these take shape under the mantle of the SCO.

## KEDO: KOREAN ENERGY DEVELOPMENT ORGANIZATION

KEDO was established in 1995 to implement the Agreed Framework between the United States and the Democratic People's Republic of Korea (DPRK) signed a year earlier to defuse the nuclear crisis that had erupted on the Korean Peninsula in the early 1990s.[59] This agreement sought to freeze and eventually dismantle North Korea's graphite-moderated reactors and related facilities in return for two new light water reactor (LWR) power plants at Kumho and to ensure the safe storage and eventual disposal of spent fuel from the country's experimental nuclear reactor at Yongbyon. The freeze of the DPRK's nuclear facilities, which was to be monitored by the International Atomic Energy Association (IAEA), was to deprive Pyongyang of future stocks of weapons-grade plutonium and hinder the North Korean leadership from reprocessing its existing stock of spent fuel rods. In return, KEDO's task has been to finance and supply the LWR project as well as to provide alternative sources of energy in the form of 500,000 tons of heavy fuel oil yearly until the completion of the first reactor.[60]

KEDO, which is based in New York with a representative office at the LWR site at Kumho, has consisted of an executive board consisting of the three founding members (Japan, Republic of Korea and the United States) and the European Atomic Energy Community, and a total membership of 13.[61] Contrary to the other regional institutions discussed in this chapter, KEDO's future has always been the most uncertain because its fortunes are bound up closely with the success of the implementation of the Agreed Framework (AF) and the political situation on the Korean Peninsula in general. A year after the onset of the second nuclear crisis, in November 2003, KEDO's activities were suspended. By this time, with only the site survey, preliminary works and the foundations completed, the project was running several years behind schedule, a fact that had already led the DPRK to demand compensation and raised questions as to who would cover the expected shortfall of funds to complete the construction of the two LWRs.

KEDO's role in fulfilling its purpose has been hampered in different ways. As regards the LWRs, delays arose because Pyongyang was reluctant to accept a strong part in the project played by South Korean industry. That said, KEDO also found it difficult to ensure a regular and predictable schedule of deliveries of heavy fuel oil to North Korea. In part, this was due to a lack of funds because expected contributions from the United States failed to materialize. Such a failure was seemingly attributable to concerns over the DPRK's alleged diversion of HFO from heating and electricity generation, which prompted Washington to ensure that KEDO and the DPRK reached agreement on a monitoring system at seven power and thermal facilities.[62] In the event, HFO deliveries depended on funds given to KEDO by the European Atomic Energy Community and other members although the United States had taken on this financial obligation (having already succeeded in committing South Korea and Japan to stomp up the vast majority of the expected construction costs for the two LWRs).

To be sure, political obstacles to the implementation of the AF and KEDO's success have not only concerned the question of the possible diversion of HFO. Particularly in the United States, the AF was one of the major subjects of significant controversy throughout the mid- to late-1990s that pitted the two Clinton administrations against a Republican-dominated Congress. To its critics, the Agreed Framework smacked of unacceptable appeasement of a brutal communist dictatorship whose survival is perceived to depend on its ability to extort concessions. In the view of these critics, the United States should never have caved in to an immoral regime that threatened nuclear blackmail.[63]

Disaffection of U.S. critics with the Agreed Framework and KEDO has focused on a number of points. For instance, critics argued that North Korea should not get nuclear power plants at all and urged the Clinton administration to replace the LWRs with thermal plants. Equally, they complained that the DPRK was not providing immediate clarity on whether Pyongyang actually ever extracted plutonium from Yongbyon that is not accounted for in its safeguards declaration pursuant to the NPT. This has been widely suspected by U.S. intelligence but has yet to be proven. Significantly, on this point the DPRK was not in contravention of the AF. According to Chapter 4 of the Agreed Framework the DPRK was obliged to come into full compliance with its safeguards agreement only upon the completion of a significant portion of the LWR project, but before delivery of key nuclear components.[64] Only then would the International Atomic Energy Agency (IAEA) begin verifying the accuracy and completeness of the DPRK's past accounting of all nuclear material. In other words, until 2002 IAEA inspectors operating in the DPRK merely rightly monitored the freeze of nuclear facilities in Yongbyon rather than ascertained that none of the material was extracted in earlier years for the production of nuclear weapons. Political events on the Korean Peninsula added to the pressure on the AF. Criticisms of the Agreed Framework reached particular highs when it appeared that Pyongyang had established a secret underground nuclear facility and test-fired a three-stage rocket over Japan in August 1998. Continued suspicions about the DPRK's pursuit of a uranium enrichment programmed reinforced the pressure.

In view of the political and congressional resistance to President Clinton's engagement strategy of the DPRK, a delay in implementing the Agreed Framework was inevitable. Although the completion of the two light water reactors was foreseen for 2003, it was only in August 2002 that the pouring of concrete for the foundations of the main power plant buildings was undertaken. Meanwhile, on the assumption that the process of verification would last approximately three or four years, American officials time and again pointed out that Pyongyang had to move speedily on the issue of ensuring inspections in order to avoid further delays in the LWR project. However, given the delays in implementing the Agreed Framework, which had already prompted North Korea to threaten that it would break out of the AF, Pyongyang — not entirely surprisingly — desisted from such a course of action.

## The Second Nuclear Crisis

If KEDO's future always seemed uncertain, its fortunes have declined precipitously since 16 October 2002, when the Bush administration announced that the DPRK had acknowledged that it was pursuing a programme to produce highly enriched uranium for nuclear weapons. In response to this development, apparently first suspected in 1997, Washington announced that the United States would no longer provide economic and political incentives to Pyongyang. Indeed, Washington declared that it would suspend negotiations with Pyongyang until such time as the latter would dismantle its nuclear weapons programme in a verifiable manner.

KEDO, at a subsequent executive board meeting, reacted to this course of events by criticising the DPRK's acknowledgement of pursuing a uranium enrichment programme as a "clear and serious violation" of its obligations under the Agreed Framework, the NPT, IAEA Safeguards Agreements and the Joint South-North Declaration on the Denuclearization of the Korean Peninsula.[65] It was moreover agreed to suspend with effect from December, rather than after the winter, as initially suggested by South Korea and Japan, heavy fuel oil deliveries to Pyongyang. The Executive Board also made future shipments to the DPRK dependent on what it called "concrete and credible actions to dismantle completely" its highly enriched uranium programme.

Washington's revelation and subsequent claims produced first a cautious and then increasingly hostile and provocative diplomatic response on the part of the DPRK. Initially, North Korea appeared to acknowledge that the country did indeed already have nuclear weapons, but this acknowledgement was marked by confusion over the precise formulation as to whether the DPRK "was entitled to have" nuclear weapons or whether it "had nuclear weapons".[66] Irrespective of whether North Korea had by then already acquired nuclear weapons or merely sought to pursue this goal by way of its uranium enrichment program, Pyongyang was seriously disturbed by KEDO's decision to suspend heavy fuel oil deliveries. Within a month of this decision the DPRK threatened to immediately resume the operation and construction of nuclear facilities necessary for electrical power generation. Ignoring the warning by the IAEA against undertaking unilateral steps and refusing to discuss practical arrangements to moving toward normal safeguards operations, Pyongyang proceeded on 21 December 2002 to cut most of the seals and impeded the functioning of surveillance equipment at the 5MW(e) reactor at Yongbyon.[67] Following the expulsion of on-site IAEA representatives, North Korea moved over 1000 nuclear fuel rods to Yongbyon in an apparent bid to reactivate the plant, drawing criticisms of "nuclear brinkmanship". On 10 January 2003, the DPRK withdrew from the NPT. In February, the regime restarted its experimental reactor and test-fired the first of two missiles. In April it claimed to have initiated the reprocessing and, in talks with the United States hosted by Beijing, admitted to having nuclear weapons. Following the scrapping of the 1992 denuclearization agreement with the Republic of Korea, Pyongyang announced in June its intention to build a nuclear deterrent. In October 2003, the regime further announced that it had reprocessed its stockpile of spent fuel rods.[68]

These moves may well have been the death knell for KEDO. By early 2003, both the United States and the DPRK had expressed the view that the Agreed Framework had been nullified. KEDO's executive board met in early November 2003 to discuss the future of the LWR project, including the question of the latter's suspension. This question was referred to the capitals, with a decision then announced in late November. Notwithstanding its suspension, KEDO preserves its construction at Kumho and has signed a Memorandum of Understanding that relevant protocols and agreements regarding the implementation of the AF remain in place. In mid-2004 indications were that KEDO's executive board would decide to extend the organization's suspension for another year until the end of 2005.

## Taking a Political Hit

Significantly, the analysis would be incomplete if this chapter would not also examine the reasons of KEDO's possible demise, particularly the role that both the administration of George W. Bush and the North Korean regime would appear to have played in this regard. This is appropriate because, from the very outset, the incoming Bush administration refused to contemplate continuing the engagement policy *vis-à-vis* Pyongyang that the Clinton administration had pursued up to late 2000 and which had almost seen a leaders' summit. Indeed, with George W. Bush in power, the United States replaced the policy of engagement with a policy of benign neglect.

This tougher line on North Korea initially manifested itself in implicit criticisms of the "sunshine policy" when meeting ROK President and Nobel Prize laureate Kim Dae Jung who visited Washington in March 2001. In June 2001, the Bush administration spelled out four objectives in relation to a further U.S.-DPRK dialogue: an improved implementation of the Agreed Framework by North Korea, verifiable constraints on Pyongyang's missile programme, a ban on its missile exports, and the adoption of a less threatening conventional military posture.[69] Although Pyongyang had previously indicated some willingness to pursue negotiations with Washington on some of these issues, this catalogue of demands on the DPRK, if it ever was a serious proposal at all, was always going to be a non-starter in view of the DPRK's threat perceptions.

Indeed, as an "alienated state",[70] the DPRK sees itself exposed to grave danger and is suspicious beyond the norm about U.S. intentions to bring about the demise of the regime and the collapse of the state. Significantly, Pyongyang's suspicions are not completely unfounded. During the Cold War, Pyongyang faced the threat of nuclear annihilation after the United States in a clandestine move introduced nuclear weapons into the Korean Peninsula in 1958. However, even after 1991, when tactical nuclear weapons were removed from the ROK, Pyongyang still has had to contend with a nuclear threat. For example, the DPRK has for years been the subject of discussions in relation to a possible pre-emptive nuclear strike by the United States as a way of dealing with the threat of North Korean Scuds armed with chemical or biological warheads reaching targets in ROK within minutes.[71] The Nuclear Posture Review Report, leaked in early 2002, identifies the DPRK as one of Washington's "chronic military concerns", whereby the U.S. government means states that sponsor or harbour terrorists and have active WMD and missile programmes. President George W. Bush of course also famously branded North Korea a part of the "axis of evil" and he suggested that doing nothing was not an option. As he remarked in his 2002 State of the Union address:

> North Korea is a regime arming with missiles and weapons of mass destruction while starving its citizens…The United States of America will not permit the world's most dangerous regimes to threaten us with the world's most destructive weapons.[72]

Given this rhetoric so conspicuous on the possibility of a resort to preventive military defence against Pyongyang, it is not surprising that the DPRK's sense of security declined after President Bush assumed office. The decline was moreover accentuated by the fact that the Bush administration seemed to completely move away from the idea of mutual recognition. This was particularly bitter for Pyongyang, as the regime has long seen U.S. acceptance of its basic right to exist as a first step towards peace on the Korean Peninsula. Mutual recognition was also at the heart of the concessions that Pyongyang thought it had extracted from Washington when signing the Agreed Framework.

How significant Bush's designation of North Korea as part of the "axis of evil" and the denial of political recognition have been in prompting Pyongyang to steer toward a second nuclear crisis will perhaps only become clear over time. However, there would appear to a lot in the argument that the DPRK leadership did indeed reach the conclusion that the Agreed Framework was little other than a "dead document" because it saw Washington as breaching all its key chapters. As noted, Washington failed to move toward realizing the DPRK's chief political objective of mutual diplomatic recognition (Article 2). Pyongyang has been able to assert moreover, not without some justification, that the U.S. policy to consider undertaking pre-emptive strikes among other against the DPRK stands in contrast to the assurances to the DPRK against the threat or use of nuclear weapons by the United States (Chapter 3). Pyongyang has also suggested that the two sides had agreed that the DPRK would allow inspections of the frozen facilities only after the delivery of the delivery of essential non-nuclear components for the first LWR unit, including turbines and generators.[73] From Pyongyang's perspective, the halting of heavy fuel oil deliveries by KEDO may thus indeed have been the final straw.[74]

## Institutionalized Cooperation and KEDO

The suspension of KEDO has not implied an end to institutionalized multilateral cooperation to deal with the DPRK's nuclear challenge. As was the case in the event of the first nuclear crisis, all of the DPRK's neighbors have a strong interest in avoiding a military escalation of the situation, an option that Washington is clearly also trying to steer clear of in favour of multilateral diplomacy. With initial tripartite talks having taken place in Beijing in April 2003, the four major East Asian powers and the two Koreas addressed head-on the second nuclear crisis in late August. Two further rounds of talks took place in February and June 2004 respectively.

Although the first six-party talks failed to achieve a major substantive breakthrough, ending only with a Chairman's Statement as in the ARF, and North Korea has intermittently signaled its aversion to a continuation of multilateral diplomacy in this framework, initial expectations whereby this format might be institutionalized in the longer term have been proved right. One reason for this development was China's evident push to promote a diplomatic solution that would not only ensure the de-nuclearization of the Korean Peninsula, but also strengthen Beijing's own hand in maintaining regional order. Another factor was the insistence on Washington's part that Pyongyang's strident demands for a non-aggression treaty, diplomatic recognition, and economic assistance could best be addressed in a multilateral setting in which other regional states would have a major stake. And institutionalized discussions may deepen. At the second round of the Six-Party Talks, for instance, it was decided to institute lower-level working groups comprising diplomats and nuclear issue experts. The third round of talks provided a basis for further negotiations but failed to overcome differences between the DPRK and other parties concerning the scope of preliminary measures (whether or not to include uranium enrichment) and verification procedures. While the DPRK reiterated its stated aim for an agreement on the freezing of its nuclear programmes and compensatory measures, the United States,

Japan, and the Republic of Korea sought an agreement on a framework that would result in the dismantlement of the DPRK's nuclear programmes.[75]

Finding a compromise acceptable to all is a tall order. Indeed, it seems that negotiations over how to address the DPRK's nuclear threat have come full circle, with the difference that Pyongyang is asked to dismantle two nuclear programs rather than just the one as in the run-up to the 1994 Agreed Framework. If a political breakthrough can be achieved, the future of KEDO is bound to be on the agenda again assuming that it remains merely suspended. At the same time, it is clear that both the circumstances and objectives have changed for all concerned. It is therefore highly unlikely that KEDO will at some point simply rise like a phoenix out of the ashes.

## CONCLUSION

Comparing ASEAN, the ARF, the SCO and KEDO, one can point to a number of similarities between some or all four institutions. First, the basic normative framework guiding intramural relations in ASEAN, the ARF and the SCO has not differed widely. Sovereignty and non-interference matter greatly to members of all three institutions even though the norm of consensus is highlighted much more in ASEAN and ARF than it is in the SCO, where the notion of joint consultations has been emphasized more specifically. Having been formed to fulfil a specific purpose and not being an inclusive organization, basic norms of international society have arguably mattered much less in the context of KEDO's task.

Second, the establishment of deeper institutional structures has been relatively slow to evolve and limited in both ASEAN and ARF. It took ASEAN a decade to set up the ASEAN Secretariat and ARF members continue to disagree about the merits of an independent ARF Secretariat. Still, whereas some of ASEAN's institutional innovations remain untried, the ARF has at least seen the steadfast practical evolution of several institutional channels such as the intersessional groups. The institutional experience of the SCO arguably has some parallels to that of the ARF, not least considering that the organization grew out of the "Shanghai Five". Significantly, however, the SCO states decided to opt for a Charter and legal personality, and to proceed with deeper institutionalization (Council of Head of State, Secretariat, RATS) rather more quickly. Designated from the outset by its Western sponsors as an organization charged with the implementation of the Agreed Framework, KEDO's particular structures of decision-making and support were never in doubt.

Third, all four regional institutions have undertaken practical multilateral security cooperation, albeit to a different extent. In the case of ASEAN, such security cooperation has for the most part focused on collective diplomacy and exchanges. In the ARF, multilateral confidence-building and cooperation in the field of preventive diplomacy continue to evolve. The SCO has also already implemented concrete practical measures of multilateral security cooperation, including anti-terrorism exercises in the field from which only Uzbekistan was absent. For KEDO, security cooperation has inevitably been firmly focused on the fulfilment of the Agreed Framework. In all cases, the limits of what individual regional security institutions have been able to do has depended in part on their financial resources and the willingness of member states to contribute to joint endeavours. One difference between the institutions under discussion is that whereas ASEAN and even the SCO (including the RATS) have boasted relatively few funds from the outset, KEDO's situation has generally been characterized by an inability of drawing on certain promised funding that was not forthcoming for political reasons.

A key difference between ASEAN and the ARF on the one hand and the SCO and KEDO on the other hand is of course the role major powers play within these institutions. ASEAN does not have a great power as one of its members and arguably has no clear leader at all, although Indonesia has a strong sense of regional entitlement and has often been considered to be *primus inter pares*. The ARF is also not led by a major power, with ASEAN instead being the "primary driving force". In contrast, China plays much more of a leadership role in the SCO. KEDO's membership has comprised more or less exclusively states from the industrialized world under the overall political leadership of the United States.

Notably, based on the four cases at hand it is not immediately apparent that regional security organizations work better if major powers take a lead role in them. As this chapter showed, ASEAN has to date repeatedly made a significant contribution to overcome hurdles blocking further institutional development, particularly when its credibility has been at stake. ASEAN has also invested significant energies to mediate between the great powers in the ARF in relation to the elaboration of legitimate understandings regarding the pursuit of preventive diplomacy. The development of the SCO has progressed quickly, but since it has yet to fully embrace substantive cooperation across the board, it seems premature to argue that major powers are *per se* better equipped to ensure the success of regional organizations. Indeed, KEDO failed to allay Pyongyang's concerns about the implementation of the Agreed Framework and it was ultimately suspended in view of political developments on the Korean Peninsula.

Washington's primacy in the international system, its emphasis on anticipatory self-defence and its long-standing strategy of strengthening bilateral relations have not always proved helpful in solving the collective action problems faced by regional security institutions discussed in this chapter. For example, those advocating the benefits of multilateral processes of cooperative security, which are subject to strict consensus decision-making, have had little alternative but to face up to the reality that from a post-September 11 perspective institutions like ASEAN and even the ARF are still not really regarded as terribly relevant by decision-makers in Washington. As this chapter has also suggested, however, even the United States cannot properly advance its security interests without participating in such multilateral endeavors in cooperative security; nor is it able to forego multilateral diplomacy as one element of a multi-dimensional strategy to deal with regional security challenges. Indeed, in view of what is at stake and the instruments Washington can rely on to effectively pursue certain particular foreign policy aims, the United States has had to acknowledge that it makes sense to work within a multilateral regional framework, if this promises to alleviate threats to regional peace and security with greater likelihood and less cost. KEDO was a relevant example and, more recently, the Six-Party Talks have become another.

Indeed, even though regional security institutions in the Asia-Pacific will remain hostage to the calculations and ambitions of the major powers, one should not be too pessimistic about their future. ASEAN has come at least as far as endorsing what may be called a weak form of "flexible engagement" on the road toward the establishment of an ASEAN Security Community. Secondly, the ARF interest in developing multilateral security cooperation continues among its membership. China may initially have been opposed to more robust forms of preventive diplomacy and conflict resolution in the ARF, but Beijing has played a leading and constructive role in the SCO from the start and, more recently, also in the arrangement of multilateral talks on Korea's second nuclear crisis. Indeed, the Chinese case suggests that when major powers see the establishment and appropriate functioning of regional organizations as enhancing both national security and winning recognition as a guardian of regional order, they will provide support, leadership and resources. Meanwhile, faced with the raw consequences of a controversial resort to force, Washington has again come to understand the limits of military power.

These trends may see some existing regional security organizations reprieved and some being revitalized or reinvented. While ASEAN's security role could evolve further, the Association is very likely to remain at least a diplomatic community and security regime. The ASEAN Regional Forum seems poised to slowly but surely manage the task of implementing preventive diplomacy and refocus its gaze on new transnational security challenges to national security, particularly in Southeast Asia. The Shanghai Cooperation Organization is likely to assume greater significance for developing Central Asian security cooperation, especially if China helps to underpin this development by further reinforcing its bilateral relations with the Central Asian states. On the other hand, KEDO is still facing collapse, and although it is possible in principle to revive the organization, it is also clear that a simple resurrection of KEDO would not provide a fully adequate institutional response to the current Korean crisis. In the meantime, however, the fledgling Six-Party Talks on Korea may well become even more institutionalized. Hence, although the actual management of regional security may still well be and remain beyond most of the security arrangements/organizations discussed in this chapter, we can nevertheless retain some optimism about the future relevance of multilateral approaches to regional security in Asia-Pacific.

## NOTES

1. This chapter has in part drawn on research undertaken in the context of the author's collaborative ESRC research project on *Transnational Challenges, Security Cultures and Regional Organizations* (RES-223-25-0072).
2. See Rosemary Foot, S. Neill MacFarlane, and Michael Mastanduno, eds., *US Hegemony and International Organizations* (Oxford: Oxford University Press, 2003).
3. See for example Arnfinn Jorgensen-Dahl, *Regional Organization and Order in South-East Asia* (Basingstoke and London: Macmillan, 1982), Michael Antolik, *ASEAN and the Diplomacy of Accommodation* (New York: M.E. Sharpe, 1990), and Dewi Fortuna Anwar, *Indonesia in ASEAN: Foreign Policy and Regionalism* (Singapore: Institute of Southeast Asian Studies, 1994).
4. See Amitav Acharya, "Association of Southeast Asian Nations: Security Community or 'Defence Community'?", *Pacific Affairs* 64, no. 2 (1991): 159–78.
5. Jürgen Haacke, *ASEAN's Diplomatic and Security Culture: Origins, Development and Prospects* (London and New York: RoutledgeCurzon, 2003).

6. See Sorpong Peou, *Conflict Neutralization in the Cambodian War: From Battlefield to Ballot-Box* (Kuala Lumpur: Oxford University Press, 1997), Michael Leifer, "The ASEAN Peace Process: A Category Mistake", *The Pacific Review* 12, no. 1 (1999): 25–38, and Shaun Narine, *Explaining ASEAN: Regionalism in Southeast Asia* (Boulder, CO: Lynne Rienner, 2002), Chapter 3.

7. ASEAN (and the ARF) would nevertheless qualify as an international organization in the sense of being a formal association of states with tasks that are partly issue area specific and partly transcend issue areas. See Henning Boekle, Volker Rittberger and Wolfgang Wagner, "Constructivist Foreign Policy Theory", in Volker Rittberger, *German Foreign Policy since Unification: Theories and Case Studies* (Manchester: Manchester University Press, 2000), p. 119.

8. See Jürgen Haacke, "The Concept of Flexible Engagement and the Practice of Enhanced Interaction: Intramural Challenges to the 'ASEAN Way'", *The Pacific Review* 12, no. 3 (1999): 581–611.

9. See Simon S.C. Tay, "Institutions and Process: Dilemmas and Possibilities", in *Reinventing ASEAN*, edited by Simon S.C. Tay, Jesus P. Estanislao and Hadi Soesastro (Singapore: Institute of Southeast Asian Studies, 2001), pp. 256–61.

10. It consists of the acting chairman of the ASEAN Standing Committee, as well as the preceding and succeeding chairs, unless otherwise agreed. For an evaluation of the troika (and other developments concerning the "ASEAN Way" up to September 11, see Jürgen Haacke, "ASEAN's Diplomatic and Security Culture: A Constructivist Assessment", *International Relations of the Asia-Pacific* 3, no. 1 (2003): 57–87.

11. It has been recognized of course that some ASEAN members have been willing to submit territorial disputes to the ICJ. In December 2002, the ICJ ruled that Sipadan and Ligitan long disputed between Indonesia and Malaysia, was to be part of the latter's sovereign jurisdiction. Significantly, the rules of procedure for the High Council could in theory also be invoked for the mediation of disputes and situations between ASEAN member states and any country that has acceded to the Treaty of Amity and Cooperation (such as China).

12. On Thai-Myanmar relations see Maung Aung Myoe, *Neither Friend Nor Foe: Myanmar's Relations with Thailand Since 1988* (Singapore: IDSS Monograph, 2002).

13. On Indonesia's condition in at the turn of the millennium, see Tim Huxley, *Disintegrating Indonesia? Implications for Regional Security* (Adelphi Paper 349) (Oxford: Oxford University Press for the International Institute of Strategic Studies, 2002).

14. On the Depayin incident and the political process in Myanmar, see Robert H. Taylor, "Myanmar: Roadmap to Where?", in *Southeast Asian Affairs 2004*, edited by Daljit Singh and Chin Kin Wah (Singapore: ISEAS, 2004), pp. 171–84.

15. This argument is developed in Jürgen Haacke, "ASEAN's Diplomatic and Security Culture: Not beyond 'flexible engagement' ", in *Regional Integration in Europe and East Asia: Convergence or Divergence?*, edited by Bertrand Fort and Douglas Webber (London and New York: Routledge, 2005), forthcoming. For the text of the Declaration, see <www.aseansec.org/15159.htm>.

16. For an overview, see "ASEAN's Efforts to Counter Terrorism", <www. aseansec.org/14396.htm>.

17. See Daljit Singh, "ASEAN Counter-Terror Strategies and Cooperation: How Effective", in *After Bali: The Threat of Terrorism in Southeast Asia*, edited by Kumar Ramkrishna and Tan See Seng (Singapore: Institute of Defence and Strategic Studies and World Scientific Publishing, 2003), pp. 216–17.

18. ASEAN-United States of America Joint Declaration for Cooperation to Combat International Terrorism, 1 August 2002, <www.aseansec.org/ 7424.htm>.

19. See Zachary Abuza, *Militant Islam in Southeast Asia: Crucible of Terror* (Boulder, CO: Lynne Rienner, 2003), Chapter 5.

20. In return, Washington secured the Mutual Logistics Support Agreement that will allow the United States better access to military supplies and facilities in the Philippines than at any time since the closure of American bases in the early 1990s.

21. For an overview of security issues in Southeast Asia, see Alan Collins, *Security and Southeast Asia: Domestic, Regional, and Global Issues* (Boulder, CO: Lynne Rienner, 2003).

22. Heiner Hänggi, *Neutralität in Südostasien: das Projekt einer Zone des Friedens, der Freiheit und der Neutralität* [Neutrality in Southeast Asia: The project of a zone of peace, freedom and neutrality] (Bern: P. Haupt, 1992). That said, in practical terms, engagement if not allied status had been and remained part of the national security strategy of several ASEAN members since the 1970s onwards.

23. Michael Leifer, *The ASEAN Regional Forum: Extending ASEAN's Model of Regional Security*. Adelphi Paper 302 (Oxford: Oxford University Press/IISS, 1996).

24. ASEAN Regional Forum, *The ASEAN Regional Forum: A Concept Paper*, annexed to the Chairman Statement of the Second Meeting of the ASEAN Regional Forum, 1 August 1995.

25. See Ralf Emmers, *Cooperative Security and the Balance of Power in ASEAN and the ARF* (London and New York: RoutledgeCurzon, 2003), pp. 36–39.

26. ASEAN Regional Forum Concept and Principles of Preventive Diplomacy, 25 July 2001, <http://www.aseansec.org/3571.htm>.

27. See Barry Desker, "The Future of the ASEAN Regional Forum", <http://www.asian-affairs.com/crisis/barrydesker.html>.

28. Building on these ideas, a collective of researchers from IDSS in Singapore later put forward twelve policy recommendations: (1) Allow a panel of the ARF Expert/Eminent Persons Group to undertake a review of the 1995 Concept Paper; (2) Moving toward frank and constructive exchange of views, and not to ignore contentious issues; (3) Pursuing a thematic and problem-oriented agenda; (4) Establishing a Secretariat; (6) Introducing greater flexibility in the relationship between the ARF Chair and the ASEAN Chair; (7) Setting up a Risk Reduction Centre; (8) Building closer relationship with the United Nations; (9) Promoting enhanced defense participation; (10) Developing closer networking with other regional institutions in Asia-Pacific; (11) ARF should pay more attention to transnational security issues, especially terrorism. [create special task force]; and (12) Strengthening links with Track II Forums. See Tan See Seng, Ralf Emmers, M.Caballero et al., *A New Agenda for the ASEAN Regional Forum* (Singapore: IDSS, 2002).

29. Future Direction of the ARF, Adopted at the Ninth ASEAN Regional Forum, 31 July 2002, Bandar Seri Begawan, Brunei Darussalam, <www.aseansec.org/16007.htm>.

30. For details see ARF Statement on Measures Against Terrorist Financing, 30 July 2002.

31. See ASEAN Regional Forum Statement on Cooperative Counter-Terrorist Action on Border Security, 18 June 2003, <www.aseansec.org/14835.htm>.

32. ASEAN Regional Forum Workshop on Managing the Consequences of a Major Terrorist Attack, Darwin, 3–5 June 2003, Co-Chairs' Summary Report, <www.15137.htm>.

33. ASEAN Regional Forum Statement on Strengthening Transport Security Against International Terrorism, Jakarta, 2 July 2004, <www.aseansec.org/16249.htm>.

34. Endorsement came from Co-Chairs' Summary Report of the Meeting of the ASEAN Regional Forum Inter-sessional Support Group on Confidence Building Measures, Yangon, 11–14 April, <www.16096.htm>.

35. Co-Chairs' Summary Report of the Second ASEAN Regional Forum Inter-Sessional Meeting on Counter-Terrorism and Transnational Crime, Manila 30–31 March 2004, <www.16101.htm>.

36. Co-Chairs' Summary Report of the Meeting of the ASEAN Regional Forum Inter-Sessional Support Group on Confidence Building Measures, Yangon, 11–14 April 2004, <www.16096.htm>.

37. Chairman's Statement, The Eleventh Meeting of the ASEAN Regional Forum, 2 July 2004.

38. The International Institute for Strategic Studies has organized in Singapore

since 2002 the IISS Asia Security Conference, also known as the Shangri-La Dialogue.

39. The Shangri-La Dialogue also addresses regional security challenges and involves regional defense ministers and armed forces chiefs. It suffers at present from the absence of high-level participation by the PRC. For details, see IISS Asia Security Conference, Singapore, <http://www.iiss.org/shangri-la.php>.

40. Chairman's Statement, Tenth ASEAN Regional Forum, Phnom Penh, 18 June 2003, <www.14845.htm>.

41. The Shanghai Five originally included China, Russia, Tajikistan, Kazahhstan and Kyrgystan. Uzbekistan only joined in June 2001 just prior to the birth of the SCO.

42. See Shanghai Convention on Combating Terrorism, Separatism and Extremism, 16 June 2001, *The Moscow Journal of International Law* 2001: 231–38, <www.unionlawyers.ru/journal/journal.pdf>.

43. See Declaration on the Establishment of the SCO, 15 June 2001, <http://missions.itu.int/~kazaks/eng/sco/sco02.htm>.

44. For an official exposition dated 1 July 2004, see "Shanghai Cooperation Organization", <www.fmprc.gov.cn/eng/topics/sco/t57970.htm>.

45. See Christian Tyler, *Wild West China: The Taming of Xinjiang* (London: John Murray, 2003).

46. Yuan Jing-Dong, "China and the Shanghai Cooperation Organization", *Politologiske Studier*, September 2003, <www.politolgiske.dk/numre/18/ps_0203_13.pdf>.

47. Declaration by the Heads of the Member States of the Shanghai Cooperation Organization, St. Petersburg, 10 June 2002, <http://russia.shaps.hawaii.edu/fp/russia/sco_20020610_4.html>.

48. Joint Statement by Ministers of Foreign Affairs of the Member States of the Shanghai Cooperation Organization, 7 January 2002, <http://missions.itu.int/~kazaks/eng/sco/sco02.htm>.

49. For details on the charter and the regional anti-terrorism centre, see Gudrun Wacker, *Gipfeltreffen der Shanghaier Organization für Zusammenarbeit: Von Worten zu Taten*, <http://www.swpaktu_22.02.pdf>.

50. See Chinese Ministry of Foreign Affairs, "Third SCO Summit Meeting Held in Moscow", 30 May 2003, <www.fmprc.gov.cn/eng/topics/hjtcf/t23117.htm>.

51. Uzbekistan did not participate.

52. See "Anti-Terror Body Launched at SCO Summit", <www.chinadaily.com.cn/english/doc/2004-06/17/content_340281.htm>.

53. For an unofficial translation of the Tashkent Declaration, see <http://russia.shaps.hawaii.edu/fp/russia2004/20040621_sco_decl_eng.html>.

54. See Ahmed Rashid, *Taliban: Islam, Oil and the New Great Game in Central Asia* (London and New York: I.B. Tauris, 2000), pp. 147–54.

55. See Xinhua, "China, Uzbekistan Issue Joint Statement", 16 June 2004, <www.china.org.cn/english/2004/Jun/98321.htm>.

56. Also see Andrews-Speed, P. Liao Xuanli and Dannreuther, R., *The Strategic Implications of China's Energy Needs*, IISS Adelphi Paper, no. 346 (London, Oxford, New York: Oxford University Press, 2002).

57. See Gudrun Wacker, "The Shanghai Cooperation Organization: Regional Security and Economic Advancement", 20 August 2004, <http://www.kas.de/proj/home/pub/37/2/year-2004/dokument_id_5210/>.

58. China's National Defence in 2002, Part VI, available online <http://www.china.org.cn/e-white/20021209/>.

59. See Leon V. Sigal, *Disarming Strangers: Nuclear Diplomacy with North Korea* (Princeton, N.J.: Princeton University Press, 1998) and Michael Mazarr, *North Korea and the Bomb: A Case Study in Nonproliferation* (New York: St. Martin's Press, 1995).

60. The Republic of Korea, Japan and the United States are reported to have spent US$1.23 billion, US$446 million and US$406 million on KEDO's activities. See Reuben Staines, "Seoul, Tokyo Seek to Keep KEDO Alive", *The Korea Times*, 6 September 2004, <http://www.times.hankooki.com/Ipage/nation/200409/kt2004090617255510510.htm>.

61. Other members are Canada, Australia, New Zealand, Indonesia, Chile, Argentina, Poland, Czech Republic, and Uzbekistan.

62. See United States General Accounting Office, Report to the Chairman, Committee on International Relations, House of Representatives: Nuclear Proliferation: Status of Heavy Fuel Oil Delivered to North Korea Under the Agreed Framework, September 1999, GAO/RCED-99-276, online at <http://www.nautilus.org/archives/library/security/gaoreports/rc99276.pdf>.

63. On the likely success of different foreign policy strategies toward North Korea, see Victor D. Cha, "Hawk Engagement and Preventive Defence on the Korean Peninsula", *International Security* 27, no. 1 (Summer 2002): 40–78; also see Victor D. Cha and David C. Kang, *Nuclear North Korea: A Debate on Engagement Strategies* (New York: Columbia University Press, 2003).

64. See Agreed Framework, <http://www.kedo.org/pdfs/AgreedFramework/pdf>.

65. Statement by the KEDO Executive Board Meeting, 14 November 2002, <http://www.kedo.org/news_detail.asp?NewsID=10>.

66. See *BBC World: Asia-Pacific*, "N Korean nuclear 'admission' in doubt", 18 November 2002, <http://news.bbc.co.uk/1/hi/world/asia-pacific/2487437.stm>.

67. See IAEA Fact Sheet on DPRK Nuclear Safeguards, <http://www.iaea.org/worldatom/Press/P_release/2002/med-advise_052.shtml>.

68. For further analysis and discussion see James Cotton, "The Second North Korean Nuclear Crisis", *Australian Journal of International Affairs* 57, no. 2

(July 2003): 261–79; and Gary Samore, "The North Korean Nuclear Crisis", *Survival* 45, no. 1 (Spring 2003): 7–24.

69. David Albright and Holly Higgins, "North Korea: It's Taking too Long", *Bulletin of the Atomic Scientist* 58, no. 1 (January/February 2002): 56–61.

70. See Denny Roy, "North Korea as an Alienated State", *Survival* (Winter 1996/97): 22–36.

71. See Hans M. Kristensen, "Preemptive Posturing", *Bulletin of the Atomic Scientists* 58, no. 5 (September/October 2002): 54–59. (Also available at <http://www.thebulletin.org/issues/2002/so02/so02Kristensen.html>.

72. For the text of the State of the Union address, see <http://news.bbc.co.uk/1/hi/world/americas/1790537.stm>.

73. See "Conclusion of Non-Aggression Treaty between DPRK and U.S. Called for", 25 October 2002, <http://www.knca.co.jp/index_e.htm>.

74. "It is the height of folly for the United States to think that the DPRK would maintain the freeze of the nuclear facilities even after the former groundlessly halted its supply of heavy fuel to the latter under the pretext of its "nuclear development". See *Korean Central News Agency*, 28 December 2002, <http://www.knca.co.jp/index-e.htm>.

75. See Foreign Ministry of Japan, Third Round of Six-Party Talks Concerning North Korean Nuclear Issues, 27 June 2004, <http://www.mofa.go.jp/region/asia-paci/n_korea/6party/talk0406.html>.

# Part Three

## Non-Traditional Challenges to Asian Security

# Chapter Seven
# Weapons Proliferation in Asia

Rod Lyon

## INTRODUCTION

Any reassessment of the changing Asian security environment must allow considerable space for the large, unresolved issues of earlier years. Despite the rush of new issues onto the Asian security agenda, at the core of many regional security problems still lies a continuing worry about an old issue: Weapons proliferation. Indeed, proliferation of weapons of mass destruction (WMD) now appears more worrying than before, precisely because of the change in the nature of war-making units that the events of September 11 have advertised,[1] and the new determination in Washington to act forcefully, and if necessary pre-emptively, to prevent terrorists from acquiring such weapons. Further, WMD remain a major concern of analysts studying the traditional state-centric balance of power in the region.

Such concerns are replicated, albeit at a lower level, in relation to the steady accumulation and qualitative improvement of conventional forces in the region. In short, the Asia-Pacific remains an area where regional institutionalization is under-developed, cross-border tensions are comparatively high, weapons capabilities are increasing, and the complex issues of WMD proliferation have not been solved. In this chapter, I will examine the issues surrounding both nuclear and conventional proliferation, by focusing on the North Korean nuclear issue and China's conventional force modernization.

## THE TWO CHESSBOARDS

Since the dramatic events of 11 September 2001, it has become clear that international security is now most appropriately depicted not as one "grand chessboard"[2] but as two interlinked chessboards. Up on the top board exist those state-centric actors who have traditionally monopolized the field of international security, and all their related concerns. On the top chessboard, the principal concern is to check great power conflict, for the simple reason that great-power wars can be incredibly destructive. On that top chessboard, we have developed, essentially since the age of Napoleon, a set of mechanisms for managing that concern, such as power-balancing, diplomacy, arms control and deterrence. Further, unipolarity suggests the basic problems of the top chessboard are currently held in check by U.S. "hyperpower".[3] Still, even a hyperpower has its limits, and the phenomenon of hyperpowerdom is itself so unusual in international relations that it might be wise to suspend judgment on whether it is stabilizing or not until further evidence is available.

But since 11 September 2001, the international community has been focusing much more sharply upon the lower chessboard. On this board, the actors are characteristically less powerful, and include the weak states, pariah states, rogue states, and non-state actors such as transnational criminals and terrorists. On the lower chessboard, the mechanisms we use to control the top chessboard do not work nearly so well. A major focus of current effort is to discern and develop mechanisms appropriate to the sort of threats found there. The National Security Strategy of the Bush administration constitutes one such attempt to address the lower chessboard security threats, albeit a controversial one that places a high emphasis on the proactive engagement of possible threats, including through the use of military power. Such action has been justified by President Bush and others as the lesser of two evils, the greater evil resulting from a policy of inaction which would allow the gradual acquisition of weapons of mass destruction by the sorts of states which might see advantage in the transfer of such capabilities to terrorists. Still, the strategy is contentious and, as the Iraq case amply demonstrates, difficult to apply. Envisaging how a strategy of pre-emption might be used against lower-chessboard proliferants in the Asia-Pacific produces some worrying scenarios.

## THE PROLIFERATION OF
## WEAPONS OF MASS DESTRUCTION

Proliferation of weapons of mass destruction is not a new problem in international security. Rather, it is a problem that has long been of particular concern to diplomats and strategists precisely because of the unique problems it poses for international stability. In the days of the Cold War, "vertical" proliferation — the steady increase in the size of WMD arsenals by states which had already crossed the threshold — was a much more common occurrence than "horizontal" proliferation — the acquisition of WMD by states crossing that threshold for the first time. Horizontal proliferation was a relatively slow-motion activity. Indeed, if we look at the pattern of history, we can see that only one or two states crossed the nuclear proliferation threshold each decade between the 1940s and the 1990s. But if vertical proliferation is the more common occurrence, horizontal proliferation is the more serious. With each new entrant to the nuclear "club", fresh waves of concern are generated within the international community over whether some form of "natural ceiling" exists in relation to the size of the club, whether deterrence will be the primary *motif* of the proliferator's strategic doctrine, and whether current high safety and security standards for nuclear weapons can be attained by the — often inadequately resourced — newcomer.

There appear to be three constraints upon horizontal nuclear proliferation. Firstly, the proliferator must have access to sufficient quantities of fissile material — either uranium-235 or plutonium — to permit fabrication of nuclear weapons. This is a serious hurdle.[4] Despite increasing talk that the collapse of the Soviet Union has made such material more freely available, gaining access to fissile material remains a difficult practical challenge for every potential proliferator. Secondly, the proliferator must have the level of technological skill that the United States possessed in about the mid-1940s. This hurdle is a non-trivial one for some potential proliferators, but it is easy to see that the importance of this barrier is shrinking as time goes by. Indeed, if we have now reached an age when states like North Korea can be regarded as serious candidates to build nuclear weapons, then the second barrier is clearly weakening rapidly. The first two barriers to proliferation are technical but the third is political. A proliferator needs a compelling motive in order to devote the time and money necessary to successfully challenge the first two barriers. It is true that motivations for proliferation may vary.[5] But this barrier is still an important one. Many states in Asia today could successfully proliferate if they chose to do so. What stops them from doing so is a lack of motivation, which arises in turn from the calculations they make about the perceived benefits and costs that such actions might incur.

What sort of state believes today that such actions are worth taking? Over the decades we have seen a fundamental change in the nature of the states attempting to build nuclear weapons.[6] During the 1940s, nuclear weapons were built by the two superpowers, the United States and the Soviet Union. In the 1950s and 1960s, they were built by a small number of great powers, Britain, France and China. In the 1970s and 1980s, they were built by regional states facing strong security challenges, Israel, India and Pakistan. Since the 1990s, the two states attempting most vigorously to cross the proliferation threshold have been Iraq and North Korea.[7] Those states, the "underdogs" of the international system, as Robert O'Neill calls them, were a security worry, including for the Asian region, before the events of 11 September 2001. Their proliferation efforts suggested that the nuclear club was rapidly losing its exclusivity, and that the doctrines of deterrence which tied together the small world of nuclear great powers — in which all had valuable assets that others might threaten to make deterrence work — might not prove a sound basis for a stable and predictable nuclear relationship between two highly asymmetric nuclear powers.

Since September 11, those worries about proliferation have increased, not decreased. The new worries are based upon a strategic calculation that says the types of state that are now most likely to be potential proliferators are also the types of states that would be most likely to offer terrorist groups access to weapons of mass destruction. That fear has highlighted the separation of the nuclear club into those nuclear weapon states who represent the older, traditional, stable, *status-quo*-oriented great powers, and those who represent the "underdogs", having interests in common with, and potential links to, other underdogs of the international system. Keeping nuclear weapons away from that second group, and devaluing the utility of such weapons if the members of that group attain them, are now ranked as high priorities on the security agenda of regional countries in general and the United States in particular.

## THE STATUS OF THE DPRK
## NUCLEAR WEAPON PROGRAMME

So far, U.S. inspection teams have found no weapons of mass destruction in Iraq following the fall of Saddam Hussein. But with the risk of Iraqi WMD proliferation now more definitely contained, attention will turn increasingly to North Korea's programmes. How far have the North Koreans managed to progress down the particularly challenging track of nuclear weapons development? Assessments on this issue must be made cautiously. We do not have full knowledge of all that has taken place. Nor is it in Pyongyang's interest to disclose the full dimensions of their programme while trying simultaneously to "sell" the programme for the highest possible price. But some markers can be laid down.

First, we know the North Koreans initially chose to pursue a plutonium route to nuclear weapons capability. Accordingly, they built and operated at Yongbyon a reactor (in which to irradiate fuel and thereby produce plutonium) and a reprocessing plant (in which they could recover the plutonium from the irradiated fuel). We know that Pyongyang had the opportunity, during 1989, to remove some or all of the fuel covertly from the reactor. We do not know for certain that they did so. We know too that some reprocessing took place at the reprocessing plant, but we are uncertain about the total quantities involved. The North Koreans' May 1992 declaration to the International Atomic Energy Agency (IAEA) acknowledged the separation of a small amount (90 grams) of plutonium in 1990 from damaged reactor fuel, but IAEA's subsequent inspections of the reprocessing facility suggested that more reprocessing had in fact taken place and over a longer time period.[8]

So the initial estimates about North Korean nuclear capability are based upon a set of conjectures. If the North Koreans did move quickly in 1989, to remove all their reactor fuel and reprocess it all, they would have sufficient plutonium for one or possibly two nuclear devices. Did they then, in the early 1990s, have available a workable design for a nuclear weapon, and was the plutonium used to build actual weapons? Here again the evidence is unclear. Some sources suggest that the North Koreans tested an implosion system as long ago as the 1980s.[9] Alternatively, have they managed to build actual weapons since then, given that they reportedly asserted their possession of such a capability in April 2003?[10] Perhaps, but that also is an area where we do not have perfect knowledge. Even the most recent statements may be duplicitous or boastful, intended to strengthen Pyongyang's negotiating position and make Washington more eager to deal with the North's list of demands.

Unfortunately, our factual knowledge of the programme has not materially advanced since the conclusion of the Framework Agreement in 1994. This is not to say that the Agreed Framework did not have other advantages. It did. It contributed to stability on the Korean Peninsula and across the broader region. And it "froze" the North Korean programme under international observation.[11] But access to the reactor's radiological history — which would have clarified what happened at Yongbyon — was never provided to the International Atomic Energy Agency's inspectors, because they were not permitted to study a selected portion of the 8,000 nuclear fuel rods down-loaded from the reactor in 1994.[12] North Korea's decision in late December 2002 to restart the reactor, to expel the IAEA's inspectors, and to recommence construction work on two larger reactors, can only heighten concern that the desire for fissile material counts more strongly with Pyongyang than does the desire for acceptance by the broader international community.

If Pyongyang makes good on its threat to return to the nuclear facilities at Yongbyon, in a worst case scenario the existing, operative reactor is of a size to permit production of sufficient plutonium to produce about five nuclear weapons from each core load of irradiated fuel. If Pyongyang reprocesses all the stored fuel rods in 1994, and those downloaded from the reactor in April 2005, it would gain plutonium sufficient for about another six to seven nuclear weapons, assuming — again — that it has a workable weapon design. Further, completion of the two larger reactors (under construction before the conclusion of the Framework Agreement) would increase substantially the amount of plutonium that could be produced each year. In short, we can reasonably expect the issue of North Korea's nuclear ambitions to become steadily more compelling as time moves on.

The programme to obtain plutonium has also been supplemented recently by a programme to enrich uranium. CIA testimony to the U.S. Congress in November 2002 noted that the North Koreans had begun "seeking centrifuge-related materials in large quantities" in 2001 and, when challenged on this point, Pyongyang admitted to American officials late in 2002 that they did have a programme to produce highly-enriched uranium. As part of that programme, they had obtained electromagnetic isotope separation (EMIS) technology from the Pakistanis. The enrichment programme would offer a different route to nuclear weapons capability, because the North Koreans would be able to use the highly enriched uranium — uranium composed almost exclusively of U-235 isotopes rather than U-238 isotopes — as their fissile material despite the freeze on their plutonium-producing facilities. Active pursuit of this second route to obtain fissile materials reinforces the judgment that construction of nuclear weapons is a high priority for the regime. Further, such pursuit diminishes our confidence in what we know about the overall dimensions of the North's nuclear activities. It is not clear whether the North has built a uranium enrichment facility to employ the EMIS technology. Nor do we know whether the North has made any attempts at actual enrichment. Nor do we know whether the regime has made any effort to build actual weapons using enriched uranium, although such construction is usually thought to be significantly easier than building nuclear weapons from plutonium.[14]

The North Korean effort to develop nuclear weapons has been matched by similar efforts to develop a robust arsenal of ballistic missiles, chemical weapons, and possibly biological weapons. The North's missile development path and testing programme have excited Japan, and raised concerns even in the United States about a growing North Korean capacity to target areas of the United States with ballistic missiles. As one South Korean analyst has observed, the attraction to Pyongyang of weapons of mass destruction is that such weapons help to offset the negative movements in the "correlation of forces" that have made North Koreans worry more about their country's and their regime's longevity.[15] But the North's efforts regarding its weapons of mass destruction programmes, when placed alongside its undiluted commitment to maintaining large conventional forces, suggest that the regime of Kim Jong Il continues to rely heavily upon a policy of force development as one of the central pillars of governance.

## THE NORTH KOREAN DILEMMA

The concern about the development of weapons of mass destruction has traditionally been felt in relation to the top chessboard, for the simple reason that the "club" of those countries wielding weapons of mass destruction has been a comparatively exclusive one. But membership of that club seems to be broadening, and as it does so, the notion of exclusivity is progressively diluted. Iraq, Iran and North Korea — all the members of President Bush's "axis of evil" — have had programmes to develop weapons of mass destruction. In Iraq's case the United Nations, galvanized by aggressive U.S. leadership, in 1992 set up a vigorous inspection regime to curb Baghdad's efforts at proliferation. Perceptions that Iraqi WMD programmes survived despite the best efforts of the inspectors prompted an invasion of Iraq in 2003 by a U.S.-led coalition of countries. But North Korea's programme has evoked a different response. President Bush has said explicitly that he sees the North Korean problem as a diplomatic problems and not a military crisis. Why? Is Pyongyang treated differently because it is seen as a different sort of international actor to Baghdad? Is it treated differently because of the threat it poses to Seoul from the large number of artillery pieces deployed immediately to the north of the Demilitarized Zone (DMZ)? Or is it treated differently because proliferation of WMD is such an idiosyncratic event that each case can be handled differently?

The last of these reasons initially seems compelling. But something must also be said about the first two reasons. In an obvious sense, North Korea does pose a distinctly different sort of threat to that posed by Iraq. Iraq is an Islamic country with a history of form on the actual use of WMD and a record of support for terrorists. Were North Korea to have similar characteristics, it is hard to imagine that international reaction to its latest behaviour would be so diplomatic. But it does not have those characteristics. Rather, it has shown in the past that its proliferation ambitions are negotiable. Still, does that necessarily mean that we can assume that Kim Jong-Il's regime is possessed of a similar delicacy of touch and diplomatic signalling as we saw from his father?

It is entirely plausible to put the events since late 2002 into an interpretive framework that emphasizes the relative poverty of the North Korean regime, and thus, the regime's need to take back off the table cards it had already played in earlier hands in order to be able to play them again. Such an interpretation would in fact be entirely consistent with North Korean behaviour during the early 1990s leading up to the negotiation of the Framework Agreement. The objective of such behaviour now could be to improve the overall terms of the bargain concluded in 1994, or to quicken the tardy fulfilment of U.S. obligations under the Framework Agreement, in particular the construction programme for the two Light Water Reactors and the fuel oil deliveries in the interim. Within this framework, North Korean provocations are perhaps most appropriately seen through a lens that shows simultaneously a shortage of bargaining channels, a paucity of assets with which to bargain, and a determination by the regime to sell the few assets it has for the highest possible price to the most affluent customer.

Following this course successfully requires Pyongyang's direct engagement with Washington. But it would also require Washington to explain such a direct engagement to South Korea, Japan and China, and leave the Americans bearing a weight of expectation that they will be willing to pay the price required to bring about an agreement. So the Six-Party Talks have been a useful vehicle for Washington, allowing the Bush administration to multilateralize a crisis in Asia while its primary attention has been focused on the Middle East. The Six-Party Talks have also been a vehicle for engaging China on the issue of North Korea. Washington's negotiating room is further reduced by the bare-faced character of recent North Korean admissions of previous transgressions, and those not merely limited to the Framework Agreement, but including the kidnapping of Japanese nationals, Pyongyang's withdrawal from the Non-Proliferation Treaty, and the repeated missile firings into the Yellow Sea.

What exactly is Pyongyang's purpose? Are those initiatives meant to cast the regime in a better light internationally or a poorer one, or does Pyongyang simply not care? Is Pyongyang merely indulging in attention-getting behaviour, or is it genuinely signalling a new commitment to develop weapons of mass destruction?[16] Certainly, the regime appears increasingly desperate in its attempts to gain outside attention and concomitant economic benefits, and is actively soliciting closer engagement with both Japan and the United States. It is possible that the continuing poor performance of the North Korean economy has driven its leadership to such an approach. Still, one alternative explanation must also be considered: That Pyongyang saw in the confusion — and weakness — of international policy towards Iraq opportunities for itself to exploit in relation to the peninsula. In short, if the United Nations were prepared to concede Baghdad's "right" to WMD, Pyongyang would have asserted that its own case be considered in identical circumstances. Obviously Pyongyang must now reassess.

A further problem for Washington is the increasing "gap" between its own view of North Korea, and Seoul's view. The North's overtures of desperation do appear to have stuck a chord with South Koreans, suggesting that a generational shift may well be under way in relation to South Korean perceptions of the North. Evidence of that shift can be found in Seoul's increased willingness to build infrastructural links to the North, and the patterns of rallies and demonstrations that can be found periodically on Seoul's streets.[17] Despite Pyongyang's recent behaviour, reconciliation between North and South looks much closer now than it did a decade ago, and the more that prospect looms as a near term possibility, the more it will drive wedges into the existing security linkages between the United States and South Korea. Further, the strains between Washington and Seoul can only be exacerbated by the recent revelations that South Korean nuclear scientists have also been "experimenting" with the production of small quantities of fissile material. The scientists appear to have conducted an experiment in reprocessing plutonium as far back as 1982, and another more recently in 2000, enriching uranium to 77 per cent.[18] Those revelations make it harder to bring pressure to bear upon Pyongyang, because they help paint the North's efforts as defensive in nature, and less anomalous than Washington had hoped to portray them.

## CHINA'S NUCLEAR AND MISSILE PROGRAMMES

The "two-chessboards" nature of the dilemmas that arise from North Korean efforts at nuclear proliferation can also be appreciated by placing those efforts alongside the continued development of the Chinese nuclear arsenal. Such development poses a different set of problems. As noted earlier, the proliferation worries that attend issues of vertical proliferation are essentially different to those surrounding horizontal proliferation. In the case of China, we see the only member of the United Nations Security Council's Permanent Five still continuing to expand the size of its nuclear weapons arsenal. China continues to make technological improvements in that arsenal and threatens to accelerate its nuclear weapon programmes dramatically in response to the ballistic missile defence deployments mooted by the United States — and possibly Japan and Taiwan later. The problem for Beijing is that Western nuclear strategies — and American nuclear strategy in particular — are moving rapidly towards greater acceptance of such ballistic missile defences. The abrogation by the United States of the Anti Ballistic Missile (ABM) treaty in June 2002 has excited Chinese concerns about the possible deployment of a theatre-range ballistic missile shield in Asia able to protect Taiwan from China's missiles deployed on the coast opposite. Such a system would have two problems for Beijing: It would simultaneously dilute Beijing's ability to intimidate Taipei and risk enticing the island's leaders to declare independence from the mainland.

Here we see a complex part of the proliferation puzzle: As continuing horizontal proliferation breaks down the notion of an exclusive nuclear club, established strategic doctrines are coming under greater stress. Ballistic missile defences are intended to compensate for the possible weakening of deterrence in relation to the newest and future nuclear actors. So the primary role of missile defences will be as a hurdle for midgets to jump. But deployment of the Ballistic Missile Defence (BMD) also plays back onto the top chessboard, aggravating great-power relationships and implying that deterrence has a limited life-span there too. Chinese strategists have made clear that their solution to the growth of ballistic missile defences lies in the proliferation of offensive missiles, thereby allowing Chinese leaders capacity to saturate any defensive system and to retain the ability to deter potential adversaries. This strategy is a sound one. It is essentially the strategy that the United States and Russia would use to overcome either side's deployment of a limited ballistic missile defence system, and exploits the technological fact that — at least for the next few decades — missile defences are not going to be effective against large-scale offensive attacks. So the region should be prepared to see a continuing expansion of Chinese ballistic missile deployments, offering Beijing greater capacity at both theatre and inter-continental ranges. But such expansion is a problem of a different order to those posed by North Korean moves to acquire even a comparatively small arsenal of nuclear weapons, precisely because of the differences between China and North Korea in the current international order.

## CONVENTIONAL WEAPONS PROLIFERATION

Conventional weapons modernization programmes are always of interest to strategists. For one thing, they have the potential to escalate into competitive arms races. Despite recent research which tends to weaken the supposed causative link between arms racing and the onset of war,[19] arms races are worrying. The Asian theatre provides considerable opportunities for such competitions, host as it is to eight of the world's ten largest armies, and three of its most volatile flashpoints: The Korean Peninsula, China-Taiwan, and Kashmir.

During the 1990s, concerns about potential Asian arms races were at their zenith. Asian economic growth left many countries well-placed to exploit the buyer's market in weapons acquisitions that followed the end of the Cold War. Regional analysts began to argue over how best to interpret the broad pattern of arms purchases. Was the region experiencing an arms race? Or were purchases better understood in terms of simple defence force modernization and the performance of new functions, such as the monitoring of new maritime economic zones?[20] Certainly some of the most important purchases were those that enhanced naval and air capabilities, but analysts have similarly disagreed about the significance of even those purchases. Some suggest that the new weaponry should be seen not merely in operational terms but as symbols of state strength, because of the particular resonance that symbolism has in Asia.[21] Others have suggested that the growth of air and naval power is actually a positive development, reflecting the growth of mature, liberal, and affluent states within the region, less reliant upon armies for repression of their domestic populations.[22] Eric Heginbotham has argued that a correlation exists between the rise of liberal political leaders within Asian countries, supported by the naval services as distinct political actors, and an increasing regional expenditure upon maritime capabilities.[23] While such positive interpretations of arms purchases are obviously possible, they need to be balanced against other interpretations, including those which stress the overall growth of capabilities and the frictions that might arise amongst a community of "maritime adolescents".[24]

Currently, worries about the proliferation of conventional weapons in East Asia are concentrated particularly around the pace of Chinese arms modernization. This focus is not caused by a paranoid fantasy about the nature and scope of Chinese strategic ambition, but by the slowing of most other regional arms modernization programmes in the wake of the 1997 Asian financial crisis, notably in Southeast Asia. Although several regional countries have again returned to more vigorous acquisition programmes, that slowing has made the continuing progress of China's modernization programme stand out rather more starkly, and encouraged a greater degree of analytical concentration on the possible implications of that effort. The resilience of Chinese programme has also underlined the unpalatable fact that regional concerns about arms acquisitions are not limited solely to those occasions in which we can detect an actual "arms race" between two or more competitors.

The usual view of Chinese military modernization is that the programme must be seen in terms of its problems and limitations as well as its successes and opportunities.[25] Chinese military forces have been characterized for decades by what Russell Howard has called "short arms and slow legs".[26] The forces lack power projection capabilities, and China itself remains much more clearly a land-based power than a maritime one. But it is important to put even that assessment within a larger comparative context. At a time when most ASEAN military modernization — Singapore might be the exception — has been all but stalled, China's military modernization has been steadily shifting the conventional military balance between China and its immediate neighbours. Further, it is too blasé to assert that Chinese forces remain ill-equipped to undertake key missions, such as launching an attack on Taiwan. The fact that their forces are ill-equipped might not deter Chinese political leaders from using them for such options if they believed that such an option was vital to China's national interests.[27]

So a key issue for regional strategists must be, "what standards do we use to judge Chinese arms modernization?" Comparison of Chinese conventional forces against Western counterparts would still leave the Chinese services looking dated and obsolete. But comparing them to the forces of countries closer to China's borders makes them look more potent. In the years ahead, they will look stronger still.

In relation to Taiwan, Chinese arms modernization has a slow but threatening quality to it. This does not mean that China can achieve military dominance over Taiwan any time soon. Planning, purchasing and introducing major weapons systems takes time, even for advanced military powers. And gaining and maintaining air superiority over the Taiwan Straits, or naval dominance on or under it, will remain beyond Beijing's capabilities for a long time yet. But Beijing is making considerable effort to be able to exert military options across the strait despite that weakness. In particular the deployment of several hundred medium-range ballistic missiles along the Chinese coastline opposite Taiwan is intended to convey a warning message to leaders in Taipei.

## ADDRESSING THE THREATS

Some of the most serious strategic thinking in coming years will be aimed at addressing the particular concerns that arise from continuing weapons proliferation. Finding solutions to those problems was not easy in the pre-September 11 world, when Asian countries and Western alliance partners focused almost exclusively upon the top chessboard. The emergence of a new series of threats posing a different genre of threat has only served to highlight the divisions over the appropriate response now to be made to pre-existing threats. The unfortunate fact is that WMD and conventional weapon proliferation is continuing as smaller and smaller groups acquire a war-fighting capability, and a capacity to wreak destruction on a scale commensurate with their ambitions. September 11 thus added more problems to the international security planner's agenda without resolving any of the existing problems.

Addressing the issue of WMD proliferation will be a major focus of regional security concerns in coming years. The attack on Iraq by the coalition of the willing in March 2003 shows that some states are prepared to countenance the use of force to address those new concerns. Such an attack upon North Korea for the purposes of effecting regime change there would be more difficult. Even a limited attack upon Yongbyon would stir up a host of new problems. So it is no surprise that some prominent regional figures, especially in South Korea and Japan, have begun to claim that the key issue for countries in the Asian region will increasingly be how to live with a nuclear-armed North Korea, rather than to how to disarm it. [28]

If North Korea cannot be deflected from pursuit if WMD, there is even less chance that China's pursuit of a better and more capable nuclear and conventional arsenal can be halted. Beijing's leaders still believe that political influence goes hand in hand with military strength, and will continue the steady expansion of China's military capability regardless of what other actors do. The foreshadowed U.S. ballistic missile defence deployments at both the regional and global level will make the Chinese pay particular attention to the size of their offensive missile forces and encourage them to build an arsenal big enough to overwhelm such defences, because by doing that Beijing can be assured that China will remain a great power on the top chessboard of international security, rather than slipping down amongst the second chessboard midgets.

## CONCLUSION

The traditional issues of force and power continue to be a focus for strategic analysis in the post-September 11 world. Although the definition of security is being tested by the adoption of wider and deeper notions of security — notions that point to the growing importance of non-military threats, and threats to actors other than states — the importance of traditional grand strategy is not waning. Asia's security problems have been compounded by the emergence of new threats, not least because they cause us to see some of the old threats in new ways. The issue of WMD proliferation, in particular the horizontal proliferation side of the problem, has taken on new urgency.

## NOTES

1. See, for example, Brian Jenkins, *International Terrorism: A New Mode of Conflict* (Santa Monica: California Seminar on Arms Control and Foreign Policy, 1975) and Martin van Creveld, *The Transformation of War* (New York: The Free Press, 1991).
2. Zbigniew Brzezinski, *The Grand Chessboard* (New York: Basic Books, 1997).
3. G John Ikenberry, "America's Imperial Ambition", *Foreign Affairs* 81, no. 5 (2002): 44–60.
4. Joseph Cirincione, *Deadly Arsenals: Tracking Weapons of Mass Destruction* (Washington DC: Carnegie Endowment for International Peace, 2002), p. 35: "By far the most costly, complicated and observable part of producing a nuclear weapon is acquiring sufficient amounts of weapons-usable nuclear materials from which the explosive power of nuclear weapons derives."
5. Scott Sagan, "Why do States Build Nuclear Weapons? Three Models in Search of a Bomb", *International Security* 21, no. 3 (1996): 54–86.
6. Robert O'Neill, "The Weapons of the Underdog", in *Alternative Nuclear Futures: The Role of Nuclear Weapons in the Post-Cold War World*, edited by John Baylis and Robert O'Neill (Oxford: Oxford University Press, 2000), pp. 191–208.
7. Joseph Cirincione, op. cit., p. 7.
8. Joel Wit, Daniel Poneman and Robert Gallucci, *Going Critical: The First North Korean Nuclear Crisis* (Washington DC: Brookings Institution Press, 2004) p. 13.
9. Joel Wit, et al., op. cit., p. 6.
10. Li Gun, a North Korean deputy foreign minister and a delegate to talks held in Beijing with American and the Chinese officials, asserted that North Korea already had nuclear weapons, and that the issue at stake was whether it should begin testing the weapons or exporting them. See Joseph Kahn, "North Korea may be Angering its Only Ally", *New York Times*, 26 April 2003, p. A13.
11. Joel Wit, et al., op. cit., p. 372.
12. Joseph Cirincione, op. cit., p. 246.
13. Larry Niksch, *North Korea's Nuclear Weapons Program: Issue Brief for Congress* (Washington D.C.: Congressional Research Service, 2003).
14. Joel Wit, et al., op. cit., pp. 372, 459. Enriched uranium enables weapons designers to utilize a simple "gun"-type assembly, rather than a more complicated implosion device.
15. Chung Min Lee, "North Korean Missiles: Strategic Implications and Policy Responses", *The Pacific Review* 14, no. 1 (2001): 85–120.

16. A good treatment of the competing interpretations of the North Korean regime is available in the book by Victor Cha and David Kang, *Nuclear North Korea: A Debate on Engagement Strategies* (New York: Columbia University Press, 2003).
17. Keith Bradsher, "Rallies in Seoul Differ on U.S., Highlighting a Generation Gap", article published on *New York Times* website at <www.nytimes.com>, 2 March 2003.
18. Dafna Linzer, "South Korea Nuclear Project Detailed", *The Washington Post*, 12 September 2004, p. A24, A28.
19. Susan Sample, "Military Build-ups: Arming and War", in *What Do We Know About War?*, edited by John Vasquez (Lanham: Rowan and Littlefield, 2000), pp. 165–95.
20. Typical of the many good analyses of this issue is the article by Amitav Acharya, "An Arms Race in Southeast Asia?", in *The Evolving Pacific Power Structure*, edited by Derek da Cunha (Singapore: ISEAS, 1996) pp. 83–88.
21. Derek da Cunha, "Asia-Pacific Security: Strategic Trends and Military Developments" in *Southeast Asian Perspectives on Security*, edited by Derek da Cunha (Singapore: ISEAS, 2000) pp. 20–34, at p. 30.
22. Sheldon Simon, "Asian Armed Forces: Internal and External Tasks and Capabilities", in *The Many Faces of Asian Security*, edited by Sheldon Simed (Lanham, Maryland: Rowman and Littlefield Publishers, 2001) pp. 49–70.
23. Eric Heginbotham, "The Fall and Rise of Navies in East Asia: Military Organizations, Domestic Politics and Grand Strategy", *International Security* 27, no. 2 (2002): 86–125.
24. See, for example, the chapter by Jean-Marc Blanchard, "Maritime Issues in Asia: The Problem of Adolescence", in *Asian Security: Instrumental and Normative Features*, edited by Muthiah Alagappa (Stanford, California: Stanford University Press, 2003).
25. David Shambaugh, *Modernizing China's Military: Progress, Problems and Prospects* (Berkeley: University of California Press, 2002).
26. Russell Howard, *The Chinese People's Liberation Army: "Short Arms and Slow Legs"* (Washington D.C.: Institute for National and Strategic Studies, 1999), Occasional Paper 28.
27. Mark Burles and Abram Shulsky, *Patterns in China's Use of Force: Evidence from History and Doctrinal Writings* (Santa Monica: RAND, 2000).
28. Doug Struck and Glenn Kessler, "Foes Giving in to North Korea's Nuclear Aims", *Washington Post*, 5 March 2003, p. A01.

Chapter Eight

# Conflicts over Natural Resources and the Environment

Clevo Wilson and Clem Tisdell

## INTRODUCTION

The need for natural resources has given rise to conflicts in many parts of the world.[1] As the World Commission on Environment and Development points out, "nations have often fought to assert or resist control over war materials, energy supplies, land, river basins, sea passages and other key environmental resources".[2] Malaquias[3] observes that it is "not accidental that some of the nastiest wars in Africa are being fought in countries richly endowed with natural resources". While there are no parallel cases in East and Southeast Asia to match the intensity and magnitude of the conflicts in some African countries, many conflicts have arisen either directly or indirectly over the control and use of natural resources.[4] The concentration of rich natural resources in outlying parts of countries, especially in large countries with weak provincial administrative structures, can be a major contributor to calls for autonomy or breakaway in some countries.

Frequently, political and social disagreements about the sharing of economic benefits of natural resources assume major significance and often exacerbate existing religious, cultural and social tensions. Security of nations may be undermined by internal or external armed conflict or by terrorism, as well as by the weakening of economic systems, thereby making nations more vulnerable to attack. Geographic cultural diversity (for example, of ethnic minorities) and geographical inequality in natural resources available within countries and in different regions add to tensions. Furthermore, more economically developed regions and nations, to sustain economic growth, tend to exploit the natural resources and environments of less developed regions and nations.[5] Perhaps as a precaution against attack from neighbours, small but resource rich countries such as Brunei spend a larger percentage of their GDP on defense than some of the larger countries such as China, Indonesia and Malaysia.[6]

This chapter discusses the security issues and conflicts (both external and internal) over natural resources and the environment in East and Southeast Asia. The first section briefly discusses the resources of the region. A map locates some of the natural resources discussed. The second section deals with the conflicts related to the use and control of natural resources in the region. The nature and the magnitude of the conflicts between and within countries are dealt with. The third section discusses the responses and possible remedial action for these conflicts and the fourth section concludes the chapter.

## OVERVIEW OF SOURCES OF RESOURCE CONFLICT

Domestic and international tensions, disputes and conflicts arise over how to manage and distribute a range of natural resources including oil, natural gas, mineral resources, forests, and irrigation water. Conflicts have also arisen from the exploitation of marine resources. Some of the disputes over natural resources and the environment are straightforward zero-sum conflicts while others are far more complex.

Many countries in the East and Southeast Asian region share common borders and this inevitably leads to the need to share certain resources, such as water. As a result, tensions and even conflicts can arise in the distribution of these resources. To take the example of water and inland fisheries, tensions may occur due to over-exploitation, the building of barriers such as dams, and pollution due to agriculture.[7] Other trans-boundary problems arise from air pollution resulting from forest fires, burning of fossil fuel and sandstorms arising from deforestation.[8]

Similar problems exist in the sharing of maritime resources in the region.[9] All countries in the East and Southeast Asian region (except Laos and Mongolia) are bordered by the sea and their maritime boundary and

Exclusive Economic Zone claims in many instances overlap.[10, 11] In such situations disputes arise in sharing resources. Some countries also dispute the control of maritime territories such as islands, reefs and coral cays.[12] The natural resources within the maritime areas of East and Southeast Asia are large and valuable and cover the Indian and Pacific oceans. The potential economic value of new mineral discoveries has a maritime dimension, for some of the off-shore zone claims include oil and natural gas.[13] The desire to exploit these potentially lucrative resources has led some countries to claim control using historical arguments[14] and "the potential [for conflict] is already apparent".[15]

Apart from oil and natural gas, the East and Southeast Asian region is also rich in fisheries. Over-exploitation of fishing resources has led to a depletion of traditional fishing grounds across East and Southeast Asia and hence more pressure is been exerted on the resources in the South China Sea where fish stocks are considered plentiful.[16] Competition leading to disputes over these declining transboundary resources is inevitable. Moreover, poaching by vessels from within these countries is a common problem and several major stand-offs and clashes are reported each year with consequent ill will towards the poachers' home governments.[17] As Dupont[18] points out "maritime incidents involving fish resources are linked to Northeast Asia's most intractable territorial disputes".

Another issue is the pollution of the seas. Because of the large area of the sea, some countries use it as a free dumping ground for dangerous wastes such as nuclear materials. An extreme example is Russia's dumping of nuclear waste in the Sea of Japan.[19] The region is also of strategic importance for commerce and military purposes, not only to the countries in the region, but also to the major powers outside the region.

As much as the issues involved between countries are complex, so too are the conflicts within countries that are connected with the use of natural resources and the environment. Although these conflicts are as violent as those arising between nations, the nature of the conflicts is different. Terrorism, civil war and separatism are some of the distinguishing features in conflicts within countries. These are consequences of the fact that East and Southeast Asia are home to many minority groups. Within the region there are more than 300 ethnic groups speaking roughly 240 languages.[20] Although conflicts among such diverse groups are well known, inequalities in benefits from natural resources exacerbate pre-existing cultural and social tensions and fuel calls for secession of provinces or regions from the central governments. Some examples that can be cited in Indonesia include

Aceh, Papua and Kalimantan. Corruption by politicians and bureaucrats from the dominant ethnic groups magnify the tensions.[21]

Desire for control over natural resources can also give rise to violence by those who extract them. Large-scale exploitation of resources not only displaces indigenous people but also creates tensions between them and the central authorities. Some of the mountainous regions' inhabitants grow opium poppies which are illegal but an irresistible source of lucrative trade in the area. The money is not only used by money launderers, but is a potential and an attractive source of revenue for rebel organizations such as the Gerakan Aceh Merdeka (GAM) and perhaps even terrorist organizations.[22] This is especially so when governments after September 11 are making an increased effort to cut off the conventional sources of terrorist funding such as from diaspora contributors and money given by some governments to the political fronts and allied organizations of some terrorist organizations.

Not surprisingly in view of the varied geography of the region, neighbouring countries have adopted sharply differing constitutions and economic systems. For instance there are military regimes (for example, Myanmar), communism (for example, North Korea), a form of monarchy (Brunei), guided democracies (for example, Singapore) and democratically elected multi-party governments (or example, Japan, South Korea, Thailand). The economic systems vary from centrally planned (for example, North Korea) to fully market-based capitalist economies (for example, Singapore and Taiwan). The religions range from countries or regions that are intensely Islamic (for example, Aceh) to Christians (for example, East Timor, most parts of the Philippines) to tribal beliefs and faiths (for example, Papua). Some of the differences between these countries, as a result of religious, ideological, and economic systems, could exacerbate existing resource-use tensions. In such situations the larger or better institutionalized groups normally prevail by using state power, but leave a legacy of bitterness among those who do not enjoy equal access to political assets. This can happen both between and within countries.

Although many conflicts can be identified as being directly or indirectly linked to the control and use of resources, other conflicts appear to overshadow resource-linked conflicts in the region, such as terrorism and the events of September 11. Furthermore, the tensions between the People's Republic of China and Taiwan from time to time, the ongoing dispute in the Korean Peninsula, and inter-ethnic strife in Myanmar have been inherited from the Pacific War and decolonization.

Resource-related conflicts have taken a back seat in these conflicts, though retaining the potential to exacerbate them, thus further destabilizing the region. Thus resource disputes remain salient insofar as conflicts arising from the control of resources and their exploitation could destabilize a country or countries or even the entire region as a whole. Such conflicts could also slow down the economic growth of the region and increase unemployment. These events could in turn have a reactive effect in the countries concerned and the region and fuel unrest. If unrest erupts into conflict, a refugee crisis could spill over into neighbouring countries, or as far away as Australia, and worsen regional inter-governmental relations.

## MAJOR NATURAL RESOURCES OF THE REGION

East and Southeast Asia are rich in mineral and energy resources, especially petroleum, natural gas, coal, tin, bauxite, gold, silver, uranium, copper, lead and zinc.[23] For instance, the largest concentration of petroleum and natural gas in the region occurs in China, Brunei, Indonesia and Malaysia.[24] Although none of the countries in East or Southeast Asia fall into the category of the world's top ten net exporters of energy,[25] Brunei, Indonesia and Malaysia are major net exporters of oil and gas in the region.[26] Furthermore, significant offshore oil and gas reserves have been discovered off the coasts of Indonesia, East Timor, Brunei, Malaysia and China[27] since major offshore oil exploration began in the region in the 1960s. Many more reserves could be discovered in the future as technology and economic factors aid such exploration.[28] For the major oil and gas producing countries in the region such as Indonesia, Brunei and Malaysia, petroleum has become a major source of domestic revenue as well as foreign exchange earnings.[29] For example, Brunei obtains as much as 90 per cent of its revenues from oil and natural gas exports.[30] China also has large reserves of coal, especially in the northern province of Shaanxi, which contains approximately 30 per cent of China's proven reserves.[31] Malaysia is well known for its large tin deposits and Indonesia is rich in bauxite.[32] The Southeast Asian region is also rich in gem stones, mainly in sapphires and rubies.[33]

Furthermore, the region produces some of the world's most important renewable natural resources such as natural rubber, palm-oil, copra and other coconut products. For example, the Philippines, Brunei, Indonesia Thailand, Malaysia and Singapore account for 82 per cent of the world's production of natural rubber, 70 per cent of copra and other coconut products and 56 per cent of palm oil.[34]

Apart from these resources, Southeast Asia contains significant tropical rainforests valuable for timber and medicinal plants.[35] Three countries in the region, namely the Philippines, Indonesia and Malaysia, accounted for approximately 66 per cent of worldwide exports of hardwoods in the past.[36] However, tropical deforestation has been widespread in the region in the last few decades, especially in the Philippines and Indonesia.[37] The region is also watered by many major rivers such as the Mekong which is shared by six countries.[38] The fresh water rivers such as the Mekong, Yellow and Yangtze provide water to large tracts of agricultural land and are used for inland transport and are important for fisheries. The seas surrounding these countries, apart from being rich in oil and natural gas and other mineral reserves, offer abundant fisheries. For example, Thailand and the Philippines are major tuna exporters.[39]

Natural resources play a significant role in the economic growth of these countries.[40] In the case of countries such as Indonesia, outlying provinces rich in natural resources contribute significantly to the national economy. Furthermore, because of the close proximity of some countries to each other (for example, common borders), some resources such as river water and other transboundary resources such as fisheries have to be divided or shared. Some countries are less endowed with natural resources and hence are dependent on renewable resources such as water, in competition with neighbouring countries. A good example is Singapore's dependence on Malaysian freshwater.[41] On the other hand, some countries such as Brunei, although small, are rich in natural resources such as oil and natural gas.

Having inventoried the region's natural resources, in the next section we discuss some of the conflicts or issues that have the potential to lead to larger conflicts or create tensions in the East and Southeast Asian region. Since each conflict that arises between countries and within countries has unique or distinguishing features, we discuss them separately under appropriate sub-headings.

## ECONOMIC MISDISTRIBUTION AND CONFLICTS ARISING FROM THE USE OF NATURAL RESOURCES AND THE ENVIRONMENT

Many conflicts have taken place in this region in the post-World War II period. These have been both within and between nations. Most inter-state conflicts between nations have been territorial disputes while the internal conflicts have been due to diverse issues ranging from the awkward geography of some countries, differences in political ideology, ethnicity, and distinct religions and languages.

It is not possible to discuss all these conflicts and the underlying issues, so in keeping with the theme of the chapter we examine only those that are directly or indirectly attributable to the use of or the existence of natural resources and the environment, both within and between countries. In the case of internal conflicts, the distinguishing feature in most cases is the misdistribution of wealth created by natural resources exploitation. In the case of inter-state conflicts, the striking feature in most instances is conflicts arising over the control of resources. Current history shows that conflicts within countries have become far more common than conflicts between countries. In certain cases, tensions have been ongoing for decades, if not for centuries. This should not be surprising inasmuch as resource scarcity conflicts were analysed two centuries ago by Malthus.[42]

## INTER-STATE CONFLICT

Given the large size of the region with many of the countries sharing common borders, both land and marine, sharing resources is a complex activity and in such cases conflicts are inevitable between neighbours and rivals. In many cases larger countries and those that are more economically affluent and politically dominant are likely to have access to more resources than smaller and weaker countries. Furthermore, weaker countries depend on larger countries for their economic survival, trade and security, so may find it imprudent to challenge misdistribution. In such cases many disputes go unnoticed or unresolved, although internal tensions may fester.

One of the most sensitive and recurring resource-related issues in the East and Southeast Asian region involves the territorial dispute over a collection of more than 200 islands, atolls, reefs and shoals in the South China Sea (see Figure 8.1). The islands are claimed in whole or part by four small-to-medium countries of the sub-region, namely Vietnam, Malaysia, Brunei and the Philippines, but also by the giant People's Republic of China and rival Taiwan from north of the sub-region.[43] The claims are based in part on the definition of the Exclusive Economic Zone which in some places overlap. While some of the claims over this territory such as Brunei's are based on the Exclusive Economic Zone concept, those of others such as China's and Taiwan's have been based on historical grounds.[44] As a result the issues have become complicated and negotiations and flare-ups have alternated

## Figure 8.1
## Map Showing Countries of East and Southeast Asia and the Location of Major Resources of the Region

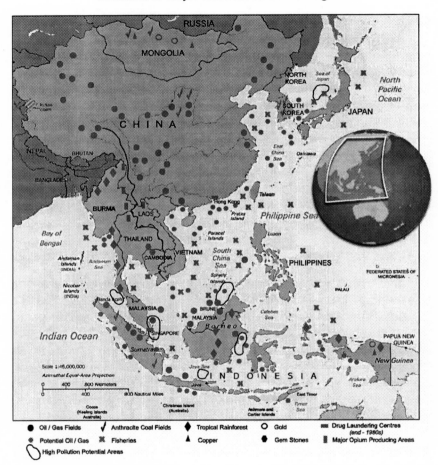

| ● Oil / Gas Fields | ✓ Anthracite Coal Fields | ◆ Tropical Rainforest | ○ Gold | ▨ Drug Laundering Centres (end - 1980s) |
| ◉ Potential Oil / Gas | ✖ Fisheries | ▲ Copper | ◆ Gem Stones | ▌ Major Opium Producing Areas |
| ◯ High Pollution Potential Areas | | | | |

*Source:* The map of the region has been adapted from *The Taiwan Documents Project* (2003). The location of resources has been taken from the following sources: Offshore oil and gas — various sources: op. cit., Ref. 7, p. 100; Harrison, S. (1977) *China, Oil and Asia: Conflict Ahead?* (N.Y.: Columbia University Press, pp. 49–56). Onshore oil and gas — various sources: op. cit., Ref. 16, p. 172; Bartke, W. (1977) *Oil in the People's Republic of China. Industry Structure, Production, Exports* (London: C. Hurst and Company, p. 15); Harrison, S. (1977) *China, Oil and Asia: Conflict Ahead?* op. cit., pp. 49–56, p. 48. Fisheries — op. cit., Ref. 7, pp. 112, 131. Oil pollution and tank discharges — op. cit., Ref. 7, p. 123. Tropical rainforests — Kurian, G.T. (ed.) (1992) *Atlas of the Third World,* second edition (N.Y.: Facts on File Ltd). Coalfields — ibid., Ref. 16, p. 172. Gold and copper — ibid. Major opium producing areas and drug laundering centres: End 1980s — ibid., Ref. 19, p. 86. Note: Location of marked resources in the region is only approximate.

for a decade. Although the natural resources of the disputed zone have been evaluated by some authors as little more than bird droppings and shelters for fishermen,[45] the zone is in fact potentially rich in oil and natural gas deposits apart from the rich marine resources.[46] The area is also a strategically important sea lane for commercial ships as well as for the security of big trading and maritime powers like the United States and Japan.[47] There has been tension between several countries in the region over the islands, mainly involving China, and sporadic military action has taken place since the 1950s.[48, 49] For example, China and Vietnam fought a short battle in the Paracels in 1974 and in 1995 China stationed armed vessels in the Philippine-claimed Mischief (Panganiban) Reef. Many other disputes have been recorded over this large collection of islands[50] as well as other unresolved maritime boundary claims to areas with high petroleum potential.[51] The potential is high for armed clashes to arise from disagreements over property rights in the course of development of these resources.[52]

Because of the large potential for oil and gas discoveries and the rich marine resources in the South China Sea, the disputes are likely to persist or even grow, depending on the proved value of the resources. If China, despite the fact that it has signed a Code of Conduct and acceded to the ASEAN Treaty of Amity and Cooperation (TAC) in 2002, will continue to consider expanding its presence in the South China Sea and if smaller states confront such moves, it could lead to a larger conflict. Until now, although the claims are contentious and important to the countries involved, no serious conflict has erupted and hence the dispute has kept a low profile. Nevertheless the disputes have strained relations between some countries and this could limit economic cooperation and outside investment, thus retard economic growth in the region. There is also a possibility that outside powers may get involved given the area's strategic importance for commercial and military purposes, with a risk of escalation.

Apart from the offshore oil and gas conflicts and the strategic importance to some countries of the seas, the sharing of transboundary resources between countries is a major challenge that from time to time precipitates conflicts. All countries, except land-locked Laos and Mongolia, engage in traditional fishing in the region and it is an important economic activity where generous incentives have been provided by the respective governments to operate in the areas.[53] However, except in the South China Sea, in many parts of the region over-fishing has severely depleted fishing stocks, and as a result many countries' fishermen compete for the fish stocks in the region, often straying into neighbouring countries' territorial waters.[54] Such disputes are frequent and in certain instances they flare into bigger conflicts.[55]

Another resource issue that could lead to an armed conflict between nations is that of the control and use of water resources in the region. Sharing of the Mekong river which supports one of the biggest inland fisheries between six countries (see Figure 8.1) is an issue that has already led to much discussion between the countries involved. The Mekong is not only an important river for fisheries with an annual income of US$1.4 billion, but is also an important source of water for agriculture, tourism, hydroelectricity, transport and freshwater fisheries. Millions of people along this stretch of the river depend on the Mekong for their livelihood. Any unequal distribution of this resource or polluting of the river could trigger a major conflict.[56] Excessive use of water by one or more upstream nations could create water shortages in downstream countries as well as affect agriculture, not only through a shortage of water but also through salt water intrusion. The recreational use of the river and the water available for generation of electricity would also be jeopardized. The health of many thousands, if not millions, of downstream inhabitants could be adversely affected if water is polluted. There is already concern in Vietnam that Thailand is drawing excessive amounts of water during the dry season thus increasing the intrusion of salt water from the sea into the Mekong delta region of southern Vietnam which is its main rice growing area.[57] However, this dispute has been resolved by the intervention of the United Nations Development Programme (UNDP) and the subsequent signing of the Mekong Agreement in 1995.[58]

Another water conflict involves Singapore and Malaysia. Singapore, because of its small size, and sandy geography, and location at the end of the Malay Peninsula, is dependent on Malaysia for half of its water needs.[59] The supply of water to Singapore is guaranteed by two agreements signed in 1961 and 1962.[60] But as water becomes scarce, especially during dry periods and when the demand for water increases, it could become an even more valuable commodity. Reduced water supply has the potential to slow down Singapore's economic growth. If there were to be a unilateral abrogation of the agreements by Malaysia, or an extortionate demand for more payment, then the potential for armed conflict between Singapore and Malaysia would rise. At present, such a conflict is unlikely, but to avert one it is important that friendly relations prevail between the two nations.

The close proximity of many countries in the region sharing common borders and the sea results in several negative externalities arising from the use of natural resources. Furthermore, illegal use of territory or resources could also occur. This has the potential to lead to conflicts if appropriate action is not taken, or compensation provided to affected parties. Maddock[61] notes that Japan and South Korea have raised concerns because the Sea of Japan is used by Russia to dump low-level nuclear waste. Nuclear waste can not only affect the health of the people but could pollute valuable fishery resources, as well as affect the recreational use of the sea. Siddayao[62] has also pointed to the potential problem of pollution arising from offshore oil fields which could affect recreational as well as wildlife and the fisheries sector. There is also considerable oil pollution from ship discharges[63] due to the region being an important international shipping lane. The pollution no doubt could affect the rich fishing and prawn grounds of the region (see Figure 8.1).

Air pollution affecting neighbouring countries is another major issue in the region. For instance, half of measured sulphur dioxide depositions in Japan is believed to originate from China and to a lesser extent from South Korea.[64] Forest fires in Indonesia in 1997 were responsible for the region's worst smoke haze, affecting Malaysia, Singapore, Brunei and Southern Thailand. The economic damage and loss of tourism revenues were estimated to be very high.[65] There was much pressure exerted on Indonesia by the neighbouring countries to curtail the fires. This is another example of transboundry environmental problems that arise because of the close proximity of the countries in the region.

## INTERNAL CONFLICTS

Conflicts over resources within countries, too, can lead to calls for autonomy or separation from the central government, especially when there is economic inequality in the distribution of resources. This is especially so when the countries are large and have weak central governments relative to local power structures.[66] The existence of a multitude of ethnic minorities with diverse languages and religious beliefs fuel such separatist issues. Corruption by politicians and bureaucrats aggravate the problems even further. Many conflicts have arisen in the region over the central government's reluctance to pass on the benefits to the provinces. As a result there is the danger of armed conflict destabilizing governments or of provinces or regions breaking away from the centre. The breakaway mentality springs from the notion that such a breakaway could self-finance separation because of the potential revenues that could be generated from natural resources in addition to other issues.

A current example is the fossil fuel-rich province of Aceh on the northern tip of Sumatra (see Figure 8.1) which is also strategically located between the Indian Ocean by the Straits of Malacca.[67] Aceh is one of the resource-rich provinces of Indonesia whose resources support the Indonesian economy.[68] The unequal distribution of revenues has fuelled the separation issue in Aceh, which has become a major conflict in recent times. Since the discovery of large deposits of oil and natural gas, Aceh was the fastest growing province in Indonesia in the 1970s and 1980s.[69] According to Ricklefs[70] it contributed as much as between US$2 billion and US$3 billion annually to the Indonesian economy. Aceh was in fact the fourth largest contributor to Indonesia's economy after the resource rich provinces of Riau, West Papua and East Kalimantan.[71] Despite the large transfer of wealth from Aceh to the Indonesian treasury, the Acehnese themselves did not benefit from their own resources.[72] For example, according to Ali,[73] Aceh received only around US$82 million annually from the central government for its economic development and very few Acehnese have been employed by the mining companies.[74] Despite its rich mineral resources Aceh remains one of the underdeveloped provinces of Indonesia.[75]

High unemployment and low economic growth can also contribute to armed conflict and terrorism. The economic issues together with political, religious and historical events in Aceh have fractured Aceh's relationship with the Indonesian Government and given increased impetus to the Free Aceh Movement (GAM) resulting in increased armed conflict and violence. The unequal distribution of economic resources has added weight to the call by the Free Aceh Movement to revert back to an independent state, similar to what existed before the occupation of Aceh by the Dutch in 1873. The abundant mineral resources and the example of the small but rich kingdom of Brunei gave credence to the belief that a small but independent Aceh could be prosperous.[76]

The recently ended armed conflict was not only a burden on the Indonesian economy, but was also weakening the economic system and destabilizing other provinces in Indonesia and it had implications for neighbouring countries. Other resource-rich provinces of Indonesia which generate substantial sums of revenue for the Indonesian economy could turn violent if resources are not more equally distributed by the central government. For example, East Kalimantan and Papua for many years have been seeking a larger share of resources from the Indonesian central government because of the huge inequality that exists in the distribution of revenues.[77] It has been estimated that East Kalimantan contributes as much as Rp70 trillion (approximately US$7.6 billion) each year to the Indonesian economy but receives only Rp6.7 trillion (approximately US$725 million) a year in return, less than 10 per cent.[78] Such unequal redistribution of revenues alone is sufficient to spark calls for separation which can turn into violent conflicts, as happened in Aceh, and could happen in Papua, where secessionist movements are growing.[79]

The existence of a large population of diverse ethnic groups in one country spilling across into neighbouring lands can result in conflicts over control of resources and their use. Natural resources could be the dominant or significant factor in such disputes, although in many cases the conflicts are complex. The East and Southeast Asian countries are comprised of more than 300 ethnic groups speaking roughly 240 languages. Half of the population of over 200 million belong to ethnic minorities or indigenous peoples.[80] In such situations the control or attempts to control the use of resources by a few dominant ethnic groups could not only lead to an unequal distribution of resources, but also lead to armed resistance and conflict from minority groups. There are many instances in this region where conflicts have arisen over the use of resources. Such conflicts have the potential to spread to other regions and destabilize governments and possibly even regions.

In the Philippines, for example, large-scale mechanized mining activities of companies, often involving open-cut mines, have disrupted the small-scale manual gold, copper and other mineral mining activities of indigenous peoples such as the Igorots.[81] This led to political unrest and sporadic conflict because large-scale mechanized mining has not only depressed the livelihood of indigenous people but also destroyed their natural environments and their traditional lands. Furthermore, in a move to accelerate economic growth and increase export earnings, the Philippines government in the mid-1990s on the advice of the World Bank passed an act that liberalized mining operations in the country. This legislation has created large mining opportunities for open-cut bauxite mining to multinational companies such as Rio Tinto Zinc (RTZ). This has already created tensions among indigenous people, such as the *Subanen,* living in Mindanao's Zamboanga Peninsula.[82] There are instances where dissatisfaction of local owners in the sharing of natural resources and the destruction of the environment have intensified the struggle of terrorist-separatist organizations in some countries. For example, Bougainville

Copper Pty Ltd's mining triggered the formation of and attacks by the Bougainville Revolutionary Army, which had its origins of dissatisfactions among local landowners in the sharing of incomes and the extent of environmental damage caused by the mining.[83]

In Indonesia, too, indigenous people and minorities in certain provinces have been affected as a result of resource exploitation. A good example is the effects of timber merchants (for example, Javanese business interests and transmigrants) harvesting tropical forests in Kalimantan. Illegal logging is a highly organized crime in many parts of Southeast Asia. Not only are such logging practices unsustainable, but such operations are also blamed for forest fires that create serious air pollution in parts of Southeast Asia.[84] Indigenous people of Kalimantan, as a result, have had to move deeper into the mountains of Central Borneo.[85] Often, these timber merchants run mafia-like operations against the indigenous people involving threats and violence.[86] In Central Kalimantan, Indonesia "kidnapping, bribery and stand over tactics are simply ways of doing business".[87] It is estimated that 70 per cent of all logging taking place in Indonesia is illegal[88] and that it is run by highly organized timber mafias with corrupt political connections to the ruling parties. The tactics used by the timber mafias are similar to those used in the drug trade dealings. They deal ruthlessly with anyone standing in their way.

There is also evidence to show that natural resources have been used to finance brutal regimes. For example, Pol Pot's Khmer Rouge did lucrative timber and gem deals with corrupt Thai military officials in order to finance their regime in the late 1970s[89] and, after their ouster by Vietnamese invasion troops, their resistance against the latter and the Cambodian government. Furthermore the opium poppy can be an attractive source for funding for terror organizations in the region since Southeast Asia is one of the major producers of opium poppy in the world. The poppy growing areas in Southeast Asia, the notorious "Golden Triangle", are in adjoining parts of highland Myanmar, Laos and to a lesser extent in Vietnam, Thailand and China.[90] Although in Southeast Asia the extent of violence and drug operations is unlike that of Colombia and Peru where separatist-terrorist groups impose taxes on illicit drug producers to finance their operations, in Southeast Asia, too, violence is used by the illicit drug operators. Financial hubs in the region have been suspected as drug-money laundering centres and all producer centres (see Figure 8.1) are important secondary markets.[91] The United Nations estimate that the global illicit drug trade is worth as much as US$400 billion annually and it is a potential and substantial actual source of revenue to terrorist groups.[92] More recently there have been accusations by Australia that North Korea is involved with smuggling drugs to Western countries, including Australia, to finance the development of nuclear weapons.[93]

Furthermore, there are instances where the security of a nation or a region could be affected due to environmental degradation and East and Southeast Asia are no exception. The Human Development Report[94] of the United Nations identifies Myanmar as one of the countries in the region affected by environmental degradation. Homer-Dixon[95] also mentions that land degradation and ecological marginalization have led to conflicts in the Southeast Asian region, and cites the Philippines as an example. Homer-Dixon,[96] citing Roque and Garcia[97] and other authors, states that:

> The country's upland insurgency — which peaked in the 1980s and still included regular guerrilla assaults on military stations in the mid 1990s — was motivated by the relative deprivation of landless agricultural labourers and poor farmers displaced into remote hills where they tried to eke a living from the failing land ....

Granting that the natural resources of a country, amongst other causes, could underpin arguments in favour of secession, there is also the danger of newly seceded states placing too much reliance on such reserves. A good example is East Timor. Amongst other reasons, the decision of East Timor to separate from Indonesia was based on the projected oil and gas reserves in the Timor Sea which was not only an issue with Indonesia, but also one of the reasons for the tense relationship between Australia and Indonesia.[98] The Timor Gap oil and natural resources will no doubt play an important role in the economy of the independent state, but there is the danger of over-reliance especially if the oil and gas is found to be less than originally estimated. In such cases, East Timor can face problems similar to those faced by Papua New Guinea when its Panguna copper mine was shut down in 1989.[99] It has been pointed out by Oxfam that in such a case East Timor would have been much better off being a province of Indonesia. Hence, falling revenue and low economic growth and unemployment could create unrest in the country. Such a situation could force people to move to parts of Indonesia for employment or as refugees. This could lead to border tensions between the two countries.

## RESPONSES AND POSSIBLE REMEDIAL ACTION

The management of conflicts arising from resource use are complex partly because of the size and diversity of the Asian region, comprising as it does several incompatible political and economic systems, make the politics of regional cooperation intricate.[100] Sharing of resources in such situations among the largest population in the world combined with the presence of multifarious ethnic groups and deep historical disputes is fraught with problems. Some conflicts in such situations become intractable. Furthermore, in the region there are a multitude of resource-linked conflicts at any given time and they spark off violence from time to time. Hence, it is difficult to discuss responses and remedial action for each conflict since it appears that conflicts need specific responses for specific problems and in some instances they are time-specific. However, an overview of some of the responses could be suggested as a starting point towards minimizing or resolving some of these conflicts.

Because most resource conflicts in the region are linked with other issues, any solutions to a problem should also take into account all aspects of the issues involved. In many cases, it is likely that when one issue is resolved the other related conflicts may also subdue in intensity.

In the case of inter-country conflicts, the Association of Southeast Asian Nations (ASEAN) is a good starting point. The ASEAN Declaration states that:

> the association represents the collective will of the nations of Southeast Asia to bind themselves together in friendship and cooperation and through joint efforts and sacrifices, secure for their peoples and for posterity the blessings of peace, freedom and prosperity.

All countries in Southeast Asia (except East Timor which participates only as an invited guest) are members of ASEAN and ASEAN have close links with countries in East Asia particularly China, Japan and the Republic of Korea.[101] Such an organization can sometimes manage local disputes and tensions more effectively than distant international organizations such as the United Nations. Since ASEAN also involves dealing with economic issues, it provides an incentive for member countries to cooperate in settling disputes when they arise.

Yet, this presupposes that ASEAN ceases to cling to its sacred principle of non-interference. Relegating resource conflicts to track two dialogues (that is, informal and unofficial expert meetings) may help to sharpen the awareness of policymakers of more innovative solutions, but does not move the problems closer to a settlement. As long as ASEAN member states are not prepared to submit for adjudication such conflicts to its dispute settlement mechanisms such as the ASEAN High Council or the Troika, they might linger on in the same way as in the past. Also the ASEAN Regional Forum (ARF) has added little to the defusing of these conflicts as it has not gone beyond the level of confidence-building measures; the prospect of a proactive role in the resolution of conflicts in the region is remote.

Nevertheless, the United Nations can still play a useful role, especially regarding international conventions such as the Law of the Sea, inasmuch as this convention provides a legal framework for rational management of marine resources, such as those in the South China Sea. Under the United Nations Convention on the Law of the Non-Navigational uses of International Watercourses of 1997 countries should utilize rivers, lakes and similar resources in an equitable and reasonable manner.[102] Countries also could use the 1992 Convention on the Protection and use of Transboundary Watercourses and International Lakes (the Helsinki Convention) to resolve disputes. Haftendorn[103] also refers to several other international organizations in addition to the International Court of Justice that could help resolve disputes between countries. Thus, in the event of a dispute, countries can have recourse to international mediators and international law rather than engaging in war.

Another organization is the Asia-Pacific Economic Cooperation (APEC) which involves a wide range of countries in Asia including the East and Southeast Asian countries. Regional organizations, especially those with economic benefits, could act as a disincentive for countries to pursue acts of aggression towards their neighbours. Economic incentives could also act as a disincentive for countries to engage in military action. For example China's entry into the World Trade Organization and a number of additional regional and international organizations[104] in many ways reduces the risk of its engagement in military actions in the region.

All countries in the region either have large or sophisticated military forces and their military expenditures are high.[105] The military capability of a country may act as a deterrent for countries engaging in resource disputes. The presence of major powers and their military assistance may also pre-empt military conflicts.

## CONCLUSIONS

Although many resource-related tensions and conflicts have arisen in the region in the past and continue to date, they have in most cases been overshadowed by higher profile issues such as the inter-Korea military confrontation, tensions between China and Taiwan, and proliferation of alleged weapons of mass destruction.

A new issue is the rise of international terrorism, which precedes the events September 11 and the Bali bombing but has assumed great prominence since then. Ironically this could help dampen resource conflicts. It is possible that because of increasing evidence of illegal drugs financing terrorism there will be pressure exerted on opium producing countries to take action to combat the growing of illegal opium poppy in the region and outside. In the case of any action being taken it is necessary to provide alternative sources of income to people, who are already engaged in such cultivation. Since the events of September 11, governments have pursued a more active role in combating terrorism. In doing so, some countries have used the campaign against terrorism more vigorously to suppress movements that are linked to natural resources and minorities in their traditional lands, for example in Aceh.

But quick results under the banner of counter-terrorism are not to be expected. In the case of intra-country conflicts many resource conflicts are continuations or offshoots of historical conflicts, usually involving ethnic divisions. In such cases, multilateral economic and political initiative could reduce the magnitude of the conflicts or ameliorate their consequences. In other cases, appropriate political devolution may help restore some degree of stability, although sometimes devolution creates new problems leading to destabilization by provoking those who oppose such moves including the military and rival ethnic groups.

Nevertheless, resources in the region, especially the potentially large oil and gas reserves in the East and South China Sea, combined with other issues such as historical disputes, ideological differences, regional rivalry and ethnic groups fragmentation could destabilize the region if conflicts flare up. Because resource-linked conflicts are often related to each other and are complex in nature, any solution or management of issues should consider the root causes of the tensions. In many cases, resolving one issue will dampen other related conflicts.

Regional organizations such as ASEAN, APEC and international organizations such as the United Nations, and international conventions such as the Law of the Sea, can contribute to defusing or managing conflicts between countries. Resource-related conflicts within countries can be less easily resolved because of the multitude of issues involved. In many cases, some issues may be intractable, at least in the short-term, and must be skilfully managed to keep the magnitude of conflicts to a minimum.

Finally, it is important that local conflicts arising from resource control and use are addressed early to prevent their flaring into larger conflicts engulfing two or more countries or an entire sub-region. Although many of the resource-related conflicts are low in intensity, or in some cases isolated incidents compared to resource related conflicts in some countries in Africa, the lure of vast resources of Asia shown in Figure 8.1 have the potential to create larger conflicts and destabilize the region. The South China Sea claims issue is a case in point, with potential to generate conflict between states of East Asia and Southeast Asia. Asian leaders have before them the dire example of how ethnic war in the former Yugoslavia threatened the stability of Europe and tested the resolve of the Western powers and Russia, and how religious-ethnic violence troubles relations between India and Pakistan, and in Sri Lanka. Lacking the security structures of Europe, such as the North Atlantic Treaty Organization (NATO) and the Organization for Security and Cooperation (OSCE), Asia would be especially vulnerable to resource clashes not only generating non-traditional security threats, such as refugee flows, but also escalating into conventional inter-state confrontations of armed forces. This is another instance of the interaction of traditional and non-traditional security issues, an interaction that will need increasingly to be dealt by Asian leaders in coming years.

## NOTES

1. M.T. Klare, "The Geopolitics of War", *The Nation* (5 November 2001), accessed at <http://www.thenation.com/doc.mhtml?i=20011105&s=klare>; T.F. Homer-Dixon, *Environment, Scarcity and Violence* (Princeton: Princeton University Press, 1999); L.T. Ghee and M.J. Valencia, eds. *Conflict over Natural Resources in Southeast Asia and the Pacific* (Oxford: Oxford University Press, 1990).
2. The World Commission on Environment and Development. *Our Common Future* (Oxford: Oxford University Press, 1987), p. 290.
3. A. Malaquias, "Diamonds are a Guerrilla's Best Friend: The Impact of Illicit Wealth on Insurgency Strategy", *Third World Quarterly* 22, no. 3 (2001): 311–25.

4. A.T. Tan and J.D.K. Boutin, eds., *Non-Traditional Security Issues* (Singapore: Select Publishing for Institute of Defence and Strategic Studies, 2001); Ghee and Valencia, op. cit.

5. N. Samaranayake, "Oil and Politics in East Asia", *Journal of Peace and Conflict Resolution* 1, no. 2 (May 1998), accessed online.

6. Central Intelligence Agency, *The World Factbook 2002*, "East and Southeast Asian Countries — Military Expenditures", accessed June 2003 at <http:// www.odci.gov/cia/publications/factbook/geos/mg.html>.

7. A. Dupont, *East Asia Imperilled: Transnational Challenges to Security* (Cambridge: Cambridge University Press, 2001).

8. Ibid.

9. Ibid.

10. M.J. Valencia, "International Conflict over Marine Resources in Southeast Asia: Trends in Politicization and Militarization", in Ghee and Valencia, op. cit.

11. Dupont, op. cit.

12. F.A. Magno, "Environmental Security in South China Sea", *Security Dialogue* 28, no. 1 (1997): 97–112.

13. C.M. Siddayao, *The Off-shore Petroleum Resources of Southeast Asia. Potential Conflict Situations and Related Economic Considerations* (Kuala Lumpur: Oxford University Press, 1980).

14. M. Leifer, *Stalemate in the South China Sea* (1999), accessed June 2003 at <http://www.prio.no/research/asiasecurity/Publications/pdf/leifer.pdf>.

15. Dupont, op. cit., p. 76.

16. Magno, op. cit.

17. N. Ganesan, "Illegal Fishing and Illegal Migration in Thailand's Bilateral Relationships with Malaysia and Myanmar", pp. 507–27, in Tan and Boutin, op. cit.

18. Dupont, op. cit., p. 106.

19. R.T. Maddock, "Environmental Security in East Asia", *Contemporary Southeast Asia* 17, no. XX (1995): 20–37.

20. G. Clarke, "From Ethnocide to Ethnodevelopment? Ethnic Minorities and Indigenous Peoples in Southeast Asia", *Third World Quarterly* 22, no. 3 (2001): 413–36.

21. For more on Southeast Asian ethnic conflicts, see also the chapter by Jürgen Rüland in this volume.

22. Drug Policy Alliance. *Drug Policy around the World* (2003) accessed June 2003 at <http://www.lindesmith.org/global/terrorism/>.

23. For example see Mbendi, *Asia Continental Profile* (2001), accessed June 2003 at <http://www.mbendi.co.za/land/as/p0005.htm ()>; Oxfam, *The Role of*

"*Gap Oil*", (2000) accessed June 2003 at <http://www.caa.org.au/publications/briefing/timor_gap_treaty/role.html ()>; Ghee and Valencia, op. cit.

24. G.T. Kurian, ed. *Atlas of the Third World* (Second edition, New York: Facts on File Ltd; Siddayao, op. cit., Ref. 9; Harrison, S., "China, Oil and Asia: Conflict Ahead?" (New York: Columbia University Press, 1977).

25. M. Kidron and R. Segal, *The New State of the World Atlas* (Fourth edition, London: Simon and Schuster Ltd., 1991).

26. *The World Factbook*, op. cit., Ref. 6.

27. Barnes, op. cit., Ref. 16; Siddayao, op. cit., Ref. 9; Harrison, op. cit.

28. Siddayao, op. cit., Ref. 9; Bartke, W. *Oil in the People's Republic of China. Industry Structure, Production, Exports* (London: C. Hurst and Company, 1977).

29. *The World Factbook*, op. cit., Ref. 6; Siddayao, op. cit., Ref. 9.

30. Ibid.

31. Mbendi, op. cit., Ref. 17.

32. E. Tadem, "Conflict over Land-based Natural Resources in the ASEAN Countries", in Ghee and Valencia, op. cit., Chapter 2.

33. Mbendi, op. cit., Ref. 17.

34. Tadem, op. cit., Ref. 27.

35. Ibid.

36. Ibid.

37. P. Dauvergne, *Loggers and Degradation in the Asia-Pacific — Corporations and Environmental Management* (Cambridge: Cambridge University Press, 2001); Homer-Dixon, op. cit.; Ghee and Valencia, op. cit.

38. M. Richardson, "Sharing the Mekong: and Asian Challenge", *International Herald Tribune*, 30 October 2002.

39. Tadem, op. cit., Ref. 27.

40. *The World Factbook*, op. cit., Ref. 6; Siddayao, op. cit., Ref. 9.

41. Dupont, op. cit.

42. R. Reuveny, "Economic Growth, Environmental Scarcity, and Conflict", *Global Environmental Politics* 2, no. 1 (February 2002), Massachusetts Institute of Technology.

43. Magno, op. cit., Ref. 8.

44. Leifer, op. cit., Ref. 10.

45. Ibid.

46. M.J. Valencia, "International Conflict over Marine Resources in Southeast Asia: Trends in Politicization and Militarization", in Ghee and Valencia, op. cit., Chapter 4; Siddayao, op. cit., Ref. 9.

47. Magno, op. cit., Ref. 8.

48. Ibid.

49. Dupont, op. cit.
50. Magno, op. cit., Ref. 8.
51. M.J. Valencia, "Building Confidence and Security in the South China Sea: The Way Forward", in Tan and Boutin, op. cit., pp. 528–70.
52. Siddayao, op. cit., Ref. 9.
53. Magno, op. cit., Ref. 8.
54. Dupont, cited above.
55. Ganesan, op. cit., Ref. 12.
56. Richardson, op. cit., Ref. 33.
57. Maddock, op. cit., Ref. 13.
58. E. Goh, "The Hydro-politics of the Mekong River Basin — Regional Cooperation and Environmental Security", in Tan and Boutin, op. cit., pp. 408–505.
59. Dupont, op. cit.
60. J. Long, "Desecuritizing the Water Issue in Singapore–Malaysia Relations", *Contemporary Southeast Asia* 23, no. 3 (December 2001): 504–33.
61. Maddock, op. cit., Ref. 13.
62. Siddayao, op. cit., Ref. 9.
63. Valencia, op. cit.
64. Maddock, op. cit., Ref. 13.
65. R. Steele, "Environmental Issues of Asia and the Pacific", in *The Far East and Australia, 2003, Regional Surveys of the World*, Europa Publications (London: Taylor and Francis, 2003).
66. R. Duncan, and S. Chand, "The Economics of the 'Arc of Instability' ", *Asia-Pacific Economic Literature* 16, no. 1 (May 2002).
67. On the conflict in Aceh, see the chapter by Jürgen Rüland in this volume.
68. Sulistiyanto, P. "Wither Aceh?", *Third World Quarterly* 22, no. 3 (2001): 437–52.
69. Sulistiyanto, op. cit., Ref. 13.
70. M.C. Ricklefs, *A History of Modern Indonesia Since c1300* (London: Macmillan, 1993).
71. Ibid., Ref. 61.
72. G. Robinson, "Rawan is as Rawan Does: The Origins of Disorder in New Order Aceh", *Indonesia* 66 (1998): 137.
73. A. Ali, "Aceh Dahulu, Sekarang dan Masa Depan" [Aceh in the Past, Present and Future], in *Aceh Merdeka dalam Perdebatan* [Free Aceh in Debate], edited by Tulus Widjanarko and Asep S. Sambodja Jakarta: Cita Putra Bangsa, 1999.
74. Ibid., Ref. 64.
75. Sulistiyanto, op. cit., Ref. 13.
76. Ibid.
77. Ibid.

78. "East Kalimantan 'might Rebel' ", *Jakarta Post*, 25 September 2001.
79. E. Aspinall and M. T. Berger, "The Breakup of Indonesia? Nationalisms after Decolonisation and the Limits of the Nation-state in Post-Cold War Southeast Asia", *Third World Quarterly* 22, no. 6 (2001): 1003–24.
80. Clarke, op. cit., Ref. 14.
81. R. Broad and J. Cavanagh, *Plundering Paradise: The Struggle for the Environment in the Philippines* (Berkeley, CA: University of California Press, 1993).
82. Clarke, op. cit., Ref. 14.
83. C. Tisdell, "The Environment and Sustainable Development in the Asia-Pacific: Views and Policies", *Asian-Pacific Economic Literature* 11, no. 1 (1997): 39–55.
84. P. Dauvergne, op. cit.
85. Clarke, op. cit., Ref. 14.
86. Four Corners, "The Timber Mafia, Produced in Conjunction with TVE", Monday, 29 July 2002, <http://www.abc.net.au/4corners/content/2002/timber_mafia/> (accessed June 2003).
87. Ibid., Ref. 77.
88. Ibid.
89. R. Garella, "The Death of Pol Pot", <http://www.garella.com/rich/camoppot.htm> (accessed June 2003).
90. Dupont, op. cit.
91. Kidron and Segal, op. cit., Ref. 19.
92. Drug Policy Alliance, op. cit., Ref. 15.
93. J. Kerin, "Safety-First for N. Korea: Howard", *The Australian*, 13 June 2003.
94. Human Development Report, "New Dimensions of Human Security", published for the United Nations Development Programme, New York (Oxford: Oxford University Press, 1994).
95. Homer-Dixon, op. cit.
96. Ibid., Ref. 85.
97. C. Roque and M. Garcia, "Economic Inequality, Environmental Degradation and Civil Strife in the Philippines". Paper prepared for the project on Environmental Change and Acute Conflict, Peace and Conflict Studies Programme, University of Toronto, 1993.
98. B. DuBois, "The Timor Gap Treaty — Where to Now?", 2000, <http://www.caa.org.au/publications/briefing/timor_gap_treaty/> (accessed June 2003).
99. Oxfam, "The Role of 'Gap Oil' ", 2000, <http://www.caa.org.au/publications/briefing/timor_gap_treaty/role.html> (accessed June 2003).
100. L.K. Tick, Competing Regionalism: APEC and EAEG, 1989–90, pp. 54–86, in Tan and Boutin, op. cit.

101. ASEAN Secretariat, Joint Statement on East Asia Cooperation 28 November 1999, <http://www.aseansec.org/5469.htm> (accessed June 2003).
102. H. Haftendorn, "Water and International Conflict", *Third World Quarterly* 21, no. 1 (2000): 51–68.
103. Ibid., Ref. 92.
104. For China's turn towards multilateralism, see the contribution by Jian Yang in this volume.
105. *The World Factbook*, op. cit., Ref. 6.

Chapter Nine

# Ethnic Conflict, Separatism and Terrorism

Jürgen Rüland

## INTRODUCTION

Politicized ethnicity "has become the most keen and potent edge of intra-state and inter-state conflict displacing class and ideological conflict, and it asserts itself today, dialectically, as the leading legitimator or delegitimating challenger of political authority".[1] This statement is as valid today as when Joseph Rothschild made it in 1981. Southeast Asia's "plural societies" — most notably Indonesia and Myanmar, but also Malaysia, the Southern Philippines and Southern Thailand — are particularly exposed to communal strife. In the Philippines and Indonesia, Islam has been a major ingredient in these conflicts, nurturing fears that they may spur Islamist militancy in Southeast Asia, a region known for a diverse but heretofore tolerant Islam.

This chapter seeks to explore the security risks posed by ethnic violence in Southeast Asia. From among a plethora of ethnic conflicts in the region, the conflicts in Aceh and the Southern Philippines have been selected for in-depth study. Both conflicts are driven by Muslim secessionist movements — albeit in one case, the Philippines, against a Christian majority, in the other case, Indonesia, against Javanese dominance, which is equated with a hegemonic Indonesian state. Although the role of Islam as the unifying factor has declined in recent years, Acehnese still perceive Indonesia as a primarily secular state and hence as a threat to their cultural identity which is strongly flavoured by Islam. Both conflicts have centuries-old roots, both have been exacerbated by modernization and globalization and both rage in peripheral regions. After sketching a framework of analysis, the chapter first discusses the underlying causes of these conflicts, and then offers options for conflict resolution. The final section links them to the wider Asian and international security arenas and the post-September 11 developments.

## CONCEPTUAL PREMISES

Few concepts are more contested than "ethnicity" and few topics have generated more theoretical approaches than ethnic conflict. Among the multitude of explanations for ethnic conflict we may distinguish the (1) primordialist, (2) political economy and (3) cognitive approaches.[2]

Primordialists use "objective" criteria for defining ethnic identities such as blood relations, race, physical features, language, religion and custom. These commonalities constitute fundamental group identities that have developed over centuries. In the words of Clifford Geertz, they are "givens", natural affinities and predispositions a person has acquired by birth, which are deepened by primary socialization and which constitute a way of life.[3] Such blood ties are more binding than identities created by changing social contexts, interests and interactions. Due to their emotional character, they are believed to be beyond rational reflection and, as argued by Shils, of an "ineffable significance".[4] Ethnic conflicts are thus an integral part of political life; the tension between "primordial sentiments" and "civil politics" is, contrary to the optimistic beliefs of modernization theorists, irreconcilable.

Critics challenge this essentialist character of ethnic identities. They argue that ethnic ties are by no means "natural givens". Ethnic identities and conflicts are the result of socio-economic structures and the mental representations of historical legacies, concrete experiences and interaction of groups. Hence, ethnic boundaries are not rigid but rather open to change. Political economists, for instance, attach great importance to the socio-economic structures defining group behaviour. For them primordial identities will be mobilized when tangible economic disparities coincide with ethnic divisions and are perceived by one group in terms of relative deprivation. If such disparities are exacerbated by social discrimination and political oppression of a group and hence constitute what has been called "internal colonialism", the likelihood of ethnic strife increases significantly.[5]

Proponents of the cognitive approach, by contrast, define a subjective concept of ethnicity. Accordingly, ethnic boundaries are defined in a continuous interactive process between self and other. These interactions shape the way other groups are perceived and they also shape group identity by interpreting what identity and interests other ethnic groups ascribe to one's own group. However, the perceptions of other ethnic groups based on previous interactions are not necessarily rational in the sense that they reflect an objective balance sheet. To a much greater extent the way other ethnic groups are viewed is subjective, as in-groups may rate out-groups on the basis of very selective perceptions. They may attach great relevance to certain singular incidents victimizing the own group. Such incidents may be atypical, if a relationship is viewed *à la longue*, but as they may have gravely offended the self-esteem of one's group, they became deeply ingrained in the group's collective memory.[6] Over time such collective memories condense into myths and stereotypes, with the effect that inter-ethnic relations will be more strained than justified by material antagonisms. Memories of such incidents may recede under more favourable circumstances (such as positive sum games caused by an expanding societal resource base or simply more accommodating policies by the center), but in times of stress and tension they can be activated, with the effect of inflaming emotions and eventually erupting into violence. This means that ethnic identities are socially and politically constructed. Ethnic boundaries may thus change over time or may even differentiate into multiple identities. Accordingly, cognitivists study the historical evolution of group beliefs, norms and institutions in concrete situations of interaction.

This chapter relies mainly on the cognitive and political economy-based frameworks of analysis. It however acknowledges that these factors do not cause inter-ethnic violence, as long as the primordialist characteristics have not been mobilized by political entrepreneurs.[7] In the following study, I borrow from an analytical framework developed by German sociologist Peter Waldmann.[8] According to Waldmann, the root causes and evolution of ethnic conflicts may be explained by four major factors. The first is the tradition and history of an ethnic group. It unveils the historical patterns of group interactions or, to be more precise, the narratives of interethnic relations, and their contribution to the formation of ethnic identities. This includes the development of norms, beliefs, myths, and symbols about the own group as a process of sharpening ethnic boundaries in response to a long asymmetric relationship with the dominant ethnic group characterized by political oppression, discrimination, and broken promises.

The second factor involves the structural dimension of ethnic group conflict. It assumes that there are deep-rooted socio-economic grievances felt by an ethnic group, which the latter perceived as relative deprivation. Such a situation is characterized by marked wealth disparities between ethnic groups and major blockades to social mobility such as limited access to education, administrative and political office.

The third factor concerns elites.[9] Because structures alone are hardly able to effect political change, change needs actors. Actors that may function as catalysts of change are elites. In societies with ethnic divisions, ethnic elites perform the important function of translating widespread sentiments of discrimination and marginalization into a coherent response to the dominant ethnic group which is viewed as the embodiment of a repressive state. Pivotal in this respect is the ability of ethnic elites to construct a shared identity which is recognized by a majority of group members. To this end elites amalgamate reminiscences of a great past, heroic myths, notions of cultural uniqueness, primordial attributes such as religion, language and race and political, economic and social grievances into an ideology of ethnic nationalism. While grievances may always lead to ethnic violence, without an ideology of ethnic nationalism it is quite unlikely that they mount to a concerted separatist challenge. Only when ethnic consciousness has reached a high level will it be possible for ethnic entrepreneurs to mobilize group members for armed struggle.

The fourth factor is singular incidents. While elites may have a long-term catalytic effect on the formation of a distinctive ethnic identity, traumatic incidents such as massacres of members of the own group by members of another group or shocking and repressive actions of the central government often have short-term galvanizing effects on ethnic solidarity. Thereafter they sink into the collective memory of the group, to be revived whenever tensions with the other group intensify. This factor comes close to Vamik Volkan's concept of "chosen trauma". By this he means "the collective memory of a calamity that once befell a group of ancestors. It is ... a shared mental representation of the event, which includes realistic information, fantasized expectations, intense feeling and defenses against unacceptable thoughts". Chosen traumas "become heavily mythologized over time and thereby act as central carriers not only of collective meaning (cognition) but also emotion and affect". In respect to social action chosen traumas "bring with them powerful experiences of loss and feelings of humiliation, vengeance and hatred that trigger a variety of unconscious defense mechanisms that attempt to reverse these experiences and feelings".[10]

## CAUSES OF ETHNIC CONFLICT IN ACEH AND THE SOUTHERN PHILIPPINES

### Tradition and History

Ethnic conflicts have a long history in maritime Southeast Asia. Most of them erupted in periods of profound political change such as colonization, decolonization and regime change which are usually paralleled by major socio-economic upheavals. The two most protracted among them are the conflicts in Aceh on the Indonesian island of Sumatra and in the islands of the Southern Philippines.

Aceh and the Southern Philippines share a peripheral location and a long history as independent sultanates. Islam was brought to Aceh in the thirteenth century by Arab and Indian traders. One century later it had also reached the Sulu archipelago and the shores of Mindanao.[11] While in Aceh Islam firmly took root, in the southern Philippines it became only a thin veneer cast over local Malay customs (*adat*). Moreover, unlike Aceh, the Muslim sultanates in the southern Philippines were deeply divided along ethnic lines and clan structures and, for most of the time between the fourteenth and twentieth centuries, entangled in fierce competition and power struggles. What united them was the common struggle against the Spanish colonizers who after 1565 had taken possession of the Visayas and Luzon. For the Spanish the warfare against the Islamic sultanates was a re-enactment of the Iberian *Reconquista* (driving the Moors out of Spain), albeit in another part of the world. However, by derogatively tagging the Muslim population of the South as "Moros", the Spanish unwittingly facilitated the construction of Moro nationalism. After the Spanish-American War in 1898 and the "pacification" of the South under American military administration (1899–1913), U.S. colonial rule (1901–35) further helped to engender a Moro identity transcending primordial boundaries. Benevolent colonial administrators such as Syrian-born Najeeb

Saleeby and Edward M. Kuder believed that only united Muslims would be able to overcome their marginalization. In their view, a sense of community would also make Muslims more amenable to the idea of becoming part of an independent Philippines.[12]

However, integration of Muslims in the emerging Philippine state did not succeed for several reasons. First, there was an accelerating migration of Christian settlers to Mindanao which was initiated and promoted by the colonial authorities. Second, with it went the introduction of alien legal concepts, especially relating to land rights, which discriminated against Muslims. Third, and perhaps most threatening from a Muslim point of view, was the loss of special rights protecting Islamic and traditional laws, the abolition of the institution of the sultanate and the termination of socio-economic programmes during the Philippine-American Commonwealth (1935–42), a kind of home rule prior to independence. For Muslims these measures foreshadowed their second-class status in a fully independent Philippine state dominated by Christian Filipinos. Consequently, when in 1946 the Philippines became independent, the Moros unsuccessfully appealed to the U.S. Government not to be incorporated into the new state.[13]

## Aceh

In Aceh, due to the fact that the sultanate was a more coherent political entity and Islam played a more pervasive role in Acehnese society, independence and religion made a substantially greater contribution to defining a common identity than in the Southern Philippines. By the seventeenth century Aceh had risen to a major power straddling the Straits of Malacca. When in the nineteenth century the Dutch advanced their colonial rule into the peripheral areas of the Indonesian archipelago, Aceh was their "wealthiest, most determined, most organized and most fiercely independent opponent".[14] Even though the Dutch quickly took Banda Aceh, the capital, Acehnese insurgents, led by religious scholars *(ulamas)*, resisted the Dutch for more than thirty years. It was thus no accident that the Dutch avoided entering Aceh when they sought to restore their colonial empire at the end of World War II. The ensuing power vacuum enabled the pro-independence *ulamas* to kill or imprison the local nobility *(uleebalangs)* which had collaborated with the Dutch and, during World War II, with the Japanese. Thereafter Aceh strongly supported the Indonesian nationalists in their struggle against the Dutch (1945–49). At the same time, the *ulamas* had become the undisputed leaders in Aceh. Moreover, the fact that they figured prominently in the anti-colonial struggle strengthened the Islamic identity of the Acehnese to an extent that after independence, Islam became a major factor defining Acehnese exceptionalism in Indonesia's *Pancasila* state.[15]

After independence, state repression and broken promises further galvanized ethnic identities of the Acehnese. Aceh, for instance, was given special provincial status in 1949. But one year later, in 1950, the decision was revoked and Aceh became part of the province of North Sumatra where Acehnese were a minority among the Christian Bataks.[16] Unsurprisingly, Acehnese viewed this as a disregard of their merits in the anti-colonial struggle. They also resented the secularist nature of the Indonesian Republic which was at variance with their aspirations for an Islamic state. In 1953, Aceh's former governor, Teungko Daud Beureu'eh joined the millenarist Darul Islam movement and declared Aceh an Islamic state. Government troops soon took control of Aceh, but once more, Acehnese resorted to guerilla warfare. By 1956, in response to secessionist movements in other parts of Sumatra, the government entered into negotiations with the insurgents. In 1957, Aceh was restored as a separate province. Two years later, in 1959, Aceh received the status of a "special region" *(Daerah Istimewa)*, which entailed autonomy in the areas of religious and customary law and education. Finally, in 1962, Daud Beureu'eh ended his rebellion.[17]

However, implementation of the law only resulted in nominal autonomy. Under the centralist New Order (*Orde Baru*) regime of President Suharto, who had wrested power from Sukarno after the aborted coup attempt of 30 September 1965, things changed from bad to worse. The wealth created by the exploitation of the province's oil and natural gas deposits bypassed Aceh and only five per cent of the proceeds came back in the form of central government grants.[18]

Before long, the Acehnese launched a new revolt. On 4 December 1976, Mohammed Hasan di Tiro, a businessman returned from the United States and member of a prominent Acehnese *ulama* family, declared the independence of Aceh and created the Aceh Sumatra National Liberation Front (ASNLF), better known as Movement for a Free Aceh (Gerakan Aceh Merdeka, GAM).[19] The uprising was quickly crushed by the Indonesian military and by 1979 di Tiro went into exile in Sweden. But restiveness in the province did not subside. A new uprising started in 1989. It was triggered by the return of Afghanistan fighters and several hundred

Acehnese who received military training in Libya.[20] Other insurgents were trained in Muslim rebel camps in the Southern Philippines.[21] The Indonesian Government responded by declaring Aceh a Military Operations Area (*Daerah Operasi Militer*, DOM) which resembles a state of emergency and gives security forces a free hand in dealing with the insurgents. Among the government forces were units of the KOPASSUS and KOSTRAD special forces which were notorious for their human rights violations in East Timor. As a result of the military campaign against the GAM, between 3,000–4,000 persons were killed or had disappeared by the end of the Suharto regime.[22]

The new opportunities for peace in Aceh that emerged after the fall of Suharto in May 1998 were overshadowed by reports in the media which, freed from censorship, publicized the atrocities committed by the Indonesian military between 1989 and 1998.[23] This forced President Habibie and Armed Forces chief General Wiranto to offer public apologies. Habibie also appointed an independent committee to investigate human rights violations in the province, although this did not lead to serious prosecution of the military officers responsible for the brutalities. In August 1998 DOM was lifted and the withdrawal of non-local military forces, including the KOSTRAD and KOPASSUS troops, was announced.[24]

But as in the 1950s and 1960s, central government concessions in the 1990s did not lead to peace. Provocations during the farewell ceremony for the withdrawing government troops stirred riots, resulting in new hostilities and intensifying clashes between military and GAM. Since then more than 2,000 persons lost their lives and between 100,000 and 200,000 persons have been displaced.[25] In the meantime, GAM gained control over major parts of the territory and a majority of Acehnese by that time seemed to support secession.[26] GAM enjoyed broad popular support, which only crumbled where the rebels in their fund-raising drives taxed the impoverished rural population too heavily.[27] Although the military arm of GAM, Angkatan Gerakan Aceh Merdeka (AGAM), was a relatively small force of about 5,000 fighters[28] with only a limited number of modern weapons, most of which were acquired from corrupt military and police personnel, or smuggled into Aceh from Cambodia *via* Southern Thailand, the government deployed over 30,000 security personnel in the province. Yet, despite its superiority, the government was unable to break the stalemate by military force alone.[29]

New hopes for a peaceful conflict resolution were raised by President Abdurrahman Wahid (1999–2001) who prior to his election promised a referendum on autonomy or independence, similar to the one held in East Timor in August 1999.[30] Such a solution was however completely unacceptable for the Indonesian Armed Forces (TNI). Although Wahid sought to strengthen his grip on the military by several reshuffles, faced with recalcitrance in the armed forces, he was forced to back-pedal. Wahid's new proposal to hold a referendum over the introduction of *shariah* law in Aceh and concessions such as the appointment of an Acehnese human rights minister, were rejected by many Acehnese as hollow symbolism.[31]

As Wahid was unable to control the military, violence continued unabated. Some progress was finally made in May 2000, when the Indonesian Government and GAM agreed to a ceasefire. Although the "Humanitarian Pause", brokered by the Geneva-based Henry Dunant Centre, was difficult to implement and armed clashes continued, the ceasefire was prolonged in September 2000. In March 2001 both sides agreed on a "Peace through Dialogue", including another ceasefire and intensified consultations to end violence. In August 2001, in an obvious concession, parliament passed an Autonomy Law for Aceh, which grants Acehnese a 70 per cent share of the oil and gas revenues generated in the province and also provides for autonomy in religious and educational matters, including the introduction of the *shariah*.[32]

However, the Acehnese viewed the *shariah* as a mixed blessing, hardly more than a thinly veiled attempt to drive a wedge between the insurgents and *ulamas*.[33] Especially after 11 September 2001, they feared the introduction of the *shariah* would brand them abroad as Islamist radicals. In the meantime, by May 2002 GAM representatives and the government agreed to negotiate a more comprehensive peace plan. Military actions, however, continued, obviously tolerated by President Megawati Sukarnoputri who succeeded Wahid after his impeachment in July 2001. Megawati shared with the military strong nationalist sentiments and an equally strong sense for unity. Finally, by 9 December 2002, preceded by massive threats of the military to launch an all out war against the rebels, the Indonesian Government and GAM signed a Framework Agreement on the Cessation of Hostilities.[34]

Less than half a year later, the agreement was in shambles, partly because it left key issues such as the disarmament of GAM and the withdrawal of government forces unresolved,[35] partly because both sides did not negotiate in good faith. The military, for instance, seems to have agreed to the ceasefire merely by bowing to international pressure. Military hardliners were thus only waiting for a pretext to resume counter-insurgency operations. After all, festering insurgencies such as in Aceh help the military to defend its corporate interests when they are challenged by democratization. They provide the rationale for maintaining the military's self-styled role as guardian of national unity and to protect the special political rights it enjoyed in the *Orde Baru*. Moreover, as only about one-third of the defence expenditures are covered by the state budget, the military must raise the rest from businesses enterprises and illegal activities. Competing with the rebels, in Aceh the military is allegedly involved in illegal logging, protection rackets, smuggling, and trafficking of marijuana.[36] A strong autonomous provincial government would thus not only curtail the military's economic interests, but also threaten its illegal activities. Under these circumstances provocations on the part of the security apparatus were likely to continue and hardening the determination of the insurgents to stick to their secessionist agenda. GAM, for its part, used the ceasefire to restock its arms supplies and to start a campaign of disinformation, portraying the truce as a major step towards independence.

In May 2003, after the collapse of another round of negotiations in Tokyo, the Indonesian Government once more imposed martial law (reduced to a civil emergency in 2004) and a news blackout on Aceh.[37] Amassing 50,000 troops in the province, the military launched a new offensive against GAM, its biggest operation since the 1975 invasion of East Timor.[38] It weakened the insurgents and claimed hundreds of deaths, bringing the entire death toll to over 12,000 since 1976, but failed to extinguish the resurrection.

The obvious failure to end the conflict by military means, inspired Indonesian Vice President Jusuf Kalla to initiate a new round of negotiations. However, a breakthrough in the deadlocked dialogue came only in the aftermath of the disastrous tsunami which hit Aceh on 26 December 2004, claiming over 170,000 lives and making more than 400,000 people homeless. Under intense pressure of the international community, which did not wish to see relief operations impaired by the conflict, both the Indonesian Government and the rebels eventually gave up their maximum demands. After five rounds of negotiations, brokered by the Helsinki-based Crisis Management Initiative, an NGO set up by former Finnish President Martti Athisaari, a peace accord was signed on 15 August 2005. The agreement called for an end of violence and the subsequent demilitarization of the province. While GAM had to hand over 840 arms until 31 December 2005, Indonesia had to reduce its troop strength in Aceh to 15,700 and its police force to 9,100. An Aceh Monitoring Mission

(AMM) composed of 200 observers from the European Union and 100 from ASEAN countries was entrusted with the task of monitoring the ceasefire, the troop reductions and the human rights situation. GAM also gave up its independence and agreed to a special autonomy which included the right to set up local political parties in the province and allocated to the province 70 per cent of the revenues from its natural resources. In the first two weeks after the conclusion of the peace accord, the government released more than 1,700 detainees associated with GAM.[39] Former rebels, GAM detainees and civilians severely affected by the conflict were promised economic assistance from a Reintegration Fund. Finally, in order to come to terms with the human rights violations and atrocities committed by both sides during the nearly thirty years of civil war, a human rights court and a truth and reconciliation commission will be set up.[40] Given the fact that most of these provisions — in particular the demilitarization — have been implemented quite smoothly, there is for the first time a real chance for an enduring settlement.[41]

## Southern Philippines

The Moro struggle against the Philippine central government resembles Aceh's case insofar as trust in the majority culture and the Philippine state has been shattered by endless cycles of half-hearted government concessions, repression and broken promises. These experiences have spurred ethnic identity-building that previously rested mainly on shared history and ascription by others.

After the Philippines had gained independence in 1946, massive government-sponsored Christian migration into Mindanao markedly changed not only the demographic balance in the region, but gradually also the political power equation. By the 1960s, Muslim Filipinos had become a minority in their own homelands. At the same time, electoral competition intensified and increasingly followed ethnic lines.[42] In the process, both sides sought to strengthen their positions by employing militias and vigilante groups. This led to increasing violence, with Christian Ilaga (rats) militias terrorizing Muslim villagers and Muslim Barracudas and Blackshirts harassing Christian settlers where the latter were a minority. The death toll resulting from politically motivated violence was thus constantly on the rise. The killings aroused the collective anger of Muslims and stiffened their resistance against the Philippine state, for the security forces often stood idly by or sided with Christians.[43] Violence, harassment by the security forces, land grabbing by Christian settlers and the loss of authority of traditional Muslim leaders in the electoral arena eventually spurred the creation of Moro organizations propagating secession. The first of them, the Mindanao Independence Movement (MIM), was formed by Datu Udtog Matalam, a traditional Muslim politician voted out of office in 1967. Although hardly being a radical organization, MIM's formation and secessionist overtones set in motion a new wave of state repression against Muslims. With spiralling violence, more radical organizations, led by a youthful non-traditional elite emerged. In 1971, Nur Misuari established the Mindanao National Liberation Front (MNLF) and its military arm, the Bangsamoro Army (BMA).[44]

The declaration of martial law by President Marcos in September 1972 triggered the outbreak of fierce fighting between Moro rebels and government troops. Moros particularly resented the order to surrender all firearms which they saw as an attempt to render them defenceless and buttress their colonization once and for all. Muslim rebels received support from neighbouring Malaysian state Sabah, where Chief Minister Tun Mustapha, a Tausug with family ties to Sulu, and angered by the Philippine claim to Sabah, provided them with sanctuary and allowed them to operate training camps. Sabah also became a conduit for arms supplies from Libya, Syria, and the Palestine Liberation Organization (PLO).[45] The governments of Egypt, Saudi-Arabia, Pakistan and Iran supported the Moro cause financially and on the diplomatic front,[46] and in 1974 the Organization of Islamic States (OIC) granted observer status to the MNLF. Massive hostilities between the MNLF, whose 30,000 fighters tied down three-fourth of the Philippine Armed Forces, continued until the mid-1970s. Until today, fighting and violence in the Philippine South claimed some 120,000 lives and displaced more than one million persons.[47]

Pressured by the OIC and Arab countries threatening with oil boycotts, the Marcos regime eventually sought a political settlement. In the Tripoli Agreement signed on 23 December 1976, the MNLF gave up its demand for secession, while the Philippine Government agreed to establish an autonomous region in the then thirteen provinces of the southern Philippines. The autonomy gave the Moros the right to set up their own administration and representative bodies, their court system based on Islamic *shariah* law and their own educational system. Details were relegated to subsequent negotiations.[48]

Due to its vagueness, disputes soon erupted over the implementation of the agreement. As the negotiations became deadlocked, the Philippine

Government implemented the agreement unilaterally. President Marcos held a plebiscite in which only ten provinces voted for autonomy. While the MNLF refused to recognize the plebiscite, Marcos argued that the autonomous region must be established in accordance with constitutional procedures. In the end, Marcos, implementing Presidential Decree (PD) No. 1618, set up two autonomous regions instead of one, covering ten provinces in Mindanao and the Sulu archipelago instead of thirteen. The local governments and the representative bodies of the autonomous regions were almost exclusively controlled by traditional Muslim politicians aligned with the Marcos regime and MNLF defectors. As a result, fighting resumed by the end of 1977, though less fiercely than before.[49]

After the ouster of Marcos in February 1986, the incoming Aquino administration resumed peace talks with the MNLF.[50] Perspectives for a peaceful settlement were enhanced by provisions of the 1987 Constitution calling for the creation of an Autonomous Region of Muslim Mindanao (ARMM). Yet, the constitutional framers left the details to be specified by Congress. To this end, the president convened a Regional Consultative Commission (RCC) with the mandate to assist Congress in drafting an Organic Act on Autonomy. Republic Act (RA) 6734 eventually authorized the creation of the ARMM which would take effect with the election of officials.[51] In 1989, in consonance with constitutional provisions, the government held another plebiscite. Its results reflected the demographic changes in Mindanao over the last forty years; only four provinces and one city (Sulu, Tawi-Tawi, Maguindanao, Lanao del Sur and Marawi City) opted for inclusion in the ARMM.[52] Unsurprisingly, the MNLF rejected the whole process which, it claimed, was at variance with the provisions of the Tripoli Agreement and also reneged on the Jeddah Accord of January 1987 where the Philippine Government had conceded an expanded area of autonomy. By 1988 negotiations were deadlocked and the MNLF went back to armed struggle.[53]

Peace talks did not resume before 1992 when newly elected President Fidel V. Ramos created a National Unification Commission with the mandate to work out new proposals for the peaceful settlement of the rebellions in various parts of the country. After several rounds of talks hosted by Indonesia and supervised by the OIC, a peace accord was signed by the MNLF and the Philippine Government in September 1996. The most intricate problem to be solved was reconciling the provisions of the Tripoli Agreement, which called for the establishment of a provisional government covering all thirteen (now fourteen) provinces, with the constitutional requirements subjecting the establishment of an autonomous region to a plebiscite. The solution found was a two-phased implementation of the accord. In the first phase a body known as the Southern Philippines Council for Peace and Development (SPCPD) was created which would resemble the provisional government called for in the Tripoli Agreement. The SPCPD would cover all provinces envisioned by the Tripoli Agreement and for a three-year trial period supervise the implementation of the Peace Accord. Nur Misuari, the MNLF chairman, was appointed chairman of the SPCPD and soon thereafter on the ticket of Ramos' Lakas-NUCD party, elected as governor of the ARMM. The agreement also facilitated the integration of thousands of MNLF fighters into the Philippine Armed Forces and the national police. Even more significant, however, were the developmental functions accorded to the SPCPD. In order to boost the legitimacy of the autonomous region, SPCPD was tasked with the attraction of national and international development funds which were expected to result in a marked improvement of living conditions in the Southern Philippines.[54]

The second phase, scheduled to begin in September 1999, would enable other provinces under the SPCPD to join ARMM. Elections would then pave the way to the establishment of a new Regional Autonomous Government which, as provided for in the Tripoli Agreement, would consist of an executive council, a legislative assembly, and representation in the national government. It would be vested with taxing powers, be allowed to set up Special Regional Security Forces, to create an educational system incorporating Islamic boarding schools (*madari*) and to set up Islamic *shariah* courts.[55]

Unfortunately, the peace accord did not result in a lasting peace. Already, phase one was saddled with problems. Consequently, the second phase only started in 2002, three years behind schedule. At least three major factors contributed to the peace accord's failure. First, the accord was rejected by Mindanao's Christian majority as well as the Mindanao Islamic Liberation Front (MILF), a break-away group from the MNLF, and the Abu Sayyaf, which were not party in the peace talks. Wooed by the Ramos administration, the MILF finally agreed to a ceasefire in 1997. However, the hardline position taken by Ramos's successor Estrada against the Moro insurgents, provoked renewed fighting in 2000. In the process, government forces overrun most MILF camps including MILF headquarters at Camp Abubakar. The MILF subsequently returned to guerilla tactics which spread out MILF forces, making it more difficult for the military to engage the rebels and affecting an even larger portion of the civilian population by the hostilities.[56] Fighting even worsened after Estrada also declared an all out war on the Abu Sayyaf following the kidnapping of twenty-one foreign tourists on the East Malaysian resort island of Sipadan. After Estrada's ouster, President Macapagal-Arroyo negotiated a new ceasefire with Malaysian mediation which is, however, very fragile and has collapsed several times.

Second, the SPCPD suffered from similar flaws as the Marcos-installed autonomous governments. Confined to recommendatory powers, it lacked meaningful authority. It "could neither initiate development planning in the region nor direct national government agencies to address the development priorities it had established", as Thomas McKenna notes. Worst of all, however, without revenue-raising and budgetary powers of its own, the SDCPD was financially strait-jacketed and entirely dependent on the President's Office.[57]

Third, the SPCPD was unable to channel the massive funding into the region that was needed to stimulate socio-economic development and combat poverty. Only a fraction of the funding promised by the central government for infrastructure development actually reached the region. Also the UN Multi Donor Programme, despite the participation of Australia, the United States, Japan, Saudi-Arabia, the EU, the World Bank and the Asian Development Bank with $8.3 million, produced only a trickle.[58] To make things worse, ARMM governor Nur Misuari was accused of corruption and negligence by his own clientele, labelled an "absentee governor" who spends only fifty to sixty days in the SPCPD capital of Cotabato City.[59] In April 2001, Misuari was ousted as MNLF chief. After ferociously opposing the plebiscite inaugurating the second stage of the Peace Accord on 14 August 2001 and the subsequent ARMM elections held on 26 November 2001, Misuari severed his ties with the government and staged attacks on military and police camps in Jolo in November 2001 that left dead scores of soldiers, rebels and civilians.[60] After fleeing to Sabah, Misuari was apprehended by the Malaysian authorities and extradited to the Philippines.[61]

At the time of the book going to print, the prospects for a settlement look bleak as ever. The peace accord signed in 1996 turned out as an agreement signed between the MNLF leadership and former President Ramos without sufficiently committing the Philippine Government as a whole.[62] The MNLF is in disarray and deeply factionalized, while progress in the peace process with the MILF is clouded by the outbreak of new fighting.[63] Moreover, the demand of the MILF to hold an East Timor-type referendum in the South, is unacceptable to the Philippine Government. Worst, the events after 11 September 2001, the stationing of 660 U.S. Special Operations Forces under the Balikatan-02 exercise in the Southern Philippines and the violence of the Abu Sayyaf do not bode well for peace.[64]

## Modernization and Socio-economic Change

While historical legacies are deeply inculcated in the collective memory of Acehnese and Moros, thus shaping their distrustful attitudes towards the central government and the majority culture, socio-economic structure also has a major bearing on interethnic relations. Social and economic contradictions, while existing previously, have intensified in recent years. The accelerated integration of Southeast Asian economies into the world market from the 1970s onward has created new incentives for the development of frontier regions. More than merely relying on the export of primary commodities, resource-based industries became a major stage in the industrialization strategies of Southeast Asian governments. Infrastructure development and the attraction of foreign investment profoundly changed the economic conditions in these regions. As the capitalist transformation of the peripheries occurred under the aegis of authoritarian central governments, their cronies and foreign partners, the asymmetries of this development caused resentment on the part of the local population.

In Aceh as well as the Southern Philippines, socio-economic change initiated by the central government deepened existing social disparities along ethnic lines. Modernization and development thus appeared as zero-sum games, benefiting outsiders over the indigenous population.[65] Apart from the experiences of political repression, broken government promises and the ethnic partiality of the authorities and the security forces, economic marginalization became a factor sharpening ethnic consciousness. Sentiments of being victims of internal colonialism were in the Southern Philippines exacerbated by the massive immigration of Christian settlers. This process started with the explicit blessing of the American colonial administration, which actively promoted the settlement of Christian homesteaders in Mindanao. The creation of agricultural colonies where Muslim and Christian farming families settled side-by-side became a facet of American policies of integrating Moros into the Christian-dominated

Filipino society. A concomitant of these early migratory movements was the introduction of a new land titling system — the Torrens system — which established individual land rights. As the new laws became the legal basis for land transactions in the South, with accelerating migration they increasingly conflicted with the existing traditional land rights. Under the *adat* system of the Moros, land was owned by the clan chiefs (*datus*) and used by the entire community.[66]

Land disputes escalated after independence, when in the 1950s and 1960s massive Christian migration drastically changed the demographic balance in Mindanao. In an attempt to ease land pressures in the agricultural heartlands of Central Luzon, the Philippine Government promised landless agricultural labourers and tenant farmers land in Mindanao.[67] Agrarian unrest had intensified in Central Luzon since the 1930s and culminated in the Hukbalahap rebellion in the decade between 1946 and the mid-1950s. The Huk rebellion articulated the growing frustration of the rural poor over grave social injustices and deepening social disparities going hand in hand with the advancement of commercial agriculture. The "exit"-option, that is, moving people to the frontier, was a convenient way for the land-owning elites of combating agrarian unrest without committing themselves to redistributive policies. While countries without land frontier such as South Korea and Taiwan implemented comprehensive agrarian reforms, which became the launching pad for a major social transformation and industrial take off, evasion of such reforms kept intact a change-resistant oligarchy in the Philippines. It must be attributed to the resilience of this oligarchy that the Philippines, though a head starter in industrialization in Asia, failed to join the tiger club of Southeast Asian economies. Transforming the frontier into a safety valve for social conflicts elsewhere in the country at the expense of the indigenous Muslims and the tribal Lumads was little more than shifting these conflicts to the periphery. In an atmosphere of centuries-old mutual distrust and intermittent warfare, mass immigration could only deepen inter-communal antagonisms. The civil war since 1972 is certainly one of the reasons why large parts of Mindanao are still economic backwaters and why the potentials of this natural resource-rich island can neither be tapped for national development nor for the indigenous Muslim population.

How profound and dramatic the demographic change in the Philippine South and the ensuing social consequences actually were, may be illustrated by the following figures. While in the early twentieth century Muslims accounted for 80 per cent of Mindanao's population, their share had dwindled to 17.5 per cent in 1990.[68] Data on land ownership closely correlate with the demographic figures. While in 1912 Moros owned most of the land in Mindanao, by 1982 their share of the land had declined to a mere 17 per cent. Unfamiliar with the bureaucratic procedures involved in securing legal land titles, Filipino Muslims became hapless victims of land grabbing by Christian settlers and TNCs. Aggravating the land problems was widespread corruption and collusion between public officials and land speculators. Their insider knowledge enabled them to buy large tracts of prime lands where roads and other infrastructure projects were being planned.[69] Coupled with the partiality of the Christian-dominated bureaucracy, which gave Christian settlers an edge in access to government services, especially credit and agricultural extension, the dispossession nourished a deepening sentiment among Muslims that Christians, even though in their majority smallholders and poor as well, were the more prosperous community.[70]

By the end of the 1960s, Muslim provinces were still the least developed of the archipelago. Sulu and Maguindanao, provinces with Muslim majorities until today, are the two poorest provinces in the entire country. Fifteen of the poorest provinces of the Philippines are in Mindanao, which also does not fare any better in other human life indicators such as literacy and life expectancy. While the literacy rate is 93.5 per cent for the Philippines, it is only 68 per cent for Mindanao.[71] Life expectancy is 69 years in the Philippines, but only 57 years in Mindanao.[72] By 2000, 62 per cent of the population of the ARMM lived below the poverty threshold, up from 52 per cent in the early 1990s.[73] Average daily minimum wages in the ARMM are the lowest in the country, reaching only two-thirds of the rate in Metro Manila.[74] Deepening ethnic divisions between Muslims and Christians and further propelling the formation of a shared Moro identity were pejorative stereotypes of the Moros cultivated by the Christian population. Christians depicted Muslim Filipinos as backward, uneducated and uncivilized and their alleged religious fanaticism explained their poverty.[75]

Failure of the central government to deliver the socio-economic development agreed in the Tripoli Agreement and the 1996 Peace Accord, was a factor which — despite factional infighting — kept alive a sense of shared identity among Moros. President Marcos, for instance, after setting up two autonomous regions in the South, announced large-scale development programmes. The outcome, however, was more than disappointing and neither overcame socio-economic disparities between Muslim and Christian Filipinos nor between the South and the rest of the country. Some of the infrastructure projects such as airport and harbour upgrading benefited the Philippine military more than the civilian population.[76] Moreover, some of the industries attracted from abroad were polluting and endangered the livelihood of the local farming and fishing communities. In a similar vein, agro-industrial TNCs circumvented the ceiling for corporate landholdings of 1,024 hectares by contract farming arrangements with smallholders. In the process, many of these farmers — Christians and Muslims alike — became increasingly indebted to these companies and in the long run went bankrupt and lost their land.

After 1996 several adverse conditions converged which stymied development initiated by foreign donors or government programs. The first was lack of government coordination and, to a considerable extent, outright disinterest and neglect. The second major impediment was the fact that the implementation of the crucial first phase of the 1996 Peace Accord coincided with the Asian currency crisis. Although the latter did not hit the Philippines as badly as neighbouring countries, it nevertheless stalled economic growth and curtailed the ability of the government to channel public investments into the South. The third major factor concerns the lack of managerial and administrative competence of the autonomous Muslim bodies. What in the second half of the 1990s eventually trickled down to Mindanao in terms of investment mainly went to the few urban centres with sizeable Christian majorities as a result of the newly launched East ASEAN Growth Area (EAGA) — a transborder development scheme covering Sabah, Sarawak, Brunei, Kalimantan, East Indonesia and the Southern Philippines.[77]

In Aceh, profound socio-economic change also deepened sentiments of discrimination and marginalization. In the early 1970s, Suharto cronies pre-empted moves of local Acehnese entrepreneurs to team up with foreign investors in the development of the province's oil and gas industry.[78] The government awarded a concession to ExxonMobil which exploits and refines the oil and gas. Revenues generated from gas and oil amounted to US$2–3 billion during the 1980s, making Aceh the fourth largest contributor to government revenues after Kalimantan, West Papua and Riau.[79] Unfortunately, the oil and gas industry and feeder industries set up subsequently, developed few linkages to the local economy. Geographically concentrated in the eastern coastal areas around Lhokseumawe, they remained enclaves accounting for 40 per cent of Aceh's GDP, but employing only 10 per cent of the workforce.[80] Resettlement, pollution and widening income disparities were other adverse consequences of industrial development.[81] Adding to Acehnese grievances was the fact that the investors brought in their own labour force — mainly consisting of workers from South Sumatra and Java. Development of plantations and the awarding of timber concessions led to the eviction, sometimes by force, of the local population. Exacerbating land disputes were the central government's transmigration projects. The Javanese settlers brought to Aceh later became a key target for GAM harassment. Schulze reports that between 2000 and 2002, alone, an estimated 50,000 migrants were terrorized by GAM into leaving their homes in various parts of Aceh.[82]

Transmigration, which intensified in the 1980s and 1990s, pursued a two-fold objective: First, to ease population pressures on Java and, second, to consolidate the regime's rule which strongly relied on Javanese symbols and values, by settling Javanese in the outer islands. The latter objective reflected the distrust of the regime and the military towards the loyalty of the population in the outer islands — certainly a legacy of the separatism of the 1950s. Moreover, agro-industrial modernization and transmigration left their imprint on the environment. Droughts and floods adversely affected the living conditions of the rural population. Modern fishing fleets from outside the province also depleted the province's maritime resources.[83]

Today, despite its wealth in natural resources, Aceh is the poorest province on the island of Sumatra. Forty per cent of its population live below the poverty threshold, one-third of its villages are classified as poor and 30 per cent of the population are unemployed.[84] The unabated violence gives little prospect for a marked improvement of the situation in the near future. In fact, given the notoriously corrupt provincial bureaucracy, it remains to be seen as to what extent the 70 per cent of oil and gas revenues accruing to the province under the special autonomy granted in 2001, actually trickles down to the grassroots. Yet, as in the case of the Southern Philippines, the perception of central-local relations as a manifestation of internal colonialism, propelling economic marginalization, has played a major role in stiffening Acehnese resistance against the central government.

## Elites

Crucial for translating political discrimination, economic marginalization and repression into separatist uprisings is the existence of an ethnic elite.

In Aceh, the elite mobilizing resistence against the Dutch and later against the Javenese-dominated Indonesian state were Islamic clerics, the *ulamas*. In the 1950s the *ulamas* under the leadership of Daud Beureu'eh were the driving force in the Darul Islam movement which fought for greater autonomy of Aceh and an Islamic state. In the New Order, *ulamas* continued to resent the quasi-secular *Pancasila* state ideology, but saw their authority increasingly eclipsed by the excessive centralism of the Suharto regime and the social transformations going hand in hand with economic modernization in the province.[85]

Even though the provincial governor and some other positions at the apex of the provincial administration were held by Acehnese, this was little more than political symbolism as in their majority these bureaucrats were closely aligned with Jakarta-based political and economic interests. The majority of bureaucrats in the local governments and national line agencies operating in the province were Javanese. Moreover, the Law 1/ 1979 which unified village government structures nationwide sidelined traditional village leaders (including the *ulamas*) and extended central control to the grassroots. Moreover, the same corporatist institutions set up by the Suharto regime to depoliticize Indonesian society were also extended to the religious sector. Acehnese *ulamas* were brought under state control through membership in the provincial branch of the Majelis Ulama Indonesia (MUI) and were increasingly instrumentalized by the government to explain to the population the development policies of the state. These changes are also illustrated by electoral results in the province. While prior to 1987, the Islam-based Partai Persatuan Pembangunan (PPP) dominated elections, from 1987 onward President Suharto's Golkar party won with growing majorities. The electoral decline of the PPP thus further curtailed what was left of the influence of the *ulama* who were aligned with the PPP.[86]

Devoid of powerful leaders and their descendants joining the technocrat urban middle class, the uprising starting in the late 1980s was fomented by a new ethnic elite. The core leaders of Hasan di Tiro's GAM were young Acehnese intellectuals. Moreover, GAM's ideological platform was more secular than previous insurgencies.[87] Nevertheless, Islam still played a major role in Acehnese identity formation. Many mid-level leaders had fought already in the Darul Islam rebellion and GAM was also joined by Afghanistan veterans and fighters trained by the MILF in Mindanao. GAM adherence to Islam was strongest at the village level, where — as Schulze in her enlightening analysis of GAM's strategies and organization shows — "it relied heavily on the mosque network and has often presented its struggle in Islamist terms".[88] Of even greater impact, however, was the emphasis GAM leaders placed on history as a central tenet of Acehnese nationalism. Like in Mindanao, the separatist leadership consciously instrumentalized the reminiscence of a great Islamic past for the construction of ethnic identity. What for the Moros was Sultan Kudarat, was for the Acehnese early seventeenth century Sultan Iskandar Muda and the heroic, *ulama*-led war against the Dutch. After the fall of Suharto, *ulama*-organized groups in the Acehnese branch of the MUI also joined students and local NGOs in their demand to investigate the human rights violations of the Army under DOM.[89]

Yet, Acehnese elites were by no means monolithic. The economic transformation, the expansion of the state and provincial bureaucracy and the increasing educational opportunities created functional elites loyal to the *New Order* state. Their identity was more Indonesian than Acehnese. The fall of Suharto later gave rise to Acehnese NGOs which share GAM's ultimate objective of independence, but unlike GAM, seek to achieve it by peaceful means. The GAM leadership, too, was split into a faction close to exiled GAM founder Hasan di Tiro, a faction based in Malaysia and two local splinter groups. These factions mainly differed in their views on Islam. Unlike the Sweden-based GAM leadership, the breakaway groups stood for more Islamist positions. Divisions also seemed to exist between the GAM leadership in Sweden and local GAM leaders regarding a peace agreement.[90] While GAM leaders in Aceh seemed to be more amenable to a peace agreement, the exiled leadership did not trust the sincerity of the Indonesian Government and military and called for the continuation of the armed struggle. Local GAM leaders viewed a peace agreement and autonomy as a pause for regrouping, without, however, giving up their long-term goal of independence. This was precisely what the Indonesian military sought to avoid and why GAM only reluctantly complied with the peace overtures of the government. Moreover, while di Tiro seemed to prefer a sultanate as the form of government of an independent Aceh, other leaders seemed to opt for a democracy.[91]

In Mindanao, the U.S. colonial administration initially pursued a policy of attraction towards Muslim leaders. *Datus* were either bought off or grudgingly accepted the superior fire power of the U.S. military and eventually pledged compliance. When in the Commonwealth period political and administrative power was laid into the hands of Christian

Filipinos, central authorities began to pursue a more assimilationist policy in the South. Yet, the power of the *datus* was not frontally challenged until the mid-1960s. The Muslim nobility was still elected into local offices and in many areas even Christian settlers voted for them.[92]

However, from the mid-1960s onwards, under the impact of modernization and rising economic stakes, the traditional *datu* elite was faced with a two-pronged challenge: First, Christian politicians aligned with the central government who successfully mobilized the growing Christian majority in the South and thus were able to beat Muslim leaders at the polls. The loss of positions exacerbated the loss of prestige which traditional leaders suffered as a result of their weakening control over land. After all, political office and land were the status symbols of the *datus*. The second, and for the dynamics of ethnic identity-building more formative trend was the rise of a non-traditional Muslim elite. This new elite was young and better educated as the majority of *datus*, though internally divided. One faction, led by Nur Misuari, a former political science instructor at the University of the Philippines, stood for a left-leaning, secular Moro nationalism, while the other faction, led by Misuari's deputy in the MNLF, Hashim Salamat, an Islamic cleric, worked towards an Islamic Moro identity. Both factions were also split along ethnic and clan divisions. While the Misuari faction was basically Tausug from Sulu, the Salamat faction consisted in their majority of Maguindanaoans and Maranaons from Cotabato and Lanao.[93]

In 1957 the Philippine Congress through RA 1888 established the Commission on National Integration. The commission embarked on a programme to uplift the living conditions of Muslims by improving their educational opportunities. As a result, thousands of scholarships were awarded to young Muslims, many of whom studied in the universities of Manila. Between 1958 and 1967, more than 8,000 Muslim students received a higher education, although only 16.7 per cent completed their courses.[94] Returned home, these students had a better education than the old leadership, but an education that was not sufficient to successfully compete with Christian Filipinos for jobs in the bureaucracy and the public sector. This, together with the high dropout rates added to Muslim frustration and turned a well-meant scheme into one exacerbating Muslim alienation. The second group got an education abroad in the religious universities in the Middle East. In the 1950s, Egypt started to provide scholarships for Filipino Muslim students which, after returning home, became religious leaders in their communities. Both groups challenged the *datus*, whom they considered corrupt and self-serving. This, however, did not hinder them to use the old political institutions associated with traditional rulers for constructing a distinct Moro identity.[95]

The educated counter elite became the driving force behind the new organizations which, from the 1960s onwards, championed Moro interests and eventually demanded an independent Moro state. For a while, after *datus* lost their political positions, and in the years after martial law, some of the *datus* like Rashid Lucman and Udtog Matalam cooperated with the new counter elite. Many traditional leaders however sided with the Marcos regime, and those who joined the armed struggle defected in increasing numbers in the 1970s. By 1980, the *datus* had laid down arms.[96]

However, the new counter elite also split. Misuari and Salamat fell out with each other shortly after the Tripoli Agreement, and in 1984, Salamat formed his Moro National Liberation Front (MILF). The MILF, influenced by the Egyptian Muslim Brotherhood and the teachings of Syed Qutb, is supported by the religious scholars which returned from the religious universities of the Middle East. Yet, in the Philippine South, the *ulamas* are much less influential than in Aceh. Although Middle Eastern missionaries came to Mindanao since the 1950s, indigenous clerics only became more influential in the 1980s when the worldwide Islamic revival also reached the Philippine South. From the 1970s onward, substantial Saudi and Libyan funding was channelled into Mindanao and used for the building of religious schools and mosques. Still, studies show that religious leaders only moderately succeeded in inculcating into Filipino Muslims a purified Wahabite form of Islam.[97]

The leadership of the Abu Sayyaf terrorist group, formed in 1991, can hardly be considered Moro elite. Even though they are descendents of the first generation of MNLF fighters, their political objective of fighting for an Islamic Moro state is only of a declaratory nature. They are plain bandits and terrorists.

Today, the outlook of the Moro elite is more Islamic than secular. The MNLF, as the organization standing for the latter, is in disarray and associated with two failed peace agreements. Yet, despite the military prowess of the MILF, which commands between 12,000 and 15,000 fighters,[98] the Moro elite is deeply divided into a number of organizations each claiming legitimacy for the group as a whole and those Moros which have in certain ways accommodated with the Philippine state. The fragmentation of the elite, however, stands in the way of a durable peace solution, because so far bringing all groups (including the Christian settlers) to the negotiating table has proven elusive.

## Singular Incidents and Constellations

While elites may have a long-term catalytic effect on the formation of a distinctive ethnic identity, traumatic incidents such as massacres of members of the in-group by members of another ethnic group also have uniting effects. However, unlike in most other ethnic conflicts in Indonesia such as in East Timor, Kalimantan and the Moluccas, it is more difficult in the case of Aceh to identify a singular incident transforming a latent into an open conflict.

Among such incidents were the massacres perpetrated by the military in the villages of Lot Jeumpa and Pulot Leupung in 1955.[99] Army massacres also occurred in Kreung Geukeueh and Bentong Ateuh in May and July 1999, when forty and fifty people were killed, respectively.[100] Among the singular incidents mobilizing Acehnese resistance against Jakarta was also the violence that broke out during and after the withdrawal ceremony of the non-local troops in 1998.[101] From the perspective of the Indonesian military it was taken as a confirmation that GAM does not respond to concessions. On the part of the GAM, which claims *agents provocateurs* of the army fomented the trouble, it was seen as another proof that the TNI and the central government are untrustworthy. The independence of East Timor may also be considered as singular incident as it strongly inspired Acehnese demands for secession. Yet, the Indonesian Government — also under pressure by concerned ASEAN neighbours — recognized the snowballing effect of East Timorese independence on other separatist movements in the archipelago and henceforth ruled out the holding a referendum as in East Timor in August 1999. The opposition of the military and the government to a referendum exacerbated frustration on the part of GAM and — in tandem with the continuing military atrocities — further radicalized the rebels.

In Mindanao several incidents can be identified as strengthening Moro nationalism. Probably the most decisive was the Jabidah massacre of March 1968. While the circumstances surrounding the massacre are not entirely known, much speaks for the version revealed by Senator Benigno Aquino in the Philippine Senate, who claimed that the Philippine Government had recruited Moros in order to train them for a secret mission to Sabah. They were to be part of a force clandestinely invading the East Malaysian state of Sabah from Sulu without implicating the Philippine military. The Philippine Government had in the 1960s repeatedly renewed its claim on the East Malaysian state of Sabah which historically belonged to the Sultan of Sulu. It seems that the recruits mutinied when they realized the purpose of their training. The Philippine military squashed the mutiny, killing over thirty of the Muslim recruits. The revelation of the massacre inspired Muslim campus activists in Manila to step up secessionist demands.[102] Soon after the *Jabidah* massacre, Moro organizations demanding independence emerged.

Further galvanizing Moro nationalism were massacres such as in Manili, a barrio of the municipality of Carmen in North Cotabato where Christian *Ilaga* militias murdered more than seventy Muslims, mostly old men, women and children, many of them in the local mosque.[103] The final straw for armed rebellion was the declaration of martial law in September 1972 which was perceived as a severe threat to the Moro way of life.[104] Even though these incidents may now be part of a more distant past of the Moros, they have become part of their collective memory and are factors upholding or even renewing the hatred and distrust of the Christian Filipinos and the central government.

## CONFLICT RESOLUTION

The main lesson to be drawn from the comparison of the civil wars in the Southern Philippines and Aceh is that despite an increasing frequency of ceasefires and peace talks, lasting settlements are extremely difficult to achieve. The long-standing nature of both conflicts, a centuries-old history of warfare and the daily experience of discrimination, repression, impoverishment and broken promises have implanted in the collective memories of Acehnese and Filipino Muslims a deep distrust *vis-à-vis* the Javanese-dominated central government and the Christian majority. Intermittent lulls in the fighting must thus mainly be attributed to the exhaustion of the population and the need for regrouping of the secessionists in the face of internal splits and military offensives. The fragmentation of Acehnese and, to a greater extent, Moro elites, aggravated a peaceful conflict resolution. Negotiated settlements falling short of the ultimate objective of secession provoke the defection of extremist splinter groups who view any concession to the government as betrayal of their struggle. Even though they may not be able to seriously challenge the government, they disturb and eventually derail the peace process by bombings, kidnappings and other terrorist acts. Lost commands[105] and criminal gangs posing as ethnic freedom fighters as well as the instrumentalization of rebels and military units by political clans for local power contests further enhance the volatility of the ceasefires.[106] Any violent incident may thus set in motion a new escalation of retaliations, also leaving the more moderate factions on both sides no other choice than to resume full-scale use of force.

Conflict resolution must in the first place end hostilities, initiate confidence-building and address the root causes of the conflicts.[107] Yet, already here we face a dilemma. Given the deep distrust of both sides towards each other, separation of the warring parties and demilitarization may only work if there is external mediation backed up by a peace-keeping force. Demilitarization means the disarmament of the separatists, the reduction of the military presence and the ultimate integration of the insurgents into the military and the police forces. While the Philippines as well as Indonesia have been amenable to third party mediation, both governments view the stationing of an international peace-keeping force as an infringement on their sovereignty. Yet, while rejecting a peacekeeping force in Aceh, the Indonesian Government nevertheless accepted an international observer mission composed of experts from the EU and ASEAN. Fortunately, and certainly a result of the high international attention paid to the peace process in the aftermath of the tsunami, the demilitarization proceeded smoothly, although the continued existence of pro-government militias remains a cause for concern.[108] Under more volatile conditions, however, such as in the Philippines, an unarmed and thinly spread observer group could hardly do anything if violations of the ceasefire agreement occur.

Only if violence is markedly reduced will amnesties and re-integration schemes become attractive for the ethnic minority. The problem with amnesties for rebels, however, is that the military demands the same for officers and men accused of human rights violations. Hence, atrocities committed against civilians must be prosecuted, no matter perpetrated by whom — certainly also including terrorist acts on the part of the rebels. The human rights courts and the truth an reconciliation commission envisioned by the 2005 peace accord on Aceh are certainly steps into the right direction. Yet, doubts linger as to what extent the Indonesian Government is prepared to prosecute military personnel involved in serious human rights violations in the province. The peace agreement leaves open whether the powers of these institutions are retrospective and also apply to the crimes committed during the three decades of civil war. While the peace accord explicitly exempts the exiled leadership of GAM from prosecution, the government announced that it also will not hold the military accountable for its human rights violations.[109]

Prosecution must also go hand in hand with condemnations of violence by the leadership of both parties and apologies to the other side. Adopting responsibility for human rights violations and their demythologization by an active approach towards the traumas they caused is a first step to change the cognitive map of the combatants and their supporters. This must be followed by educational programmes, intensified social interaction and a relentless campaign for tolerance, supported by government authorities, religious and civil society organizations and in the schools with the objective of isolating the militants.

Apart from long-term measures aimed at changing the cognitive map of the people and their leaders, the material conditions must improve markedly for broad sections of the minorities. A first step is the rebuilding of the war-torn infrastructure and the repatriation of refugees. Still, this process is fraught with many difficulties. Given Indonesia's economic crisis and sluggish growth in the Philippines, much of this funding must come from external sources. While in Aceh the devastation of the tsunami has mobilized external resources in an order of nearly US$2 billion (compared to the US$4 billion needed for the reconstruction of the province),[110] the Philippine ARMM has been virtually starved off from development funding both by the central government as well as from foreign donors. Moreover, the Peace Accord of 1996 has shown how difficult it is for a movement that fought a civil war for decades to build up a an effective civilian administration. Aggravating the administrative problems is the expectation of the rebels to be compensated for their sacrifices in the armed struggle by being given preferential access to development funds and opportunities. Here the downward spiral commences: Charges of corruption will be levelled against the autonomous government, factional infighting intensifies and leaders bypassed by appointments and spoils defect. Those rejecting the peace negotiations feel confirmed in their opposition and step up armed struggle. With growing instability, badly needed investments are not coming and foreign donors scale down their assistance. With resource flows reduced to a trickle, the peace accord looses its last vestiges of credibility which rested on the promise of better living conditions. At this point the peace accord has once more degenerated into broken promises, thus further deepening distrust, adding to the sentiments of betrayal and prolonging the conflict.

Granting a major share of the revenues from oil and gas to the Acehnese may mollify their leaders and the population, but creates new problems on a national scale. It weakens the central state, which resource-strapped further looses steering capacity, thus cementing the soft state syndrome characterizing Indonesia after the demise of the Suharto regime. And it creates new socio-economic imbalances among the provinces. As income levels between resource-rich provinces and provinces without natural resources markedly diverge, the disparities may trigger a wave of protests from the poorer provinces. In other words, the new revenue sharing formula for natural resources will be perceived in provinces without natural resources as discriminating. It may exacerbate tendencies among rent-seeking provincial elites to compensate for these losses by indiscriminately increasing local taxes and fees, thereby seriously damaging Indonesia's attractiveness as a destination for investments.

While the Indonesian and the Philippine governments ruled out an East Timor-type referendum and, hence, any prospect of independence for Aceh and Moroland, the only viable option is genuine autonomy which comes close to self-rule and only leaves key functions such as national defence and foreign policy with the national government. Although the August 2005 peace accord on Aceh provides for such a wide-ranging autonomy, we know that the successful implementation of far-reaching decentralization schemes is usually fraught with enormous technical problems.

The special autonomy granted by the Indonesian Government to the Acehnese remains within the confines of the unitary state. While replacing the unitary state by a federal system of government as presently discussed in the Philippines is a theoretically plausible, yet hardly viable alternative. In Indonesia, federalism runs against deeply ingrained beliefs of the national political elite and the military. Especially among Indonesian nationalists, federalism is discredited by the Dutch attempts in the late 1940s to prolong their colonial rule by creating puppet states in a Federation of Indonesia.[111] Moreover, the separatist rebellions of the 1950s have been attributed to the decentralization that gave provincial and local governments much greater independence from Jakarta than under Sukarno's "Guided Democracy" and subsequently the centralist Suharto state. Against this background, the creation of a second chamber based on territorial representation, the Dewan Perwakilan Daerah (DPD), which becomes operational by 2004, is a move into the right direction as are the other consociational ingredients of the Indonesian constitution. They strengthen the participation of the outer parts of the archipelago and of minorities in national decision-making.

No less gigantic are the practical problems facing the introduction of a federal system in the Philippines. These problems become almost intractable, if the introduction of a federal system goes hand in hand with change from a presidential to a parliamentary system. Even taking into account proposals to introduce the federal system gradually until 2010, there is no precedent anywhere in the world where such a radical change of the government system has been attempted. While sections of the Moro leadership may agree to a federalist system in principle, disputes will inevitably emerge over the jurisdiction of one or even more Moro states. Moros will use such a discussion to extract concessions from the central government that a Moro state as part of a Philippine federation will cover the whole territory defined by the Tripoli Agreement. The past has shown that such a demand faces fierce opposition from Mindanao's Christian majority, the central government and the military. In other words, already the demarcation of a Moro state would bring the conflict back to square one. No less daunting are the other problems going hand in hand with federalization: The sharing of powers and revenues between central state, state and local governments as well as the number and jurisdiction of states to be created. A committed and serious implementation of the 1996 Peace Accord by all parties, and the inclusion of the MILF and the Christian majority into the accord, would most likely be a more promising solution than a federalization of the Philippines. In sum, thus, and at least for the moment, the perspectives for a lasting peace seem better in Aceh than in the southern Philippines. Yet, even here, as shown in the previous section, the obstacles towards this objective are formidable and much depends on how smoothly the peace agreement can be implemented in the coming months. Another failure, however, would set bad precedents not only for peace in Aceh but in other simmering conflicts in Indonesia, too.

## ETHNIC SEPARATISM AND INTERNATIONAL TERRORISM

After 11 September 2001 Southeast Asia came into the focus of U.S. anti-terrorism strategists. Catching their attention was the Islamic revival in the region that spilled over to Southeast Asia from the Middle East in the

1980s and gained momentum in Indonesia in the 1990s as a result of deliberate state policies. Challenged by military factions loyal to army commander General Benny Murdani, a Christian, Indonesian President Suharto gave up his policy of containing political Islam and aligned himself with modernist Islam. Although the regime continued to control Islam by co-opting it into corporatist arrangements, state patronage enhanced the legitimacy and symbolic capital of Islam.[112]

After Suharto's resignation in May 1998, political space for militant Islamist groups widened. The socially and economically disastrous consequences of the Asian financial crisis further prepared the ground for Islamic militancy, since the economic slump was widely portrayed as a Western conspiracy designed to weaken Muslims and to thwart the rise of Asia's emerging economic power houses. In the process Islam became a vehicle for mobilizing the population against neo-liberal globalization which was perceived as part of a Western and, in particular, American scheme to establish hegemony over Muslims. All this occurred against the background of a fragile democratization process in which the rules of the political game had to be renegotiated by the Indonesian political elite. As the tug-of-war between the rivalling elite factions dragged on, a weak state, unsure of the loyalty of the security apparatus, was unable to effectively curtail Islamist activities. In an unholy alliance, some radical Islamic groups were instrumentalized by military factions and the remnants of the Suharto regime out to destabilize the fledgling Indonesian democracy.

Pentagon planners, think-tank strategists and the American media were thus quick to portray Southeast Asia's future in gloomy terms. Some of them went so far as likening Indonesia to another Afghanistan and the Abu Sayyaf to the Taliban. After the U.S. military action against the Taliban, reports circulated that Al Qaeda operatives and Arabs fighting with the Taliban were fleeing to Southeast Asia and getting involved in the ethnic conflicts in the Moluccas and Central Sulawesi.[113] In short, Southeast Asia was proclaimed as the "second front" in the war against international terrorism.[114]

American concerns that Southeast Asia might turn into a hotbed of Islamic extremism and a haven for international terrorism, were furthered by apprehensions that Al Qaeda-linked Islamic extremists exploit the separatist insurgencies in the region for their own purposes. Apart from Aceh and the Southern Philippines separatist and ethno-religious conflicts involving Muslim groups raged in the Moluccas, Central Sulawesi and West Papua. A conflict believed to have been pacified resurfaced in Southern

Thailand in early 2004,[115] claiming more than 4,000 lives since then. In the eyes of security analysts these conflicts seemed to represent the eminent danger of state failure and thus provide ideal conditions for Islamic extremism to thrive.[116]

Terrorism experts have since made great efforts to expose alleged links between separatist organizations in Southeast Asia and Al Qaeda. At the centre of their concerns is MILF which — together with Abu Sayyaf — has been labelled by Rohan Gunaratna an "associate group" of Al Qaeda.[117] MILF is accused of providing training in its camps for recruits of Jemaah Islamiyah, the Southeast Asian group with the closest links to international terror networks, and for other militant Islamic groups such as Laskar Jihad and Laskar Jundullah which have been involved in the ethno-religious conflicts of the Moluccas, Central Sulawesi and West Papua.[118] The *Far Eastern Economic Review* cited intelligence sources who, based on photographic material, say Philippine government troops killed several Middle Eastern and Pakistani trainers and demolition experts when they overran MILF's Camp Abu Bakar in 2000. MILF is also said to have received funding from Osama Bin Laden. Such links to Al Qaeda are traced back to the war in Afghanistan where in the 1980s several hundred Muslim Filipinos received military training and fought with the Afghan *mujahidin* against the Soviets. It is further assumed that in the 1990s Bin Laden's brother-in-law, Mohammed Jamal Khalifa, had set up charities and Islamic foundations as a conduit for financing the Moro war against the Philippine central government. Abu Sayyaf was also linked to the operations of Ramzi Yousef, one of the masterminds of the first bombing of the World Trade Tower in New York in 1993 and the architect of other terrorist designs such as the assassination of Pope John Paul during his visit of the Philippines in 1994 and the blowing up of eleven American airliners over the Pacific.[119]

As far as Aceh is concerned, breakaway splinter groups of GAM such as the Front Mujahidin Islam Aceh (FMIA) and Republik Islam Aceh (RIA), which were at loggerheads with the exiled GAM leadership over the role of Islam in GAM's ideology, have been linked to Al Qaeda. Reports claim that their leader, Fauzi Hazbi, has met Omar al Faruq, an Al Qaeda operative later arrested by Indonesian authorities, and to have been in contact with Ayman Zawaheri when he went to Aceh in June 2000. Allegations have also been made about links to alleged Jemaah Islamiyah leader Abu Bakar Ba'asyir and Agus Dwikarna, a JI activist, apprehended in 2002 in Mindanao. The Singapore Government went even further, claiming that GAM guerrillas undergo regular training in Mindanao with the implicit assumption that there contacts to international terrorists are willy-nilly established.[120] Finally, GAM and other separatist groups have occasionally been suspected of being involved in piracy acts in the strategically important Straits of Malacca or in aiding terrorists planning to block the Straits by blowing up one of the super tankers passing the waterway.[121]

A more sober analysis, however, suggests that not only the "second front" thesis, but also the threat perceptions emanating from alleged links between separatism and international terrorism are exaggerated.[122] This is not to belittle terrorism and separatism as security threats, but is a plea to view them in proper perspective. The proven links between Al Qaeda and Southeast Asian Islamist organizations are too well documented as to dismiss them.[123] Yet, it is uncertain how intensive they are. It seems, for instance, that JI operations chief Riduan Isamuddin alias Hambali was the only Southeast Asian belonging to the inner circle of Al Qaeda. With Hambali and others with alleged contacts to Al Qaeda caught or killed in recent years, it is unclear as to what extent the new leadership of Jemaah Islamiyah, Kumpulan Mujahidin Malaysia, Laskar Jundullah and other militant militias are still able to maintain such links. Much of the evidence on which the "second front" thesis is based, rests on murky intelligence material which in some cases did not hold up to deeper scrutiny, on unsubstantiated claims or on the uncritical repetition of outdated information.

Moreover, MILF as well GAM have been adamant in dissociating themselves from international terrorism. MILF repeatedly rejected charges of terrorism, denying links to Al Qaeda. The MILF leadership vocally condemned the September 11 attacks and other terrorist acts with mass casualties committed in the name of Islam, pointing out that such savage acts contradict the Koran and Islam.[124] Moreover, as has been mentioned before, Islam was hardly more than a mobilizing factor in a war of "national" liberation, even though deceased MILF leader Hashim Salamat propagated an Islam with Wahabite leanings. Much thus speaks for David Wright-Neville's judgment that "rather than seeing itself as a religious movement, most MILF members tend to see their struggle less as a religious-based insurgency and more in terms of semi-conventional war of liberation."[125] The same applies to the GAM whose leadership displayed a rather ambiguous relationship to Islam.[126] Moreover, even though the Indonesian Government labelled GAM a terrorist organization, GAM was never implicated in bombings and other terrorist acts outside Aceh. Proven links to terrorist organizations would have diametrically contradicted GAM's strategy to muster international attention and support for its political objectives.[127] Of course, given the decentralized nature of separatist organizations, which was exacerbated after the death of Hashim Salamat in 2003, it cannot be ruled out that individual leaders on the ground do have contacts to trainers and operatives of international terrorist organizations, but it would be wrong to implicate with them the entire organization. Even less convincing is the evidence for a link up between separatist, terrorists and piracy in the maritime zones of the region.[128] While piracy is certainly on the rise in Southeast Asia, only a fraction is occurring in the Malacca Strait and evidence hardly exists that GAM or any other separatist organization was involved in it.

## CONCLUSION

The Aceh and Moro cases illustrate the wider themes of this book, namely, that the security of Asian states, societies, and even individuals depends on ethnic harmony, or at least peaceful coexistence. Virtually every country of Asia save Korea is riven by ethnic interfaces, and thus the potential for disharmony leading to violence is evident throughout the region. The security-policy problem is to manage ethnic pluralism so it does not erupt into armed conflict, separatism, or terrorism, whether locally or internationally supported. Nevertheless I have argued here that ethnicity in and of itself does not produce violence. As Waldmann's framework above has spotlighted, violence is the outcome of unsettling historical experiences and stressful socio-economic conditions inflamed by elite leadership and triggered by situational disappointments or outrages.

The prescription I have suggested is thus to address each factor in its own terms. Concessions and peace talks initiated by governments or rebels are a necessary first step but hardly sufficient to assuage the deep-seated grievances welling up from the past and roiled by the rhetoric and reaction by leaders of both sides, some of whom have an unscrupulous interest in continued conflict. A multi-faceted and long-term strategy must be envisioned by responsible leaders and carried out with patience, sensitivity, and substantial resources. The advent of the war on terrorism is an unfortunate complication inasmuch as it draws outside players, mainly the

United States, into the Asian arena, disturbing delicate local balances, cutting across nuanced negotiations, and allegedly stimulating more recruits for terrorist cells from among aggrieved anti-Western youth.

As argued in this book, state security is only part of the security spectrum, with comprehensive and human security comprising parts of rising salience. Therefore, the threats of Al Qaeda and other international terrorist movements in Asia should not be exaggerated to the point where they becomes an excuse for repressive actions by local governments, drawing attention away from real ethnic injustices and the failures of governments and ethnic leaders to deal with them at the economic, social and individual levels. Policies of denial and deceit will not only violate the tenets of human security but also erode the legitimacy of states in the longer term, and thus undermine the benign stability that has allowed Asian countries to achieve ever-higher levels of political and economic security in recent decades.

## NOTES

1. Joseph Rothschild, *Ethnopolitics. A Conceptual Framework* (New York: Columbia University Press, 1981).
2. For a comprehensive overview on theoretical approaches, see Stefan Ganter, *Ethnizität und ethnische Konflikte. Konzepte und theoretische Ansätze für eine vergleichende Analyse* (Freiburg: Arnold-Bergstraesser-Institut, 1995).
3. Clifford Geertz, The Integrative Revolution. Primordial Sentiments and Civil Politics in the New States, in *Old Societies and New States*, edited by Clifford Geertz (New York: Free Press of Glencoe, 1963), pp. 105–57.
4. Edward Shils, "Primordial, Personal, Scared and Civil Ties. Some Particular Observations on the Relationships of Sociological Research and Theory", *British Journal of Sociology* 8, pp. 130–45.
5. Michael Hechter, *Internal Colonialism. The Celtic Fringe in British National Development, 1536–1966* (London: Routledge & Kegan Paul, 1975).
6. On the concept of "collective memory", see Jan Assmann, *Kollektives Gedächtnis. Schrift, Erinnerung und politische Identität in frühen Hochkulturen* (München: Beck'sche Reihe, 4th edition, 2002).
7. For the concept of "ethnic entrepreneurs", see Rothschild, op. cit.
8. See Peter Waldmann, Ethnischer Konflikt und Klassenkonflikt — ein Diskussionsbeitrag zu widersprüchlichen Theorieansätzen, in *Ethnizität im Wandel*, edited by Peter Waldmann/Georg Elwert (Saarbrücken/Fort Lauderdale: Verlag breitenbach Publishers, 1989). For directing my attention to Waldmann's parameters, I am indebted to Julia Karg.
9. On the role of elites in ethnic conflicts see David Brown, "From Peripheral

Communities to Ethnic Nations: Separatism in Southeast Asia", *Pacific Affairs* 61, no. 1 (Spring 1988): 51–77.

10. Vamik Volkan, *Blood Lines: from Ethnic Pride to Ethnic Terrorism* (New York: Farrar/Straus/Giroux, 1997), cited in Peter Kreuzer, *Applying Theories of Ethno-Cultural Conflict and Conflict Resolution to Collective Violence in Indonesia* (Frankfurt: Peace Research Institute Frankfurt, PRIF Reports no. 63, 2002), pp. 9–10.

11. Peter Gordon Gowing, *Muslim Filipinos — Heritage and Horizon* (Quezon City: New Day Publishers, 1979), p. 17f.; M.C. Ricklefs, *A History of Modern Indonesia since 1300* (Second edition, Houndmills, Basingstoke: MacMillan, 1993), p. 3f.

12. Thomas M. McKenna, *Muslim Rulers and Rebels. Everyday Politics and Armed Separatism in the Southern Philippines* (Manila: Anvil Publishing Inc., 1998), p. 104f.

13. Daniel Joseph Ringuet, "The Continuation of Civil Unrest and Poverty in Mindanao", *Contemporary Southeast Asia* 24, no. 1 (April 2002): 36.

14. Ricklefs, op. cit., p. 143ff.

15. Sylvia Tiwon, "From East Timor to Aceh: The Disintegration of Indonesia?", *Bulletin of Concerned Asian Scholars* 32, nos. 1 and 2 (2000): 101; Piyambudi Sulistiyanto, "Whither Aceh", *Third World Quarterly* 22, no. 3 (2001): 438.

16. Klaus H. Schreiner, "Regionale Konflikte in Indonesien: Eine Krise des Nation Building?", in *ASIEN*, no. 75 (April, 2000): 9.

17. Tim Kell, *The Roots of Acehnese Rebellion, 1989–1992* (Ithaca: Cornell University, 1995), p. 11.

18. Tiwon, op. cit., p. 98; "Aceh: Why Military Force won't Bring Lasting Peace", Jakarta/Brussels: ICG Report no. 17, 12 June 2001a, p 3.

19. Kirsten E. Schulze: *The Free Aceh Movement (GAM): Anatomy of a Separatist Organization, Policy Studies* 2 (Washington, D.C.: East-West Center), p. 4.

20. The number of Libyan trained fighters ranges from 250 to more than one thousand. See Schulze, p. 30.

21. Kell, op. cit., p. 73.

22. Tiwon, op. cit., p. 98–99; International Crisis Group 2001a, op. cit., p. 3.

23. Sulistiyanto, op. cit., p. 444.

24. Tiwon, op. cit., p. 98; Sulistiyanto, op. cit., p. 444.

25. Tiwon, op. cit., pp. 98–99; International Crisis Group 2001a, op. cit., p. 3.

26. International Crisis Group (2001b): "Aceh: Can Autonomy Stem the Conflict?", Jakarta/Brussels: ICG Asia Report no. 18, 27 June 2001, p. 2.

27. *Far Eastern Economic Review*, 13 December 2001, p. 22.

28. International Crisis Group 2001a, op. cit., p. 7; *Far Eastern Economic Review*, 25 September 2003, p. 22.

29. Ibid., pp. 8, 11; Schulze, p. 33.

30. Ibid., p. 4.

31. International Crisis Group 2001*b*, op. cit., p. 4; *Far Eastern Economic Review*, 18 November 1999, pp. 17–18; 22 August 2002, p. 14.
32. International Crisis Group 2001*a*, op. cit., p. 1.
33. Edward Aspinall, "Modernity, History and Ethnicity. Indonesian and Acehnese Nationalism", *Autonomy and Disintegration in Indonesia*, edited by Damien Kingsbury/Harry Aveling (London/New York: RoutledgeCurzon, 2003), p. 142.
34. *Südostasien aktuell*, Januar 2003, p. 17.
35. International Crisis Group, "Aceh: A Fragile Peace", Brussels, 27 February 2003 <http://www.intl.crisis-group.org/projects/showreport.cfm? reportid=907> (accessed 8 May 2003).
36. International Crisis Group 2001*a*, op. cit., p. 14; Schulze, p. 27.
37. *Far Eastern Economic Review*, 5 June 2003, p. 16.
38. *Far Eastern Economic Review*, 5 June 2003, p. 16; 25 December 2003, p. 21.
39. *Spiegel Online*, 31 August 2005 (http://www.watchindonesia@snafu.de) (accessed 27 October 2005); *Süddeutsche Zeitung*, 31 August 2005, S. 7.
40. Anett Keller, "Frieden für Aceh? Perspektiven nach dem Abkommen zwischen indonesischer Regierung und GAM, Kurzberichte aus der internationalen Entwicklungszusammenarbeit". (Asien und Pazifik, Bonn: Friedrich-Ebert-Stiftung, November 2005), p. 2.
41. *Süddeutsche Zeitung*, 30 December 2005, p. 8.
42. McKenna, op. cit., p. 113.
43. Hans U. Luther, Der Mindanao-Konflikt: "Interner Kolonialismus" und regionale Rebellion in den Südphilippinen, in *Regionalkonflikte in der Dritten Welt. Ursachen, Verlauf/Internationalisierung, Lösungsansätze*, edited by Kushi M. Khan/Volker Matthies (Munich/Cologne/London: Weltforum, 1981): 183–282; Nathan Gilbert Quimpo, "Options in the Pursuit of a Just, Comprehensive, and Stable Peace in the Southern Philippines", *Asian Survey* XLI, no. 2 (March/April 2001): 275; McKenna, op. cit.
44. McKenna, op. cit., p. 155; Jolob, op. cit., p. 8.
45. McKenna, ibid., p. 157; Jolob, ibid.
46. Jolob, ibid.
47. Lela Garner Noble, "The Moro National Liberation Front in the Philippines", *Pacific Affairs* 49, no. 3 (1976): 405–24; Luther, op. cit.; McKenna, op. cit., p. 4; Quimpo, op. cit., p. 278.
48. Carmen A. Abubakar, "SPCPD and Economic Development in SZOPAD: High Expectations, Low Output", in *Kasarinlan* 15, no. 2 (2000): 125; Jolob, op. cit., p. 11. See also 1976 Tripoli Agreement <http://www.incore.ulst.ac.uk/cds/agreements/pdf/phil20.pdf> (accessed 9 April 2003).
49. McKenna, op. cit.; Abubakar, op. cit., p. 126; Natasha Jolob, Reference Dossier. Moro Rebel Groups — South Philippines, London: NSA Database, December 2000, p. 12.

50. *Far Eastern Economic Review*, 11 September 1986, pp. 18–19.
51. Frederico V. Magdalena, "The Peace Process in Mindanao. Problems and Prospects", *Southeast Asian Affairs 1997* (Singapore: Institute of Southeast Asian Studies, 1997), pp. 245–59.
52. Abubakar, op. cit., p. 127.
53. Jolob, op. cit., p. 12.
54. Abubakar, op. cit., pp. 128f.; Jolob, op. cit., p. 12.
55. See 1996 Peace Agreement with the Moro National Liberation Front. <http://www.incore.ulst.ac.uk/cds/agreements/pdf/phil16.pdf> (accessed 9 April 2003).
56. *The Manila Times*, 14 February 2003, p. 3.
57. Thomas M. McKenna, "Muslim Separatism in the Philippines: Meaningful Autonomy or Endless War?" <http://www.asiasource.org/asip/mckenna.cfm> (accessed 9 April 2003); Jacques Bertrand, "Peace and Conflict in the Southern Philippines: Why the 1996 Peace Agreement is Fragile", *Pacific Affairs* 73, no. 1 (Spring 2000): 42.
58. Abubakar, op. cit., p. 153.
59. Ibid., p. 148; Bertrand, op. cit., p. 46.
60. <http://www.cyberdyaryo.com/features/f2001_1120_01.htm> (accessed 8 June 2003).
61. Abubakar, op. cit., pp. 140f.; *Business World*, 24 January 2003, p. 11.
62. Ibid., p. 161.
63. *Business World*, 24 January 2003, p. 11; *Today*, 23 January 2003, p. 3.
64. Report of the International Peace Mission to Basilan, Philippines: "Basilan: The Next Afghanistan?", 23–27 March 2002, p. 4.
65. Brown, op. cit., pp. 51–77.
66. Luther, op. cit.; McKenna, op. cit., p. 90; Jolob, op. cit., p. 7.
67. Luther, op. cit., p. 216; McKenna, op. cit., p. 115.
68. Quimpo, op. cit., p. 274.
69. Luther, op. cit., p. 219f.; Bertrand, op. cit., p. 44.
70. McKenna, op. cit., p. 117.
71. <http://www.census.gov.ph/data/pressrelease/2003/pr0301tx.html> (accessed 8 June 2003).
72. *Far Eastern Economic Review*, 25 May 2000, p. 20.
73. Report of the International Peace Mission to Basilan, Philippines, op. cit., p. 5; *Today*, 23 January 2003, p. 4.
74. <http://www.mindanao.org/mindanao/overview/muslim1htm> (accessed 8 June 2003).
75. Luther, op. cit., p. 241; McKenna, op. cit., p. 60.
76. McKenna, op. cit., p. 166.
77. *Far Eastern Economic Review*, 25 May 2000, p. 20.
78. Tiwon, op. cit., p. 98.

79. Sulistiyanto, op. cit., p. 439.
80. International Crisis Group 2001*a*, op. cit., p. 8; International Crisis Group 2001*b*, op. cit., p. 10.
81. For a detailed analysis of the socio-economic changes in Aceh under the New Order regime, see Kell, op. cit., p. 13f.
82. Schulze, op. cit., p. 39.
83. Tiwon, op. cit., p. 98.
84. Ibid.; International Crisis Group 2001*b*, op. cit., p. 10.
85. Kell, op. cit., p. 47f.
86. Ibid., p. 28f.; Sulistiyanto, op. cit., p. 439.
87. Kell, op. cit., p. 65.
88. Schulze, op. cit., p. 8.
89. Jacques Bertrand, *Nationalism and Ethnic Conflict in Indonesia* (Cambridge: Cambridge University Press, 2004), p. 174.
90. Schulze, op. cit., p. 19f.
91. Sulistiyanto, op. cit., p. 447; Schulze, p. 10.
92. McKenna, op. cit.
93. Jolob, op. cit., p. 8.
94. Gowing, op. cit., p. 184.
95. McKenna, op. cit., pp. 139, 143, 164.
96. Ibid., p. 162.
97. Ibid., p. 205f., 228–33; Jolob, op. cit., p. 14.
98. Jolob, ibid., p. 19.
99. Bertrand 2004, op. cit. p. 167.
100. Mike Heed, A Military Massacre in Aceh <http://www.wsws.org/articles/1999/jul1999/aceh-j29.shtml> (accessed 22 November 2003).
101. Sulistiyanto, op. cit., p. 444.
102. McKenna, op. cit., p. 141.
103. Quimpo, op. cit., p. 275.
104. Ibid., pp. 155–57.
105. *Far Eastern Economic Review*, 20 September 2001, p. 30.
106. For an excellent analysis of the mélange of conflicts in the Southern Philippines, see Peter Kreuzer, *Politische Clans und Gewalt im Süden der Philippinen* (Frankfurt a.M.: Hessische Stiftung Friedens-und Konfliktforschung, 2005).
107. Clemens Jürgenmeyer, "Möglichkeiten friedlicher Regelung ethnischer Konflikte", *Nord-Süd aktuell* (2/2000): 330.
108. Keller, op. cit., p. 3 and Felix Heiduk: Der Aceh-Konflikt und seine Auswirkungen auf die Stabilität Indonesiens und Südostasiens (Berlin: Stiftung Wissenschaft und Politik, *SWP-Studie*, February 2004), p. 14.
109. Süddentsche Zeitung, 31 August 2005, p. 7.
110. *Neue Zürcher Zeitung*, 20 January 2005.

111. Ricklefs, op. cit., p. 232; Schreiner, op. cit., p. 13.

112. For details, see Douglas E. Ramage, *Politics in Indonesia. Democracy, Islam and the Ideology of Tolerance* (London/New York: Routledge, 1995).

113. Joshua Kurlantzick, "Tilting at Dominos: America and Al Qaeda in Southeast Asia", *Current History* 101, no. 659 (December 2002): 421.

114. Martin Wagener, "Second Front: Die USA, Südostasien und der Kampf gegen den Terrorismus, Trier: Universität Trier", ZOPS Occasional Paper no. 16, October 2002.

115. Marco Bünte, Gewalt in Thailands Süden: Ursachen und Wege zur Konfliktlösung, *südostasien aktuell*, September 2004, pp. 447–56.

116. On the relationship between state failure and international terrorism see The U.S. National Security Strategy. See <http://www.whitehouse.gov/nsc/nss.pdf> (accessed 27 December 2005).

117. Rohan Gunaratna, *Inside Al Qaeda. Global Network of Terror* (Melbourne: Scribe Publications, 2002).

118. Ibid., *Far Eastern Economic Review*, 12 September 2002, pp. 15–22.

119. Jolob, op. cit., p. 26; Report of the International Peace Mission to Basilan, Philippines, op. cit., p. 17; *Far Eastern Economic Review*, 27 September 2001, p. 22.

120. Schulze, op. cit., p. 23.

121. Heiduk, op. cit., p. 19.

122. For a critique of the "second front" thesis, see Jürgen Rüland, "Südostasien nach dem 11. September 2001. Islam, Sicherheit und Demokratie in einer strategischen Weltregion", *Zeitschrift für Politikwissenschaft*, no. 1 (2003): 143–63 and David Wright-Neville: Dangerous Dynamics: Activists, Militants and Terrorists in Southeast Asia, *The Pacific Review* 17, no. 1 (March 2004): 27–46.

123. Abuza, op. cit.

124. Wright-Neville, op. cit., p. 37.

125. Ibid.

126. Schulze, op. cit., p. 8.

127. Schulze, op. cit., p. 3, 51; Heiduk, op. cit., p. 17.

128. Adam Young/Mark J. Valencia, "Conflation of Piracy and Terrorism in Southeast Asia: Rectitude and Utility", *Contemporary Southeast Asia* 25, no. 2, pp. 269–83.

Chapter Ten

# Irregular Migration as a Security Issue

Stephen Hoadley

## UNREGULATED MIGRATION AS A SECURITY THREAT

Migration has long been a security-policy concern to Asian governments. But during the Cold War it was discounted by realist theorists as a social or economic problem, and thus relegated to "low politics", in contrast to the "high politics" of defence and diplomacy.[1] The rise to prominence of concepts of comprehensive security and human security has brought migration into clearer view as a security threat in the post-Cold War period.[2] This is most obvious in the cases of disorderly migrations forced by government oppression or expulsion, or precipitated by war, ethnic violence, or famine. Furthermore, illegal movement by economic migrants facilitated by document forgers, people-smuggling and people-trafficking gangs, and illicit employer networks, and other law-breaking activity such as labour exploitation, extortion, and forced prostitution, have made migration a central topic for security studies. Because realists and liberals differ on the cause and nature of migration problems and the proper policies to address them, political controversy is endemic.

Migration is an Asian security concern from the perspective of not only the migrants but also the source and host states. Migrants, particularly illegal migrants, are at physical risk during their perilous transit and at legal risk and vulnerable to economic exploitation until their status is regularized in their new abode and their rights protected by governments. Migrants' unauthorized or sudden appearance in the host country can inflame social tensions, raise costs of public services, and unsettle traditional institutions of administration and law enforcement. However, under certain circumstances migration can increase individuals' security, as in the case of escape from famine in North Korea or joblessness in Indonesia or ethnic war in Myanmar. High-skilled or wealthy migrants can be long-term economic assets to their new home countries. Moreover, migration can help a poor and overcrowded source country by relieving pressure and generating remittances. Conversely, it can threaten the source country by depleting its human capital or providing resources for insurrection. Herein lies the six-fold paradox of migration: It can enhance the security of both the migrant and the source and destination countries, or jeopardize the security of all three, or produce good outcomes for one and simultaneously negative ones for the others. This chapter is concerned with the negative outcomes, for they are associated with security risks and threats.

## OVERVIEW OF MIGRATION IN ASIA

The following passages have several aims. The first is to sketch the demographic dimensions of migration in Northeast and Southeast Asia. Initial attention is paid to the movement of refugees because that phenomenon is monitored by the United Nations High Commission for Refugees (UNHCR) and international non-governmental organizations (NGOs), and is thus reasonably well documented. Second, illegal migration is spotlighted and related to security concerns by the destination governments, with examples. In this analysis, facts and figures become sparse and give way to anecdote and speculation. Third, the particular problems of people smuggling and people trafficking are spotlighted, and some responses by Asia-Pacific governments are described and their effectiveness is assessed. Finally, the security implications of emerging migration trends and the responses of governments are summed up and the chapter ends with speculation on future trends and policies.

At the outset one should be aware that there are no "countries of immigration" in Asia. There is no counterpart in the Far East to the United States, Canada, Australia, New Zealand, South Africa, or Argentina, under-populated lands whose governments extend an official welcome to selected categories of immigrants. There are however, several counterparts to Germany inasmuch as the governments of Japan, China, Taiwan and South Korea maintain an open door to ethnic Japanese, Chinese or Koreans, respectively, who wish to return to their fatherlands after absences that may span generations. And there is a qualified counterpart to France and Great Britain inasmuch as Thailand has traditionally been a haven for political refugees from its neighbours Cambodia, Laos, and Myanmar. In the past Hong Kong played that role but it ceased doing so since its return to China's jurisdiction, and the authorities do not permit migration even from China, out of concern for the scarcity of Hong Kong's space and the efficiency of its economy.

At the other end of the spectrum, there are several countries that firmly discourage immigration except for co-ethnics or strictly limited occupational categories of persons. These include Japan, China, South Korea, Taiwan, and Singapore. North Korea and Myanmar stand as extreme examples of a closed-door policy. Other Asian countries attempt to regulate immigration but their maritime geography and the permeability of their borders due to ineffective enforcement allow substantial migration, much of it illegal; these countries include Indonesia, Malaysia, the Philippines, Vietnam, Cambodia, Laos, and Myanmar.

Besides migration within Asia, one must acknowledge also migration to Asia from the Middle East, and from Asia to Europe, North America, and Australia and New Zealand. These links with Asian migration also have security implications, and will be discussed as appropriate.

## REFUGEES AND PERSONS OF CONCERN

Turning to the issue of refugees, one notes first that its impact on Asian societies differs, and the responses of Asian governments vary. Figures compiled by the UNHCR show that "persons of concern" numbered nearly twenty million at the start of 2002. The largest number, totalling nearly nine million, was found in Asia.[3] These totals include not only registered cross-border refugees and others whose status in a country not of their birth was legally insecure or irregular, but also persons internally displaced in their own homelands. But most were in South Asia or Southwest Asia, principally refugees from Afghanistan and Iraq taking refuge in Iran and Pakistan, and others in India and Sri Lanka displaced by armed conflicts and ethnic clashes.

Refugees in the countries of Northeast and Southeast Asia on which this book focuses were relatively fewer in number, totalling just over one-half million. Table 10.1 shows the numbers recorded in each country. Note the relatively large numbers in China due to internal displacement by economic hardship, and in Thailand as a result of permissive asylum policies regarding its neighbours. Note also the relatively small numbers in Hong Kong and especially Singapore, reflecting their restrictive policies and efficient management of displaced persons. One would expect small

**Table 10.1**
**Number of Persons of Concern to UNHCR**
**at the Start of 2002, by Country of Asylum**

| | |
|---|---|
| Cambodia | 1,100 |
| China | 295,000 |
| Hong Kong SAR | 1,900 |
| East Timor | 18,000 |
| Indonesia | 74,000 |
| Japan | 3,530 |
| Korea (South) | 80 |
| Korea (North) | (n.a.; est. 50,000) |
| Malaysia | 51,000 |
| Myanmar (Burma) | 280 reported (est. 1,500,000) |
| Philippines | 2,180 |
| Singapore | 0 |
| Taiwan | (n.a.) |
| Thailand | 111,000 |
| Vietnam | 16,000 |
| TOTAL | 624,070 |

Source: Table 10, *2001 UNHCR Population Statistics (Provisional)*, Geneva: UNHCR Population Data Unit, 7 June 2002. Found at <www.unhcr.ch>. Data for North Korea found in *Country Report: North Korea 2002*. Washington, D.C.: U.S. Committee on Refugees, 2002, found at <www.refugees.org/world/countryrpt/easia_pacific/north_korea.htm>.
Data for Myanmar is vastly under-reported because of the secretive nature of the regime. Data for Taiwan not available.

numbers also in Taiwan for similar reasons, but data are unavailable. The U.S. Committee on Refugees estimates internally displaced persons at one million and refugees in neighbouring countries from ethnic and civil wars and oppression by the regime at another half-million.[4] One suspects there are many more persons of concern in Cambodia and Laos than reported. And the U.S. Committee on Refugees estimates there are twice as many refugees and asylum seekers on temporary permits in Japan than reported by the UNHCR, although to be fair the reporting criteria of the two organizations differ.[5]

## LABOUR MIGRATION

The situation of refugees blurs with that of undocumented labour migrants when economic hardship sends people abroad in search of a livelihood. Labour migration can be beneficial to the security of both the migrant and the host economy, and indeed the economic growth of many countries, not least the United States, can be attributed to this convergence of benefits. But unless labour migrants' rights are recognized and their status legalized, they can remain insecure in the longer term, and social insecurity can rise in times of economic downturn, when pressure to expel labour migrants rises. East Asia is the site of much labour migration, and much of it is non-legal. While some of East and Southeast Asia's labour migration prior to the 1980s was destined to the West and the Middle East, more recent migration flows were predominantly intra-Asian. Much of this migration is non-legal. Some estimates of undocumented labour migration in Asian host countries are summarized in Table 10.2 below.

Labour migration generally reflects the economic change in the region.[6] Accordingly, three types of countries can be discerned. First are the receiving countries. These are economically advanced countries such as Japan, South Korea, Taiwan and Singapore and, prior to its re-integration into the People's Republic of China, Hong Kong, despite many restrictions imposed on labour immigration. Second, fast-growing Southeast Asian economies like Malaysia and Thailand, previously labour exporters, that have become receiving and sending states at the same time. Third, the economically less successful economies such as the Philippines and Indonesia are mainly labour exporters. Myanmar, Laos, Cambodia and Vietnam may also be classified as sending states, though at a lesser scale than the Philippines and Indonesia.[7]

**Table 10.2**
**Undocumented Labour Migrants in Asia in 1999**

| Receiving country | Estimated number | Sending country |
|---|---|---|
| Malaysia | 1.3 million | Indonesia, Bangladesh, India, Philippines |
| Thailand | 0.75 – 1.0 million | Myanmar, China |
| Japan | 0.33 million | China, S. E. Asia, South Asia, Mid East |
| Taiwan | 0.10 million | China, S.E. Asia |
| South Korea | 0.085 million | China, Philippines |
| Singapore | 0.010 million | Malaysia, Philippines, Thailand |
| Cambodia | 1 million | Vietnam, China |
| Myanmar | 0.5 – 1.0 million | China, Bangladesh |

Source: Alan Dupont, *East Asia Imperilled: Transnational Threats to Security* (Cambridge: Cambridge University Press, 2001), Chapter 8, "People-Smuggling, Undocumented Labour Migration and Environmental Refugees".

## SECURITY IMPLICATIONS OF UNREGULATED AND ILLEGAL MIGRATION

It is unregulated and especially illegal migration, not legal migration, which poses a security threat to governments, and is the concern of this chapter. Legal migration is regulated migration, wherein governments issue passports, visas, residence permits or other documents to approved persons, and refuse entry to all others. The numbers involved are usually manageable. This is the prerogative of every legitimate government. But the administration of legal immigration procedures often does not preclude entry by unregulated means, such as infiltration by job-seekers or a stampede of people fleeing civil strife, or illegal means, such as individuals deliberately avoiding or defrauding authorities to gain entry. Regarding prosperous countries, the more strictly their governments impose formal entry requirements, the more widespread and cunning become the attempts to evade those requirements by illegal means.

Examples of unregulated or illegal migration abound in Asia as shown in Table 10.2. But note that "illegals" can become "legals" overnight; host governments may decree blanket refugee status, or grant temporary visas, or simply announce that the "illegals" can stay *pro tem*. Then unregulated entry becomes regulated entry, which legitimates both the entrants' presence and the governments' authority over them. And "legals" can be transformed into "illegals" by similar means, for example when Malaysia in the wake of the Asian currency crisis in 1998 and more recently, in 2002, decreed summarily that Indonesian workers return home. The problems generated for the labour migrants by this policy reversal were compounded by the reluctance of Indonesian authorities to repatriate the expelled workers and the inability of the ailing home economy to accommodate the returning job-seekers.

With unregulated and illegal entrants come a variety of threats.[8] These range from infiltration by criminals or insurgents to transmission of human, animal, or plant diseases, and include also economic costs, social tensions, and violent disturbances. The spread of AIDS in Myanmar through sex workers returning home from Thailand is just one recent example. Threats include also the smuggling of prohibited goods, funds, and even ideas and individuals, as in criminal and terrorist networks.

A case in point is Indonesian migration to Malaysia. Indonesian immigration was long tolerated by Malaysian authorities because ethnic Malay Indonesians were believed to assimilate easily with the local *bumiputra* population. They would thus help to tip the demographic balance in favour of the Malays over the Chinese and Indian immigrant population. In the face of increasing labour shortages in the plantation,

**Table 10.3**
**Examples of Illegal Migrants**

North Koreans in China and South Korea
Koreans in Japan
Chinese in Japan, Taiwan, Thailand and Cambodia
Filipinos in Taiwan
Burmese in Thailand
Filipino Muslims in Malaysia
Vietnamese in Cambodia and China
Cambodians and Laotians in Thailand
Indonesians in Malaysia

construction and manufacturing sectors, illegal immigrants working for less than the officially stipulated minimum wages were tolerated as part of a tacit policy to preserve the competitiveness of the Malaysian economy. In the last decade, in view of a swelling flow of illegal Indonesian immigrants, and as a result of a high crime incidence among Indonesian immigrants, repeated riots involving Indonesian workers, and economic recession in the aftermath of the Asian financial crisis, Malaysian attitudes toward Indonesian immigration turned negative. The 11 September 2001 attacks exacerbated these resentments, for Indonesians played a major role in organizing terrorist groups such as Kumpulan Mujahedin Malaysia (KMM) and Jemaah Islamiyah (JI), both operating in Malaysia.[9] The expulsion of tens of thousands of Indonesian migrant workers in the first half of 2002, and their rude treatment in detention centers by Malaysian police and humiliating penalties meted out to them, instigated heated responses by the Indonesian media and politicians and led to a serious deterioration of bilateral relations. Earlier expulsions of Thai migrant workers from Singapore, and the execution of a Filipina maid convicted for murder, triggered similar emotional responses in the home countries of the migrants and soured diplomatic relations.

Even when migrants are law-abiding, they can threaten social stability by tipping the demographic balance between residents and newcomers, or between one ethno-religious group and another, or between job-holders and job-seekers, raising the potential for struggle for space, services and economic opportunities, and generating social strife. Unwanted entry from particular countries can sour relations between the destination and source governments as the former protests and the latter prevaricates. In the event of conflict the migrant communities will be under suspicion of sympathizing with their country of origin or even of espionage, sabotage and insurrection. They may also be recruited, or infiltrated, by the source country government for these purposes. During the Cold War period, for instance, Chinese minorities in Southeast Asia were suspected of serving as Beijing's "fifth column" in the region. And in Cambodia the genocidal Khmer Rouge tagged Vietnamese immigrants as agents of the government in Hanoi.

Finally, the very fact of illegal entry undermines the credibility of the destination government by showing that its borders cannot be protected. This may be exacerbated by blackmail, bribery or other forms of corruption which will erode the probity of administration and law enforcement of the destination government.

## PEOPLE SMUGGLING AND PEOPLE TRAFFICKING

Governments are increasingly pitted not only against the ingenuity of individual aspiring migrants but also the cunning and adaptability of international criminal conspiracies engaged in moving people across national borders illegally. These activities are named people smuggling and people trafficking. They arise out of similar "push" circumstances such as civil disorder and economic deprivation but are analytically distinct in terms of means and consequences. People smuggling is the facilitation of voluntary illegal migration for profit. It is, in effect, an illicit travel service for economic migrants and refugees with money. People smuggling has grown into a major international business in the past decade. Some estimates place the number of smuggled persons annually at four million and the revenues earned by smuggling networks at over US$5 billion.[10]

People trafficking involves fewer persons but is more insidious, particularly for the victims. It is the moving of people under false pretences or by coercion, for the purpose of exploiting them, as in the trafficking of children for inappropriate work and young women for prostitution. The U.S. State Department estimates up to 900,000 victims are trafficked annually. This earns up to US$10 billion for the traffickers, putting this criminal activity in the same league as drug and gun smuggling in profitability.[11] And it takes its toll. The evils accompanying trafficking include not only the harmful effects on the victims' human security but also the undermining of public health and social order and the encouragement of organized crime and terrorism. Table 10.4 summarizes the U.S. State Department's inventory of the threats to security posed by human trafficking.

**Table 10.4**
**People Trafficking Threats to Security**

| |
| --- |
| Trafficking is a human rights violation |
| Trafficking increases social breakdown |
| Trafficking deprives source countries of human capital |
| Trafficking undermines public health |
| Trafficking subverts government authority |
| Trafficking promotes organized crime |
| Trafficking can finance illicit activities and terrorism |

Source: Abridged from *Trafficking in Persons Report, June 2004* (Washington: U.S. Department of State Bureau of Public Affairs, 14 June 2004), found at <www.state.gov>.

While distinct in conception, in practice the smuggling and trafficking networks tend to overlap in routes, organization, personnel, and methods. Their structures are decentralized, segmented, and flexible. Typically, these structures put down roots in three venues: First, countries of out-migration, second, countries of transit, and third, countries of destination. The latter especially applies to people-trafficking networks. A simplified pattern would be thus: First, recruiters in countries of out-migration make contacts, collect initial payments, coach migrants, provide travel and identity documents (often fraudulent or forged), and introduce the migrants to their travel escorts. The second group conducts the migrants by land, sea, or air through intermediate countries to the port of destination. The transit organization may in fact be several segmented organizations and include different modes of transport, such as trucks, boats, or airlines. The organization at the destination point may be rudimentary in the case of people smugglers, whose main job is to retrieve the fraudulent documents for recycling to the next bunch of migrants, and who often abandon the migrant at the port of entry or at a desolate beach, jungle, or mountain wasteland. People traffickers by contrast have a permanent presence in the destination country. They may bribe officials, meet new arrivals, and physically escort their hapless "clients" to prospective employers, from whom they get payment, and then watch over the illegal migrant-worker, often extorting money and threatening or meting out violence to assure compliance and secrecy.[12]

In Asia, the overwhelming bulk of illegal migrants originate in China, whence they attempt to move to Europe, the United States, Australia, or other countries of the Asia-Pacific. According to a U.S. estimate, three-quarters of a million Chinese migrated illegally in the early 1990s, 200,000 to the United States, 100,000 to Europe, 150,000 to Russia, and 200,000 to the Asia-Pacific. The business was worth US$3 billion to the smuggling and trafficking networks.[13] Those who do not leave by air tend to exit by two main routes. The first is *via* the Fujian coast in Southeast China. From there, Taiwan fishermen turned smugglers transport them to Taiwan, Southeast Asia, or directly to the United States. The second is overland through Yunnan Province south through Laos or Myanmar to Thailand and thence to Western destination countries by air or boat. Bangkok is a notorious way-station for illegal migration not only from China but also from Southeast Asia, and as a transit point for the numerous refugees from Afghanistan and the Middle East that proliferated in the 1990s.

## UNILATERAL POLICIES TO CURB ILLEGAL MIGRATION

National governments have the primary responsibility to curb not only people smuggling and people trafficking but also to manage unregulated refugee and migrant labour flows.[14] Their goal is mainly to protect their own national security and stability. But the rising profile of international human rights standards, backed by the initiatives of the UNHCR and the human rights agencies, has induced governments to pay closer attention also to the protection of the security of the victims, the migrants. As suggested above, governments fall into three categories depending on whether they have jurisdiction in source countries, transit countries, or destination countries.

- The source country governments have the hardest task. They are obliged not only to outlaw and police the illegal networks facilitating the migrant outflow but also to create stable and secure political conditions and economic opportunities so as to minimize the incentive for emigration. But closing the border to keep people in is not practical, nor is it legal in international law.
- Transit country governments are obligated to monitor and manage cross-border migration and curb illegal organizations; they are also obliged to treat the migrants humanely. They must refrain from returning them to harm in their countries of origin or irresponsibly pushing them on to the next country.
- Destination country governments are likewise obliged to observe the human rights of the migrants, provide for their basic welfare, and grant them political asylum if necessary. Once they grant visa, refugee or protected status, they are obliged to facilitate the permanent settlement and integration of the new migrants, to maximize both the migrants' welfare and the stability and prosperity of the destination society and economy. And governments should act against the criminal smugglers or traffickers based or operating in their country, including supporters such as document forgers, financiers, couriers, escorts, enforcers, and employers and landlords.

Australian scholar Andreas Schloenhardt offers a comprehensive inventory of illegal migration activities which is summarized in Table 10.5.[15] He also surveys the governments of the Asia-Pacific and finds that laws prohibiting these activities are spotty and often non-existent. These lacunae suggest

**Table 10.5**
**Migration Activities to be Outlawed**

| |
| --- |
| Mobilizing migrants by false promises |
| Offering illegal migration |
| Organizing illegal migration |
| Facilitating illegal migration |
| Transporting illegal migrants |
| Harbouring and concealing illegal migrants |
| Immigration fraud by false statement |
| Forgery and falsification of documents |
| Transfer of documents to unauthorized migrants |
| Conspiracy to commit a crime |
| Criminal organization |

Source: Abridged from Andreas Schloenhardt, "Trafficking in Migrants in the Asia-Pacific: National, Regional, and International Responses", *Singapore Journal of International and Comparative Law* 5 (2001): 696–747.

that a valuable first step by governments keen to curb illegal migration activities would be to legislate comprehensively against them. This would set standards publicly, deter illicit migrants and operators, and provide a legal basis for detection, apprehension, and prosecution of smugglers and traffickers.

Governments serious about curbing illegal migration networks and activities must go beyond providing a legal basis for cracking down on particular offenders. They are well advised to strengthen their capacities for intelligence gathering and processing, immigration administration, border control, non-corrupt and effective law enforcement, expeditious execution of justice, and public education.

## INTERNATIONAL EFFORTS TO DEAL WITH ILLEGAL MIGRATION

The roles of the UN High Commission for Refugees and the International Organization for Migration (IOM) are central to monitoring and ministering to refugees, many of which become illegal migrants in the course of their flight. Numerous other international and national organizations deal with localized or specialized aspects of the refugees' plight such as the World Food Programme (WFP), the World Health Organization (WHO), and the International Labour Organization (ILO). And a myriad of churches and NGOs contribute to ameliorating the refugees' conditions and advocating their claims in transit and destination countries. These organizations have done much to raise the security of the migrants en route. Their initiatives also assuage the fears of transit governments that the refugees might stay forever, stimulating political hostility and precipitating in the extreme case summary expulsion or refusal of entry despite the hazards to the vulnerable migrants, and recriminations with neighbouring governments.

But as people smuggling and people trafficking emerged as serious new threats to security, and governments found it impossible to cope alone with increasing illegal flows outside the Refugee Convention paradigm, leaders began to search for more cooperative and comprehensive responses. These took three forms: (1) standard-setting and law-making by treaty; (2) coordination through international organizations, and (3) Asian regional policy consultation through *ad hoc* conferences and bilateral diplomacy.

## (1) Treaties

Because smugglers and traffickers exploit discrepancies in law and policies between countries, international treaties to harmonize laws function to narrow differences and thus opportunities for manipulation. An overarching treaty finalized in December 2000 is the Convention Against Transnational Organized Crime. This major convention is bolstered by two subsidiary agreements, the Protocol Against the Smuggling of Migrants by Land, Air and Sea and the Protocol to Prevent, Suppress and Punish Trafficking in Persons.

Other treaties, some recent, some mature, have been brought to bear on the new threats posed by illegal migration. These include the:

- ILO Convention on the Elimination of the Worst Forms of Child Labour,
- Optional Protocol to the Convention of the Rights of the Child,
- Optional Protocol on the Sale of Children, and
- Optional Protocol on the Rights of the Child in Armed Conflict.

In addition, many conventions outlawing slavery can be applied to trafficking.

Over all these international agreements stands the International Bill of Human Rights. This includes Universal Declaration of Human Rights, and its two principal buttresses the International Convention on Civil and Political Rights and the International Convention on Economic, Social and Cultural Rights. The Refugee Convention 1951 applies their provisions to persons fleeing persecution. Unfortunately, not all Asian states have adopted these instruments. For example, as of mid-2003 seven East and Southeast Asian states had neither ratified nor signed the Protocol on People Smuggling: Brunei, Myanmar, China, Laos, Malaysia, North Korea, and Vietnam. The Philippines was the only state to both sign and ratify; the remainder have signed but not ratified. And of seventeen Asian states, only three, South Korea, Hong Kong, and Taiwan, were judged by the U.S. State Department as complying with the U.S. Trafficking Victims Protection Act, and seven (Japan, Singapore, Malaysia, Indonesia, Nepal, Sri Lanka, and Cambodia) were judged to be non-complying but making efforts to comply. But seven (India, Japan, Laos, Pakistan, Philippines, Thailand, Bangladesh and Vietnam) were placed on a watch list indicating significant abuses despite good intentions, and two — Myanmar and North Korea — were condemned as neither complying nor making efforts to do so.[16] It is apparent that until acceptance of the People Smuggling Protocol and other relevant instruments becomes more widespread, international legal gaps will remain in which smugglers and traffickers will operate with impunity.

## (2) International Organizations

Treaties set legal standards, but these can be made effective only by institutions to monitor, implement, and enforcement them. These responsibilities rest on states in the first instance. But states increasingly work together to share risks, costs and administrative burdens, and to match the multi-national character of smuggling and trafficking networks. A number of multilateral institutions have been established in recent decades; those of especial relevance to the migration issue include the following:

- The UNHCR, the IOM, the ILO, and the UN human rights agencies have adapted their work in part to take into account intensifying refugee and migrant worker issues, in Asia and elsewhere.
- The G-8 governments at their 1999 Moscow summit adopted common principles and an action plan to combat people trafficking.
- In parallel, around fifty states have cooperated voluntarily for the past several years in the Inter-governmental Consultations on Asylum, Refugees and Migration Policies in Europe, North America, and Australia.

- In 2002 the UNHCR convened a meeting of 127 member states to endorse the Agenda for Protection and a Programme of Action to coordinate refugee policies; the agenda also distinguished between legitimate and refugee movements and illegal migration by means of smuggling and trafficking.[17]

## (3) Asian Initiatives

But these efforts needed to be supplemented to focus on illegal migration as manifested in particular regions of the world such as Asia where the problems were unique in magnitude and complexity. Out of these needs emerged a number of Asian regional and *ad hoc* meetings, supplementing international treaties and institutions. Many have become regular events despite the absence of headquarters or formal organizations, with member governments providing leadership, hosting, and secretarial services. These include the following:

- The Asia-Pacific Consultations on Refugees, Displaced Persons, and Migrants (APC), organized originally in the mid-1990s by the UNHCR and the IOM with encouragement by Australia, now includes twenty-four member states with a focus on population movements generally.
- "The Manila Process". This annual meeting of seventeen regional governments, with a focus on irregular migration and migrant trafficking, has been coordinated by the IOM with the help of the Philippines since 1996.
- The Bangkok Declaration on Irregular Migration was conceived by the IOM in consultation with concerned Asian governments in the mid-1990s. The government of Thailand convened the meeting at which fifteen Asian region governments adopted the Bangkok Declaration. This instrument set legal goals and standards and provided a common vocabulary to encourage convergence of national laws on smuggling, trafficking, and organized crime.
- The Association of Southeast Asian Nations (ASEAN) proclaimed its Declaration on Transnational Crime in 1997 and followed that up by drafting a Plan of Action on Cooperation on Immigration Matters and organizing an officials working group that continues to meet periodically.

Indonesia, a major transit country between the Middle East and Australia, in the early 2000s hosted (with Australian support) two major Asian regional meetings to address the problems. Each was attended by representatives from over fifty governments from Asia and neighbouring regions. These meetings were:

- the Regional Ministerial Conference on People Smuggling, Trafficking in Persons and Related Transnational Crime, in 2001, and
- the Regional Conference on People Smuggling, in 2002.

## SHORTFALLS

It was noted above that a number of governments had not acceded to major international agreements on refugees and trafficking, notably Brunei, Myanmar, China, Laos, Malaysia, North Korea, and Vietnam, and that others such as Indonesia, Bangladesh, Cambodia, and Thailand were lax in policing their borders and otherwise meeting their international obligations. These were the same governments whose attendance at the Asian regional meetings and other initiatives was irregular and unenthusiastic. The reasons were several. For the poor countries with porous boundaries, lack of resources was a practical obstacle. For governments sceptical of the West, illegal migration was conceived as a problem for the West, not themselves; for others it was a private affair not requiring government attention. Some governments tacitly welcomed out-migration as a means of reducing overcrowding and eventually generating remittances from successful emigrants. Endemic corruption and collusion with smugglers and traffickers reduced incentives to cooperate with international and regional efforts to curb these activities, and some governments regarded them as legitimate sources of income.

When international and regional efforts fell short, some concerned governments took bilateral action, notably Australia, an attractive destination for thousands of illegal migrants in the 1990s. Australia has become especially active as a result of a surge of unauthorized arrivals by air and sea from Asia and the Middle East in the late 1990s.[19] The Australian Government was particularly worried by what it regarded as lax law enforcement by Indonesia, at whose southern ports many illegal migrants bound for Australia have embarked, often with the knowledge and tacit permission of local authorities. In the late 1990s and early 2000s the Government of Australia undertook not only to tighten up its regulations on asylum seeking and to enforce them stringently, but also to make direct approaches to governments of countries from which migrants came, or through which they passed en route to Australia.

In the past five years Australia has engaged at government-to-government level source and transit countries such as China, Indonesia, Vietnam, Pakistan, Afghanistan, and Iran. Australia's ministers enjoined the cooperation of their counterparts in retarding illegal migrant flows and sharing information with Australia. In many cases written pledges of mutual cooperation were made in Letters of Exchange or Memoranda of Agreement. Australia has given aid to train partner country migration and law enforcement officials to raise standards of information-gathering and management of migration flows in their countries. Australia has provided funding bilaterally and through the UNHCR and the IOM also, and controversially, to support migrant and refugee processing camps in Southeast Asia and the South Pacific to deflect the movements of asylum seekers away from Australia. Those illegal migrants who manage to reach Australian soil are subject to compulsory detention while their claims are being authenticated. These policies have attracted criticism at home and internationally for their adverse consequences for human rights and their insensitivity to partner governments, but have proved effective in reducing numbers of fraudulent arrivals, and show no signs of easing.

## CONCLUSION

It is evident that unregulated and illegal migration in and through Asia will continue, given the combination of push factors of political disruption and economic deprivation in source countries, the pull factors of stability, jobs, and prosperity in destination countries, and the lure of easy profits for smugglers and traffickers in between. Countervailing policies are being discussed, devised, and implemented throughout Asia and also in Australia, North America, and Europe, all destinations affected by Asian migration flows. Many of the policies involve interception, deflection, detention or expulsion of migrants. But these policies, entailing tougher laws and stricter enforcement, are becoming controversial inasmuch as they infringe on rising human rights standards and humane sensibilities in liberal countries, and are yielding only short-term results. Longer-term policies are emerging amongst progressive governments; these involve relief aid, economic assistance, support for good governance, and bilateral and multilateral cooperation to reduce the motives for migration. But emerging also is a concern to take the critical focus off the migrants and put it on the smugglers and traffickers and the governments who allow them to operate with impunity. Liberal theorists and NGO activists prefer to recast migration as a human rights issue rather than just a law enforcement issue.[20] While acknowledging the security dimensions of the problem for governments, they would emphasize the need to criminalize the smuggler or trafficker but not the migrant, who should be protected. Thus the concepts of state security and human security are seen once again to interact, this time on the issue of irregular migration. The policy challenge is to balance them humanely as well as effectively so as to protect the rights of individuals as well as the integrity and stability of governments.

## NOTES

1. Astri Suhrke, "The 'High Politics' of Population Movements: Migration, State, and Civil Society in Southeast Asia", in *International Migration and Security*, edited by Myron Weiner (Boulder: Westview Press, 1993).

2. Suhrke (above) and many of the chapters in *The Cambridge Survey of World Migration*, edited by Robin Cohen (Cambridge: Cambridge University Press, 1995), show that unregulated migration is hardly a new threat but, as described in Chapter One of this book, it is now appreciated in a new security policy context.

3. *Basic Facts: Information about UNHCR: Refugees by Numbers 2002.* Geneva: UNHCR, 2002. Found at <www.unhcr.ch>.

4. *Country Report: Burma 2002.* Washington D.C.: U.S. Committee on Refugees, 2002. Found at <www.refugees.org/world/countryrpt/easia_pacific/burma.htm>.

5. *Country Report: Japan 2002.* Washington DC: U.S. Committee on Refugees, 2002. Found at <www.refugees.org/world/countryrpt/easia_pacific/japan.htm>.

6. The Asia Pacific migration system with reference to theories of economic motivations is surveyed by Douglas S. Massey et al., *Worlds in Motion: Understanding International Migration at the End of the Millennium* (Oxford: Clarendon Press, 1998), pp. 160–95.

7. Suriya B. Prasai, "Intra-Asian Labor Migration", *Asian Survey* XXXIII, no. 11 (November 1993): 1055–70; Joseph Liow, "Malaysia's Illegal Indonesian Migrant Labor Problem: In Search of Solutions", *Contmporary Southeast Asia* 25, no. 1 (April 2003): 44–64.

8. Peter Chalk, *Non-Military Security and Global Order* (Macmillan, 2000), especially Chapter 6 on "Mass Unregulated Population Flows", is a useful introduction to the problem. Also see Warren Zimmerman, "Migrants and Refugees: A Threat to Security?" in *Threatened Peoples, Threatened Borders*, edited by Michael S. Teitelbaum and Myron Weiner (New York: W.W. Norton, 1995 and Myron Weiner, "Introduction: Security, Stability and

International Migration" in *International Migration and Security*, edited by Myron Weiner (Boulder: Westview Press, 1993), especially pp. 9–21.

9. See Rüland in this book, p. 240.

10. Prime Minister's [of Australia] Coastal Surveillance Task Force Report, Executive Summary, June 1999 found at <www.dpmc.gov.au>.

11. *Trafficking in Persons Report, June 2004* (Washington: U.S. Department of State Bureau of Public Affairs, 14 June 2004), found at <www.state.gov>. The International Organization for Migration offers a similar estimate, found at <www.iom.int>.

12. Alan Dupont, *East Asia Imperilled: Transnational Threats to Security* (Cambridge: Cambridge University Press, 2001) Chapter 8, "People-smuggling, Undocumented Labor Migration and Environmental Refugees".

13. Graeme Hugo, "Illegal International Migration in Asia", in *The Cambridge Survey of World Migration*, edited by Robin Cohen (Cambridge: Cambridge University Press, 1995), p. 398.

14. James F. Hollifield, "The Politics of International Migration: How Can we 'Bring the State Back In'?", in *Migration Theory: Talking Across Disciplines*, edited by Caroline B. Brettell and James F. Hollifield (New York: Routledge, 2000).

15. Andreas Schloenhardt, "Trafficking in Migrants in the Asia-Pacific: National, Regional, and International Responses", *Singapore Journal of International and Comparative Law* 5 (2001), pp. 696–747.

16. *Trafficking in Persons Report, June 2004* (Washington: U.S. Department of State Bureau of Public Affairs, 14 June 2004), found at <www.state.gov>.

17. *The Agenda for Protection* arose from the Global Consultations on International Protection. See <www.unhcr.ch>.

18. Australia's policies have become notorious amongst media commentators and humanitarian NGOs, for example see Peter Mares, *Borderline: Australia's Treatment of Refugees and Asylum Seekers* (Sydney: University of New South Wales Press, 2001). For the Australian Government's view of illegal migration problems besetting the country and its policies to meet them see <www.immi.gov.au>.

19. Ibid.

20. William Malley, "Refugees and Forced Migration as a Security Problem" in *Asia's Emerging Regional Order: Reconciling Traditional and Human Security*, edited by William T. Tow, Ramesh Thakur, and In-Taek Hyun (Tokyo: United Nations University, 2000); Andreas Schloenhardt, "Migrant Trafficking and Regional Security", *Forum for Applied Research and Public Policy* 16, no. 2 (Summer 2001): 83–88; Myron Weiner, *The Global Migration Crisis: Challenge to States and to Human Rights* (New York: HarperCollins College Publishers, 1995); Bill Jordan and Franck Duvell, *Irregular Migration: The Dilemmas of Transnational Mobility* (Cheltenham: Edward Elgar, 2002), especially Chapter 10, "In Search of Global Justice".

Chapter Eleven

# Globalization and Asian Financial Insecurity

Mia Mikic

## INTRODUCTION

In the past decade we have witnessed a number of financial crises in Asia and elsewhere. None was predicted but all imposed great economic and social costs on the countries involved directly or indirectly in the crises. The stability of states and the security of their inhabitants were jeopardized. Greater openness of economies, a facet of globalization, thus entails greater instability, vulnerability, and costs not only in the economic sector but in society, politics, and international relations as well. Financial integration has spread, outdistancing methods or mechanisms for assessing the state of countries' financial sectors and economies in general so that crises could be predicted and costs either prevented or minimized. However, more is learnt from bad experiences than from good ones. This chapter is thus a stock-taking exercise about where we stand today with respect to financial crises, that is, what we know about their causes and how to respond to them.[1] Answers to such questions are essential for providing stability and predictability to the markets, which in turn are necessary (although not always sufficient) conditions for Asian security.

The chapter begins with giving a brief overview of the process of globalization and its different aspects. The rest of the chapter is organized as follows. An overview of potential benefits and costs of open financial markets is given prior to discussing the nature and types of financial crises as one of the more serious globalization-driven threats to security. This is followed by a detailed account of the Asian crisis of 1997–98. While the Asian crisis was indeed triggered by an overvalued Thai baht in July 1997, there is a host of contributing factors leading to this triggering moment and inducing the crisis to spread. There is a broad consensus on what caused the Asian crisis. It was different from other crises because its origin was found in imbalances of the private sector across the region. Nevertheless, the crucial question remains why the policymakers in the East and Southeast Asian countries, which managed their economies so well before, and not at all so badly since, did not see the crisis coming. There is a set of policy prerequisites that may allow governments better to manage the risks while still letting their countries enjoy the benefits of open financial markets. The final section of the chapter offers a reconsideration of the International Monetary Fund's (IMF) response to financial crises and some elements for strengthening the architecture of the international financial system.

## GLOBALIZATION AND ITS MANY FACETS

Globalization has become one of the most written-about topics in recent years, and rightly so. The impacts of globalization have become more forcefully felt than ever before. Both, the benefits, like reduction of aggregate global poverty and inequality, and negative impacts, such as crises and security threats, grew stronger as larger shares of the world's population and more economies got enmeshed in the interdependent "global" economy.[2]

There are several facets of globalization, all part of the same process which results in the deeper and fuller connectedness over national borders of the real and financial markets:

- Trade liberalization;
- Liberalization of financial flows and capital movements;
- Accelerating labour movements (legal and illegal migration); and
- Easier diffusion of knowledge, information and technology (information technology).[3]

Not all of these elements play equally important roles, but vary with historical circumstances. A number of research studies have pointed to two main surges of globalization in the modern era: A first wave lasting from 1890 until 1914, and after the retrogression of the inter-war period, a second wave beginning in the 1950s. The two waves of globalization are found to differ with respect to flows of labour and knowledge. Labour migration was very much a part of the first wave of globalization; in contrast, the direct or visible flows of information (except flows of knowledge embodied in labour) were negligible. At the present time it is labour that is being kept behind national borders, while information flows across borders without significant restrictions.[4] But the key difference between the two surges was the existence of a gold standard regime in the first one. Its breakdown was followed by the cessation of trade among the largest trading nations, thus contributing to the great depression in Europe and Americas and to debt crises in Latin America. Globalization was halted for a number of years until it took off again in the 1950s, supported by the partial return to the gold standard (by establishment of the Bretton Woods international monetary system) and liberalization of trade (by establishment of the multilateral rules for trade through the General Agreement on Tariffs and Trade, GATT).[5] These fundamentals of globalization shifted dramatically in the early 1970s when the Bretton Woods system collapsed, drastically reducing restrictions on international flows of capital. At the same time, liberalization of trade continued at its stop-go pace, while in contrast almost no additional freedom in international movements of labour was noticeable.

Obviously this uneven and shifting contribution of particular forces of globalization had to affect the overall process of globalization: Inter-dependence of markets cannot be achieved only by deepening integration in a single sector. In fact, as the narrative will show below, instability and crisis are much more likely when one of these sectors gets out of balance with the others. Thus when financial liberalization surged ahead of other aspects of globalization in Asia in the 1997, as in other parts of the world at other times, we had a stability problem that resulted in a crisis. In future, the gains from further globalization can be consolidated only by governments' ability to combine and synchronize all the elements of market integration.

## IMPACT OF FINANCIAL OPENNESS IN ASIA

The surge in flows of private capital into Asian economies in the 1980s and 1990s can be explained by a combination of two forces, one characterized as a pull factor and the other as a push factor.[6] A key pull factor was liberalization of financial markets in developed and developing countries alike. In particular, many Asian developing economies, just as those of Eastern Europe a few years later, were moving from regimes of financial repression to regimes without capital control and with deregulated domestic financial markets. On a push side, a search by Western, Middle East (petro dollars), and Japanese capital for higher rates of return and diversification of risk played an important role. Together they caused a sudden increase in capital inflows into the developing economies, and Asian developing economies attracting the lion's share. While growth of foreign direct investment (FDI) was stable throughout this period, growth of foreign portfolio investment and other private capital flows started to behave quite erratically in the second half of the 1990s, stimulating the *Trade and Development Report 1997* to claim that the volatile financial flows and international financial instability "constitute the single most important impediment to attaining steady and rapid growth".[7] (See Figure 11.1) Furthermore, the dependence on private flows of capital compared to official flows remained very high. This dependence on private capital flows was welcome as it was consistent with the approach to development based on efficient markets, that is, the idea that private capital would be more inclined than public flows to find its most efficient use, thus contributing to higher growth rates.[8]

This correlation between financial openness and high economic growth is in fact only one of the benefits that are associated with the free capital movements. Other benefits include:

- Counter-cyclical role in risk sharing and consumption smoothing,
- The positive impact on domestic investment,
- Enhanced macroeconomic discipline, and
- Increased efficiency and greater stability of the domestic financial system which is penetrated with foreign banks.[9]

Financial openness does not bring only positive effects but also negative ones, as some detrimental experiences have shown in Asia, Mexico, the Russian Federation, Brazil, Turkey, and Argentina, to mention only the

Figure 11.1
Private and Official Capital Flows (net) in Asia 1995–2002

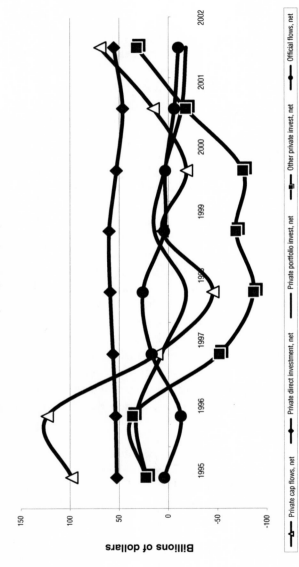

crises of the 1990s. Economic theory acknowledges that financial openness can render a country vulnerable to the risk of volatility and abrupt reversals in capital flows, causing high, widespread, and prolonged costs due to likely herding and contagion effects. Other potential costs of open financial markets include a high degree of concentration of capital flows and crowding-out of small companies, an inadequate allocation of financial flows with an adverse effect on growth, the loss of macroeconomic stability, pro-cyclical movements in short-term capital flows, and risks associated with foreign bank penetration.[10]

A comparison of benefits and costs listed above implies that open financial markets with high penetration of foreign banks in the domestic financial system can do an economy good (by increasing the depth of financial markets, lowering the costs via an increased competition and an increase in efficiency of the financial intermediation process) or bad (rationing of credit to SMEs or to the firms in nontradable sector, pressuring domestic banks into mergers causing concentration, or non-lending to domestic firms in crisis). One cannot make a definitive *a priori* determination of the net effects of the open financial system.[11] One could compile a list of factors similar to those of the theory of regional trade agreements, which might lead to a margin of potential benefits outweighing potential costs. But ultimately the net impact of financial openness is an empirical question.

## FINANCIAL CRISES AND REASONS CAUSING THEM

A financial crisis is typically defined as a loss of confidence in a country's currency or other financial assets causing international investors to withdraw their funds from the country. It is rarely caused by a single source; it involves various combinations of (1) currency crisis (or foreign exchange crisis), (2) banking crisis and (3) debt crisis. These three crises are described in Box 11.1.

The Bretton-Woods system set up after World War II rested on pegging exchange rates of all the important world currencies to the American dollar, and on fixing the price of American dollar in terms of gold, usually US$35 per ounce of gold. This was known as a "gold-exchange" standard which was meant to encourage the international exchange of goods and services but keep labour and capital behind national borders. There were a few currency crises in this regime, mainly in Latin America where they

---

**Box 11.1**
**Currency, Banking, and Debt Crisis Described**

A foreign exchange, or **currency**, crisis occurs when a speculative attack on a country's currency results in a devaluation or sharp depreciation or forces the central bank to defend the currency by selling large amounts of reserves or by significantly raising by selling large amounts or reserves or by significantly raising interest rates. These as a rule have severe consequences on a real side most notably output fall and rise in unemployment.

> *Old-style or slow motion currency crises*
> These occur after a period of overspending and real appreciation that weaken the current account, frequently under a regime of capital controls, and result in devaluation.

> *New-style currency crises*
> These happen when investors are concerned about the creditworthiness of the balance sheet of a significant part of the economy (public or private) which in the integrated financial and capital markets can lead very rapidly to pressure on the exchange rate.

A **banking** crisis occurs when actual or potential bank runs induce banks to suspend the internal convertibility of their liabilities or force the government to intervene to prevent this by providing banks with large-scale financial support ("bail-outs"). Banking crises tend to last longer than currency crises and have more severe effects on economic activity. They have become more common since the 1970s with countries abandoning capital and financial control.

A **debt** crisis occurs either when a borrower defaults or when lenders believe default is likely and therefore withhold new loans and try to liquidate existing ones. Debt crises can be associated with either commercial (private) or sovereign (public) debt. A perceived risk that the public sector will cease to honour its repayment obligations is likely to lead to a sharp drop in private capital inflows and a currency crisis.

Source: "Currency, Banking and Debt Crises", *Finance and Development* 39, no. 4 (2002), Box 1.

---

were severe in part because that region was not fully part of the gold-exchange system.[12]

When the Bretton-Woods gold-exchange system collapsed in 1973, it was replaced by various types of currency floats. This new flexibility in the international monetary system was accompanied by large-scale capital mobility. The rest of the story has been told many times: In the era of avalanching international capital mobility many serious financial crises took place in the 1980s and 1990s in cases when countries opted for less flexible exchange regimes. This led many commentators to claim that globalization of the post-Bretton-Woods times brought too much financial openness and capital mobility.[13] This, in turn, resulted in a renewed preference for restricting capital flows by imposing "clever" capital controls. Alternatively recommendations have been made for more appropriate managing of the financial sectors. For example, Brad DeLong believes that:

> we should... have our cake and eat it too: to reap the benefits of international capital mobility, and to minimize the human costs of recurrent crises through appropriate and well-funded international central banking institutions and practices".[14]

The overarching cause of most financial crises is misaligned fundamentals, that is, unsustainable current account deficits, overvalued domestic currency, excessive short-term foreign borrowing, and growing fiscal deficit. A prolonged occurrence of any or a combination of the above should be a signal to policymakers to undertake corrective measures. And if they delay doing so, sooner or latter they will be forced to act because uncorrected imbalances in fundamentals are very inviting for speculators whose manipulations could cause further instability.

## MISALIGNED FUNDAMENTALS IN FINANCIAL CRISES

The role of fundamentals in the Asian financial crisis as manifested in each Asian country is summarized in Table 11.1. This table is valuable also to show how the Asian financial crisis was a manifestation of a larger phenomenon and not just an Asian problem.

However, in some cases crises erupt not only because of imbalances of fundamentals but also because of "the inherent instability of international financial markets and the risks that cross-border financial transactions pose for countries with relatively fragile financial system and weak regulatory and supervision structure".[15]

Furthermore, as the title of Charles Kindelberger's rediscovered book, *Panics, Manias and Crashes*, suggests capital flows are vulnerable to non-financial logic. This means that destabilizing speculation followed by a panic is possible whenever the speculators decide to bail out even with the

Table 11.1
Misaligned Fundamentals in Financial Crises in the 1990s

| | Unsustainable current account deficit | Overvalued exchange rate | Large fiscal deficits | Large debt | |
|---|---|---|---|---|---|
| | | | | Public | Private |
| Mexico | ++ | ++ | | | |
| Asian countries | | | | | |
| – Thailand | ++ | + | | | ++ |
| – Indonesia | + | + | | | ++ |
| – Malaysia | + | + | | | |
| – Philippines | ++ | + | | | ++ |
| – Republic of Korea | | | | | + |
| Brazil | | ++ | ++ | ++ | |
| Russian Federation | ++ | ++ | ++ | | |

++: strong impact
+: medium impact
Source: Author's compilation based on literature of financial crisis causes.

fundamentals are sound because the fundamentals themselves will be destabilized as a result of the speculation, validating the action of speculators.[16]

Post-Bretton-Woods globalization has created fluid financial markets with short-term capital being much more mobile and moving freely in and out of most countries. A combination of new markets and new forms of finance (such as hedge funds) have facilitated capital mobility. In general this is a good thing. Moving idle capital or capital earning low returns in some economies to economies where it could be utilized earning high returns must bring benefits to everyone. However, in practice this chase for new profit opportunities is often overdone resulting in over-lending and over-borrowing, with familiar results of debt-crises. As explained above, these are almost always combined with currency crises and often with banking crises too.

In summary, we can offer some common features of financial crises bearing in mind that each one has special characteristics on its own. Most crises:

- Will be preceded by financial deregulation and liberalization of capital account;
- Follow after excessive lending on certain categories of assets such as property stocks;
- Are in economies where the banking system operates with weak financial regulation and supervision;
- Will be preceded by sharp increases in capital inflows (attracted by a combination of high interest rate differential and stable exchange rates) which result in a large increase in liquidity, over-extension of lending, a decline in the quality of assets and increased laxity in risk assessment;
- Happen after local currency appreciation and worsening of the current account; and
- Are triggered by or result in reversals of capital flows associated with a deterioration of macroeconomic conditions.

A financial crisis, particularly a currency crisis, rarely remains constrained within national borders. Instead a phenomenon known as "contagion" expands a national crisis to a regional or even global crisis. Furthermore an effect known as "herding" could also take place, whereby investors move together. Keith Maskus describes it as a "wake-up call" to investors in other markets who start looking at their investments more closely after an occurrence of banking and currency crisis in a neighbouring economy.[17] Quickly they notice similarities in weaknesses between the markets and start exerting pressure on their currencies. The process of "competitive devaluations" could be triggered with governments' attempt to maintain relative commodity prices of tradables intact through the adjustment of exchange rates. But this policy has negative consequences for investments and may precipitate a stampede of investors.

## UNDERSTANDING THE ASIAN CRISIS OF 1997–98

What is understood by the Asian financial crisis in this chapter is a crisis that began at the end of June 1997 in Thailand. It ended in 1998 not because the crisis was over, but because it spread out of Asia into the Russian, Brazilian and other Latin American economies and threatened to become almost a global crisis. Luckily this threat never materialized but it should not be a reason for complacency. Instead all parties should use this experience to understand how to better read signals of distress in future and even more, how to manage national and international financial crises. Because we do have a consensus about what happened in Asia to cause and trigger the crisis of 1997–98, here we can provide a stylized chronology of most important events leading to the crisis.[18] Figure 11.2 gives a schematic bird's eye view of the linkages between the main causes leading to the crisis.

### The Asian Financial Crisis Unveiled

High domestic savings rates led to rapid physical and human capital formation and high growth. In a closed economy, growth based on capital accumulation might have slowed down once the supply of capital was exhausted. However as the supply of foreign capital was freely available (given the slower growth rates and returns on investments in other markets) once the Asian economies allowed for capital account liberalization, this foreign capital freely flowed in, adding to domestic capital accumulation. An apparently virtuous circle was created whereby the inflow of foreign capital aided the high growth rates which in turn attracted more foreign capital. It is important to note that the biggest source of foreign capital was found in Japan. High wages but mostly high yen value pushed many Japanese manufacturers and exporters to relocate production overseas, mostly in "second tier" newly industrialized economies of East Asia. This started a build-up of productive capacity in the Asian developing economies.

## Figure 11.2
## Crisis Enfolding

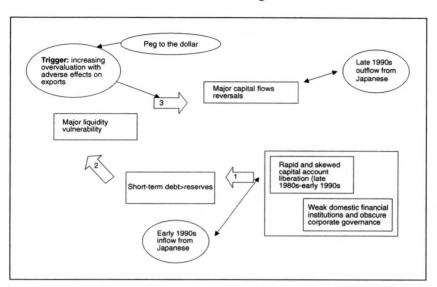

An additional lure to the inflow of capital was the choice of hard-currency-linked foreign exchange regimes in these countries. Most of them pegged their currencies to the American dollar (Hong Kong, China has a currency board with the dollar). These fixed exchange rates encouraged rapid capital inflows which in turn created a fast monetary growth. All these developments took place in an environment of imperfect financial intermediation. Indiscriminate selection and moral hazard only contributed to rapid monetary growth. The result eventually was both over-investment and misallocation of capital. Furthermore, because of the relatively successful inflation targeting, prices of goods and services were kept under control but not the prices of assets, which because of the rapid monetary growth went into an upward spiral.

However, asset inflation cannot persist forever. As soon as banks start putting more realistic values on collaterals and limiting bank bailouts, the asset inflation turned into asset deflation. Already existing high debt ratios combined with asset deflation led to debt servicing difficulties. In fact by this stage the telling signs of "fundamentals imbalance" were flashing and the likelihood of reversals of capital flows was increasing sharply. This created additional pressure on local currency values. But the monetary authorities could not correct the exchange rates. This imbalance raised the local-currency value of debts denominated in foreign currency, and without local earnings able to cover foreign debt servicing costs, many enterprises defaulted or declared bankruptcy.

The above story can be interpreted in two different ways. One is that the crisis occurred because the unrestricted capital flows combined with Asian style of macro and micro governance (that is "Asian capitalism") created an "extremely volatile combination". In fact, *Trade and Development Report 1998* states "the crises occurred because governments failed to manage integration into global capital markets with the same prudence and skill they had earlier shown in managing trade liberalization."[19]

This interpretation of the crisis became known in the literature as "government failure". But it begs the question of why otherwise competent policy makers allowed such high risks without adequate mitigating actions.

The alternative interpretation is one of a "market failure", which finds an ultimate cause for the crisis in unrestricted capital movements and therefore provides a simple cure of the problem: Return to restricting (short-term) capital movements. At present there is more weight given to the first interpretation, leading to the prescription of placing more importance on domestic financial disclosure, supervision and regulation than on regulation of capital movements. Kenneth Rogoff sums up the current policy prescription very clearly:

> Experience has shown that there are real risks in lifting longstanding exchange controls before the internal regulatory structure can handle the resulting capital flows. And even in countries that have largely dispensed with capital controls as a regular mechanism, there may still be a role for limited and temporary controls, particularly on inflows, but in some cases on outflows.[20]

## Tracking the Asian Contagion

Unlike the other crises in the developing countries in 1990s, the Asian financial crisis which started in Thailand spread to other countries in the region: Investors who were hurt by developments in Thailand but also investors in other regional markets in Indonesia, Malaysia, Philippines, Hong Kong, China started to question the soundness of the fundamentals there, perhaps too harshly. Very rapidly the currencies of these countries came under pressure because after the baht depreciation those currencies looked even more overvalued. Similarity with a spread of disease led commentators to call this extension of the Thai crisis into the other markets of the region a "contagion". However, the Asian contagion could have been driven by other exogenous factors such as a rise in the U.S. dollar, trade linkages, competition in third markets, or market sentiments.[21] It is also necessary to differentiate between real contagion and just a simple case of coincidental correlation of similar developments in different markets. Markets that are normally very interdependent will have a high degree of cross-correlation at any given time: This simply means that markets are reacting to each other's changes as per their ordinary relationship. The contagion occurs only if these correlations change substantially after the onset of the crises.

The fact that currencies in the Asian region depreciated one after the other led many to belief that a contagion effect was at work. Analyses done subsequently do not support this finding unanimously. Nevertheless, there is enough evidence to claim at least weak contagion in the currency markets between Thailand, Malaysia, Indonesia, Republic of Korea and Philippines. This was enhanced by herd-like behaviour of investors, who followed the markets and each other rather than trusting their own assessments of each countries' fundamentals.

## Asian Policy Responses

Obviously policy errors were very much at heart of the accumulated vulnerability of the Asian economies before the crisis was triggered. As noted above, exchange rate mismanagement, lack of financial regulation and weak supervision of the banking system in addition to misallocation of funds were among the biggest policy errors leading up to the crisis. However there were also some questionable responses to the crisis itself. Almost invariably governments adopted the floating exchange rate regime after futile attempts to maintain the currency values through market intervention and increased interest rates. Raising interest rates might have worsened the situation by causing more corporate and bank bankruptcies, but not raising interest rates would have pushed the currencies even lower. Ironically, the most controversial response at that time, the introduction of temporary capital control by the Malaysian Government, proved to be the most effective. In orthodox theory, controls on short-term capital flows are considered by many a dangerous weapon in the hands of governments, but this time they worked.

In summary, a country has different possibilities to respond in case of an attack on its currency and/or if facing debt-problems:

- Response by domestic policies, especially by monetary policy;
- Maintaining sufficiently high level of precautionary foreign reserves and credit lines;
- Recourse to an international lender of last resort;
- Imposition of debt standstill and exchange restrictions, accompanied by initiation of negotiations for rapid debt workout.[22]

## THE ASIAN FINANCIAL CRISIS AND SOCIAL INSECURITY

For the most part of the second wave of globalization, the Asian second layer of the newly industrializing economies (Indonesia, Malaysia, Thailand) and of course frontrunners (Republic of Korea; Taiwan, Province of China; Hong Kong, China and Singapore) had an impressive record of economic performance — fast growth, low inflation, stable macroeconomic environment with high saving rates, open export-led economies, and increasing standard of living and quality of life. In this environment, these countries did not work hard on design and maintenance of social safety nets. After all, only several years before this crisis unfolded, the whole region was labelled as a "miracle".[23]

Therefore, without "cover-all" safety nets, massive currency devaluations had very severe impacts on the region's poor because they raised inflation and made imported foodstuffs, which were normally cheap, unaffordable. Unemployment rose sharply and all income groups started to feel the teeth of the recession, including the "rich" (whose net wealth fell due to sharp drop in equity and real estate prices). Many Thai investors lost their life savings because the stream of baht earnings on their investments were not enough after the devaluation was insufficient to pay off loans in foreign currencies. Investors in Hong Kong, China, Taiwan, Province of China, Republic of Korea and Southeast Asian economies suffered correspondingly. The worst affected countries were Thailand, Indonesia and the Republic of Korea where deterioration of employment and social conditions resulted in civil unrest and riots, resulting in death and prolonged impact on security.

To the great surprise of many commentators, Asian countries rebounded faster than expected. Figure 11.3 captures the changes in the GDP growth before and after the crisis and it is obvious that once again most of these economies, and China in particular, are set on a high growth path. It is to

Figure 11.3
GDP Growth in Asia

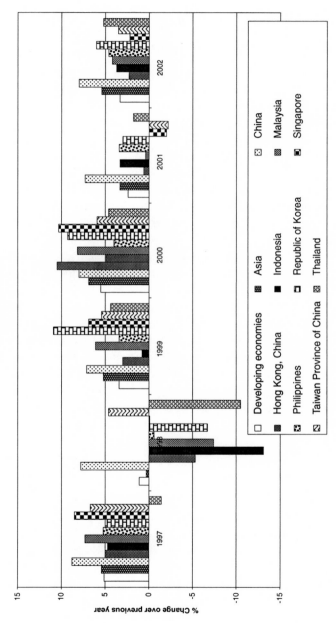

be hoped this growth will relieve some of the social and political stresses that threatened the security of Asia at the end of the last decade.

## LESSONS FOR PREVENTION

Empirical evidence shows that access to global capital markets in principle closes up whenever a (developing) country is in distress. Thus an argument in favour of a complete financial openness in order to use capital markets for increased diversification and for consumption smoothing, as hedge against adverse shocks, does not necessarily hold. Moreover, as the experience of many countries demonstrates, international capital markets tend to swing between too much optimism in good times and excess pessimism in bad times. This is an aspect of the volatility of financial markets that has been stressed repeatedly as one of the bigger risks of financial openness and which could easily offset many of the benefits otherwise arising from the capital inflows.

Notwithstanding this, there is still sufficient evidence that FDI and the integration of a national economy with international financial markets provide positive dynamic effects on its growth. However, to make this openness work for rather than against the economy, it is necessary to accompany financial liberalization by financial regulation which will impose adequate standards for domestic financial and capital markets. This includes requirements for information disclosure, more transparency, better supervision, better corporate governance and enhanced banking sector supervision. Furthermore, changes in style of macroeconomic management including greater exchange rate flexibility, better surveillance and quicker responses with appropriate monetary and fiscal policies are also required.

Even though crises are inevitable, some preventive measures could be adopted to reduce economies' vulnerability and help them deal with crises more effectively:[24]

- Avoiding real exchange rate misalignment;
- Limiting fiscal imbalances;
- Preventing an excessive build-up of domestic debt;
- Maintaining a monetary policy consistent with low inflation;
- Ensuring that the ratio of unhedged short-term foreign currency debt over official reserves remains sufficiently low;
- Strengthening supervision and prudential regulation; and
- Fostering risk management capacities in banks and non-financial firms.

Generally, governments lacking technical expertise and experience in dealing with open financial markets should proceed cautiously with capital account liberalization. Alternately, during the transition period they should resort to additional instruments such as restrictions on short-term capital flows to prevent excessive volatility from adversely affecting domestic stability.

We now know that the prescription of fiscal contraction applied without discrimination to all economies in distress was too strong for those economies without solvency problems. Indeed there is a strong belief that the international policy response to the crisis has contributed to the severity of the crisis by failing to appreciate the full gravity of the situation, and by placing too much faith in conventional policy prescription.[25]

## THE IMF ROLE

In most cases the International Monetary Fund (IMF) is able to assist countries to overcome balance of payments difficulties without involving private creditors. During 1997–98 the IMF provided US$36 billion to support reform programmes in the three worst hit Asian countries, Indonesia, Republic of Korea and Thailand, as part of international packages worth almost US$100 billion in total. To calm private investors it was frequently sufficient to work out an agreement on economic adjustment and reform programme which restores a country's access to foreign private capital. In more serious situations where a country needs a large injection of foreign currency or faces a liquidity problem, a framework for restructuring sovereign debts is necessary. The IMF has advanced two such frameworks: The contractual approach and the statutory approach. The former involves the use of contractual provisions in international sovereign bonds. The latter aims to create a legal foundation for collective action by creditors.

For countries facing a capital account crisis, access to IMF resources is now guided by the following rules:[26]

- A country must be experiencing exceptional capital account pressures resulting in need for financing outside the normal limits for IMF financing;
- A country's debt must be sustainable;
- There must be good prospects for a country to regain access to private capital markets within the timeframe of the IMF led borrowing; and
- Programme of policies, including adjustments and institutional and political capacity for their implementation should be deemed successful.

## CONCLUSION

Many commentators still believe that even after the experience of crises in Asia and elsewhere in the 1990s and all the learning associated with them, the world nonetheless lacks clear rules for dealing with and preventing the occurrence of such crisis. The IMF has not managed to transform itself into a proper lender of last resort, nor do we have a solution for effective standstill on unserviceable debt. The biggest obstacle in creating these is moral hazard, a phenomenon described as reckless behaviour by borrowers, lenders and investors due to liberal access to the international community's financial assistance. Despite some imaginative suggestions for solving this problem (such as introducing private insurers) a debate is still alive.

Furthermore there are two other policies that are essential: Capital controls and an exchange rate regime. With respect to short-term capital controls, it was noted above that they are sometimes effective if applied so as not to restrain capital flows excessively. Opinions on an "optimal" exchange rate regime are still sharply divided. What we can say with certainty is that there is no single exchange rate regime to fit all economies at all times.

Thus restraint by speculators, prudence by national financial managers, and discrimination by international financial regulatory agencies are still essential qualities to enhance financial stability in Asia and elsewhere. Without stability in the economic sphere, whether internationally, regionally, nationally, or at the level of small businesses and individual entrepreneurs, social and political stability are in jeopardy and individual security is in peril. In recent decades Asian economic crises have often become social and political crises. Sound economic management is thus seen to be an essential requirement for security, paralleling sound border defence and domestic law and order policies. Both as a policy goal and as a security concept, prudent economic management by governments is a bridge between traditional concerns with state security and newer concerns with human security.

## NOTES

1. When preparing this chapter, data was available up to end of 2002.
2. This process was accelerated with China and India both increasingly opening up towards the end of the millennium.
3. There are of course many more elements and forces that one could associate with globalization. There are also political, military, cultural, religious and

other sides of globalization but this chapter focuses on economic aspects even though they are not always most relevant when discussing impacts of globalization on security.

4. See for example, papers written in preparation for the Expert Group Meeting on Market Access Issues on Mode 4 (Movement of Natural Persons to Supply Services) and Effective Implementation of Article IV on Increasing the Participation of Developing Countries, Geneva 29–31 July 2003, and a note by the UNCTAD secretariat (TD/B/COM.1/EM.22/2), 18 June 2003.

5. James W. Dean, "Exchange Rate Regimes for the 21st Century: Asia, Europe and the Americas", Discussion paper (October 2003), Carleton University, mimeo., p. 3.

6. For an excellent overview, see in a recent article by Pierre-Richard Agénor, "Benefits and Costs of International Financial Integration: Theory and Facts", *The World Economy*, August (2003): 1098–118.

7. UNCTAD, *Trade and Development Report 1997* (New York and Geneva: United Nations).

8. However, as it turned out, in periods of crisis private flows tend to be quite "footloose" and in the case of the Asian crisis, the outflows compounded the problems in the private sectors of Thailand, Indonesia and Malaysia making things much worse. See also Charles Wyplosz, "How Risky is Financial Liberalization in the Developing Countries?" Graduate Institute of International Studies, Geneva and CEPR (mimeo.), 2001.

9. See Agénor (2003), pp. 1092–96 for more details.

10. Ibid., pp. 1096–101.

11. Except that Wyplosz, op. cit., shows that financial liberalization is "considerably more destabilizing in developing countries than in developed countries". (pp. 3–4).

12. James W. Dean, op. cit.

13. Perhaps one of the most passionate advocates of this view is Jagdish Bhagwati. Alan Deardorff (2002) "What Might Globalization's Critics Believe?". Discussion paper no. 492, University of Michigan, p. 10, summarizes this position well: " ...it appears that less globalization and even less freedom of markets would be desirable: short-term capital flows. Changes in technology have accompanied changes in policy during the last thirty years or so to permit financial capital to flow among countries at speeds and in quantities that are almost impossible to comprehend. If markets were static and came at all close to the ideal of fully informed, perfect competition, then the case could easily be made that these markets enhance efficiency, transferring capital from those who have it to those who need it, to the benefit of all. But if ever there were markets that were not static, these are them. And the assumption that there is full information in these markets is laughable. Instead, the large swings in fashion and expectations that cause short-term

capital to flow into and then out of vulnerable countries seem most unlikely to be beneficial for the world, and they certainly are not beneficial to the countries that become their victims."

14. In "Reply to Jagdish Bhagwati", published on Brad DeLong's website 5 January 1998. Downloaded 15 November 2003 from <http://www.j-bradford-delong.net/Comments/Bhagwati_reply.html>.

15. Agénor, op. cit., p. 1091.

16. Jagdish Bhagwati, "Why Free Capital Mobility may be Hazardous to Your Health: Lessons from the Latest Financial Crisis", NBER Conference on Capital Control, Cambridge, Massachusetts, p. 2 (mimeo.), 1998.

17. Keith Maskus, "The East Asian Currency Crisis" Policy Paper 5 (mimeo.), 2001.

18. When the Asian crisis first happened there was no agreement on the main causes of the crisis. There were two main candidates: One, inherent instability of open financial markets, and two, "Asian" crony capitalism. See more on this in James W. Dean, "East Asia Through a Glass Darkly: Disparate Lenses on the Road to Gamascus" in *Editing Economics: Essays in Honour of Mark Perlman*, edited by Geoffrey C. Harcourt, Hank Lim and Ungsuh Ken Park (Routledge, 2001). This section of the paper borrows heavily from the above paper.

19. UNCTAD, *Trade and Development Report 1998*, p. II.

20. Kenneth Rogoff, "Four Challenges for 40 Years", *OECD Observer*, 12 June 2003.

21. Taimur Baig and Ilan Goldfajn, "Financial Market Contagion in the Asian Crisis", *IMF Staff Paper*, vol. 42, no. 2 (June 1999).

22. UNCTAD, op. cit. p. VIII.

23. World Bank, *Asian Miracle* (Washington: The World Bank, 1993). This was questioned persuasively by Paul Krugman, "The Myth of Asia's Miracle", *Foreign Affairs* (November/December 1994): 62–78.

24. Agénor, op. cit., pp. 1114–15.

25. UNCTAD, op. cit. (1998) p. II.

26. Inutu Lukonga, "Riding Out the Storm" *Finance and Development* 39, no. 4 (December 2002). Downloaded 8 November 2003 from <http://www.imf.org/external/pubs/ft/fandd/2002/12/lukonga.htm>.

Chapter Twelve

# Challenges to Human Rights and Civil Liberties

Anja Jetschke

## SECURITY CONCEPTS AND HUMAN RIGHTS IN ASIA: PAST AND PRESENT

Within the framework of human security sketched in the introductory chapters of this book, this chapter describes and assesses security threats at the interface between the state and the individual in Asia. Post-independence Asian security policy has focused on internal security, that is, the strengthening of state capacity and nation-building has been emphasized more than the defence against an external aggressor. For example, in the 1960s Indonesia's then President Suharto popularized the concept of "national resilience" (*ketahanan nasional*). National resilience encapsulates the idea that only stable, prosperous states will be peaceful states and will not pose a threat to their neighbours.

Though formally independent, many Southeast Asian states were weak states and therefore not capable of dealing with political turbulence such as secessionist movements, challenges to the central government posed by Communist or Islamic movements and border disputes. Cases in point are Indonesia's *konfrontasi* against Malaysia and Singapore (1963–66) and the

Philippine–Malaysian dispute over Sabah. These developments and Southeast Asia's precarious situation during the Cold War prompted Indonesia, Malaysia, Thailand, Singapore and the Philippines to found the Association of Southeast Asian Nations (ASEAN), a regional organization to promote cooperation in the economic, cultural and security area, in 1967 in an attempt to regionalize "national resilience". The Bangkok Declaration, the founding document of ASEAN therefore emphasized the principles of non-interference and economic development.

With regards to human rights, the emphasis on state-building appeared most rational, given the fact that an effective promotion and protection of human rights first and foremost requires the existence of a capable state. As such, much of the current debate on state capabilities and good governance has been anticipated by the concept of national resilience, except that national resilience heavily relied on each state's own ability to manage state-building and did not build on active international financial support. In other words, regional resilience rested on the assumption that in order to achieve truly national independence, Southeast Asian governments had to guarantee themselves a considerable measure of autonomy and abstain from intervention. This included the assurance that they would not interfere in each other's affairs and that they would equally prevent great powers, such as China, the United States and the Soviet Union from interfering in the region.

Regional resilience has since lost much of its relevance given that ASEAN member states, and Asian states more generally, have prospered over the past decades and most of the countries have developed stable political systems. In fact, it has been argued (at least prior to the Asian financial crisis) that ASEAN is one of the most successful regional organizations in the Third World. Yet, when national resilience was envisioned ASEAN governments could not anticipate that challenges to their political legitimacy would emerge from globalization rather than from military interference or economic dependence. International models of good governance and standards of good behaviour, of which standards for human rights practice constitute the core, soon provided challenges to the political legitimacy of Southeast Asian governments which also threatened the traditional Asian concept of security. Moreover, in the age of globalization the dual process of economic integration and cultural fragmentation has also led to a reaffirmation of cultural identity among Asia's many ethnic minorities and revived the idea of national self-determination. These developments present Asian governments with the dilemma of preserving their relatively new nation-states and maintaining their political legitimacy on the one hand and choosing means which are in accordance with international models for good behaviour, particularly human rights standards, on the other.

## HUMAN RIGHTS AFTER SEPTEMBER 11

The link between security and human rights has become even more visible after 11 September 2001. Shortly after the terrorist attack, many Asian governments introduced new security or anti-subversion legislation and explicitly referred to the new threats posed by allegedly terrorist organizations. Almost immediately after the enactment, human rights organizations complained about the detrimental effects of this legislation on human rights. In a recently released report, Amnesty International concludes, for example, that in the case of India, a "breakdown of the rule of law in relation to the Muslim minority" has occurred.[1] Asian human rights organizations complained that Southeast Asian governments are using the war against terror as an excuse to step up political repression and crack down against their own citizens.[2] This is most likely to result in a radicalization of the political opposition, most importantly Muslim groups, which might seriously jeopardize the process of democratization.

These developments seem to reverse the process of human rights improvement that has taken place in several Asian countries during the 1990s, when human rights and democracy were high on the international agenda. Several studies have documented how international campaigns and pressure against human rights violations in Asian countries have yielded tangible results in terms of a gradual improvement in human rights practices. For example, the Indonesian and Chinese governments' abuse of power against political dissidents has attracted worldwide attention and led to significant concessions in the area of human rights.

This chapter argues that the international pro-human rights and democracy atmosphere of the 1990s has stimulated processes of political change which have been uneven and might even be reversed. For example, in the early 1990s, when Indonesia and China responded to criticism of the repression of political dissidents, the military regime in Myanmar has shown a surprising ability to ignore similar demands. This suggests that the international context alone is only a necessary condition, but by no means sufficient for human rights change, and that additional factors have to be taken into account.

In this context, it is quite interesting to note that a similar anti-Islamic atmosphere prevailed at the end of the 1970s, when the Iranian revolution shocked the Western world and the Iranian hostage crisis in the U.S. embassy in Teheran proved to be a traumatic experience for the U.S. Government. Although little research exists about the relationship between the suppression of alleged extremist Muslim activities and backlash of democratization in Muslim countries at the end of the 1970s and the beginning of the 1980s, the available evidence suggests that Western governments condoned the installation of authoritarian or military governments to prevent the spread of radical Islam in Muslim countries. As such, the probability that anti-Islamic mood might jeopardize democratization processes in Muslim countries might be higher now. In other words, walking the tightrope between fighting extremist Muslims and fostering democracy might become more difficult.

This chapter will therefore try to provide a more nuanced picture of the processes which lead to human rights change and isolate and describe the variables that have pressured Asian governments such as China and Indonesia to improve human rights laws and practices. Then it will be possible to evaluate how the new focus on terrorism has affected human rights and to make predictions about the direction the protection of civil rights and liberties will take in the future. In sum, the chapter will address the following questions:

- Given internationally institutionalized human rights norms, how do these rights affect Asian governments which have a record of human rights violations?
- What are the processes through which these norms become embedded in Asian political systems?
- How does the current anti-Islamic atmosphere among Western countries affect international pressures on Asian governments to change their policies?
- How do the September 11 attacks affect the Muslim sectors of society, that is, their civil and political rights?
- What strategies are likely to work best to ensure the protection of human rights and progress along the path of democratization?

In answering these questions I will, first, provide an overview of the status of ratification of major human rights treaties by Asian governments. The Asia-Pacific region is one of the regions in which only very few governments have signed and/or ratified international human rights instruments, such as the International Covenant on Civil and Political Rights (ICCPR) and the Convention Against Torture and Other Cruel and Degrading Treatment.

Second, I will provide a brief overview of recent research on the promotion of international human rights. This research suggests that sustained human rights changes come about as a result of pressure mobilized at both international and domestic levels. I will then present the case of China to illustrate the argument. Before speculating about how the terrorist attacks in the United States of 11 September 2001 will affect these dynamics and consequently the human rights situation in several Asian countries, I will recount a human rights campaign in Indonesia in the 1970s as a forerunner of today's developments, wherein demands for political liberalization essentially fell victim to the growing anti-Islamic atmosphere prevailing in the international community after the Iranian Islamic revolution in 1979.

While I do not believe that this comparison is perfect, I do want to argue that there are important lessons to learn with regard to human rights and democracy. The main lesson is fairly simple: Attempts to suppress political dissent by violating human rights in order to save democracy are most likely doomed to fail and have a serious price: The loss of democracy.

## THE INTERNATIONAL CONCEPT OF HUMAN RIGHTS

Today, human rights basically include three types of rights:

1. The classical liberal rights designed to protect an individual against violations of his personal integrity by a state government, such as torture and other inhuman and degrading treatment, involuntary disappearances, extrajudicial killings and arbitrary detention. These liberal rights or so called first generation human rights are internationally institutionalized in the International Covenant on Civil and Political Rights, which entered into force in 1976. A particular feature of these rights is that their respect is closely tied to an independent judiciary which monitors state practice and issues individual rulings in case a citizen complains about a violation of his or her human rights.

2. The second type of human rights are economic, social and cultural rights which establish certain standards of living such as appropriate housing a state has to provide for. These are the so called second

generation rights which have entered into force together with the ICCPR but have been institutionalized in a different convention, the International Covenant on Economic, Social and Cultural Rights (ICESCR), in 1976.

3. A third type of rights represents rights protecting particularly weak sections of the society, such as women, children and minorities.

Of the three types of rights just mentioned, it is the first generation of human rights which is particularly sensitive to governments, since they affect the nature and perception of political order and legitimacy and if used by civil society to criticize a government, are an effective instrument to question the power of ruling elites. As such, these rights have an inherent critical impetus to political rule (*herrschaftskritisch*) which many governments view as particularly threatening.

In this chapter, I shall focus on the first generation of human rights, because these are the rights which have been most controversial in the Asian human rights discourse. It may be remembered at this point that in the 1990s Asian governments and intellectuals have passionately rejected a human rights concept that primarily focuses on individual political rights. Such a human rights concept was suspected as part of a Western strategy to establish value hegemony over Asian societies. The Asian value hypothesis, which was developed as an ideational and relativist alternative to Western universalism, argued that Asian culture places greater emphasis on authority, hierarchy and communitarian values than Western culture. Hence, also taking into account the need for economic development (but one may add also the importance economic success has for the legitimacy of the rulers), collective social and economic rights were seen as playing a much greater role in Asia than in the West.[3]

## THE STATUS OF HUMAN RIGHTS AND POLITICAL FREEDOM IN ASIA

Asian countries have a fairly good record of signing and ratifying second and third generation human rights. This is by no means a characteristic only of Asian countries, however. The International Convention on the rights of the Child, for example, has been signed by an overwhelming majority of states.

If it comes to the classical civil and political rights, Asian states exhibit great variation in the ratification of the individual conventions. In general, it can be said that the more liberal the particular government and the more democratic the political system, the more likely it is that it has signed and or ratified the ICCPR or the Anti-Torture Convention. This correlation becomes most evident when one compares the status of ratification of major human rights treaties with indices on political freedom. For this end, it is particularly helpful to have a look at one index evaluating political freedom, namely the one of Freedom House. Freedom House is a non-profit organization based in the United States, which has developed a method to judge a country situation according to several indicators. Freedom House's survey of civil and political freedom encompasses two general sets of characteristics grouped under political rights and civil liberties. Political rights enable people to participate freely in the political process, and include the right of all adults to vote and compete for public office, and for elected representatives to have a decisive vote on public policies. Civil liberties include the freedoms to develop views, institutions, and personal autonomy apart from the state. These two sets of freedoms are then rated separately and the numerical results added. The political rights and civil liberties ratings are then averaged and used to assign each country and territory to an overall status of "Free", "Partly Free", or "Not Free".[4]

According to this index, Asian countries have been rated overwhelmingly as not free, with ratings ranging between five and seven. If one was about to make categories of countries, Australia, Japan and New Zealand would find themselves in a category consisting of those countries having consistently free political systems since the 1970s and a relatively high number of ratified human rights conventions. In a second category, we would find those political systems which have undergone political liberalization or transitions to democracy (and partly reversals) whose status of political freedom therefore varies considerably and which exhibit an inconsistent ratification of human rights treaties, such as Indonesia, Thailand, Malaysia, the Philippines, Cambodia and South Korea. And a third category would be made up of those countries which have been consistently rated as not free, such as China, Laos, Vietnam, North Korea, Myanmar, Brunei Darussalam and Singapore and which have hardly signed any human rights conventions.

Yet, there are exceptions to this rule, suggesting that other factors such as culture or historical experience might play a role. States like North Korea and Vietnam have both signed most human rights conventions although rating agencies such as Freedom House regard their political systems as not free. It is also interesting to note that many of the ratifications have occurred during the 1990s, when many transitions to democracy occurred in Asia. Here, Cambodia and South Korea come to mind.

As we have seen, there is a fairly obvious relationship between political freedom and the ratification of human rights treaties. But these are mainly correlations rather than statements about political processes. To evaluate how the September 11 attacks have affected the promotion of human rights, it is in order to first specify the mechanism through which Asian governments have increased their compliance with international human rights standards. Using these mechanisms as a starting point, it is easier to describe which features of the mechanism have changed or are likely to change in the future and how they might affect human rights in the region.

## THE MECHANISMS OF HUMAN RIGHTS PROMOTION

If one looks at the recent literature on the international enforcement of human rights standards, a similar mechanism seems to be at work: Rather than being promoted by international organizations or individual states, it is international civil society which monitors and sees to it that human rights are being put into effect. The prevailing mechanism is rather one of shaming than of sanctioning, rather one of morally castigating human rights violations than of exploiting financial dependence to force the target government to change its behaviour. Individual states have tied their development assistance to human rights performance, but the mechanism has been used rather inconsistently.

Several studies describe very richly how networks of human rights organizations generate international attention to particular abuses, create international solidarity with victims of human rights abuses and mobilize other states to take action against a target state. Two studies are particularly illuminating in this regard. The first one is Margaret Keck and Kathryn Sikkink's book *Activists Beyond Borders* (1998) which vividly describes how domestic activists can take advantage of the norms tying international society together to create attention and exert moral pressure on their own governments. The authors basically argue that an international normative structure provides an opportunity structure for activists to pressure their government from above and achieve policy changes they would not have attained without international support. They call this the "boomerang pattern". In a similar vein, the study *The Power of Human Rights* (1999) edited by Thomas Risse, Kathryn Sikkink and Steve Ropp shows how networks of human rights organizations have flourished since the 1970s and have had a similar impact on the human rights practice of otherwise culturally quite diverse countries such as Indonesia, South Africa or Uganda. This study places emphasis on the international and domestic processes alike that lead to a promotion of human rights in a specific target state and suggests that international moral pressure alone is not sufficient to engender a sustained improvement in human rights. Rather, international mobilization must be followed by a domestic mobilization to pressure a target government from below and sustain the international mobilization. The authors refer to the interaction pattern as "spiral model".

Since the publication of these two studies, numerous other studies have shown this dynamic with regards to Asian countries. In the following, I will quickly describe the results of these studies in order to provide the empirical data that will serve as a basis for separating the key variables that need to be in place to promote human rights. For example, China came onto the international human rights agenda in the late 1970s, when international human rights organizations started international campaigns to shame the Chinese Government within an international human rights community.[5] The initial concerns of human rights organizations were the thousands of political prisoners who had been imprisoned during the Cultural Revolution as well as human rights violations in Tibet. However, it was the massacre at the Tiananmen Square in 1989 which began to roil the interaction between China and international actors. Apart from pressures by China's donor countries such as the United States and Japan (the U.S. Government tied China's Most Favoured Nation status to improvements in its human rights policy), the Chinese Government came under increasing pressure by the United Nations Human Rights Commission, which passed a resolution criticizing human rights violations. The resolution was the first to criticize a permanent member of the Security Council.[6]

Although the Chinese Government denied all charges against it, it also took several steps to address human rights issues and invested some energy to defend its public image in an international community. This included not only concrete measures to address human rights problems, but also the publication of a White Paper on human rights in 1991 and attempts to shape the global discourse on human rights in terms of a priority on culturally specific rights (cultural relativism) and developmentalism. Despite these efforts, the Chinese Government remained under pressure to change policies and did so if only to improve its poor international image. In the words of Rosemary Foot: "The various forms of experience and pressure between 1992 and 1995, therefore, had proven to be effective in bringing about some discursive change, in wedding Beijing publicly to a series of legal reforms that were related to international standards, and in playing some role in prompting China to introduce those legal changes in the first place."[7]

I have elaborated elsewhere how this specific mechanism also worked in the case of Indonesia in the 1990s.[8] As indicated above, however, Indonesia also provides an example of an aborted process of human rights change. Since the failure of human rights networks then was related to political Islam, the case might serve as an example of the problems of promoting human rights and preserving democracy.

## INDONESIA IN THE 1970s: POLITICAL ISLAM AND THE PROMOTION OF HUMAN RIGHTS

The claim of this historical section on human rights in Indonesia in the 1970s is that both the mobilization of fundamentalist Islamic groups in Indonesia and a widespread Anti-Islamic atmosphere in Western countries worked to disrupt the impending international and domestic mobilization against the Suharto regime in Indonesia and eventually led to the consolidation of the authoritarian system. Before the Iranian revolution, international pressure for human rights improvements had hitherto led to gradual changes in the Indonesian Government's human rights policy, most importantly the release of suspected communist prisoners. The event of the Iranian revolution planted the seed of fear among Western countries that Indonesia might become a second Iran and so they stopped pressure on the Indonesian Government to continue improving its human rights record. This negligence effectively enabled the Indonesian Government to suppress the political opposition and led to the institutionalization of authoritarian rule, for example, an expansion of the political role of the Indonesian army. In sum, the process of liberalization was disrupted and could only be revitalized in the late 1980s.

Indonesia came on the international human rights network's agenda early in the 1970s due to its huge number of political prisoners detained without charges and/or trial in several prisons scattered over the Indonesian archipelago. Human rights organizations estimated that within the two years after the communist coup attempt against Sukarno in September 1965, about a quarter of a million people had been taken into custody by the Operational Command for the Restoration of Security and Order

(Kopkamtib).[9] Kopkamtib was the army intelligence and security command which had been established in October 1965 and which had virtually martial law powers. The government claimed that the prisoners were members of the Communist Party of Indonesia[10] and had been detained on the grounds that they were involved in the attempted coup. Ten years after this coup, tens of thousands of them were still awaiting charges to be levelled against them, while others were awaiting their trial.

While Western governments were initially reluctant to criticize the Suharto government's political prisoners (*tahanan politik*: tapol) policy, non-governmental organizations early on started campaigning for a release policy. In 1968, human rights and church groups, such as Amnesty International, the International Commission of Jurists and the World Council of Churches, journalists and scholars started to assemble and distribute information on the political prisoner problem.[11] International mobilization against the Indonesian Government's political prisoner policy emerged against the backdrop of a domestic mobilization against the Suharto regime in the early 1970s. The drive towards an increasingly authoritarian style of rule had aroused the open opposition of several political groups in Indonesia.[12]

Thus, Suharto's decision to "simplify" the political party system by forcing all parties to merge into two political parties, the Partai Demokrasi Indonesia (PDI), and the United Development Party (PPP) provoked their opposition. Rising corruption among the military which was officially promoted by Suharto, the Suharto government's leaning toward Western development models and its reliance on Western funds raised the level of political discontent. By 1973, issues of corruption, patronage, and the benefits perceived to be accruing to Indonesia's Chinese minority led to anti-Chinese riots in Bandung, the so-called Malari riots.[13] While the Indonesian Government at this point of time was still able to control the domestic opposition, on an international level the mobilization against Suharto continued.

In 1975, a coordinated network of Amnesty International sections in West Germany, Austria, the United States, Australia, the Netherlands and Canada conducted an international campaign on behalf of the female political prisoners in Indonesia. During this campaign, Indonesia became known as the country with the greatest number of female prisoners in the world.[14] The publication of Amnesty International's second report, exclusively dedicated to the communist political prisoners in Indonesia, proved to be a major foreign policy challenge to the military-backed

Suharto regime. The human rights campaign of the transnational network proved to be extraordinary successful. Amnesty International not only managed to engage the Indonesian Government into a substantial dialogue over its imprisonment practice, it also succeeded in mobilizing other states to put some pressure on the Indonesian Government to free the political prisoners. Individual donor countries threatened to withhold financial aid to the Indonesian Government, if the prisoners were not released. By 1979, most of the over 10,000 political prisoners were freed.

If compared to other countries such as South Korea and the Philippines at that time, the crucial question emerges why the Indonesian Government was able to get away with such an — admittedly large — tactical concession and did not face more pressure to change its authoritarian system. In order to account for this outcome, that is, no sustained change of human rights practices, one has to take a closer look at how domestic opposition groups took advantage of the emerging transnational public sphere, which was generated by the international pressure and how the international campaign shaped discourses at the domestic level.

As I will argue, the collective understanding that the Indonesian Government faced an Islamist threat provides the crucial variable, which accounts for the lack of reinforcement of international and domestic pressure which characterizes the spiral model. International mobilization did create domestic space for domestic protest. Yet, domestic opposition groups articulated their protest in terms of Islamic democracy, rather than a rule of law state. This seemed to raise the concern of secular-oriented groups in Indonesia that their rights might be jeopardized, but most importantly provided a convincing justification for the Indonesian military and the government to justify authoritarian rule in terms of the need to suppress Islamic radicalism.

## DOMESTIC MOBILIZATION, INTERNATIONAL DEMOBILIZATION AND REPRESSION

The international pressure which was put on the Suharto regime added leverage and legitimacy to the demands of the domestic opposition, for the student protests of the 1974–75 period briefly revitalized in 1977–78, and coincided with the election campaign scheduled for 1977. Demands for the resignation of Suharto resurfaced. Public dissent eventually began to rally around the Muslim party PPP, which had become a major critic of the Suharto regime. The alienation of the Muslim community led to a risk that the PPP might be able to threaten the absolute majority of Golkar in the parliamentary elections of 1977, which would also have threatened Suharto's nomination as president in 1978. Regional military authorities as well as the bureaucracy applied heavy pressure on voters before and during the campaign through intimidation, coercion and vote rigging, in order to ensure a big vote for Golkar.

Despite the manipulation, the PPP gained political strength relative to the results of the 1971 elections. Golkar suffered humiliating defeats in Jakarta and in the strongly Muslim province of Aceh, where opponents of the regime supported the PPP. The political demands of the students and the "soft liners" in ABRI diffused into the Indonesian parliament, where calls for a greater respect for human rights were regularly aired.[15] The PPP became one of the most consistent critics of the Suharto regime on human rights issues. Benedict Anderson noted that there "was strong evidence that for the first time in modern Indonesian history, sizeable numbers of 'statistical Muslims', and even Protestants and Catholics, had cast their ballots in favor of a Muslim party, evidently holding the view that it was the only credible focus of opposition to the regime."[16]

Yet, on a transnational level, the international campaign and domestic mobilization remained strangely disconnected. The most vocal critics of Suharto's regime, the student opposition, did not take up the treatment of the alleged communist political prisoners as a human rights problem. There was an explicit agreement among the student organizations not to support the issue. As Lukman Hakim, the chairman of the student union of the Universitas Indonesia between 1976 and 1979, admitted, the communist political prisoners were regarded as the "public enemy".[17] International human rights organizations noted with puzzlement this disconnectedness. A reporter, who interviewed the famous human rights lawyer Adnan Buyung Nasution in 1977 remarked that there seemed to be very little attention or concern on the part of the Indonesians she had met for the political prisoners who had been stuck in jail for more than ten years. Nasution's answer is equally telling, for he stated: "Yes, I know many people who want to make an exception for the Communists, to exclude them from our concern. I tell these people that by making an exception of any group, they are opening the door to their own loss of rights."[18]

Nasution's verdict proved to be accurate, for the Suharto government cracked down violently on the domestic student opposition. In January 1978, the government imposed limits on freedom of opinion and temporarily closed down the most outspoken newspapers *Kompas* and

*Sinar Harapan*.[19] In February 1978, troops broke up a student boycott at the prestigious Bandung Institute of Technology (ITB) and started their nation-wide crack down on student protest. The clamp-down was formally institutionalized through a policy of "campus normalization" which forbade students any political activity at universities.[20] The government introduced a compulsory educational programme, which spelt out ways of "properly" understanding and implementing the state ideology *Pancasila* (the P4 programme) and definitely stamped out any other "confessional", that is, Islamic interpretation. On a domestic level, the military and Suharto justified their harsh reaction by arguing that radical Muslims were masterminding the student unrest. They alleged that fundamental Parmusi activists had started to dominate the PPP. These "fundamentalists" were, in the government's view, also manipulating the student organization HMI,[21] which was dominating the student bodies at many universities.[22] Several leading Muslim politicians were arrested in April 1978 on the ground that they had instigated the student demonstrations.[23] The military establishment let the public know that it would not retreat out of politics, if "fanatical Muslims" filled the political vacuum.[24]

Internationally, the Indonesian Government managed to soften pressure on the communist political prisoner issue by releasing the prisoners, while it succeeded in closing the ranks in its policies against (alleged) Muslim radicals in 1978–79. In 1978, the *Far Eastern Economic Review* carried an article which warned against political liberalization in Indonesia, as this would ultimately bring Islamic forces to power whose only aim was to pursue an Islamic state.[25] In the Indonesian province of Aceh, the radical Darul Islam movement revived briefly in 1978, and renewed its call for an Indonesian Islamic state. Only one year after an alleged attempt by a fanatical group striving for an Islamic state, the Commando Jihad, to overthrow the government, the revival of Darul Islam in Aceh added credibility and leverage to the military's concerns. Even the *New York Times* reported that the Suharto government was concerned about a replication of the Iranian revolution in Indonesia, given the heightened activities of Muslim political organizations. Press reports in the *New York Times* drew an explicit comparison between Iran and Indonesia and noted the politicization of the Indonesian students, and the Indonesian Foreign Minister Adam Malik explained on a visit to the United States that the Indonesian Government's principal task was to strengthen national unity against Islamic extremists.[26] This double strategy seemed to pay off. In May 1978, U.S. Vice President Walter Mondale visited Indonesia. Mondale's visit "left the Indonesians in a jubilant mood", as they had expected sharp criticism of their illiberal policies. Instead, according to press reports, Mondale gave Suharto the American Government's "stamp of approval on human rights".[27]

## CONCLUSION: LESSONS TO BE LEARNED

What are the lessons that can be learned from the experiences of the 1970s that could be applied to current Asian human security concerns? Similar to the attacks on the World Trade Centre by members of Al Qaeda, the Iranian revolution in 1979 shocked the Western world and instilled a widespread anti-Islamic atmosphere. This atmosphere provided an ideal pretext for the Indonesian Government to suppress the Islamic community and to outmaneuvre some of its most consistent critics in the political debate. Similar to the current political situation in many Asian countries, the government tightened its surveillance of the public to deal with so-called Islamic extremists. In the end, it was the Indonesian people who paid the bill because preventing an Islamic state (a development which was by no means determined) came at the price of weakening democracy.

The interesting parallels to the 1970s are that the attacks in the United States have led to a mobilization of Islamic forces in Indonesia and in other countries with a Muslim population. Since the bombings of a discotheque in Bali in October 2002, the Marriott Hotel in Jakarta and several other violent attacks, it is almost undisputed that there exists an Islamic terror network operating in Indonesia. It is also obvious that the Indonesian army, which was notorious for its human rights violations during the Suharto era, aspires to a new political role and has used the revitalization of Islam in Indonesia to justify this aspiration.[28] As Indonesia was heading for presidential elections in 2004 individual politicians were trying to exploit political Islam for their campaign. Megawati Sukarnoputri and other nationalist politicians shied away from denouncing criminal acts allegedly committed by radicalized Muslims because this might have put them in line with the Bush administration's war on terror. Although there are politicians who hope for an Islamic state of Indonesia, it appears that if Indonesia's democratic project fails for a third time (after the 1950s and 1970s), it might ultimately fail for two reasons. First, because the curtailing of the political rights of Muslims might lead to a radicalization of Muslim opposition which in turn provides more justification for those groups who see the continuing political domination by TNI as the only bulwark against the rise of an Islamic state. Second, because of the indulgence in regard to criminal acts perpetrated by radical groups that some political leaders patronize which is obviously fuelled by a concern that if they denounce these acts they might lose political power; this indulgence might lead to a widespread perception of a lack of governmental authority and enforcement power that equally plays into the hands of those who want to see TNI's role maintained. In the face of — in the words of Amnesty International — a partial breakdown of the rule of law with regards to Muslims, it is by no means astonishing that Muslims look for laws that protect them from state interference and enable their self-determination, that is, the *shariah*.

Indicative of such a development in Indonesia is a recent gathering of approximately 200 extremist Muslim clerics in Bandung. The participants of the two-day meeting were expected to agree on support for presidential candidates who were committed to promoting the implementation of *Shariah* in Indonesia. The committee chairman was quoted as saying: "We don't want the next president to be someone who arbitrarily arrests Muslim activists but rather someone who allows Muslims to institute sharia."[29] As this statement makes clear, the introduction of *Shariah* law is not tied to religious fanaticism, but justified by human rights violations, that is, "arbitrary arrests". It basically seems to confirm the impression of human rights groups in ASEAN that the tightening of security legislation in the name of the war on terrorism, in the words of one human rights activist, "seems to be contributing to more repression and terrorism in the region."[30] In other words, by suppressing the rights of Muslims, governments such as Indonesia provoke the very developments they want to prevent, the radicalization of the Muslim community.

This raises the question of what strategies Asian governments — or the Indonesian Government in this case — should pursue to deal with threats to the secular state. In this regard, it is important to remember that human rights norms not only provide a yardstick for how a state should treat its citizens, that is, that they should be free of torture and arbitrary arrests, but that it also demarcates norms of appropriate behaviour for citizens, that is, the articulation of political dissent. Bombing discotheques, hotels and police stations is clearly not an act of peaceful articulation of political dissent but constitute criminal acts. Having said this, the best strategy would certainly be to pursue these criminal acts by the means of rule of law and make as transparent as possible the charges which are levelled against suspected criminals.[31] It does not imply issuing new internal security acts which blur the line between legitimate political opposition and terrorism.

## NOTES

1. Amnesty International: India (2003). Abuse of the law in Gujarat: Muslims detained illegally in Ahmedabad, AI INDEX: ASA 20/029/2003, 6 November 2003, available from <http://web.amnesty.org/library/Index/ENGASA200292003>, last accessed on 16 November 2003.
2. "Rights Groups Say Political Repression Rising within Asean", *Associated Press*, 6 October 2003.
3. For details, see Kishore Mahbubani, "The Dangers of Decadence", *Foreign Affairs* 72, no. 4 (1993): 11–14 and Kishore Mahbubani, "The Pacific Way", in *Foreign Affairs* 74, no. 1 (1995): 100–11.
4. For more details, see <http://www.freedomhouse.org/research/freeworld/2000/methodology.htm>, accessed on 15 December 2003. While the index and its method have been the issue of considerable debate of scientific and ideological nature alike, the index has considerably gained in status since the end of the Cold War and is now regarded as one of the most established ones to measure political freedom.
5. See for the following: Rosemary Foot, *Rights Beyond Borders. The Global Community and the Struggle over Human Rights in China* (Oxford: Oxford University Press, 2000). and John F. Copper and Ta-Ling Lee, *Coping with a Bad Global Image. Human Rights in the People's Republic of China* (Lanham: University Press of America, 1997).
6. Foot, op. cit.
7. Ibid.
8. Anja Jetschke, "Linking the Unlinkable? International Norms and Nationalism in Indonesia and the Philippines," in *The Power of Human Rights. International Norms and Domestic Change*, edited by Thomas Risse, Stephen Ropp, and Kathryn Sikkink (Cambridge: Cambridge University Press, 1999).
9. Komando Permulihan Keamanan dan Ketertiban: Kopkamtib.
10. Partai Komunis Indonesia: PKI.
11. See, for example, Amnesty International, *Background to Indonesia* (London: Amnesty International, 1968).
12. Damien King, *The Politics of Indonesia* (Melbourne: Oxford University Press Australia, 1998), pp. 101–06; John Bresnan, *Managing Indonesia. The Modern Political Economy, Studies of the East Asian Institute* (New York: Columbia University Press, 1993); Jamie Mackie and Andrew MacIntyre, "Politics", in *Indonesia's New Order*, edited by Hal Hill (Sydney: Allen&Unwin, 1994).
13. Harold Crouch, *The Army and Politics in Indonesia* (Ithaca and London: Cornelly University Press, 1978); King, op. cit., p. 103.

14. Amnesty International, *Indonesien. Ein Bericht Von Amnesty International November 1977* (Baden-Baden: Nomos Verlagsgesellschaft, 1977).

15. Leo Suryadinata, "Indonesia in 1979 — Controlled Discontent", *Southeast Asian Affairs* (1980).

16. Ben Anderson, "Last Days of Indonesia's Suharto?", *Southeast Asia Chronicle*, no. 63 (1978).

17. Interview with Dr. Lukman Hakim, Jakarta, 26 February 1999.

18. Charyl Payer, "Indonesia's Human Rights Lobby", *Tapol Bulletin* 1977.

19. Anderson, op. cit.

20. David Jenkins, "The Storming of the Basketball Court", *Far Eastern Economic Review*, 24 February 1978.

21. Himpunan Mahasiswa Indonesia: Indonesian Student's Organization.

22. David Jenkins, "Warning Shots to Students", *Far Eastern Economic Review*, 13 January 1978.

23. Indonesian authorities detained Mahbub Djunaide, the deputy secretary of the PPP, Ismail Suny, a professor of constitutional law, and Sutomo and held them for one year without trial. See David Jenkins, "Accounting for Human Errors", *Far Eastern Economic Review*, 27 July 1979.

24. David Jenkins, "Where the Generals Reign Supreme", *Far Eastern Economic Review*, 13 January 1978.

25. Interestingly, and contrary to the common usage of the *Far Eastern Economic Review*, the article concealed the author's name. This leaves a lot of room for speculation over who wrote the particular article and with what intention.

26. *New York Times*, 18 April 1978, p. 9; 3 June 1979, p. 3; 17 June 1979, IV, p. 3.

27. Richard Jenkins, "Mondale Sows the Seeds", *Far Eastern Economic Review*, 5 May 1978.

28. See, for example, "TNI and War on Terrorism", *The Jakarta Post*, 20 August 2003.

29. "Clerics Meet to Push for Sharia Law", *The Jakarta Post*, 8 October 2003.

30. "Rights Groups say Political Repression Rising within ASEAN", *Associated Press*, 6 October 2003.

31. For a very good explanation of this standpoint, see Sidney Jones, "Facing the Enemy Within. The Indonesian Government Must Tell the Whole Truth About Organized Terror", *Time Asia* 162, no. 14 (2003).

# Part Four

## New Concepts of
## Asian Security

# Chapter Thirteen

# Asian Security as a Global Public Good

Hermann Schwengel

## INTRODUCTION

Asia is beset by security dilemmas.[1] These dilemmas have their origins in the collective memories of Asian societies, and were sharpened by colonial experience and intensified by interaction patterns of the Cold War period. These pre-colonial, colonial, and post-colonial experiences still influence the perceptions of contemporary actors. Present day security dilemmas appear to be embedded in the driving forces of technological change, globalization and cultural diffusion.[2] Policymakers need conceptual tools to resolve these dilemmas, or at least manage them by bridging the different ways of thinking about them. This chapter is an attempt to construct a conceptual bridge by proposing the idea of global public goods.

To conceptualize security dilemmas in terms of globalization, structural change, or the polarities of realist versus liberal political theory is a start. But more concrete results are needed, for example, good governance, sustainable growth and cultural resilience. Reaching consensus on the best route from diagnosis to reform is, however, more difficult than ever. In the years since the fall of the Berlin Wall, those advocating Kantian agendas for peace have suffered disenchantment, but so too have those proposing new Hobbesian world orders. The expectation of an era of fresh opportunity for international peace and security [3] which characterized the early years of the post-bipolar world definitely has gone. Those in the moderate centre advocate pragmatic means of conflict management, including early attention to potential conflicts, confidence-building measures, negotiated peace-making, pre-emptive containment of disputes, and the threat or use of military force as a last resort.[4] Others support a benevolent hegemonial strategy to allow free markets, sustainable development, and democracy to flourish. Policies abound but a vision is needed to direct them.

## TOWARDS A FRESH DISCOURSE

The time is ripe for a fresh discourse on security frameworks. If new concepts of global growth can be manifested to stabilize and strengthen Asian economies, then new comprehensive concepts may be able to meliorate security dilemmas, too. This search for comprehensive concepts should be motivated not by optimism but rather cool political calculation. I propose the concept of global public goods to interpret the dynamics of international relations, security dilemmas and the opportunities of regions such as Asia. One should not confuse this idea with a renaissance of ambitious human security ideals, worthy though that is, but see it clearly as a concept reflecting:

- The persistence of strong states;
- The growing flexibility and cosmopolitanism of leaders;
- The strengthening of non-state actors;
- The formation of multiple inter-relationships, allowing
- Emergence of "regional states" and "multiple regionalisms".[5]

Global public goods theory is a way to encompass the experience of structurally expanding global markets demanding new modes of public regulation without waiting for inter-governmental institution-building. Asia thus may become one of the key laboratories for region-building because it is located between the well-established attraction of American global market-building and the new European state-building experience. Southeast Asian regionalism, as manifested in the evolution of the Association of Southeast Asian Nations (ASEAN) has in part been inspired by and compared to the growth of the European Union (EU) even as academic analysts distinguish it from the European model. At the same time, Southeast Asia has had to adapt to the influences of two large nation-state neighbours, China and India, each representing unique economic, political and cultural institution-building experiences, and to the impact of United States hegemony.[6] The reaching out by China, Japan, and Korea to ASEAN in the ASEAN+3 (APT) initiative is the most recent manifestation of a growing Asian regional consciousness. The literature on globalization carefully distinguishes between the three different levels of globalization, namely, the international, transnational and global levels.[7] But if one places the historical experiences of China, India, Europe and the United States in the same context, then one may discern new patterns that have much to teach. Policymakers trained in realist think tanks or state bureaucracies will have to expand their thinking to take these unique patterns into account.

## THE CONCEPT OF GLOBAL PUBLIC GOODS

Kaul, Gruneberg, and Stern provide a starting point for global public goods analysis when they asserted that "To understand better the routes of global crisis, whether loud (financial crashes) or silent (poverty), we propose to look at today's policy challenges through the lens of global public goods".[8] To appreciate the usefulness of this concept, we have to look at its intellectual history. The main properties of public goods are non-rivalry in consumption and non-excludability of users.[9] The idea of public goods may be most easily understood in terms of the contrast between markets and states, the former providing private goods, the latter public goods. Furthermore, if we interpret public goods in terms of globalization, that is, transcending the neo-classical contrast of market *versus* state, we may be able to demonstrate how classes and groups, nations and generations, regions and local communities are managing the consequences of economic uncertainty, political reshuffling of power and cultural differentiation.

But one needs to go beyond the radical-liberal discourse of the 1970s or the conservative-libertarian challenge of the 1980s to make conceptual progress. Too many people in Europe are still stuck in this alternative: Security as a global public good in the first instance has to provide all the benefits people have already come to expect from the global economic order, that is, rising prosperity. Global public goods defined by global movements and humanitarian advocates in the language of United Nations agencies are growing without limit in response to global social problems, which are limitless by nature. If one wants to confine the concept of global public goods to only those areas where private enterprise desperately needs the support of public institutions, that is, during shortfalls or failure, then there is no conceptual advance, only reaction. Liberal economists have seen public goods only as an institutional means to gain greater efficiency that cannot be provided by private markets, that is, the legitimacy and sovereignty of the state, the predictability of law, the security of property, and the provision of unprofitable public infrastructure. Within these contexts of public choice and institutional competition, the role of public goods will always appear very limited. In contrast, the contemporary interest in global public goods is born out of the original globalization experience but is growing beyond it. If developed, public goods theory could offer pragmatic tools for policymakers not only at the national level but also to sub-national actors — even though controlling governance costs may remain a concern.

## THREE ADVANTAGES AND THREE GOODS

Three conceptual advantages accrue to the creative use of public goods concepts in framing global private goods markets. First, in the concept of global public goods, the breakthrough of private-market-led institutionalization of global exchange is encompassed. This is the realization that public goods theory is leaving socialism behind while taking its motives and values into a new era. Different levels of public goods provision can be distinguished, each offering well-ordered local, regional, national and continental supply structures, private-public joint production of goods and services and legitimation by global middle classes accepting loyalties not only to local, regional and national public institutions but to responsible transnational political bodies as well. People will have to learn to move between local, national and global levels of identification, interchange, and investment and this will make attractive a public goods theory that provides a map of the pathways.

Secondly, the provision of public goods offers flexible standards because public goods are different from human needs, class solidarities and national identity. In general, public goods can be defined as basic resources or needs for human life. Their other characteristics are access to means of communication, labour and business markets or life chances and — last but not least — the empowerment of people, groups and entrepreneurship to join, to shape and to use markets to develop their own way of life. Current policymakers have to take into account this liberalization of economic behaviour much more than two decades ago. Even the Asian financial crisis has not destroyed this dynamism of economic behaviour.

Thirdly, public goods can be provided not only by the state or state agency in public-private-partnership but also by the activities of civil societies in making health care work, enriching education and broadening social communication. Many activities of welfare states, local communities and transnational institutions and movements therefore contribute to a production of public goods making the concept rich and open at the same time. Security, financial stability or sustainability may be provided in fact by local, regional, national and a variety of transnational institutions, but it is necessary to develop public goods at the global level as well. Global public goods cannot be provided without global structure-building. Therefore global public goods are not only defined by their global character but also need explanation as to which level the good is manifested on and at which level the production is coordinated and legitimated. The advantage of the concept of public goods is the ability to link the different territorial and functional levels that are necessary for the production of global public goods.[10] One can no longer cling to a "realist" or a "liberal" ideology because the provision of public goods on different levels demands different attitudes at different times. As in Europe, this conscious flexibility in Asia will be a result of historical experience transformed by the cooperation of policymakers and historians.

Global public goods are manifold but may be grouped into three bundles: Security, sustainability, and education, with social justice possibly added in future. After World War II, security was the primary global public good. It was visualized as an answer to global depression, political authoritarianism and war. Three decades later, sustainability had become a modern global public good of equal importance, addressing the crises of global industrialism with protection of the environment, fair trade rules, and stable financial frameworks. A new global public good being developed and institutionalized today is education, which gives global citizens the basic resources, the necessary access and empowerment to manage their own lives. Other public goods like social justice are important but will not be provided on the global level in the near future as there are local and national regulating structures, public bodies and institutions of law capable of doing so. In the longer term social justice as a public good may move from the national to the transnational level, as it is doing cautiously in

Europe, but will probably remain on a national or even local and family level in other regions. These national public goods may vary between different levels of development, historical and cultural traditions or political struggle. And local public goods institutions may have to bear the burden of compensating for the failure of global, regional or national provision of public goods. In keeping with the theme of this book, the following passages focus on the public good of security.

## SECURITY AND REGIONAL STATES

The public good of security appears at all levels. The language of public goods is flexible enough to identify the different contributions to security on each level. States remain as key mediators and nodes of the networks between local, regional, national and transnational levels even, if they do not provide public goods themselves. Joint public-private enterprises need the sovereignty and legitimation of states even more than before. Because of globalization, states are losing and gaining importance depending on their circumstances but all are adapting one way or the other.[11] Their transformation makes the traditional military-political and the commercial state[12] more like what I will call a "regional state" on the global level, one defining itself from the beginning as a dynamic entity moving between federal differentiation and global inclusion. A regional state is a national state whose leaders adopt a regional vision within a global framework and succeed in providing public goods. Adopting the concepts of regional states and public goods will not impose the same stress on policymakers as conventional regional institution-building, which challenged deep commitment to sovereignty held by nationalists. I suggest below that China, India, and the more cosmopolitan states of Southeast Asia may be regional states in embryo.

Thus the modern regional state is capable of offering advanced public goods, contribute to transnational and global public goods and encourage the provision of local public goods. In accepting this role, the regional state becomes linked to powerful civil societies, and they undertake community-building as to secure their positions. For the provision of public goods, international civil societies need the regional state like the old liberal domestic society needed the national state in order to flourish. Consequently the discourse on global public goods is part of a global intellectual effort as challenging as the work after the end of the two world wars when the interdependence between private production and politically managed demand, industrial culture and consumerism, interventionist state and open class society had to be re-thought.[13] Historical perspective offering more global options is necessary in order to free the contemporary debate from the context of the last two decades, during which policy-makers were trapped by the concept of sovereignty.

## THE PROVISION OF SECURITY AS A GLOBAL PUBLIC GOOD

Building on the above observations, we are now ready to analyse security as a global public good. Insofar as we accept global free markets, we must perforce accept both opportunity on the one hand and insecurity, risk and conflict on the other. The liberalization of markets for goods and services, capital and money offers chances for established actors to gain — or lose — even more. The distribution of wealth, income and life chances is more unequal than ever. Economic globalization furthermore poses the risk of destabilizing key structures of democracy, and market-driven globalization also deepens ecological crises in many respects.[14] These are reasons to enlarge the concept of security to embrace human security, including the consequences of poverty,[15] cooperative development strategies, and human rights. Human security might be identified indeed as a public good characterized by non-rivalry and non-excludability.

But all good reasons have their limits. One is that hegemonial leaders may co-opt human security to legitimize a war on terrorism or their own power position. A second is that the enlargement of security as a global public good is limited by other global public goods such as sustainability and education because different agencies are responsible and the aggregation of security, sustainability and education and do not coordinate to take collective action automatically. And third, if security does include all moments of a safe life, then the concept may help to alert people to the risks of the neo-liberal world of privatization, deregulation and risky individualization. But at the same time, this warning does not give any political answer to the structural uncertainties of the post-bipolar world, only a vague wariness and paralysing scepticism.

The fact is that security as a global public good is provided neither exclusively from above, that is, United Nations arrangements or global movements, nor from below, that is, national democracies or enlightened administrations opening space for grass-roots self-organization. Rather, global security is provided from within by multiple regions and overlapping networks of active groups, that is, the multi-dimensional interaction of state and agencies, civil society representatives and cultural mediators all understanding their status in relation to a globalized world. Sustainability may be much more organized from above, by transnational corporations, high politics and high-specialized global movements — quite different from the origin of Western environmental movements — whereas education is probably organized much more from below because the cultural character of education needs the dense interaction of national or even local values and societies — against the imagination of global cultural industries and education managers. Different public goods are provided by different constellations of global, national, regional and local authorities, electorates and people. The concept of public goods does acknowledge competition, choice and democratic decision between different types of political producers. Previously, public goods theory assumed that the distinction between private markets and public authorities would be useful for both. Now, public-private partnership, co-production by producers and consumers and intermediary powers between states and markets are becoming the rule for a global mixed economy.[16] Increasingly, liberal economic elites as well as producers of public goods can discourse in ideological debates in the same language and in front of the same audience.

The provision of security as a global public good organized by regional institutions may engender the following benign effects for other public goods.

- Regional security arrangements may retard the spillover of trade disputes into political domains,
- Trade patterns may follow investment patterns made safe by regional security arrangements,
- Pursuit of prosperity may benefit from well-designed security environments,
- Secure trade arrangements will retard conflicts by imposing higher opportunity costs.

In the provision of global public goods by regional security-building, the instability provoked by rising great powers like China[17] may be better neutralized than in a more competitive environment. Rising regional powers may contribute to the joint production of the security public good on more than one level — subregional, regional, or global — proportionate to their size, resources, and prosperity. Regarding Southeast

Asian region-building, the rise of Chinese as well as Indian power interpreted in terms of the provision of global public goods can signal more alternatives instead of fewer.

To sum up thus far, all territorial levels are involved in the provision of public goods, but one level — in the case of security the regional level — will have to take the lead, the anchor role and the goalsetter of regime-building. This division of labour between multi-level actors structured around anchor levels depends on the mobilization of overlapping civic communities in and between the states and societies of global regions. The organized multi-level provision of security as a global public good does need the organized mobilization of civic communities corresponding to this political structure. By an irony of history the idea of a politics of global public goods may lead to modern regional differentiation of global society necessary for any political representation of the world as a whole.

Such thinking would certainly have consequences for the structure of the United Nations Security Council. A reformed Security Council would have to represent regions and not only nation states as in the post-World War II period. It must take the associations of regional states and their active civil communities increasingly into account. This would require a virtual second chamber of the Security Council that includes global movements, activities and networked civil societies ready to work with global administrations, global firms and public spheres. If Security Council membership were extended to regionally representative members as India, Brazil, Japan, Germany and an African nation, the demand for the representation of public goods providers would remain. This is because public goods are no longer provided only by states monopolizing political and military power but by civil society agencies networking the activities of various local organizations. Their constituent people are interested not only in institutional and military security but also in the security and safety of everyday life.

## SOUTHEAST ASIA AS AN EMERGING MODEL?

Security as a global public good is encouraging the interaction between global region building and vocal local communities. In this context China, conceived as a nascent regional state, is not necessarily a threat to enlightened power holders but rather — like European, Latin American and African associations — may offer a new focus for the provision of public goods. There are five ways in which the organized provision of public goods, and especially the enhancement of security as a global public good inspired by regional organizations such as ASEAN in association with regional states such as China (and possibly India) might contribute to resolving security dilemmas:

(1) Building transparency and trust in unstable state-society complexes,
(2) Managing political frictions arising from region-building processes,
(3) Stabilizing the interaction between large states and differently composed associations of regional states in the same geopolitical area,
(4) Promoting inclusion of Asian region-building models in other parts of the world, and
(5) Coping with cultural hegemony, market dependence, and power-political pressures.

Globalization, modern information technology, and overlapping public spheres have created something like the end of secrecy.[18] Security as a global public good may then include the mobilization of sources of transparency and build trust by revealing the rival and even the enemy in a less threatening light.[19] Responsibility for this regime of transparency can be apportioned between public and private actors so as not to burden one state or group. Obviously, governments have to build up or negotiate structures of friendly interaction between countries and at the same time be on guard against states that might threaten their national interests and survival. Residual scepticism about the intention of others, even of those whose friendship is being sought, is normal in international discourse. But, if security as a global public good provided by associations of regional states is identified and raised in priority, then a system of systematically interacting regional transparency agencies might fill the gap between universalist expectations and real distrust. To put it another way, one can aspire to the transformation of the Westphalian order of states into a Westphalian order of societies. This aspiration is particularly applicable to Asia, given the region's overlapping ethnicities and nationalities is reflected most obviously in Southeast Asia but also in what I am calling nascent regional states like China or India.

The Asian financial crisis of 1997–98, for all its short-term damage to economies, was a long-term tonic to the new Asian regionalism. Regional organizations have become energized in all parts of the world and more differentiated in their levels of interaction, and Asia was no exception. Of course, this motivation can no longer be driven by the aspirations of middle-range states defending their status against global as well as local powers, as exemplified by France, but has to be built into the world of multiple regionalism, pragmatic policymakers and a cultural consciousness of the time necessary to work with the dynamics of states, civilizations and cities. Furthermore a political conjuncture between "soft" and "deep" institutionalization became more visible, as did the convergence of central or decentralized ways of coordination, and legalization and legitimization. As everywhere, Asian actors before the Asian financial crises were structurally hesitant to move beyond certain levels of trade and exchange because opportunity costs were difficult to predict and manage.[20] The crisis produced a "nothing more to lose" syndrome that facilitated restructuring.

Security as a global public good engendered by associations of Asian regional states holds the promise of making costs more calculable and stabilizing the private-political interface. In this way "thick" networks of regional interaction may reduce uncertainty. Even some regional Asian cosmopolitism could be defined in opportunities and costs and thereby understood, communicated and translated by political and economic elites as well as by cultural or religious leaders. In Europe and, to a lesser degree in the United States, political interfaces have been stabilized by deeply structured party systems channelling social movements, modulating conflicts, and offering inclusion opportunities to previously neglected minorities. While the provision of security as a global public good directed by regional interaction may be more comprehensive and potentially more effective than national political party structuring, just as multilateral agreements are more comprehensive than bilateral agreements, security provision on a global or even regional level is still weak. In the interim, this systemic supply of security as a public good by national party systems and inter-state networks of civil societies may be a beneficial model for Asia. Policymakers may understand the challenge to substitute the historical European party-building by well organized elite communication and "Eurasian" think tanks may organize the discourse on different historical experiences.

## LINKING SOUTHEAST ASIA, CHINA, AND INDIA

Security as a public good defined in this way may offer different views on the power, rationality and future of large regionally active states like China and India. One can envision a regional space of overlapping communications focused on mutual security issues linking the Chinese experience to the

Southeast Asian experience, transcending the national, ethnic and religious differences that have separated the parties heretofore. Societal elites and intellectuals may be well placed to carry out this very selective, limited and flexible initiative, but only if the context of public good provision by governments allows safe and sustainable networking and freedom for flexibility in and between global regions so different as China, India and Southeast Asia. The emerging concepts of global social and political sciences and cultural studies already offer valuable insights into the mutual interpenetration of social knowledge that is a concomitant of this networking and a prerequisite of a security community.[21]

Regarding regional institutions, ASEAN has often been compared to the European Union and to the Mercado Común del Sur (MERCOSUR) in South America. In the bipolar world, the interests of middle range power states like Brazil, France or Indonesia were interpreted as the driving force for region-building, not least in pacifying deep historical conflicts and rivalries and providing leadership for the building of organization superstructures for growing regional markets. In the post-Cold War world, the discussion between neo-realists and neo-institutionalists on the one hand and sociologists and culturalists on the other is shifting towards the latter. In the Westphalian system of societies that is moderating the Westphalian system of states, multi-level politics is not constrained to political institutions. It involves deeply penetrating social interactions, too. There are overlapping state-society complexes making the nascent associations of regional states in Asia more and more dependent on the inclusion of civic communities to manage different patterns of cultural identity.

In contrast, it is argued here that the top-down neo-institutional model of European integration is in decline. In certain areas the old European foundational societies interact more deeply than in others, and in some the new European societies are the most vital driving force. In maybe the most interesting case — the interaction between Western European core societies and the new "periphery" from Russia and Central Asia to the Middle East and Northern Africa — social interaction is the key force for advanced networking, migration structures and interdependence. Even this model is not complex enough to describe the interaction of societies, communities and groups that regional states can only manage, lead and coordinate but not ignore or suppress. There is an analogy to be drawn between core-periphery interaction in Europe and the incipient processes of regionalization in Asia. And there is the possibility of mutual learning between regional state associations in Southeast Asia,

South America, Europe and hopefully Southern Africa. Again, the framework of security as a global public good may be a vital cultural-intellectual element alongside political and economic institutions and their interactions.

## CONCLUSION

The provision of security as a global public good by associations of regional states and their vital communities may contribute to the benign transformation of hegemonial relations based heretofore on superior economic, political and cultural power. Japan, Australia and New Zealand are ambivalent as regards their situation in, and their identity with, Asia. Even the United States displays hesitation about its Pacific orientation as contrasted to its Atlantic or Southern orientations and its exceptionalism. The military, political and financial costs of the benevolent hegemony exercised by the United States, Japan, and Australia in parts of Asia are rising dramatically. But the costs and risks of withdrawing and abandoning Asia to unknown and unpredictable future hegemons are even greater. Europeans are experiencing a similar dilemma regarding the peripheries of the Mediterranean and Russia.

The way out of the dilemma is to invest in security as a public good. The debate on the provision of global public goods is growing[22] and no policymaker can afford to ignore the opportunities offered by this discourse. While it was initiated by the United Nations Development Programme, among others, the discourse has expanded beyond an exercise of transnational experts. If security is defined as a global public good to be provided by associations of regional states and their overlapping civic communities, then the United States, the European Union, India, China and East Asia, Southeast Asia, South America and Africa could work together to stabilize the existing pattern of regions even though their systems of governance and society, their historical experiences, and their modes of cultural communication are very different. The capstone of this structure of public security must be reflected in, and steadied by, the institutions of the United Nations. This may entail reforming the composition of the Security Council and by establishing a global public body representing the variety of civic communities within and beyond the associations of regional states they constitute. In this process, the nascent associations of Asia may constitute a laboratory in which new concepts of security as a global public good may be tested.

## NOTES

1. Alan Collins, *The Security Dilemmas of South East Asia* (Basingstoke: Macmillan, 2000); Alan Collins, *Security and Southeast Asia: Domestic, Regional and Global Issues* (Boulder: Lynne Rienner, 2003).
2. Compare Karl Polanyi's famous configuration of "opening" and "closing".
3. Stephanie Lawson, *The New Agenda for Global Security. Cooperation for Peace and Beyond* (Canberra: Australian National University, 1995).
4. See Gareth Evans, *Cooperating for Peace: The Global Agenda for the 1990s and Beyond* (St. Leonards: Allen & Unwin, 1993).
5. Paul Bowles, "ASEAN, AFTA and the New Regionalism", *Pacific Affairs* 70, no. 2 (1997): 219–34.
6. The Australian experience should be added here for comparative perspective.
7. Michael Mann, "Has Globalization Ended the Rise of the Nation State?" *Review of International Political Economy* 4 (1997).
8. Inge Kaul, Isabelle Grunenberg and Marc A. Stern, *Global Public Goods. International Cooperation in the 21st Century* (New York: Oxford University Press, 1999). See especially the Introduction.
9. "Defining Global Public Goods", in Kaul et al. eds., cited above, p. 3ff.
10. The high degree of abstraction is also a source of risk in this concept.
11. Michel Mann, cited above.
12. Richard Rosecrance, *The Rise of the Trading State: Commerce and Conquest in the Modern World* (New York: Basic Books, 1986).
13. Ethan Kapstein, "Distributive Justice as an International Public Good. A Historical Perspective" in Kaul et als. eds., cited above.
14. Annual Report, UNEP, 2002.
15. Mahbub Ul-Haq, *The Poverty Curtain: Choices for the Third World* (New York: Columbia University Press, 1999).
16. This global mixed economy has to be distinguished from the industrial mixed economy although there is some intellectual relationship.
17. Hung-Mao Chien, in *The Security Environment in the Asia-Pacific*, edited by Tun-yen Cheng (Armonk, New York: M.E. Sharpe, 2000), p. 8ff.
18. N. Florini, "The End of Secrecy", in *Foreign Policy* 111 (Summer 1998).
19. Jefrey M. Ritter, "Know Thine Enemy: Information and Democratic Foreign Policy", in Bernhard I. Finel and Kristine M. Lord, *Power and Conflict in the Age of Transferency* (New York and Houndmills: Palgrave, 2000), pp. 83–114.
20. Jürgen Rüland, "Dichte oder schlanke Institutionalisierung? Der neue Regionalismus im Zeichen von Globalisierung und Asienkrise", in *Zeitschrift für Internationale Beziehungen* 9, no. 2 (2002).
21. See Schirmer, Chapter 14 in this volume.
22. Inge Kaul, Pedro Conceição, Katell Le Goulven and Ronald U. Mendoza, *Providing Public Goods. Managing Globalization* (New York: Oxford University Press, 2003).

Chapter Fourteen

# Communities and Security in Pacific Asia

Dominique Schirmer

## INTRODUCTION: CHANGE AND SOCIAL INSECURITY

Political and scientific discourses about security in Pacific Asia[1] refer most often to political and institutional factors. As a rule these focus on questions of public security or — more often — of military threats coming from outside the state. However, public security and domestic security are concerns of growing interest. The prior focus on institutions is beginning to broaden from state, military and police-oriented viewpoints to include a broader range of issues. As discussed in other chapters of this book, the wider range of problems includes environmental questions such as the region-wide haze caused by forest fires in Indonesia that peaked in 1997, illegal border crossings and associated crime, maritime piracy, and the aftermath of the Asian financial crisis.[2] Countries like China and Vietnam have experienced social unrest, especially in the countryside, and the specter of eroding stability is feared as much by the people as by their governments.[3] In the majority of the countries in the region, poverty and social disparity on the one hand, and religious or ethnic conflicts on the other, are ever-present conditions not only threatening governments, but also threatening to disrupt social order and societal stability.

Furthermore, what looks like stability and continuity in the eyes of governments often means stagnation or even repression in the eyes of the opposition and individuals. Corruption, political disputes, a dearth of democracy, a surfeit of poverty and social disparity, and ecological degradation are ancillary breeding grounds for dangerous forms of social unrest in most of the countries in the Pacific Asia region.

## INDIVIDUAL CONCEPTS OF SECURITY AND STATE LEGITIMATION

It must be acknowledged here that security for most ordinary people seems to be neither institutional nor communal in nature but first and foremost a private issue involving things like having a home, job, and good economic prospects, and a stable social environment of friends, family and neighborhood. External threats do not loom large in the thoughts of most people most of the time.[4]

People often feel stressed when social change impacts suddenly on the social climate and social relations in new ways. Governments are often thought of as being unwilling or even unable to cope with such social upheaval, and politics is thought to be self-serving. A play of words in the Thai language illustrates this: "'politics' (*kanmuang*) resonates with 'eating the country' (*kinmuang*)".[5] It is well known that dissatisfaction grows in countries in transition, so it follows that dissatisfaction is endemic in the rapidly changing countries of Pacific Asia. The implication is that asking for stability and security in the region involves more than just asking for further economic development. The quest for stability is an important value and integral to all societies, although for different reasons, reflected for example in Confucian or religious traditions and the popular understandings of recent political history. But stability may be co-opted by governments to legitimate power. The number of Pacific Asian governments championing national security and stability and for the sake of this objective oppressing the population in order to retain power may be in decline, but is far from disappearing.[6] For governments such as the People's Republic of China and the Socialist Republic of Vietnam, appeal for stability to guarantee political continuity and economic prosperity is a tool with which they seek to discipline and ideologically convert the people to the leaders' worldviews.[7]

## COMMUNITIES AND SECURITY

When regional security or stability in East or Southeast Asia is under discussion, often the pessimistic diagnosis is that the region is riven by a dizzying plurality of cultures and styles of life and of conflicting national interests. It is said that there are but few common interests and that there is little hope that the fragments can be linked to form a regional community.[8]

But as indicated throughout this book, recent experiences have brought new concepts such as human security into focus, not least in Pacific Asia.[9] These new concepts not only take into account a broader range of possible security challenges in the region, but also question common assumptions of political non-interference. As a consequence they are more and more part of the discourse on security. At the same time the conviction is growing that the creation of a community would help resolve conflicts inside countries and manage threats coming from the region and beyond.[10] From this flows my premise that to enhance stability and security in the countries of East and Southeast Asia, it is necessary to establish some form of socio-cultural community. So the objective of this paper is to identify and encourage research in areas fruitful for community-building in the region, including causes, possible forms, and consequences of community-building. This chapter is less about formal institutions than about socio-cultural communities, their theoretical character, and their contribution to security in the Pacific Asia region.

In my view, socio-cultural communities are more than accessories of regional and national security. Rather, they are prerequisites inasmuch as they comprise the necessary foundation of political or economic measures. A sociological viewpoint is needed to understand this foundation. Because concepts of security are changing, researchers from political and international relations disciplines are beginning to incorporate sociological concepts into their analyses. When talking about factors guaranteeing or threatening security and when asking what security implies, non-military questions like the economic and ecological impacts of globalization or the economic, ecological and technical aspects of a situation are increasingly acknowledged.

As far as security conceived as domestic socio-political stability is concerned, this is widely recognized and discussed, for example when talking about the causes of crime and its impact on the security of society. This shift is evident in the academic discourse of Pacific Asian security, as reflected in this book. Authors like Amitav Acharya who have embraced the concept of "security community" (referring to Karl Deutsch's early concept of security community and to Benedict Anderson's notion of "imagined community") have proved to be well equipped to detect and analyse forms of collectivity in the Southeast Asian region.[11] Their concept is grounded on the constructivist idea that an ASEAN or regional collective identity is some sort of imagined community, preceding rather than resulting from political, strategic and functional interactions and interdependence. For Acharya, the ingredients of such a community are:

- Common vulnerability,
- Shared consciousness,
- A we-feeling,
- Interactions and adjustments,
- Regional elites' idea of an ASEAN way, and
- A norms-creating culture.[12]

Acharya's concept is, like others in political science, for example Nischalke's, mainly based on the concept and function of institutions.

## SMALL COMMUNITIES, NETWORKS, AND REGIONS

Community enhances security: this is agreed. But what does that mean? What is community in this context? The question is not whether there is a single regional community but rather whether a growing network can encompass different forms of community and numerous small communities. Research on such small communities and their interrelationships thus transcends the importance of each small community taken solely by itself, and provides hints about ways by which wider forms of community develop. Research on particular areas is already available (see below), but it needs to be consolidated. Study of possible conceptual components of a wider Pacific Asia community such as intensified forms of communication and mutually experienced realities seems promising. I am not looking for some completed community but for specific ways in which Pacific Asia is developing a regional network of communities, and the areas being covered by this network. Following this, the questions that arise are:

- What kind of communities already exist?
- What will strengthen and consolidate them?
- Do they develop and link up over the course of time?

The process and instruments of globalization can bring together the small communities of Pacific Asia by precipitating political and economic institutionalization to cope with challenges. Hence countries in the Pacific Asia region already engage in a sort of community-building to cope with increasing global pressure in the political, economic and sociocultural arenas. Community-building is manifested not only in institutional cooperation and contracts, but also in debates about democracy, human rights, the world market, the Asian finanical crisis, global media, and the Westernization of popular cultures. Global economic development which helped create the Asian economic miracle, the Asian financial crisis, and an "Asian rebirth" is one of the most important driving factors here. The impact of the Asian financial crisis of 1997–98 can be seen in the "minds of the societies" as well as the economic and social spheres. Even before this period a reaction had emerged in the invention and discussion of an Asian or Eastern identity, as implied by the "Asian values" debate. The debate was fuelled by multiple circumstances including, among other things, geographic proximity, the challenge of globalization, negotiating regional blocks such as ASEAN, the West-East conflict, and the West-rest conflict.

Sceptics insist that there is no chance that a Pacific Asian community will be anything more than a dream.[13] Their argument is based on static ideas of culture. Traditional culture and the tradition of culture have been used — often implicitly — by many regional experts as strong arguments against the evolution of community. Associations that mix "unnatural" combinations of ideologies, tastes or viewpoints (for example Chinese and Indonesian) are discounted from the start, based on the assumption that the different cultures do not fit together and never will. This is, in turn, based on the implicit assumption of the existence of static, homogeneous cultures and civilizations, like the Asian, the Islamic, or the Western civilization. As a result of the strength of this "culture" argument, the ideology of the clash of cultures has been applied to the Pacific Asia region. It is often overlooked that culture is a dynamic and performative concept that changes in relation to current contexts. While there is no intention here either to invent or deny a Pacific Asian culture, it is asserted that when looking at this region and talking about its future social climate, security endeavours and well-being, a regional dynamism cannot be ignored. Regional community-building at a holistic level will be overlooked if the focus is only on concrete facts within a national framework. Fresh attention should be given to phenomena in popular cultures, for example like the "Kim chic" that is sweeping in East Asia in the new millennium, or Kung Fu fiction or films popular even in the West, and also older discourses like the many "Asian values" debates going back to the nineteenth century. These should be seen not as single phenomena or as incident limited only to some groups but rather recognized as parts of a whole that fit together.

But how can we speak of a "Pacific Asian community" when attempts to establish community institutions experience so many difficulties? Political institutions like ASEAN regularly hit the headlines with conflicts and alleged failure.[14] And it is argued that much communication is strongly limited to particular spheres and elite discourses within Pacific Asia, and as such may create a superficial regional community for a small, elite group only. Perhaps such mostly governmental constructions of community do not function the way they are supposed to because of the original motives of the actors involved. Governments or political elites may proclaim "Asian values" to legitimize and secure their national power base and not to discuss values at all. Cooperative ventures have also been undertaken only when the partners come to see a common threat and not because regional actors were eager to cooperate for the sake of building a regional community.[15] Therefore, most cooperative activities can be seen more as preventive measures aimed at countering some threat, and as such can be seen to be based on negative or reactive grounds. Although they may fulfil their defensive task, they do not to constitute community-building.

## COMMUNITIES AND SOCIETIES

I therefore want to direct the question of community towards the societal level and the socio-cultural sphere. I believe there is a change occurring in the socio-cultural relationships and dynamic of societies in Pacific Asia. While governments assert the importance of the national interests when shaping inter-state cooperation, I would argue that parts of everyday culture are often closer to each other than governments and formal institutions are. In recent years, an intensification of cross-boundary discourse can be seen. This does not mean disregarding political and economic or institutional communities, but rather, recognizing their inherent separate points of view. Officially proclaimed communities may, in social terms, work against true community.

There is another viewpoint: Regional forms of identity can be based on the growth of cultural networks, popular culture and common social experiences like the Asian economic miracle, the Asian financial crisis (and its gradual overcoming), common measures facing globalized markets and also anti-Western sentiment. This positive view may also entail a negative side: Latent and manifest armed conflicts within the region spurred by persistent intra-regional threats. In contrast, true community at different levels would entail a regional network, constructed through communication across national borders (communication including the exchange of words, ideas, goods, and fashions) and through equally felt realities building common grounds of experience. Although these communities might be institutionalized, market-oriented or imagined communities,[16] or even communities by chance, it does not matter who or what stimulated such common grounds or community, be it invented in discourse, like the Asian values debates, or experienced directly, like the Asian financial crisis.

It is my contention that beneath the political and economic community-building by official proclamation and pressure, there are subtle forms of voluntary community-building in the region occurring within the socio-cultural spheres. It is important to emphasize that tracing socio-cultural communities does not mean "uncovering" hidden cultural communities. On the contrary, it means that all sorts of community-building whether conscious or unconscious, political, institutional, or economic, imply some *gemeinschaft*, some sort of affective community. They presuppose, assume or have as a consequence cultural and social relations of emotional identity. There are many forms of *gemeinschaft* as demonstrated by the trend towards a variety of networks, alliances and other forms of integration. Technical strategies used to expand and consolidate community at a political level and targeted at economic or security solutions will need to be embedded both socially and culturally in a regional community if they are to last. A deeper investigation of sociocultural community means a deeper investigation of such an embeddedness. This is why investigation on the socio-cultural level is also especially interesting to assess the resilience of communities of instrumental rationality and for clearly constructed communities.

## TWO AVENUES TO COMMUNITY-BUILDING: COMMUNICATION AND MUTUALLY EXPERIENCED REALITIES

The development of small communities in Pacific Asia displays two interacting modes, one based on communication, the other on mutually experienced realities. Both influence the "minds of the societies". It is neither common culture nor material cooperation that form communities, but rather the combination of communication on the one hand, and commonly experienced realities on the other. My thesis is that this combination of a thickening of very different forms of communication, together with an increase in mutually experienced realities, constitute the ingredients of possible community-building in Pacific Asia. I will discuss each in turn, giving some examples where research needs to be extended.

## Communication

Communication here refers broadly to all exchanges: Human, material as well as verbal.[17] It is communication in the sense of discourses, of the exchange of goods — including cultural goods, of the exchange of ideas, thinking, things, symbols and of travelling people, being all exchanged through the facilitation by media, mobility and migration. Of course, the exchange of material things alone has no direct function in community-building. Only if something is seen as a symbol or bears a symbol (a cultural product) itself, can it be said to produce community. As such, communication can be seen as the most important means of community development.[18]

If we added up all the different types of communication within Pacific Asian we would see a thickening of communication which, together with a clear and noticeable increase in experienced realities as described in this text, can be a vehicle for the development of some community. Both are forms of implicit community building, in contrast to the explicit top-down cooperation of elites. The focus of research and discourses should thus center on the examination of implicit and not merely explicit community building which would help make this subtle picture clearer.

### Official Communications and Official Community

On an institutional or even governmental level, many different forms of political or economic cooperation exist, for example, the ASEAN Free Trade Area (AFTA), ASEAN, ASEAN+3, the ASEAN Regional Forum (ARF), and the Council on Security Cooperation in the Asia-Pacific (CSCAP), as other chapters such as Haacke's and Schwengel's have pointed out. The motives and targets of such cooperation lie in the economic or strategic sphere and are dominated by national interests and bilateral or multilateral conflict and cooperation. But interference is taboo, as reflected in the Treaty of Amity and Cooperation of 1976.[19] These regional cooperation initiatives are prime elements in analyses of the region's conflicts and in the alleged lack of mutual understanding between the countries concerned. They are, nevertheless, communities by communication and have, over the last ten years, evolved into a regional community based on common rules and a common code of conduct as well as on a growing number of shared interpretations.[20] Nischalke demonstrates that these sorts of communicated communities are gradually becoming commonly experienced realities, based not on cultural history but on consciously "shared interpretations".[21] One can say, in some respect, that the conscious creation of a regional identity by national leaders, usually the main actors, and their assertion of an Asian identity, does gradually bear fruit, but only indirectly.

## Communication and Asian Values

The early 1990s saw the rise of discourses emphasizing the difference between "the Asian" or "Eastern cultures" and "the West".[22] Many such discourses explicitly construct community, often to dissociate the actor from "the West" or to resist the pressure of globalization (economic competition, democracy discourses) with the objective of strengthening national identity and consciousness. Although the motives behind such opposing constructions are mainly political (to legitimize a government, for example, or establish a multipolar international order) and have governmental protagonists like, for example, Singapore's Minister Mentor Lee Kuan Yew, former Malaysian Prime Minister Mahathir Mohamad or former Indonesian President Suharto, there is some economic motivation as well. Furthermore, opponents of the authoritarianism of Asian values proponents are disputing a specific manifestation, not the existence of Asian values as such. Korean dissident and later President Kim Dae Jung, a champion of democracy, contradicted former Singapore Prime Minister Lee Kuan Yew when he referred to a "myth of Asia's anti-democratic values" and in stating "that Asia has a rich heritage of democracy-oriented philosophies and traditions".[23]

Contrary to the sorts of cooperation described in the section above, the debates on Asian values, Confucian capitalism or Eastern civilization do rest on the logic of some regional Pacific Asia socio-cultural community, although such a community is not explicitly mentioned.[24] This can be seen as implicit community-building where the different societies construct Pacific Asian communities in different areas based on values and styles of life. Such implicit communities can be found in the development of new socio-economic values and lifestyles typical of some of the countries in the region, which are then declared to be "Asian values". In this respect the discussion of business modes is very popular, for example the way to organize business relations, or the fostering of some corporate identity among employees.[25] Often different societies use their own terms, for example "socialist market economy" in China[26] or "Eastern civilization" in other countries. Such communities are talked of and created by intellectuals, politicians or business people, and as such are limited to certain spheres or groups within the region.

The rise of such discourses claiming a specific, almost homogenous "Asian" (meaning East and Southeast Asian) culture and, as such, an "Asian" political understanding (for example, of "guided" democracy), accompanied the emergence in the region of the "Asian economic miracle". Researchers tried to identify and understand "the values motivating East Asian people to outstanding achievements in the areas of creation of capital, industrial management, commerce, technological innovation…."[27] Arguments and motives are closely linked to concepts like that of Suharto's Pancasila ideology in Indonesia[28] or of Confucian capitalism, which first became popular among Chinese scholars in the West and are now being discussed and adopted in the Peoples Republic of China.[29] The national, social and cultural histories of the different Asian nations have, therefore, been brought together under this common roof. Although these elite discourses often have very concrete and clear interests behind them, they are not without any social background and are sometimes appreciated by the ordinary public. Because most observers assume that nation-building and the legitimating of governmental prerogatives are the main motives of these discourses, meaning "policing culture, controlling change",[30] they tend to ignore their inter-connectedness to other phenomena. Such concepts intend to prove the inter-connectedness of economic success with "Asian culture" and "Asian" cultural values. This debate weakened with the Asian financial crisis but is alive today throughout the region, although on another level. For example, in China the popular idea of bearing Chinese characteristics [you Zhongguo tese] today often shows remarkable similarity to the Asian values debates elsewhere. For Dieter Senghaas, similarities are due to the concrete historical situation and not to culture.[31] This historical situation is indeed the common ground, shaped by the commonly experienced reality in the region.

In the case of the Asian values debates, this reality is underlined and moulded by the continuous communication of this concrete Asian identity. An early example of this are the popular books expressing "national" debates or circumstances such as The Japan that Can Say No,[32] The Asia that Can Say No[33] and The China that Can Say No.[34] These are conceptually connected even though their authors and intentions are very different; Morita Akio of Sony did not want to be listed as author in the English version of his book in 1991, while Ishihara Shintaro, a Japanese nationalist, published further books under this "say no" genre, one together with

Mahathir Mohamad of Malaysia.[35] In China a group of authors published such a book; it enjoyed huge popularity in the country, provoking the government to react to it ambivalently, first allowing it to be published but later forbidding it.

The relations between such discourses and debates have not yet been thoroughly investigated, but the background sketched above demonstrates that a convergence of values in the region resulting from many different forms of communication as well as other phenomena, situations and problems, is probable.

## Communication and Asian Popular Cultures

Popular cultures in the region — films, videos and music, fashion, food or lifestyles — represent areas in need of deeper comparative research. Two preliminary assessments can be made. First, an Asianization, as some call it, is taking place, reducing the influence of the United States, but also of Japan (which is often seen as an Eastern-West or Western-East country) in popular cultures and producing growing Pacific Asian markets (for example, for Hong Kong films).[36] This is a fact not welcome by all. Accordingly, Lii Ding-Tzann speaks of them as just another economic imperialism, perhaps even another cultural imperialism in this respect.[37] Experiences like "Kim chic" or "Korea fever" sweeping East and partly Southeast Asia half a decade ago may be a temporary product of hype, but they are nevertheless part of a process of "pan-Asianism" capable of reasserting an "Asian identity" as Habib Khondker calls it.[38] Secondly, similarities in seemingly separate markets develop, like Indian-style pop-music and East Asian-style pop-music; Charles Hamm calls this very obvious phenomenon a generic "Pacific Pop" with characteristic features.[39] Such communities and communications come about either by accidental market interchanges, or as a mixture of "chance" and a conscious search for identity, sometimes fostered by government policies. Community-building is thus either a by-product, or it is made by will, forming or backing up identity; most of the time it is both. An effect produced by these common cultures and cultural centers is the growing alignment in the looks and habits of many people in the region. Again, a certain style (of expression, using things or thinking) must not be taken as sufficient evidence of a community, particularly if it is contradictory to a regional, national or group style, but this can be common signs of everyday life which are helpful in creating a (sense of) community.

## Mutually Experienced Realities

The "minds of societies" (a term encompassing shared values, discussions, topics, fears, and knowledge) are shaped by the many realities experienced by their members. Cultures are shaped differently as a consequence of different realities. (This observation can be co-opted by those claiming the existence of a clash of civilizations as well as by those denying a Pacific Asian community based on the claim that cultural realities in the region are too heterogeneous, but I would resist this usage.) Besides the communicated forms of communities, discussed here under the title of communication, there are "separately" experienced events and realities that do not involve direct communication.[40] The Asian financial crisis is an example of an indirect experience molding a very large group of people in Pacific Asia. Like communication, commonly experienced realities are a prerequisite and a ground for community development in Pacific Asia but without being a guarantor of it.

### *Mutually Experienced Realities: Countries in Transition*

Today, most of the countries of the region are witnessing socio-economic change. They are countries in transition with many of the characteristic effects in the social, political and economic spheres.[41] These are countries with noticeable "Pacific-Asian characteristics" as far as the following features are concerned. Economic development is not only one of the main topics of concern for Pacific Asia but also a very important aspect of stability. "Getting rich" (as it is called in China where Deng Xiaoping announced that "getting rich is glorious" and "some must get rich first" to underline the policy of reform and opening up) seems to be the main concern of people in the middle and elite classes while keeping out of poverty is the main concern of the rest. Even "the former command economies of Vietnam, Laos, Cambodia and Myanmar [...are...] firmly embarked on the market road".[42] North Korea, one of the poorest countries worldwide, cut off from the rest of the world, is showing signs of interest in the models adopted by China or Vietnam.

However, economic development means not only rising living standards as shown in statistics, but also an adoption of capitalist principles. And the more capitalist principles are adopted, the less assurance there seems to be for personal security. Economic growth has had a second, indirect effect in many of the Pacific Asian countries and probably even more in the former socialist countries where it changes the socio-political dynamics, that is, how society works. In countries like China and Vietnam people experienced a sharp transformation of society and politics in the direction of capitalist principles.[43] According to Lulei many people do not want to accept that progress is to be measured only by increased production and consumption.[44] For them social situation, social conduct, culture, education, ecology, and morals are just as important, and these are endangered by capitalism.

## Mutually Experienced Realities: The Asian Economic Miracle

The "Asian economic miracle" signifying the years of enormous economic development seemed to produce a sense of invulnerability, at least for the winners of the economic upturn. Beginning with the "tiger economies" of Taiwan, Singapore, South Korea and Hong Kong, more and more countries in the region succeeded in jumping onto the bandwagon, or tried to. Statistics show that the majority of the people in the different countries of the Pacific Asia region have experienced a clear improvement in their living conditions. The impact of this novel feeling of success on this majority is, however, ambiguous. What is evident, though, is that the climate of economic and social change had some impact on all societies in the region.

## Mutually Experienced Realities: The Asian Financial Crisis

The remarkable economic growth in the region that took place two decades before the Asian financial crisis helped lift a huge number of people out of poverty. There had been high rates of employment growth and growing wealth. The years of 1997–98 witnessed a U-turn with a massive recession that sent shockwaves through the whole region. Did the euphoria of the Asian economic miracle aggravate the shock of the Asian financial crisis or were the people inured to poverty and uncertainty? For the economic elites, often exempted from the worst implications of the crisis, it might be particularly threatening as it confounded their assumption of the inevitability of the economic success. For many, a glorious dream was shattered in 1997. In countries like Indonesia, Korea and Thailand, those most struck by the Asian financial crisis, poverty had been reduced enormously in the 20 years before the Asian financial crisis, as a result of remarkable growth rates. With the Asian financial crisis, unemployment rose faster in these countries than in Mexico in 1994,[45] and hunger came back. Newly unemployed people suffered a drastic drop in income and living standards and for those still employed, price increases lowered real wages considerably. This was an enormous economic and social shock that loosened the foundations of societies in this region.

## Communication and Experiences Converge: The Example and Role of China

China provides an example of the inter-connectedness of culturally diverse parts of the region as evidenced in Northeast and Southeast Asia. Today China is eager to be part of and take part in the globalizing world.[46] It is an actor in ASEAN+3, ASEAN Dialogue Partners, ARF, APEC, WTO, the Anti-Terror-Coalition, Olympia 2008 and many other initiatives. From the Chinese point of view, a Pacific Asian community is helpful or even required in adapting to the risks of globalization, to meet economic and political challenges and to promote China's policy of reform and opening up. In addition to the fact that China is part of many regional communities through the agency of communication and experienced realities, the country has a characteristic and perhaps unique position and is preparing to take a leading role in the region. The country is watched with suspicion by much of the region mainly because it is seen as a possible political and military threat as it has been throughout history.[47] Culturally this threat of regional domination by China is credible even if not intended because of the sheer size of the country and the huge number of Chinese both within and outside China, and also because China occupies an exceptional position providing a special cultural context regionally and internationally, as it is the core of a global Chinese culture.[48]

China indubitably plays an important role in political, economic and socio-cultural spheres. These may be summed up as follows:

- First, in economic terms China is becoming more and more important in the region and worldwide, even surpassing Japan.
- Second, China also represents an important military factor.[49]
- Third, global Chinese culture, the ethnic, cultural and economic networks in the region of "Greater China" and the inter-connectedness of Chinese communities in Pacific Asia are very important for the Chinese economy and for China's relations with external actors.
- Fourth, "Confucian culture" connects some of the countries in the region with China seeing herself as some sort of "Confucian mother culture".

- Fifth, elements and values of an "Eastern civilization"[50] are closely connected to the elements and values of Confucian culture. These play an important role in the legitimation of "Asian" patriarchal polity in both Confucian and non-Confucian countries.[51]
- Sixth, the effort to fight U.S. hegemony and establish a multipolar international order is a very important motive for the Chinese Government — one which is shared by other leaders and countries.

However, despite the alleged virtues of establishment of a multipolar order, the possible retreat of the United States from Asia in future, together with the threat of dominance by China, raise the specter of a sort of community fostering Chinese hegemony, one not welcomed by leaders of the smaller nations in the region.

## CONCLUSION: TOWARDS A PACIFIC ASIA COMMUNITY?

While it may be strictly true to say that there is no one community but rather many forms of communities in the region, one may use socio-cultural analysis to discern that community development has taken place in Pacific Asia. Alongside the considerable pressure by political or economic leaders to develop from above a regional community, there are subtle forms of internal community-building occurring from below, within the sociocultural sphere, in diverse places. The small communities I mentioned above develop through communication and common grounds, referring to equally experienced realities, and emerge in many different areas. Despite the many differences in Pacific Asian societies, it can be stated that the region is experiencing a thickening of communication as well as an expanding range of common realities on a daily basis. This is true for phenomena like the Asian miracle or the Asian finanical crisis, as well as for popular music and lifestyles. Focusing on the socio-cultural issues that are a prerequisite for creating an integrated regional community rather than on how and where governments improve security within a given region, this chapter argues that regional common grounds, that is equally experienced realities throughout the region, build a basis for a better understanding and for an improvement of communication in the region. This is a prerequisite to the development of a broader regional community which is arguably even more necessary than political institutions to establish and guarantee security and stability.

In any case, the growing number of communications and other shared experiences and the connections between the different forms of communities must be investigated more thoroughly. All forms of community development should be considered. Heretofore research has concentrated on the prevalence of governments and national interests in regional cooperation and other forms of explicit community building, while social phenomena are seen as contextual or subordinate facts less worthy of close study. Regrettably, a synthesis of results of analyses in a wider array of disciplines is seldom attempted. It is this author's view that a comparative analysis of some of the community-building concepts described in this chapter can shed valuable new light on how to enhance security. It is necessary to take a closer look at these concepts and to study Pacific Asian communities from a socio-cultural perspective.

What can be concluded is that the paired phenomena of (1) thickening of communication and (2) commonly experienced realities have a decisive role to play in community-building, which in turn is a step towards ensuring stability and security in Pacific Asia. This conclusion carries the policy implication that governments, if they are serious about regionalism, should minimize barriers to domestic and cross-border communication by their citizens, taking the term communication in its broadest sense of exchange of material things as well as symbols. Furthermore, encouragement of sub-governmental associations, commonly known as NGOs, with the potential to coordinate common interests of people and groups, would also follow as a policy recommendation. Some analysts call this process the growing and thickening of civil society. Regardless of the terminology, the fundamental point is that community-building from the top down and by inter-governmental relations such as ASEAN, however necessary a first step it may be to counteract nationalism, is incomplete and potentially insubstantial. It must be matched and complimented by community evolution from the bottom up, wherein ordinary people communicate and share common experiences with their fellow citizens and with their counterparts in other countries. To facilitate this process of authentic community building without manipulating or distorting it should be a project of leaders concerned to enhance national and regional security.

## NOTES

1. In this chapter I concentrate on Northeast and Southeast Asia without specifically including or excluding any particular Asian country, thus subsuming them under the term *Pacific Asia*. My focus is on the broad Asian socio-

cultural sphere in which forms of communications and communities distinguish themselves from those of Western countries.

2. Sheldon W. Simon, "Evaluation Track II approaches to security diplomacy in the Asia-Pacific: The CSCAP Experience", *The Pacific Review* 15, no. 2 (2002): 167–200.

3. Wilfried Lulei, "Politische und soziale Aspekte der 'Erneuerung' in Vietnam. Zum Spannungsfeld von Reform und Beharrung im außerökonomischen Bereich", in *Vietnams neue Position in Südostasien*, edited by Vu Duy Tu and Gerhard Will (Hamburg, 1999), p. 213. For Vietnam's long tradition of protest see Long Ngo Vinh and Daniel C. Tsang, "Vietnam Today", *Critical Asian Studies* 34, no. 3 (2002): 459.

4. Ekkehard Lippert, ed. *Sicherheit in der unsicheren Gesellschaft* (Opladen: Wertdeutsche Verlag, 1997).

5. Duncan McCargo, "Security, Development and Political Participation in Thailand: Alternative Currencies of Legitimacy", *Contemporary Southeast Asia* 24, no. 1 (April 2002): 60.

6. The Asian values debate is a well-known example (see section *Communication and Asian Values*), the situation in China and Russia is often compared.

7. This could be seen in Spring 2003 in the debates about the People's Republic of China's handling of the infectious illness SARS. A Shanghai-based respiratory specialist, who sat on an advisory committee dealing with epidemic diseases, was quoted in the TIME Asia internet edition: "Our primary concern is social stability, and if a few people's deaths are kept secret, it's worth it to keep things stable", in <http://www.time.com/time/asia/covers/501030421/story.html>. This is not at all unusual.

8. See Brunhild Staiger, "Einleitung" in Brunhild Staiger, *Nationalismus und regionale Kooperation in Asien* (Hamburg: Institut für Asienkunde, 1995), pp. vii–xi; DouglasWebber, "Two Funerals and a Wedding? The Ups and Downs of Regionalism in East Asia and Asia-Pacific after the Asian Crisis", *The Pacific Review* 14, no. (2001): 343, 351, passim; Peter Franke, "Konkurrenz oder Kooperation. Im Wettlauf um die Ressourcen sind Konflikte vorprogrammiert", in *blätter des iz3w*, no. 204 (March 1995), pp. 27–30. For critical but partly optimistic views, see Tobias Nischalke, "Does ASEAN Measure up? Post-Cold War Diplomacy and the Idea of Regional Community", *The Pacific Review* 15, no. 1 (2002): 89–117 or Hanns W. Maull, Dirk Nabers, "Einleitung" in Hanns W. Maull, Dirk Nabers, *Multilateralismus in Ostasien-Pazifik. Probleme und Perspektiven im neuen Jahrhundert* (Hamburg: Institut für Asienkunde, 2001) pp. 14–17.

9. Sheldon W. Simon (2002).

10. See Masakazu Yamazaki, "Asia, a Civilization in the Making", in *Foreign Affairs* 75, no. 4 (1996): 107; Chris Dixon, "Regional integration in South

East Asia", in Jean Grugel, Wil Hout, *Regionalism across the North-South Divide* (London: Routledge, 1999), p. 131 or Hanns W. Maull, *Regionalismus in Asien-Pazifik* (Bonn: Europa-Union-Verlag, 1998), p. 1, passim.

11. Amitav Acharya, *Constructing a Security Community in Southeast Asia. ASEAN and the Problem of Regional Order* (London: Routledge, 2001). Also see Sorpong Peou, "Realism and Constructivism in Southeast Asian Security Studies Today: A Review Essay", *The Pacific Review* 15, no. 1 (2002): 124, 131. Also see endnote no. 16.

12. Amitav Acharya (2001), pp. 22–30, 63–73, who also discusses Southeast Asian community in terms of regional elites' activities and the idea of an "ASEAN Way"; Tobias Nischalke (2002); also see Peou (2002), pp. 127, 131–32.

13. See above, endnote no. 8.

14. Nevertheless, this institutional level is part of the production of community, as will be shown later.

15. The PRC became a member of ASEAN+3 and as such a partner of ASEAN states because the country is thought to pose a threat to ASEAN security and stability.

16. Benedict Anderson, *Imagined Communities: Reflections on the Origin and Spread of Nationalism* (London: Verso, rev. ed., 7th impr., 1996).

17. See Liu Ben, "Jiaowang yu Wenhua" in *Zhongguo Shehui Kexue*, no. 2 (1996), pp. 61–75; Heinz Starkulla, *Marktplätze sozialer Kommunikation. Bausteine einer Medientheorie* (München: Fischer, 1993).

18. This is true for one direction of the argument, not necessarily for both: There is no community without communication but there is communication without community.

19. See Sheldon W. Simon, (2002), pp. 167–200; Tobias Nischalke (2002). Among liberals, human rights concerns may legitimize some intervention.

20. Tobias Nischalke (2002), p. 107.

21. Ibid.

22. See, for example, Fareed Zakaria, " 'Culture is Destiny'. A Conversation with Lee Kuan Yew", *Foreign Affairs* 73, no. 2 (1994): 113; Kim Dae Jung, "Is Culture Destiny? The Myth of Asia's Anti-democratic Values. (A response to Lee Kuan Yew)", *Foreign Affairs* 73, no. 6 (1994): 189–94; Tu Wei-ming, "Asian Values and the Asian Crisis: A Confucian Humanist Perspective" at *URL: <http://www.ruf.rice.edu/-tnchina/commentary/tu1098.html>* (October 1998); Francis Fukuyama, *Konfuzius und Marktwirtschaft. Der Konflikt der Kulturen,* (München: Kindler, 1995); Masakazu Yamazaki, "Asia, a Civilization in the Making", *Foreign Affairs* 75, no. 4 (1996): 106–18. See also Mark R. Thompson, "Was ist mit den 'asiatischen Werten' geschehen?", in *Leviathan. Zeitschrift für Sozialwissenschaft* 29, no. 4 (2001): 218–36; Adolf Kimmel, *Vor dem pazifischen Jahrhundert?* (Baden-Baden: Nomos, 1996); Simon S.C. Tay, "Globalisation, Crises and Change: Nations and International Society in the

Asia-Pacific", *Panorama*, no. 3 (1999): 21–41 or Werner Draguhn, Günter Schucher, *Das neue Selbstbewußtsein in Asien: eine Herausforderung?* (Hamburg: Institut für Asienkunde, 1995).

23. Kim Dae Jung (1994), pp. 189 and 191.

24. See Chen Xianda, "The Modern Value of Traditional Chinese Culture", *Social Sciences in China*, no. 1, (1999): 80–89; Li Youzheng, "The Identity of Chinese Philosophy: New Confucianism and its International Context", *ASIEN*, no. 63 (1997): 71–75. Also compare Lin Yifu, Cai Fang, Li Zhou, "Comparative advantages and development strategy. A reinterpretation of the 'East Asian Miracle'", *Social Sciences in China*, no. 4 (2000): 16–27, HeXianming, "A Discussion on the Relationship between Confucianism and Industrialization in East Asia", *Social Sciences in China*, no. 3 (2000): 61–71, Peter L. Berger, Michael Hsin-Huang Hsiao, *In Search of an East Asian development model* (New Brunswick: Transaction Books, 1988).

25. Long Denggao, "Haiwaihua Shangjingying Moshi de Shehuixue Pouxi ('A Sociological Analysis of Overseas Chinese's Mode of Operation and Management')", *Shehuixue Yanjiu* (Sociological Research), no. 2 (March 1998): 75–82; Chen Xianda (1999), p. 83 discussing "East Asian Characteristics"; Robert W. Hefner, *Market Cultures. Society and Morality in the New Asian Capitalisms* (Boulder: Westview Press, 1998), also discussion on characteristic Asian or East Asian business modes like the often mentioned Chinese "*network* capitalism", p. 12ff.

26. Chen Xianda (1999).

27. Tu Wei-ming, "Der industrielle Aufstieg Ostasiens aus konfuzianischer Sicht", in Silke Krieger, Rolf Trauzettel, *Konfuzianismus und die Modernisierung Chinas* (Mainz: v. Hase & Koehler, 1990), p. 43, (translated from German, DS). See also, among others, Peter L. Berger, Michael Hsin-Huang Hsiao, *In Search of an East Asian development model* (New Brunswick: Transaction Books, 1988).

28. A concept deriving from India and adopted by Sukarno which was later instrumentalized under President Suharto as a political tool.

29. See, for example, Chen Xianda 1999, Dominique Schirmer, "Das Fremde als Vorbild? Die Teilung der chinesischen Kultur", in *Der Alteritätsdiskurs des Edlen Wilden*, edited by Monika Fludernik, Peter Haslinger und Stefan Kaufmann (Würzburg: ergon, 2002), pp. 329–50.

30. Simon S.C. Tay, "Globalisation, Crises and Change: Nations and International Society in the Asia-Pacific", *Panorama*, no. 3 (Manila, 1999): 27–29.

31. Dieter Senghaas, *Zivilisierung wider Willen. Der Konflikt der Kulturen mit sich selbst* (Frankfurt: Suhrkamp, 1998), pp. 178–84.

32. Morita Akio and Ishihara Shintaro, *"No" to ieru Nihon: shin Nichi-Bei kankei no kodo* (Tokyo: Kobunsha+Kappa-Holmes, 1989); Ishihara, Shintaro, *The Japan that Can Say No* (New York: Simon & Schuster, 1991).

33. Mahathir bin Mohamad and Ishihara, Shintaro (1994).

34. Song Qiang, Zhang Zangzang, Qiao Bian, et al., *Zhongguo Keyi Shuo Bu. Lengzhan Hou Shidai de Zhengzhi yu Qinggan Jueze*, revised edition (Beijing: Zhongguo Wenlian Chuban Gongsi, 1996).

35. Werner Pfennig, "Asiatisierung und asiatische Werte: Positionen innerasiatischer Debatten", in *Das neue Selbstbewußtsein in Asien: eine Herausforderung?*, edited by Werner Draguhn and Günter Schucher (Hamburg: Institut für Asienkunde, 1995), pp. 58–76, see p. 58, passim.

36. See, for example, Tu Wei-ming, "Cultural China: The Periphery as the Center", *Daedalus* 120, no. 2 (1991): 1–32; Thomas B. Gold, "Go With Your Feelings: Hong Kong and Taiwan Popular Culture in Greater China", in David Shambaugh, *Greater China: The Next Superpower?* (Oxford: Oxford University Press, 1995), pp. 255–73.

37. Ding-Tzann Lii, "A Colonized Empire: Reflections on the Expansion of Hong Kong Films in Asian Countries" in *Trajectories: Inter-Asia Cultural Studies*, edited by Kuan-Hsing Chen (London: Routledge, 1998), pp. 122–41.

38. Dean Visser, "'Korea Fever' Sweeps Asia's Pop Culture", *Associated Press* (CNN.com, 24 January 2002), see <http://www.ugcs.caltech.edu/~takoyaki/vault/articles/AP_KoreaPopCulture.html>.

39. Thomas B. Gold (1995), p. 261.

40. The sociological concept of generations refer to this idea supposing that certain events leave their marks on the group of people experiencing them, without forming a social group with their members communicating with each other.

41. The entanglement or identity of old and new economic and political elites is one of them, bringing corruption and high differences in economic and social status.

42. Jonathan Rigg, *Southeast Asia. The Human Landscape of Modernization and Development* (London: Routledge, 1997), p. i.

43. For Vietnam, see Thomas Heberer and Arno Kohl, "Privatisierungsprozesse in Vietnam und ihre soziopolitischen Konsequenzen", in *Vietnams neue Position in Südostasien*, edited by Vu Duy Tu and Gerhard Will (Hamburg: Institut für Asienkunde, 1999), p. 194.

44. Wilfried Lulei (1999), p. 216.

45. United Nations Development Programme, Human Development Report 2002, Occasional Paper 33, <http://hdr.undp.org/docs/publications/ocational_papers/oc33c.htm>, III, p. 3.

46. Zheng Yongnian, *Discovering Chinese Nationalism in China. Modernization, Identity, and International Relations* (Cambridge: Cambridge University Press, 1999), pp. 111–59.

47. See Leonard C. Sebastian, "Southeast Asian Perceptions of China: The Challenge of Acheiving a New Strategic Accomodation" in Derek da Cunha,

*Southeast Asian Perspectives on Security* (Singapore: Institute of Southeast Asian Studies, 2000), pp. 158–81; Chris Dixon (1999), p. 119.

48. Dominique Schirmer, "Globale chinesische Kultur? Überlegungen zu Ort und Raum der 'chinesischen Identität' ", in *Regionale und nationale Identitäten. Wechselwirkungen und Spannungsfelder im Zeitalter moderner Staatlichkeit*, edited by Peter Haslinger (Würzburg: ergon, 2000), pp. 183–98. See also David Shambaugh, *Greater China. The Next Superpower?* (Oxford: Oxford University Press, 1995).

49. Gerald Segal, Jusuf Wanandi, Jukio Satoh, Jin-Hyun Paik, "The Security Setting", in *Europe and the Asia Pacific*, edited by Hanns Maull, Gerald Segal, Jusuf Wanandi (London: Routledge, 1998), pp. 107–34.

50. Fareed Zakaria (1994), p. 113.

51. See Mahathir bin Mohamad and Ishihara Shintaro, *The Voice of Asia, Two Leaders Discuss the Coming Century* (Tokyo: Kodansha International, 1995).

## Chapter Fifteen

# Traditionalism and Change in the Asian Security Discourse

Jürgen Rüland

## INTRODUCTION

The chapters of this book have shown that the Asian security discourse is in flux. The negative impact of the energy crisis and the positive encouragement of *détente* in the 1970s, have shifted security thinking from a focus on military power of states to a more comprehensive conception of security. As explained in Chapter 1, comprehensive security is a much broader security concept that seeks to cope also with non-military threats caused by energy shortages, trade and financial crises, and international institutional instability. After the end of the Cold War there was another conceptual shift, albeit within narrow limits, towards human security policies to take account of new challenges of arms proliferation, environmental degradation, intra-state and inter-ethnic violence and terrorism, irregular migration flows, and human rights violations. More recently organized crime, cyber crime, and epidemics such as AIDS, SARS and bird flu have entered the security agenda. Yet, Asian policymakers and analysts are still far from abandoning state-centric outlooks to see security in terms of community-building as envisioned by Dominique Schirmer

(Chapter 13), or a global public good as called for by Hermann Schwengel (Chapter 14). Security cooperation has never transcended "soft institutionalism" and is mostly confined to institutional balancing. It ends where states fear the loss of national sovereignty. If the options of policymakers are defined by a continuum where power politics and military strength constitute one pole and supranational cooperation marks the opposite pole, Asian security is still found to be closer to the realist pole.[1] Jürgen Haacke's discussion of regional security institutions (Chapter 6) and the other contributions to Part II of this book indirectly confirm this characterization.

This concluding chapter seeks to identify reasons why this is the case. What are the major ideational and material impediments to comprehensive and human security in Pacific Asia? The chapter begins with an analysis of the ideas and experiences that influence the security culture prevalent among Asian decision-makers and the broader public. I then take a closer look at the domestic preconditions for cooperative and human security, the institutional prerequisites and the actors involved in the security discourse. The next section discusses the costs related to institution-building in the security sector. The chapter ends with a discussion of the impact of systemic influences on security thinking in the region.

## SECURITY RATIONALISM AND WORLDVIEWS

The realist and liberal schools of international relations theory often assume that security policies are the result of rational choices by foreign policy elites and security analysts who carefully evaluate what they consider as the national interests and who search for the most cost-effective means to achieve their policy objectives. While this view is not entirely wrong, it overlooks the fact that often decision-makers must base their decisions on incomplete information. Confronted with this handicap they cease to be exclusively rational utility-maximizers. Instead, they often seek or unconsciously succumb to worldviews informed by the collective or "cultural memory"[2] of their society, that is, ideas that over time have become deeply ingrained, partly as a result of experience, but also of selective memory.[3] This means that their thinking and consequently their actions are shaped to a considerable extent by mental representations of the past, of self and others, including collective images which are formed by singular events, and perpetuated by symbols, narratives and myths. Although ideas and values may undergo change over time, collective identities normally change slowly and they may even be reinforced when people find them confirmed in social interactions and political constellations, or by specific events. The merit of the constructivist approach to the study of international security is to highlight the importance of such cultural influences on security policies. Although cultural analysis is always confronted with the danger of essentializing culture and suggesting cultural conformity where diversity exists, the ideas and value patterns that distinguish the societies of Pacific Asia cannot be ignored when explaining the region's relatively low level of institutionalization of security policies. My argument is that these cultural values strongly support realist notions of security.

## PRE-COLONIAL SECURITY CONCEPTS

Ideas about security in much of Pacific Asia are still influenced by perceptions that can be traced back to pre-colonial times.[4] They correspond with key elements of the realist worldview such as anarchy (or chaos in the terminology of the region), self-help (or self-reliance/national resilience) and balance of power. Such an essentially realist worldview is inherent in the Hindu-Brahmanic idea of geometrical politics and the *mandala* concept as its ideational core and it may also be found in the Sinic world in the stratagems of the Sun Tzu. While exploration of these ideas in detail is beyond the scope of this book,[5] it suffices to state that their legacies constitute an elaborate ethnocentrism, which added to the traumatic colonial experiences became a driving force of post-independence nationalism. They depict the home territory as the centre of the world around which all other states are grouped. Sometimes this ethnocentrism is exacerbated by religious connotations such as in the Theravada Buddhist idea of the *Cakravartin*, a world conqueror. Although Buddhist scriptures portray the *Cakravartin* as a benevolent and peaceful ruler, the claim of a ruler to be a *Cakravartin* inevitably leads to conflict when he seeks to realize his ambitions by military conquest. In a seminal study Bechert has shown that rulers who derive their legitimacy from divine sources are hardly inclined to respect treaties and agreements.[6] Moreover, politically and religiously motivated ethnocentrism is a powerful source of national exceptionalism which pervades the collective identities in virtually all major powers of the region. Among the other legacies of these worldviews is the apprehension of notoriously unstable inter-state relations. The threats emanating from them must be contained by balancing, bandwagoning, and establishing of buffer zones as well as husbanding one's own national power assets.

Thus ethnocentric geo-political concepts are still very much alive in the region, especially among military elites, right-wing politicians and nationalist movements. Examples are the Thai vision of *"Suvannaphume"* (domination of a Golden Peninsula), the Japanese *"kokutai"*, the Korean *Tang'un* myth and Indonesia's archipelagic hegemony doctrine of *"Wawasan Nusantara"*.[7] Underlying them is traditional political thinking, which views power as indivisible[8] and which may even go along with racist overtones and notions of cultural superiority. Ethnocentric worldviews are without doubt a breeding ground for hegemonic ambitions; they are at variance with institutionalist conceptions of international relations and cooperative concepts of security.

Many of these ancient traditions and worldviews are preserved through media such as in the Hindu-Brahmanic Indianized culture of Southeast Asia the widely known *Ramayana* and *Mahabharata* epics as well as other art genres using their figures, symbols, language and mythology. In Thailand, for instance, they still form part of the school curriculum.[9] And the Chinese, including the Southeast Asian overseas Chinese, are still familiar with plays such as *Sam Kok* (The Three Kingdoms). The way in which they socialize the public with images of a power-driven, hostile and amoral external world, exposed to Machiavellian machinations by the powers that be, should not be underestimated. Thinking in these terms can be witnessed in everyday dialogues and political statements alike. They are still very much present on the minds of policymakers.[10]

Perceptions of inter-state relations in terms of anarchy not only reflect selective reminiscences of a far distant past, but also gain reinforcement by recent history, including the humiliation by colonialism, the devastation and human loss suffered in the Second World War, the Cold War which in Korea and Vietnam erupted into hot wars, civil wars, the chaos created by the Asian financial crisis and most recently international terrorism. Examples abound in Bernd Martin's chapter.

## LOOSELY STRUCTURED REGIONALISM

Constructivists and even some institutionalists explain the low institutionalization of the Association of Southeast Asian Nations (ASEAN) and other Asian cooperation schemes such as ASEAN+3 (APT), and the ASEAN Regional Forum (ARF) as a unique response to the great diversity of the region in terms of territory, population, power, culture, level of economic development and political systems.[11] While values such as pragmatism, flexibility, personalism and social harmony in themselves may not be amenable to deep institutionalization, they are nevertheless seen as being widely shared across the region and hence fostering a regional identity — in one of its manifestations called the ASEAN Way — which may eventually become an enabling factor for closer cooperation.[12] In short, traditional values are mutable and can be shaped selectively to underpin inter-state cooperation and common security.

In contrast to the more optimistic constructivists, I argue here that the core values of the Asian security culture are resilient and will persist in preserving a realist worldview. I believe that the values regarded by constructivists as the glue of the ASEAN Way are more convincingly interpreted from a realist perspective. Personalism, pragmatism and flexibility are primarily values shaping domestic policy processes. They are legacies of long periods of pre-modern monarchic absolutism (which suppressed the growth of autonomous institutions), the imposition of alien and hence illegitimate institutions during the colonial period and post-independence authoritarian regimes with their strategy of depoliticizing society. In the new democracies of the region they further reflect the political transition in which institutions are contested and in flux. And they are readily transferred to the arenas of regional and international politics.

Political institutions in the region often appear as loosely organized in the form of personal followings. This is not a rehearsal of Embree's loosely structured society hypothesis,[13] but rather a reminder of a widespread penchant for flexible behaviour and pragmatism. Personal relations are flexible and can be revoked, if the patron is no longer able or willing to satisfy vital interests of followers and has lost charisma and legitimacy. In such circumstances, the obligation of loyalty expires, and the clients can move to a new patron.

If clienteles are internally instable, so are the relationships between clienteles on which domestic power dynamics often rest. The typical form of cooperation between clienteles is the short-term alliance which can be dissolved at any time when interests so dictate. Ideology, principles and shared values are only of a subordinate priority for the cohesion of such alliances. They are of an ad hoc nature and instrumental, rapidly changing and by bringing together strange bedfellows, they often lead to unexpected constellations. This predilection for short-term alliances and pragmatic policy shifts is projected from the domestic domain to foreign policy and thus has a bearing on the conduct of regional security relations.

It is a truism that extreme flexibility creates distrust. Suspicion always looms that the other side will not honour agreements. Alliances and coalitions therefore tend to operate on the lowest common denominator. If they are broken, the costs should be kept minimal. Law and legal norms provide only limited protection against defections. As legal norms are often contested and manipulated for short-term gain, they fail to determine the rules of the game in a predictable way. Moreover, in many Asian societies law has a different connotation compared to liberal democracies of the West. While in the latter it is designed to provide protection against interventions of the state into the private sphere, in Asia it is traditionally regarded as something that arouses fear because it is in the first place an instrument of the state to punish non-compliance with the authorities.[14] In international relations "hard law" is eschewed because governments worry that they can not implement it. Non-implementation may lead to sanctions and loss of face.

More values standing in the way of closer cooperation could be discussed. For instance, the familism inherent in the organic state theories popular in Asia also creates clear ingroup-outgroup boundaries which reduce the propensity to cooperate. However, given the limited space, we may summarize at this point that all these worldviews and values have in common a deep-seated insecurity *vis-à-vis* the outside world.

On the other hand, substantive cooperation is not ruled out, but it can flourish only where long personal relations have created a modicum of trust. Even then it takes a long time until the threshold of symbolic and declaratory cooperation is eventually crossed. The desire to familiarize oneself with the other side is a major reason for convening meetings of regional leaders in which the meeting is an end in itself. This is at variance with Western efficiency concepts and explains why Asian forums are often criticized by the West as "talkshops". Aversion to open criticism and the fear of the loss of face associated with it are behind the efforts to create a semblance of harmony and the concomitant tabooization of conflicts. This is what constructivists call "rhetorical action" (that is, communication where arguments are only exchanged without a change or accommodating diverse positions), in contrast to "communicative action" which denotes a rational discourse characterized by mutual understanding facilitating compromise solutions and reasoned consensus.[15] Unfortunately, constructivists analysing security cooperation in

Asia have not yet considered the "realist dimension" of the values underlying "soft institutionalization" seriously.

## DEMOCRACY, DOMESTIC POLITICS, AND REGIONAL SECURITY

A major precondition for the peaceful management of international relations is democracy. The democratic peace hypothesis for instance suggests that democracies are less aggressive than non-democracies or, at least, less likely to go to war with other democracies. As democracies have developed mechanisms of peaceful dispute settlement and compromise, they are expected to transfer their preference for institutions and rule-based behaviour to the international arena. Moreover, due to this culture of peaceful conflict resolution based on the rule of law, democracies are believed to respect human rights more than autocracies and thus provide better conditions for human security.[16]

A closer look at the situation in Pacific Asia however shows that the foundations of democratic peace are still shaky because democracy itself is ambiguous. On the one hand, democracy has made headway in the region in the 1980s and 1990s when the so-called Third Wave of democratization[17] reached Asian shores. The Philippines returned to democracy in 1986, Taiwan and South Korea became democratic in 1987. In the 1990s, Thailand's fledgling democracy stabilized, too, weathering an attempt by the armed forces to restore a semi-authoritarian order, while in Indonesia, the thirty-two-year old regime of President Suharto collapsed under the impact of the Asian financial crisis in 1998. Mia Mikic's chapter on economic insecurity illustrates the point. On the other hand, however, many semi-authoritarian and authoritarian regimes remained intact, communist regimes have liberalized only economically and North Korea remains totalitarian and continues to pose a major threat for regional peace as a nuclear rogue state. And even where electoral democracies emerged, their consolidation faces many obstacles. They are thus better categorized as political systems *sui generis* which still display many vestiges of authoritarianism.[18]

While in the 1990s few armed inter-state conflicts have been registered, in all cases where they occurred they were provoked by non-democratic states. The clashes at the Thai-Burmese border were triggered by incursions of the Burmese military in hot pursuit of ethnic insurgents on Thai territory and in the South China Sea the People's Republic of China's People's Liberation Army (PLA) Navy took possession of islets and atolls claimed by the Philippines. In 1996 it was again Beijing which took a belligerent attitude by firing missiles near Taiwan on the eve of the island's presidential elections and on the Korean Peninsula all violent incidents were provoked by North Korea. However, below the level of naked military aggression, democratic states, too, did not always act according to theory. They too occasionally resorted to more or less veiled threats, as the repeated verbal assaults by Indonesia under the Habibie and Wahid governments against Singapore, and actions in East Timor, show.

Moreover, because the domestic power equation is in flux, governments are weak and the rules of the political game are still contested, new democracies are characterized by frequent policy shifts. Good examples are the various Thai governments after 1992, the Indonesian governments after the ouster of President Suharto and to a lesser extent also the Philippines and South Korea. The resulting see-saw policies impact on foreign and security policies and reduce the predictability of states' international behaviour. These erratic swings are motivated in part by the temptation to deflect domestic criticism by pursuing an activist and sometimes even risky foreign policy. Regional trust and security are undermined accordingly.

Young democracies, lacking an established participant political culture, have in common with authoritarian regimes, albeit for different reasons, a vulnerability to populist policies, a tendency which is exacerbated if regime change goes hand in hand with a profound economic crisis. While populism often targets ethnic and religious minorities such as the Chinese or Christians in Indonesia as scapegoats for domestic problems, it may adversely affect foreign relations if these minorities are under the tutelage of an external power, if it responds to the discrimination of nationals abroad or if other states are blamed for policy failures at home. In the case of Indonesia, relations suffered with the People's Republic of China over the pogrom against ethnic Chinese during the ouster of Suharto, with Malaysia as a result of the expulsion of Indonesian labour migrants from Malaysia, and with Singapore which was blamed by the Indonesian Government for the flight of Sino-Indonesian capital following the Asian financial crisis. Thailand's relations with Cambodia have been tense since the Cambodian Government failed to control anti-Thai riots in Phnom Penh. The acrimonious, often inflammatory nationalist language concomitant with these disputes was a major reason why ASEAN found it so difficult to contain the damage to the grouping's reputation caused by its paralysis during and after the Asian financial crisis.[19]

Today, most armed conflicts in the region are internal conflicts such as ethnic separatism, communist insurgencies and terrorist attacks, some of which Jürgen Rüland's Chapter 9 details. However, the track record of democratic governments in handling these security challenges is hardly better than that of non-democratic regimes as they, too, seek to end rebellions mainly by military force. Indonesian military operations after 1998 in Aceh, Papua and East Timor did not differ much from the Suharto era and have cost the life of thousands, displaced hundreds of thousands and given rise to accusations of severe human rights violations. In the war zones of Mindanao and the Sulu archipelago where the Mindanao Islamic Liberation Front (MILF) fights for an independent Muslim state, the reputation of the Philippine Armed Forces is hardly better and the escalation of the conflict between the Thai Government and Islamic insurgents has also been attributed to the indiscriminate use of force by state agents.[20]

Anti-democratic veto players such as right-wing elements in the military are also responsible for the persistence of realist concepts of security and the relatively slow advancement of cooperative and human security. This is particularly the case in countries such as Thailand and Indonesia in which the transition to democracy was negotiated, that is, the new political rules were part of a bargain between the democrats and representatives of the *ancien régime*. In such countries, but also in countries exposed to immediate military threats such as South Korea, the armed forces have retained much influence in the formulation of security doctrines and foreign policy-making. The traditional ethnocentric worldviews discussed in the previous section are particularly represented among military officers. Not surprisingly, the Thai vision of *Suvannaphume* enjoyed its greatest popularity in military circles. Military officers also dislike the growing interdependencies of a globalized world because economic interdependence jeopardizes their cherished goal of autarky. Other veto forces such as ethnic separatists and Islamic *jihadis* also impede progress toward cooperative and human security as they give the military a *raison d'être*, a cause to reassert its self-styled role as a guardian of national unity and integrity, by fighting real or imagined challenges to state authority. However, with the gradual shift from authoritarian to democratic regimes, and the concomitant diminishing of military influence, a major pillar for unprincipled realpolitik is gradually weakened. In this respect the Thai case is illustrative, as it demonstrates how new functions such as peace-keeping can provide fresh legitimacy and self-respect to the armed forces, increase their professionalism, shift their attention from national to cooperative and human security and curtail their aspirations for political power.

The picture is thus not totally bleak. Even if the armed forces still exert considerable influence on security policy, it is undeniable that democratization has gradually widened the political space for the advocates of human security. It has also given foreign policy-making a more pluralistic flavour and exerted pressure on governments for greater responsiveness. Adherents of human security are mainly found in the civil society, in particular among think tanks, the media and non-governmental organizations (NGOs). Think tanks and journalists form a fledgling epistemic community of security experts and international relations specialists. They are the ones who address issues related to human security.

Some of these civil society initiatives are also finding their way into the growing number of so-called Track II dialogue meetings taking place in the region, as suggested in Chapter 1. The Track II dialogues, initiated by the ASEAN Institutes of Security and International Studies (ISIS) and the Council for Security and Cooperation in the Asia-Pacific (CSCAP) with informal governmental assistance, played a minor role in stimulating the creation of the ASEAN Regional Forum (ARF) and in proposing items for the latter's agenda. Yet, the effectiveness of these dialogues should not be overstated, because think-tank experts are often beholden to the government and often themselves socialized in the paradigms of realism. Only more recently has generational change facilitated a gradual opening of these circles towards liberal and cooperative concepts of security. Examples of governmental policy innovations directly traceable to the Track II processes are thus relatively few. In the media only a few elite, mostly English language dailies and magazines regularly report on security-related themes and foreign policy issues, thus reaching only a comparatively small portion of the population. Their impact on official security policy, insofar as they champion cooperative and human security, is likewise limited.[21]

More tangible is the impact of NGOs and other civil society groups on security policy. Inasmuch as they are linked to transnational networks, they have initiated changes in the governments' human rights policies which have facilitated subsequent regime change as shown by Anja Jetschke for the Philippines and to a lesser extent Indonesia (see Chapter 12).[22] These changes can be explained by the so-called "spiral model", which combines constructivist "communicative action" with rational choice theory and posits five stages of change in human rights policies.[23] Again, however, the impact of these groups, remarkable and growing as it is, should not be overstated. In hardly any Asian country is there a peace movement comparable to Western Europe and North America in the last decades of the twentieth century, which would oppose the quickening trends of arms procurement and military modernization in much of Asia. Quite to the contrary, military modernization and the ability to power projection is widely approved in Asian societies as an attribute of national sovereignty and resilience.

Greater human security is also on the agenda of articulate civil society groups concerned with the pathologies of economic globalization. Their thinking is informed by dependency theory and they often belong to the radical camp according to the categories set out in the introductory chapter. Many of them view globalization as a process driven by the United States and cementing U.S. hegemony in Asia through the control Washington exerts over international financial organizations. The austerity and structural adjustment policies prescribed by International Monetary Fund's (IMF) and the World Bank for crisis-ridden economies are blamed for the seemingly accelerating erosion of the economic policy-making autonomy of the respective governments. These NGOs, which strive to put a human face on globalization by advocating workers rights, environmental protection and poverty alleviation and by exposing questionable business practices of transnational corporations (TNCs), have organized parallel summits to the meetings of international forums such as the World Trade Organization (WTO), the G-7/8, the Asia-Europe Meeting (ASEM) or the Asia-Pacific Economic Cooperation (APEC). Governments, though seeking to insulate themselves from the public pressures created by these groups, can less and less afford to ignore them. Nevertheless, events such as ASEAN's People's Forum still have mainly symbolic character and exert limited influence on the agenda of the leaders or ASEAN's numerous ministerial rounds.

## "OPPORTUNITY COSTS" AND "GOVERNANCE COSTS"

Another argument for the reluctance to adopt cooperative and human security policies in Pacific Asia can be derived from rationalist institutionalism. David Lake, writing on collective action problems, proposed a distinction between costs arising from opportunistic behavior of states and costs associated with containing opportunistic behaviour.[24]

Costs caused by opportunism denote costs which arise for one's own state and for other states as the result of free-riding of members of a cooperation agreement. Free-riding may constitute non-compliance with individual items of a cooperation agreement, temporary boycotts or full-scale defection. The damage varies according to the significance of the policy fields affected and the intensity of the cooperation.

Governments interested in cooperating seek to protect themselves against high opportunity costs by concluding binding contracts with their prospective partners. International cooperation treaties based on "hard law" usually include mechanisms of arbitration and dispute settlement and, for the worst case, even provide for sanctions against non-compliance. Governments hope that such provisions would enhance the likelihood that contractual obligations are met.

The drawback of such protective contractual arrangements are "governance costs", that is, costs incurred in order to build up institutions which will be able to monitor and restrain the free-riding and exit behaviour of members. States must, for instance, create the domestic institutions, laws and budgets to implement the obligations they incur as a result of international cooperation. This may arouse opposition which may only be placated by concessions in other policy sectors. Governments may also face resistance by nationalist groups criticizing the loss of sovereignty caused by subjecting the state to international dispute settlement and arbitration mechanisms. Moreover, many cooperation agreements include the establishment of an organizational apparatus which collects information, monitors the implementation of the agreement, conducts meetings, coordinates the policies of members and proposes improvements of the cooperation agreement, all time- and resource-consuming activities.

The willingness of governments to accept governance costs for international institutions depends on several contextual factors. It is higher in times of economic boom than in times of depression. This is in the first place, but not exclusively, a question of perception as well as capacity. In periods of economic boom the perception of absolute gains dominates, while in times of decline the perception of relative losses determines the behaviour of partners. But beyond the perceptions, governance costs rise objectively in times of crisis: The resources available for institution-building shrink, competing with other more urgent priorities. Moreover, governance costs rise because more than in boom times exit behaviour of others must be prevented, possibly by costly concessions.

Another economic factor determining the inclination of states to shoulder governance costs is the level of economic development. Wealthy states are more likely to take over governance costs than poor states. Finally, the willingness to bear governance costs is related to structural factors such as the size of the institution, the level of interdependence and the intra-institutional power equation. It may be argued that strongly interdependent states are more willing to bear higher governance costs. The same may be hypothesized of the members of small groupings, where defection of one or several members causes high opportunity costs and may even jeopardize the entire cooperation agreement. Governance costs may also be borne by a hegemon which has an interest to create a cooperative security environment.

A closer look at security cooperation in Pacific Asia shows that while regional organizations are large, governments are hesitant to subscribe to their costs. The ASEAN Regional Forum (ARF), for instance, has presently twenty-four members, the Asia-Pacific Economic Cooperation (APEC) which in recent years also increasingly adopted functions of a security dialogue, has twenty-one, and the Asia-Europe Meeting (ASEM) have been enlarged to thirty-nine members at its fifth summit in Hanoi in October 2004. Informal security arrangements such as the Track II dialogue under CSCAP also have more than twelve members. This means that costs arising from opportunistic defection by individual states (except for political and military heavyweights such as the United States, China or Japan) may not be overly prohibitive to other members or damaging to the institution. Moreover, the majority of members belong to medium-income or poor countries and in the light of scarce resources and conflicting priorities they are not willing to invest heavily in institutions. Interdependence is also low-to-moderate. If we take ASEAN as an example, even after the completion of the ASEAN Free Trade Area (AFTA) intra-regional trade has not increased markedly. Intra-ASEAN trade still hovers around a moderate 25 per cent compared to about 20 per cent in 1967. This shows that interdependence with external partners remains predominant and ASEAN members — at least in the economic domain — perceive themselves more as competitors than as partners. Moreover, there is no benign hegemon in Pacific Asia. Indonesia is economically too weak as to adopt such a position and other ASEAN members resist Indonesia's attempts to take a leadership role in the organization. Recent Indonesian proposals for strengthening cooperative and human security through an ASEAN Security Community which fosters democracy and establishes an ASEAN peace-keeping force have been dismissed by other ASEAN members.[25] China lacks the "soft power"[26] to become an accepted benign hegemon in the region, Japan is disqualified for historical reasons (see Chapters 2 and 3) and economically weakened since the burst of the "bubble economy" in the early 1990s. The United States is not prepared to take over governance costs and thereby subsidize the economic rise of major competitors in the region.

Given the fact that Asian governments are not willing to bear high governance costs and for a variety of historical and cultural reasons are not prepared to subject themselves to hard law and binding rules, they seek to compensate for the lack of institutional cohesion through participation in many, often overlapping regional institutions. This is what Paul Bowles has called "multiple regionalism".[27] Multiple membership in regional institutions is a way to balance institutional and economic changes inside and outside the region and to some extent even a response to changing threat potentials. In short, this strategy minimizes cost and risk by hedging.

## MULTILATERALISM AND BACKLASH

Finally, the structure of the international system influences the propensity of Asian governments to move towards cooperative and human security. It is no accident that especially in the post-Cold War period, Pacific Asia experienced a proliferation of cooperative institutions, not only in the economic sector but also in the security domain. With the end of the Cold War some of the conflict lines in the region blurred and even the United States seemed willing to explore more multilateralism. The enhanced role of the UN, the proliferation of regional institutions and the emerging contours of a multi-layered system of global governance increased confidence in institutions, providing new opportunities for political learning and paving the way for the diffusion of norms such as democracy and human rights which are favourable to cooperative and human security.

It should not be overlooked however that this was never a one-directional change. The influx of new liberal norms and the erosion of existing political orders in the region which was seen by conservatives in the region as accelerating through the intensifying interaction with Western partners also caused a backlash. One of these backlashes was the Asian values "hypothesis". This was partly a defensive reaction against what was perceived as a Western grand design to establish a value hegemony over the rest of the world, and partly a triumphant rationalization of the enormous economic successes much of the region had achieved. Stressing values such as power, hierarchy and authority as well as collective over individual rights, the Asian values "hypothesis" curtailed the political space of the advocates of human security and to a lesser extent also of cooperative security. Broadly speaking, the Asian values "hypothesis" may be regarded as a revaluation of the paradigms inherent in political realism.

The overall relatively favourable structural conditions for cooperative and human security changed with the outbreak of the Asian financial crisis. The crisis was widely viewed in the region as a confirmation of the anarchical and chaotic nature of international relations. Some voices even spoke of an "economic war" imposed on Asian economies by the West. This was exacerbated by the perception that regional institutions had no answer to the crisis and that international financial institutions such as the IMF are dominated by the United States which was seen as using them to reestablish its hegemonial position in world politics. The Asian financial crisis was widely viewed in the region through the realist lens as a conspiracy of the West in order to contain the rise of new formidable economic and, in the long run, strategic competitors.

## WAR ON INTERNATIONAL TERROR

The war on terror has further reconfirmed the convictions of those who view the world through the prism of realism. The United States as the world's only superpower is now seen as creating a world order in which unilateralism, pre-emption and — as the Iraq war has shown — even prevention are acceptable. These developments challenge the cherished belief held by neo-liberal institutionalists since the 1970s that military power is unable to produce desired political outcomes and that wars cannot be won only by high-tech armies and a minimum of own casualties. Yet, more than the ready defeat of Saddam Hussein undermines these beliefs, for more damage has been done to internationalism. Non-authorized military interventions by the United States and NATO in Iraq in 1998, Kosovo in 1999 and again in Iraq in 2003 have delegitimized the UN and other international institutions. Harsh policies by Russia, China, and Indonesia towards defiance by peoples in their peripheries suggests they, too, will act unilaterally with force if their governments so decide. Multilateral bodies are regarded as factious, weak and unable to deal decisively with aggressors and tyrants. This perception leads to reemphasis on the virtues of national resilience and self-help. Even more deplorable is the return to Manichean worldviews of the Cold War period; the division of the world into good and bad, which then pervaded the less sophisticated realist interpretations of world politics.

Multilateral cooperation and cooperative security are thus delegitimized as policy options of the weak,[28] while for great powers they are only one option among many in the toolbox of foreign and security policies. Moreover, there is also a tendency to misrepresent as multilateralism what is in reality coalition building. Multilateralism "American style",[29] "selective," or "imperial"[30] multilateralism as Washington's overtures to create a "coalition of the willing" have been occasionally termed, are misleading. This "multilateralism with adjectives" differs from an institutionalist version of multilateralism in two important aspects: (a) it does not produce durable institutions, and (b) as a consequence of (a), it does not create the actor predictability that multilateral frameworks are expected to provide. Coalitions such as the anti-terror coalition have the advantage of being flexible and adaptable to changing circumstances. They are of limited duration, tend to change with the issue, impose fewer commitments on their members than more cohesive institutions, and do not generate the governance costs[25] usually associated with institution-building. These coalitions have much in common with the international institutions already existing in Pacific Asia.

At the domestic level the war against terror is strengthening the security apparatus which — as we have seen above — is only reluctantly moving in the direction of cooperative and human security. Many governments in Pacific Asia have passed anti-terrorism laws or revitalized internal security acts. To what extent they are abused to curtail democratization in the region remains to be seen, but this danger should not be taken lightly. The security sector is further strengthened by the resumption of U.S. military aid which is given as a reward for loyal allies in the war against terror such as the Philippines. In the region's new democracies the war against terror will slow down the ability of their parliaments and other civilian institutions to control their militaries and to curtail the "reserved domains" of the security sector.[31] If enhanced homeland security becomes the overriding priority of governments in the region, it is inevitable that the "collateral damage" will be less democracy and more human rights violations. Those struggling for more human security will then be on the defensive for some time to come.

Despite occasional suggestions in the region, the fight against international terrorism has not become a new external stimulator for regional organizations such as ASEAN, jolting them out of the paralysis of the Asian financial crisis.[32] The non-binding trilateral Agreement on Information Exchange and Establishment of Communication Procedures signed by Indonesia, Malaysia and the Philippines in February 2002 and later joined by Thailand and Cambodia does not have much integrative potential.[33] It is an agreement very much in the tradition of "soft law" and glossing over divisions in the security outlook of ASEAN members. The same holds true for ASEAN and APEC declarations of cooperation in the fight against international terrorism.

After 11 September 2001, the threats of terrorism and the ensuing new geo-political constellations have given military modernization and arms purchases new legitimacy. While the post-September 11 arms build-up is mainly confined to conventional weapons, there are more worrisome prospects related to the proliferation of weapons of mass destruction. One is what Rodney Lyon in Chapter 7 has called "horizontal proliferation". In fact, all states which in recent years have for the first time crossed the nuclear threshold are located in Asia. The Bush doctrine of preemption may even accelerate horizontal proliferation. For "rogue states" such as North Korea there can be only one lesson from the Iraq war, namely that even abandoning a programme to develop weapons of mass destruction does not spare a country from punitive military action by the United States. The more cautious response of the United States after the North Korean admission of its nuclear weapons programme, on the other hand, suggests that the possession of such weapons may pay a dividend in deterrence. Already prior to the Iraq war, North Korea had justified its nuclear programme as an act of "self-defence", citing the U.S. withdrawal from the 1972 Anti-Ballistic Missile (ABM) Treaty with the former Soviet Union, Washington's intention to develop a missile defence system and its naming of North Korea as a member of the "axis of evil".[34] If, however, North Korea goes ahead with its nuclear and missile programs, other East Asian states such as South Korea and even Japan may feel compelled to develop their own nuclear capabilities.

The war on terror has also triggered a new round of balancing in Pacific Asia. The renewed military presence of the U.S. in the region and intensifying diplomatic activities have led China to speed up plans to create a free trade area with ASEAN.[35] Initially designed to pre-empt Japan in Southeast Asia, the move, though engineered on the institutional chessboard, was clearly guided by thinking in geo-political and geo-economic terms, as a subsequent Chinese proposal to create a "Strategic Partnership" with ASEAN reveals.[36]

The China-ASEAN FTA was followed by similar overtures to ASEAN by Japan and India. While not allowing it to regain its pre-Asian crisis role of what Haacke in Chapter 6 calls an "aspirant manager of regional order", these initiatives nevertheless gave ASEAN some leverage to respond to the geopolitical changes in the region by balancing the influence of regional great powers on Southeast Asia. The Shanghai Cooperation Organization (SCO), often depicted by hopeful liberals as an example for Beijing's seeming paradigmatic shift toward multilateralism, mainly serves as a device for balancing growing U.S. influence in Central Asia and countering Washington's suspected intentions of encircling and containing China. Central Asian states, on the other hand, perceive the SCO as a means of balancing Russia and making sure that U.S. influence in the region does not become dominant.

## CONCLUSION

The contributions of this volume have spotlighted a gradual shift from realist to liberal, cooperative, comprehensive, and human security concepts of security in Pacific Asia. This shift however is by no means uniform and one-directional. Indeed, there is evidence that several ASEAN countries and increasingly the United States and — to a lesser extent — Japan are moving in the opposite direction, a trend which in the wake of the war against international terrorism may spill over to other countries in the near future. China's shift to multilateralist policies may only be tactical in the wake of the overwhelming American military superiority. Nevertheless, at the conceptual level, the security community has left behind the simplistic and narrow power-based tenets of national security of the Cold War period and adopted more complex concepts of security such as cooperative, comprehensive, and human security. Yet, day-to-day decision-makers have only hesitantly accepted the consequence of this shift, namely the need for a deepening of institutions, allocation of scarce resources, and redefinition of national sovereignty. Institution-building has certainly taken place since the end of the Cold War, but as the Asian financial crisis demonstrated, these institutions are shallow and fragile.

Developments of the post-September 11 period are thus more reassuring to those in Asia who favour realist caution than to those who hope for liberal cooperation. As Jorn Dosch hints, United States multilateralism under presidency of Bill Clinton, and parallel moves toward comprehensive and human security thinking, are seen in the perspective of the Bush presidency as not an inevitable evolution, and possibly a stillborn episode. In the long run the alleged Chinese adoption of multilateralism (or more precisely — multipolarism) may also be viewed as either a diplomatic tactic or an historic digression. It is most plausibly a strategy adopted to compensate for a position of inferiority *vis-à-vis* the United States, as hinted by Jian Yang in Chapter 4. This tactical or *à la carte* multilateralism will not be pursued as an end in itself but only as a manoeuvre that is politically advantageous for Beijing. Likewise, Japan's military cooperation with the United States is strengthening, as Julie Gilson in Chapter 3 makes clear, suggesting a blurring of the prior focus on comprehensive security. The rivalry of the Asian regional powers and the presence of the U.S. superpower will more likely be a catalyst for power-balancing policies and conventional state coalition-building than for the deepening of cooperative or human security cooperation.

In this context and faced with many obstacles, the advocates of cooperative and human security will make only incremental advances. But they are not without hope or options. In order to advance their agenda, reformers must solicit the attention of decision-makers and encourage them to broaden their agenda to take account of new security threats and new security policies to deal with them. While sensible liberal analysts readily concede that military and economic aspects of power are essential to support orderly progress, they must also draw the non-conventional aspects of security discussed in this volume into the conceptual matrix, and to recommend this broader view to policymakers. In this regard the insights of a classic functionalist, David Mitrany, may be of help. Mitrany recommends initiating cooperation and (in modern language) regime-building in the "low politics" sectors as an avenue to building up trust among the leaders and encouraging cooperation in the security domain, broadly conceived, as well.[37] Academics and analysts can assist by illuminating positive experiences of cooperation and thereby contribute to conceptual broadening of the process of political learning. Teachers and researchers could accelerate the process of political learning by reforming the curriculum where many decision-makers receive some of their political socialization: The universities and military academies.[38] Journalists, NGO leaders, clerics and other opinion shapers can play important roles in drawing attention to new security challenges and making suggestions to their governments as to how to address them.

This multifaceted ideational process, by which the growing hazards of inattention and the potential rewards for progressive policy innovation are made more visible to policymakers, can continue despite political setbacks, and can be expected to shift towards the latter. If reformers believe that power must be guided by vision to the enhancement of human values, they are obliged to continue shaping the intellectual atmosphere to encourage policy shifts when the time is right. The legitimate goal of their efforts is a judicious blend of power, vision, and values in the pursuit of Asian security with an increasing comprehensive and human emphasis.

## NOTES

1. Typical is the cover theme of the IIAS Newsletter entitled "East Asian Geopolitics Revisited." *IIAS Newsletter*, No. 34, July 2004. The editorial authored by Koen de Ceuster and Kurt Radke captures well the intertwined nature of national self-assertion, balancing and institution-building in the region. Ibid., p. 3.
2. For the concept of "cultural memory" see Jan Assmann, *Das kulturelle Gedächtnis. Schrift, Erinnerung und politische Identität in frühen Hochkulturen* (Munich: C.H. Beck, 2002).
3. Judith Goldstein/Robert O. Keohane, eds., *Ideas and Foreign Policy: Beliefs, Institutions, and Political Change* (Ithaca: Cornell University Press, 1993).
4. Jürgen Rüland, "Ethnozentrismus, Nationalismus und regionale Kooperation in Asien", in *Nationalismus und Regionale Kooperation in Asien*, edited by Brunhild Staiger (Hamburg: Institut für Asienkunde, 1995): 1–40.
5. For more details, see Rüland, ibid., no. 243 (1995): 1–20.
6. Heinz Bechert, *Buddhismus, Staat und Gesellschaft in den Ländern des Theravada-Buddhismus*, vol. 2 (Frankfurt und Berlin: Harrassowitz, 1966), p. 9.
7. Donald G. McCloud, *Southeast Asia. Tradition and Modernity in the Contemporary World* (Boulder: Westview 1995); C.T. Allen, "Northeast Asia Centered Around Korea: Ch'oe Nam-son's View of History", *Journal of Asian Studies* 49, no. 4 (1990): 787–806; Karel van Wolferen, *The Enigma of Japanese Power: People and Politics in a Stateless Nation* (New York: Knopf, 1989).
8. Benedict Anderson, "The Idea of Power in Javanese Culture", in *Culture and Politics in Indonesia*, edited by Claire Holt (Ithaca: Cornell University Press, 1970): 1–70.

9. Meechai Thonthep, *Ramakien. The Thai Ramayama* (Bangkok: Naga Books 1993), p. 5.
10. Christianto Wibisono, Jabakan Kemelut "Sam Kok", <http://www. Indonesiamedia.com/rubrik/opini/opini00february-jebakan.htm> (accessed 17 October 2004).
11. See Miles Kahler, "Legalization as a Strategy: The Asia-Pacific Case", *International Organization* 54, no. 3 (2000): 549–71 and Kenneth W. Abbott/ Duncan Snidal, "Hard and Soft Law in International Governance", *International Organization* 54, no. 3 (2000): 421–56.
12. Nikolas Busse, "Constructivism and Southeast Asian Security", *The Pacific Review* 12, no. 1 (1999): 39–60.
13. John F. Embree, "Thailand — A Loosely Structured Social System", *American Anthropologist* 52, no. 1 (1950): 181–93.
14. Oskar Weggel, *Die Asiaten. Gesellschaftsordnungen, Wirtschaftssysteme, Denkformen, Glaubensweisen, Alltagsleben, Verhaltensstile* (München: C.C. Beck, 1989).
15. Thomas Risse, "Let's Argue!: Communicative Action in World Politics", *International Organization* 54, no. 1 (Winter 2000): 1–39; Gabriela Manea, Asian-European Dialogues on Human Rights: The Case of the Association of Southeast Asian Nations (ASEAN)-European Union (EU) Interregional Relations and the Asia-Europe Meeting (ASEM), Masters' Thesis, University of Freiburg, 2003.
16. On the relationship between democracy, peace and stability, see Anja Jetschke, "Democratization: A Threat to Peace and Stability in Southeast Asia", in *Asia-Pacific Economic and Security Cooperation. New Regional Agendas*, edited by Christopher Dent (Houndsmills, Basingstoke; Palgrave Macmillan, 2003), pp. 167–84.
17. Samuel Huntington, *The Third Wave: Democratization in the Late Twentieth Century* (Norman/London: Oklahoma University Press, 1991).
18. Steve Levitsky and Lucan Way, "The Rise of Competitive Authoritarianism", *Journal of Democracy* 13, no. 2 (2002): 51–65.
19. Jürgen Rüland, "ASEAN and the Asian Crisis: Theoretical and Practical Consequences for Southeast Asian Regionalism", *The Pacific Review* 13, no. 3 (2000): 421–51.
20. *The Nation*, 29 and 30 April 2004.
21. Hermann Kraft, "The Autonomy Dilemma of Track Two Diplomacy in Soputheast Asia", *Security Dialogue* 31, no. 3 (2000): 343–56.
22. Anja Jetschke, "International Norms, Transnational Human Rights Networks, and Domestic Political Change in Indonesia and the Philippines", Ph.D. Thesis, European University Institute, Florence, 2001.
23. For details on the spiral model see the presentation by the Forschungsgruppe Menschenrechte, in *Zeitschrift für Internationale Beziehungen*, 1998.

24. David Lake, "Global Governance: A Relational Contracting Approach", in *Globalization and Governance*, edited by Aseem Prakash/Jeffrey A. Hart (London and New York: Routledge 1999), pp. 31–53.

25. *Far Eastern Economic Review*, 6 May 2004, p. 19 and 10 June 2004, p. 20.

26. For the term "soft power", see Joseph S. Nye, *The Paradox of American Power: Why the World's Only Superpower Can't Go It Alone* (Oxford: Oxford University Press, 2002).

27. Paul Bowles, "ASEAN, AFTA and the New Regionalism", *Pacific Affairs* 70, no. 2 (1997): 219–34.

28. Robert Kagan, *On Paradise and Power: America and Europe in the New World Order* (New York: Knopf, 2003).

29. Andrew Denison, "Unilateral oder multilateral? Motive der amerikanischen Irakpolitik", *Aus Politik und Zeitgeschichte* 24–25 (2003): 24.

30. For a distinction between "cooperative", "selective" and "imperial multilateralism", see Jochen Hippler, "Unilateralismus der USA als Problem der internationalen Politik", *Aus Politik und Zeitgeschichte* 31–32 (2003): 20.

31. See Heiner Hänggi/Theodor Winkler, eds., *Challenges of Security Sector Governance* (Münster: Lit Verlag, 2003) and Hans Born/Heiner Hänggi (eds.), *The "Double Democratic Deficit". Parliamentary Accountability and the Use of Force Under International Auspices* (Aldershot: Ashgate, 2004).

32. Ralf Emmers, "ASEAN and the Securitization of Transnational Crime in Southeast Asia", *The Pacific Review* 16, no. 3 (2003): 419–38.

33. Rommel C. Banloi, "The Role of Philippine-American Relations in the Global Campaign Against Terrorism: Implications for Regional Security", *Contemporary Southeast Asia* 24, no. 2 (August 2002): 306.

34. Kay Möller, *Pyöngyang bekennt sich zur Bombe. Ende der internationalen Einbindungspolitik* (Berlin: Stiftung Wissenschaft und Politik, SWP aktuell, October 2002).

35. John Wong and Sarah Chan, "China-ASEAN Free Trade Agreement. Shaping Future Economic Relations", *Asian Survey* XLIII, no. 3 (May/June 2003): 507.

36. *Far Eastern Economic Review*, 17 July 2003, p. 29.

37. David Mitrany, *The Functional Theory of Politics* (New York: St Martin's Press, 1976).

38. The curricula of international relations courses are still dominated by realist thinking. They should be modernized and cooperative security given more space.

# Index